Unless otherwise stated all the photographs were taken by the author.

MAPS

# LIST OF ILLUSTRATIONS

v

# CONTENTS

## To Mary

First printed, 1965
Fourth impression 1977
ISBN 0 631 08750 8

Printed in Great Britain by offset lithography by
Billing & Sons Ltd, Guildford, London and Worcester

# POLITICS, LAW AND RITUAL IN TRIBAL SOCIETY

*By*

## MAX GLUCKMAN

*Late Professor of Social Anthropology in the*
*Victoria University of Manchester*

**BASIL BLACKWELL**
**OXFORD**
1977

*a.* A Zulu wife, caught in the conflicts of her position, who was ill because she was possessed by an ancestral spirit.  (see pp. 248 f.)

*b.* A contemporary survival of the traditional Eskimo song contest.
(see pp. 303 f.)

*Photograph by R. Spencer*

# ACKNOWLEDGMENTS

THE following colleagues have kindly loaned me as yet unpublished photographs: Professor M. Fortes, Dr. M. J. Meggitt, Mr. B. Sansom, and Professor R. Spencer.

I am grateful to the following for permission to reprint photographs: Professor P. J. Bohannan and the International African Institute, on the Tiv; Professor R. Firth and Messrs. Allen and Unwin, on the Tikopia; Professor M. Fortes and the International African Institute, on the Tallensi.

I am grateful to Messrs. Sampson, Low, for permission to republish illustrations from H. Capello and R. Ivens, *From Benguella to the Territory of the Yacca* (1882) and E. Holub, *Seven Years in South Africa* (1881); and to Messrs. Longmans, Green, for an illustration from F. Nansen, *The First Crossing of Greenland* (1890).

# GLOSSARY

I USE very few technical terms. The most frequently used are:

*affinal*: relationship through marriage.

*agnatic:* reckoning descent in the male line, hence 'agnates', those related thus.

*clan:* a large number of persons who consider themselves to be related to one another by descent in either the male or the female line, but who cannot always reckon their genealogical ties.

*cognatic:* a relationship by blood, hence 'cognates', those related thus.

*exogamy:* a practice by which members of a certain group do not marry one another.

*extended* (or *joint*) *family:* an association of families, related by near descent of one of the spouses.

*lineage:* a group of persons who are putatively linked together by common descent in either male or female line, and who are able to recount their genealogical ties. Lineages have varying genealogical depth, and larger lineages are composed of smaller segments which nest within them.

*matrilineal:* relationships through women.

*matrilineage* a lineage (see above) reckoning matrilineal descent.

*omnilineal:* relationships through all lines of descent.

*patrilineal:* a synonym for 'agnatic' (above).

*patrilineage:* a lineage (see above) reckoning agnatic descent.

# DRAMATIS PERSONAE

I HERE locate and summarily describe the principal tribal societies analysed in the text, referring to the characteristics stressed in this book.

By 'tribal society' I mean the kind of community which was once described by the term 'primitive society', a term now rightly rejected. Others call this type of community 'pre-literate' or 'pre-industrial'. These are appropriate terms also, but I prefer 'tribal', since 'tribe' was used to describe most of the communities of Europe, virtually up to feudal times. And forms of social organization akin to those communities, are what I am dealing with: though the lessons we learn can be applied to all societies. I begin with hunting bands, and consider many African states to be tribes—but not the great nations of West Africa. Basic to a tribal society is the egalitarian economy, with relatively simple tools to produce and primary goods to consume. The powerful and wealthy use their might and goods to support dependants; for they are unable to raise their own standards of living with the materials available (see Chapters I and II).

ANUAK: An agricultural people who live across the Sudan-Ethiopian border in the region of the Pibor River. One set of Anuak live in isolated villages, each riven by constant rebellions to oust the headman. The other villages are linked together in constant fighting to obtain certain 'royal' emblems for a noble who is associated with a particular village. The nobles are a special clan apparently devoted to pursuit of a position with few rewards. Studies by Evans-Pritchard have been followed up by Lienhardt.

AZANDE: A number of kingdoms in the Sudan near the Congo border. Evans-Pritchard made his pioneer interpretation of witchcraft and magical beliefs as philosophies of causation and of morals among them.

BAROTSE: A large kingdom on the Upper Zambezi, dominated by the Lozi tribe. Dwelling in a flood-plain, they have an intricate administrative system radiating out from their capital. Studied by Gluckman.

BEMBA: A powerful state of Congo origin, established east of Lake Bangweolu, with a ritual and secular paramountcy. Their matrilineal system of succession seems to contain seeds of dissension. Richards has given fine accounts of how they make their living, of their domestic organization, and of girls' initiation ceremonies.

BUSAMA: A village in New Guinea where World War II enabled a local 'big man' to become a tyrant. Hogbin analyses this case in his *Transformation Scene* (1951).

BUSHMEN: Hunters of South Africa, who have since 1600 been reduced and compressed by Whites, Hottentots and Bantu, till they subsist mainly in small bands in the arid lands of the west. Great painters. Standard works are by Schapera, Thomas, and Marshall.

CHEYENNE: One of the best organized of the Red Indian tribes which, after obtaining horses, moved into the Great Plains to live off the buffalo. Four thousand people were organized in several systems of intersecting secular and ritual ties. Their fighting ethos has been often described, and Hoebel and Llewellyn have analysed their varied 'law-ways'.

COMANCHE: Another tribe which used the horse to become hunters of the buffalo. They lacked the organization of the Cheyenne, and their community bonds, analysed by Hoebel, were more tenuous.

DAHOMEY: The most bureaucratized state in Africa south of the Sahara, with an elaborate administration, under the king, controlling much of the economic as well as political life. In the past, great slave-traders. The standard recent works in English are by Professor and Mrs. Herskovits.

ESKIMO: Probably the people with the tightest adaptation to their environment, they dwell in Greenland and round the Arctic Ocean. Hunters and fishermen, they live in small communities, always threatened by feud; but they too have social mechanisms to achieve trade and peace. They have been studied by many, and several authorities are used.

IFUGAO: A Philippines tribe, living off rice cultivated in magnificent rice terraces. Headhunters, but with highly developed laws and systems of social control involving the rich men who rise temporarily, but are always in danger of falling. Studied by Barton.

KALINGAS: Neighbours of the Ifugao in the Philippines, in the main similar but with a very different kinship system. Also studied by Barton.

KWAKIUTL: Red Indians of British Columbia, they are among the few rich hunters and fishermen—because of the fur trade. They compete with one another in aggressive feasting—the *potlatch*. Codere sums up the voluminous literature on them.

LOZI: See Barotse.

LUGBARA: A Uganda people, with an agnatic lineage system, in which men compete for the privilege of cursing their juniors with misfortune, for failure to acknowledge their seniority. Analysed by Middleton.

LUNDA OF LUAPULA: Studies by Cunnison illuminate ideas of history and deal with foreshortening of genealogies.

MAE ENGA: A Central New Guinea Highland tribe, recently brought under Australian rule. Without chiefs, they are organized on a framework of agnatic descent; but this framework, as studied by Meggitt, has to sustain many shocks because of heavy pressure on the land.

MAKAH: A southern outlier of the group of tribes here represented by the Kwakiutl. Their interest for this book arises from Colson's study of how they have maintained independence within the American nation.

MAMBWE: A tribe of cultivators and herdsmen living south of Lake Tanganyika. Watson's study of them analyses how a tribal system can maintain itself under great change.

MURNGIN: Australian Aborigines living in the richer north of the continent; hunters and collectors with complex social and religious systems. Studied in the 1930s by Lloyd Warner.

NDEMBU: A group of emigrant Lunda, with very elaborate rituals, whose organization and symbolism have been investigated intensively by Turner.

NGONI: Powerful states established by armies of conquest coming north from Zululand (see below). These armies absorbed those conquered en route, and the inhabitants of the region west of Lake Nyasa, where they settled. Barnes and Read have studied various of these 'snowball states', as Barnes named them.

NUBA: A congeries of people living in the Nuba Hills of the Sudan: split into many communities, with diverse languages and cultures, they are discussed here chiefly in relation to the problem: 'What is Law?' raised by Nadel, who carried out the difficult task of studying them in all their diversity.

NUER: A militant, pastoral people who depend also on millet. They dwell in the great flood-plain of the Sudanic Nile and its tributaries, and move between higher ground in the floods and lower watering-points. Evans-Pritchard's study of their polity, based on an extended lineage framework, is the classic which revealed the form of this type of polity. Their law has been studied also by Howell.

NUPE: One of the Emirates created by Fulani (Muslim) conquest of an indigenous state. Possessing a large capital, exploiting slave labour, with much trade, they are not a tribal state. Studied by Nadel.

NYAKYUSA: They practise mixed husbandry in the Livingstone Mountains of S.W. Tanganyika. Organized in small chiefdoms, they are marked by a dichotomy between their organization into agnatic lineages, which hold cattle, and their residential distribution into age-villages composed of coevals of a neighbourhood. The effects of this situation enter every aspect of their life as described by G. and M. Wilson.

RUANDA: One of a number of kingdoms to the west of Lake Victoria, created by cattle-keeping Tutsi establishing dominance over Hutu peasants, to establish a caste-like system. Peasants and pastoral elite were connected in diverse ways with the king to give a network of countervailing allegiances. Independence has seen a rising of the Hutu. The standard anthropological study is by Maquet.

SHILLUK: A people who dwell in a narrow strip along the Nile near Fashoda. They have a 'divine kingship', since it is believed that the king's physical and moral condition influence the welfare of the nation and that he should be killed if his powers begin to fail. Evans-Pritchard has analysed the political system within which this kingship operates: he used others' data for this.

SOLOMON ISLANDERS: Typical Melanesians, they show the constant struggle of aspiring men to build up networks of supporters through ceremonial and other exchanges, through marriages, and through debt. Studied by, among others, Hogbin and Oliver.

SWAZI: A kingdom in Southern Africa created by one small tribe conquering its neighbours. Kuper has provided on it one of our best studies of a kingdom of this type, with all its conflicts and its integrating organization and ritual.

TALLENSI: An agricultural people of Northern Ghana, with a very complex system of lineages, linked to one another by overlapping kinship and ritual ties. Studied by Fortes.

TIKOPIA: A small isolated Polynesian island, inhabited when studied by R. Firth by 1300 people. Yet they had an elaborate economic and political organization and highly developed religious cults.

TIV: A Nigerian tribe organized in an agnatic lineage system, whose legal and ritual institutions have been studied by the Bohannans.

TONGA OF THE N. RHODESIAN PLATEAU: A people without chiefs, who are of great interest since individuals and groups are interlinked together through a variety of different types of ties, all enforced by various pressures, including mystical sanctions. The crosscut of these ties, studied by Colson, is so complicated, that it is virtually impossible for permanent hostilities to continue, despite the absence of chiefly authority.

TROBRIANDERS: Inhabitants of a group of islands lying off the S.E. tip of New Guinea. Made famous by the many books on them by Malinowski. Possessing some inheritance of position, they are unusual for the area. They participate in the wide network of ceremonial exchanges of shell ornaments, which involves many islands of the region.

TSONGA (THONGA): The recent indigenes of Mozambique, reports on whom by Junod, a missionary, are great classics of the early twentieth century. He has given elaborate and well-analysed data on their ritual, mystical beliefs, modes of divination and ancestral-cult.

TSWANA (BECHUANA): A group of tribes living in the W. Transvaal and Bechuanaland. The need for water compels them to concentrate in 'towns'. Schapera has published a series of illuminating studies on many aspects, traditional and modern, of their lives.

WALBIRI: A tribe of Central Australian Aborigines, living in very arid conditions, as hunters and collectors, but with a very complex social and religious system. Recently studied by Meggitt.

XHOSA: One of a number of smallish chiefdoms, lying to the south of Zulu. Here, unlike among Zulu and Swazi, no fight for hegemony occurred, though tribes at times combined behind prophets to resist the Whites moving east from the Cape of Good Hope. Studied by many scholars.

YAO: A Muslim African tribe of S. Nyasaland. They are organized in small matrilineages, and struggles between brothers and their sisters' children for control of the group are acute. Further struggles result from the multiplication in a village of diverse matrilineages as the wives of headmen of villages found their descent-groups. Mitchell has analysed this process, and its relation to mystical beliefs.

ZAZZAU: A state similar in type to the Nupe: studied by M. G. Smith.

ZULU: A kingdom of South-east Africa, of a people akin to Ngoni and Swazi. It was created by Shaka in six years of conquest, 1816–1822. Its polity was marked by frequent civil war, rooted in its basic structure. They are strongly patriarchal and the position of Zulu women raises fascinating problems. Many scholars have studied the Zulu: their studies are here pulled together in the light of Gluckman's field studies.

# INTRODUCTION

In 1934 I moved from South Africa to Oxford to continue my study of social anthropology. My teacher at Oxford, the late R. R. Marett, once said to me—presumably to console me—that the great French scholar Marcel Mauss had told him of anthropology: 'In that mighty ocean anyone can catch a fish!' A lot of fishes of many species have been caught by anthropologists. The catches were made originally in the tribal societies, and more recently in Western industrial society.

A relatively short book cannot hope to be a guide to the whole anthropological aquarium. Books attempting this run into several hundred thousand words, and this is not what I have attempted. This book first discusses the origins of anthropology as a subject, and how its development was influenced both by its data and its theories. I show how general anthropology broke up into several specialized disciplines. As I am myself a social anthropologist and not a cultural or psychological anthropologist, I concern myself only with social anthropological studies.

Out of the field which social anthropologists have studied, I have for this study demarcated the region of political struggle and order, of law and social control, and of stability and change in tribal societies. I discuss first what rights to land and other property are recognized in these societies with their relatively undifferentiated economies. This economic situation influences the whole system of social relations so that wealth is produced and distributed in order to acquire personal followings. Competition is as marked as co-operation, but it is severely restricted by the type of tools used, the limited amount of trade and the kinds of goods produced. The effect is that society is dominated by status. Particular kinds of property are valued in terms of their roles in status relations. Economic exchanges similarly tend to be set in general status relations, and types of goods in these exchanges may move in relatively isolated circuits.

The following two chapters deal with the maintenance of order despite struggles for power, and disputes. In societies without governmental institutions, the major problem is to see how rights are enforced and wrongs are redressed. Here emphasis is laid on the effects of conflicts of loyalty and allegiance which prevent factions within a tribe mobilizing in whole-hearted opposition by all of their members. The unifying force of ritual symbols is most important. But the polity is dominated by the wide spread of population under their methods of husbandry. This situation also dominates politics in those tribes which have developed systems of authoritative rule. I expand this by setting out a series of chieftainships ranging from a weak, isolated village under a headman, to the powerful kingdoms of West Africa. Territorial segmentation and other principles of organization are seen to be in conflict with the principle of government: this conflict produces frequent rebellions in the idiom of defending the kingship against an unworthy king. The ritual value of kingship is high. As the economic system becomes differentiated, and a horizontal stratification of the population emerges, 'cities' of some size develop. Attacks on the king and other dynastic struggles are not direct reflections of territorial divisions. Palace intrigues become more isolated from the main mass of people. Contenders rely more on 'mercenaries', clients and men pressed into arms. In the big cities there are suggestions that there is a 'city mob' whose support each party must seek to win. Africa shows a picture similar to that of Europe and Asia in their earlier history.

I have spoken above of 'conflict' between principles of social organization. I want to stress that I apply the word 'conflict' only in this context. Where persons or groups come into 'conflict', in another sense of the word, I speak of competition, strife, disturbances, disputes, quarrels and struggles. Similarly, I confine 'cohesion' to underlying social process, and use ties, bonds and co-operation to define surface relationships.

This specializing of the use of various words out of the riches of English gives a different slant to the next chapter, on *Dispute and Settlement*. The problems here have become deeply involved in a question which has provoked considerable controversy through the centuries: 'What is Law?' In this chapter I argue, as others have, that we must accept that all words which deal with important social facts are bound to have many meanings. If we are to use ordinary words in social science, and not invent a special vocabulary, we must accept this multiplicity of meanings. It is sterile then to argue that such words can only be applied in one sense and not in another. We can only agree in mutual tolerance to specialize series of words, perhaps organized in hierarchies, to deal with complex sets of facts such as those involved in the total process of social control. Hence this chapter is written rather more argumentatively, with some effort at persuasion, than are earlier chapters where there is more agreement among anthropologists both on terminology and on conclusions. Yet I think that even in those earlier chapters I at times approach the frontiers of our understanding, and indicate new problems for research.

The discussion of terminology in the study of 'law' and social control also leads me to take issue with those anthropologists who consider that because there is something unique about any culture, we cannot translate the concepts of one society into the concepts of another society. I show that the concepts of each tribe's law are similar to those of other tribes, and indeed to early Roman and European law. Against this background, I analyse modes of settling disputes, the nature of rewards and punitive sanctions, and the sense of rightness and justice.

Not all disturbances of social relations arise from open breaches of rules of right conduct. A marked characteristic of tribal society is that 'natural' misfortunes are ascribed to the evil wishes of witches or sorcerers, to the anger of spirits affronted by neglect of themselves or of the sufferer's obligations towards kin, to breaches of taboo and omission of ritual, and to rightful curses by appropriate persons. This situation can partly be ascribed to the hazards of life in 'subsistence' economics. But we still have to explain why these hazards are associated with the moral relations between the members of a group. The discussion of mystical agencies of social control, and how they operate in the life of a group, leads to an analysis of this situation. The analysis also explains why, in tribal societies, rituals are organized by requiring persons to act their secular roles, or to reverse these roles. In making this exploration we are led to concentrate again on the deep discrepancies and conflicts between principles of social organization which inevitably produce surface disturbances and needs for readjustment. Rituals cloak these processes from their practitioners.

In the course of this analysis, I examine again how the subject developed after professional anthropologists went into the field to collect their facts, instead of relying on the reports of others. They acquired new and richer ranges of data. I show that as our understanding of problems has deepened, anthropologists have been able to make greater use of these riches. This has led to the analysis of 'extended-cases' covering the relations of persons and groups through a fair period of time. We are able to see how people manipulate in their own interests the very customs and beliefs which constrain their actions. Moreover, each later worker builds on the conclusions of his predecessors: anthropological knowledge is cumulative. Hence anthropology is a science, not an art.

The last chapter considers problems of stability and change in society, with particular reference to 'custom', which remains the focus of interest of all types of anthropology. This leads to a discussion of how social anthropology is related to other social and human sciences, and of the significance which our studies of tribal societies have for general understanding of the nature of social life.

This book is not a summary statement of all the findings of social anthropology. It is a statement of how one social anthropologist, working in the full tradition of the subject, sees the general problem of rule and disorder in social life. It is written largely in the first person. At some points—as when I discuss 'What is Law?'—I argue what is for our subject a somewhat personal view. But it will be clear to any reader that I have been stimulated throughout by the work of my predecessors, my contemporaries, and my successors. I am deeply indebted to my fellow-anthropologists for their contributions to the march of our subject and for a personal comradeship which marks our co-operation—despite disagreement.

But it behoves me here to say which of their works I have neglected. Reluctantly I had to omit any discussion of domestic relations and personal ties of kinship, though this is a field where anthropologists have made most important contributions. To deal at any depth with 'politics and law' has involved me in oversimplification of many rich analyses. It would require another book to cover domestic relations even as cursorily.

This has also meant that I have not referred to much work that has been done in building systematic models of kinship systems and in trying to compare traits of kinship with other social facts.

Secondly, to develop the analysis to some depth, I have concentrated on the results of research on single societies. I have viewed the results of this research comparatively, against a scale of increasing complication, to illustrate the various studies quoted. I try to show how this enhances the significance of each study. It also poses new problems for study.

Thirdly, I have throughout concentrated on a single approach to the analysis of all action and belief: an approach from the context of social relations. I try to demonstrate that this is always illuminating and clarifying for certain purposes. I have not therefore used work which is by persons who are called social anthropologists but which does not have this emphasis. Particularly this means that I do not refer to a number of highly regarded studies on religious and philosophical ideas.

In this way I show that there is a systematic interdependence running from the structure of economic and social relations, to ideas of property and types of economic exchange, political processes, ideas of law and morals, and ritual beliefs and practices. Hence there is a fourth limitation. The book concentrates on tribal society. I made occasional references, where it seems appropriate and illuminating, to studies of peasant villages in India or elsewhere. But on the whole I judged that the study of peasants was another field. The study of tribal society has stimulated, and been stimulated by, the study of peasants. It would have produced a far more superficial book had I tried to draw on the wealth in this somewhat distinctive field, even though many of the social processes with which I am concerned are represented there.

These limitations have also led me to concentrate on African material. In my initial chapters I use reports from tribal societies throughout the world. But save for studies of tribal law in North America, 'politics' have been best investigated in Africa, for reasons I need not here detail. Having concentrated on Africa for political analysis, I found it simpler for readers if I used this as a background to my analysis of law and ritual. But I also refer to many tribes living in other continents.

Concentration on tribal politics, and hence on Africa, has also meant that British social anthropology is here over-represented. A book on domestic relations and kinship systems, and a book on peasants, would redress this balance by bringing in much more work by Americans.

I have not cited the work of French, Belgian, Italian, Dutch, German, Soviet, and other national anthropologists because this book is intended for general readers in English-speaking countries. I have learnt from them, as from the writers in English, but it would not have been appropriate for me to draw the attention of many readers to studies in languages which they could not pursue.

My bibliography may appear long, but I decided that it was best to give readers references to enable them to follow any leads they wished to. Footnotes to the books cited give important details—author, title, date: place of publication and publisher are given in the bibliography. I have as far as possible concentrated on easily accessible books, and reduced references to articles and 'obscure' sources. These will be found in the 'standard' books cited. Where I needed crucial facts or analyses to develop my theses, I had to depart from this tenet. When good summaries of a mass of references, or of long books, are available, I have cited these. This book was virtually completed by mid-1962; books published in 1962 and later are therefore barely used (e.g. Mair's *Primitive Government*—1962), since I was abroad throughout 1963.

Another problem arose. Was I to write in past or present tense? Many anthropologists analyse in a timeless present, for reasons considered at the end of the book. The statement of general principles also reads better in the present than in the past. But many of the processes considered—e.g. the waging of feud and warlike rebellion—do not occur nowadays. Where it seemed appropriate, I have described these processes in the past tense. This does not mean always that the social processes concerned no longer operate. Indeed they are more often still of great importance in the modern life of the tribes, though denied expression in armed fighting.

In addition, I note that as I write, Northern Rhodesia and Nyasaland have not yet changed their names to Zambia and Malawi respectively: I am therefore bound to use the former names.

Finally, I am grateful to Dr. Martin Southwold who spent a long sunny weekend reading through the whole book. He also helped me draft the section on the kingdom of Buganda, which he has studied. I am responsible for the final form of this section. Mr. L. Cooper helped me with the chapter of economics, and I owe much in the final chapter to Dr. I. Cunnison's work. A generous personal grant from the Ford Foundation financed research on many themes. Dr. M. Tyson, Librarian at Manchester

University, helped me in many ways. Miss S. M. Davies, Miss S. J. Perrin, Mrs. E. Ruhemann and Mrs. D. Sansom worked on the manuscript. Professor I. Schapera, as always, has helped me substantially. My wife has assisted me by reading a mass of background literature in anthropology and history, and has read and improved each draft of the book to its final form. I dedicate the book to her in acknowledgment of this help, and her help in my field research and with my other books.

MAX GLUCKMAN

Victoria University of Manchester
England
February, 1964

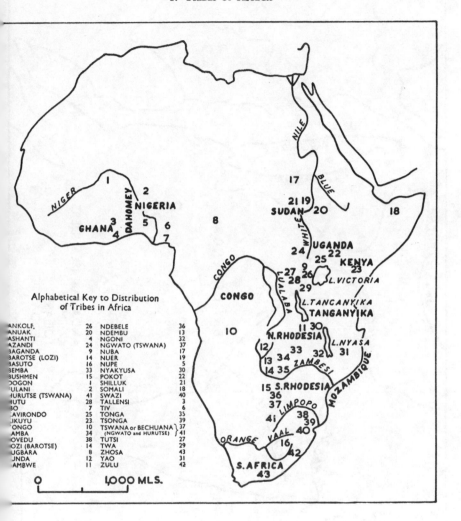

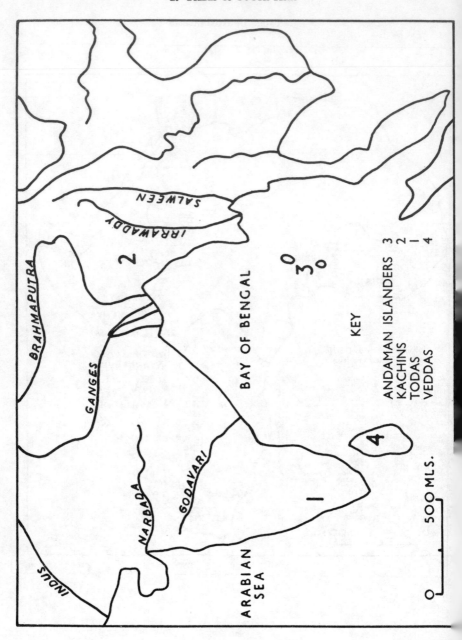

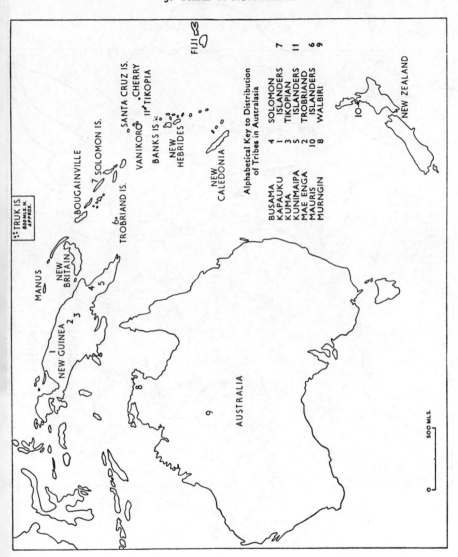

TRUK IS. :•:
800 MLS. N.
APPROX.

MANUS

NEW
BRITAIN

BOUGAINVILLE

SOLOMON IS. 7

SANTA CRUZ IS.
.CHERRY
VANIKORO° •TIKOPIA
11

BANKS IS. :•:
NEW
HEBRIDES

FIJI ∅

NEW GUINEA

TROBRIAND IS. 6

NEW
CALEDONIA

NEW ZEALAND

Alphabetical Key to Distribution
of Tribes in Australasia

| | | | |
|---|---|---|---|
| BUSAMA | 4 | SOLOMON ISLANDERS | 7 |
| KAPAUKU | 1 | TIKOPIAN | 11 |
| KUMA | 3 | TROBRIAND ISLANDERS | 6 |
| KUNIMAIPA | 5 | WALBIRI | 9 |
| MAE ENGA | 2 | | |
| MAURIS | 10 | | |
| MURNGIN | 8 | | |

AUSTRALIA

0   500 MLS.

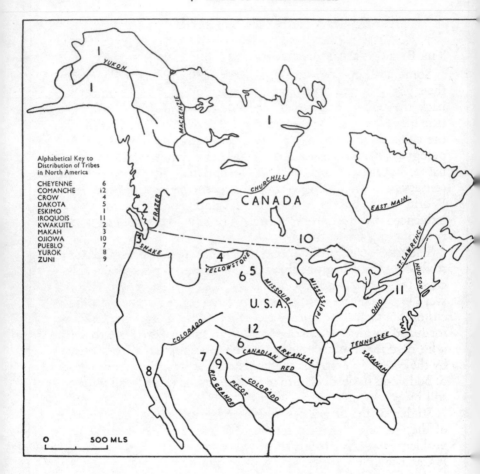

Alphabetical Key to
Distribution of Tribes
in North America

| | |
|---|---|
| CHEYENNE | 6 |
| COMANCHE | 12 |
| CROW | 4 |
| DAKOTA | 5 |
| ESKIMO | 1 |
| IROQUOIS | 11 |
| KWAKUITL | 2 |
| MAKAH | 3 |
| OJIOWA | 10 |
| PUEBLO | 7 |
| YUROK | 8 |
| ZUNI | 9 |

0    500 MLS

# CHAPTER I

# DATA AND THEORY

## THE BEGINNINGS OF ANTHROPOLOGY

Some anthropologists, like other folk, have tried to lengthen their pedigree and they have traced the origin of the subject far back through the centuries—indeed, as far as Herodotus. It is true that Herodotus was interested in describing the societies and the cultures of men and these are the fields of study of anthropology. But the subject as a specialized discipline, with its own name, began to develop in the second half of the nineteenth century. It has changed radically, particularly since the First World War, but as a science's development continues to be influenced by its history, I survey briefly how modern social anthropology has evolved.[1]

The anthropologists of the second half of the nineteenth century studied a mixed bag of subjects: skull-shapes, types of hair, folk-tales, the material objects of the so-called simple peoples which were beginning to be assembled in Western museums, wedding customs, magical practices, as-yet unwritten languages, and so forth and so forth. Looking back, I can sympathize with the wit who described anthropology as 'the investigation of oddments by the eccentric'.[2] In this chapter I consider how the investigation of oddments has broken into several disciplines, maybe all pursued still by eccentrics.

Studies of the origin of religion and magic were characteristic of the era, and the most famous of those who worked on this problem was Sir James Frazer, who wrote *The Golden Bough*. Frazer began his study, in twelve volumes, by setting out to explain the ritual of the priest-king of the grove of Nemi in ancient Italy: '. . . in this sacred grove there grew a certain tree round which at any time of the day, and probably far into the night, a grim figure might be seen to prowl. In his hand he carried a drawn sword, and kept peering warily about him as if at every instant he expected to be set upon by an enemy. He was a priest and murderer; and the man for whom he looked was sooner or later to murder him and hold the priesthood in his stead. Such was the rule of the sanctuary. A candidate for the priesthood could only succeed to office by slaying the priest, and having slain him, he retained office till he himself was slain by a stronger or a craftier.'[3] In order to understand this ritual, Frazer was led to consider priestly kings in general, different kinds of magic, worship of trees, sexuality and marriage in ritual, taboos of all kinds, the soul and its perils, the killing of divine animals and propitiation of slain game, the treatment of the last sheaf of corn, scapegoats and sacrifice, fire, first fruits and the mistletoe and peasants' games.

Frazer brought order into this varied set of data by connecting them with one another in terms of an evolutionary theory, since that type of theory was dominant at the time. Anthropologists were then largely interested in so-called primitive societies and their customs because they saw these as representing earlier stages of civilization, antedating our historical knowledge of early European society, from which there had been steady progress up to the high peak of Victorian civilization. Some primitive customs had indeed survived, and at times threatened to be revived.[4] But on the whole these were being left behind in the march of reason. They recognized that the societies which were being observed in Africa, Asia and the Americas, in Australia and the Pacific Islands, had long histories, and they tried to penetrate through extant customs to the ultimate original circumstances in which custom and culture were born. To do this, in many cases they used a mode of reasoning which a great social anthropologist, Professor A. R. Radcliffe-Brown (1881–1955), called the 'if-I-were-a-horse' argument.[5] This refers to a story of a Middle West farmer whose horse strayed out of its paddock. The farmer went into the middle of the paddock, chewed some grass, and asked himself: 'Now if I were a horse, where would I go?' It is undoubtedly caricature to apply this joke to the very learned and intelligent books of many early anthropologists; but there is also a sad element of truth in this—as in many—caricatures. The anthropologist in effect asked himself: 'Now if I were a man, just becoming a man, and not quite a man, still without a culture, what would I think in such-and-such circumstances?'

Take the passage in which Frazer introduces 'The Myth of Adonis' into the argument of *The Golden Bough*:[6] 'The spectacle of the great changes which annually pass over the face of the earth has powerfully impressed the minds of men in all ages, and stirred them to meditate on the causes of transformations so vast and wonderful. Their curiosity has not been purely disinterested; for even the savage cannot fail to perceive how intimately his own life is bound up with the life of nature, and how the same processes which freeze the stream and strip the earth of vegetation menace him with extinction. At a certain stage of development men seem to have imagined that the means of averting the threatened calamity were in their own hands, and that they could hasten the flight of the seasons by magic art. Accordingly they performed ceremonies and recited spells to make the rain fall, the sun to shine, animals to multiply, and the fruits of the earth to grow. In the course of time the slow advance of knowledge, which has dispelled so many cherished illusions, convinced at least the more thoughtful part of mankind that the alternations of summer and winter, of spring and autumn, were not merely the result of their own magical rites, but that some deeper cause, some mightier power, was at work behind the shifting scenes of nature. They now pictured to themselves the growth and decay of vegetation, the birth and death of living creatures, as the effects of the waxing or waning strength of divine beings, of gods and goddesses, who were born and died, who married and begot children, on the pattern of human life.

'Thus the old magical theory of the seasons was displaced, or rather supplemented, by a religious theory. For although men now attributed the annual cycle of change primarily to corresponding changes in their deities, they still thought that by performing certain magical rites they could aid the god, who was the principle of life, in his struggle with the opposing principle of death.' Hence they now performed ceremonies which were religious or 'rather magical dramas' setting forth '. . . the fruitful union of the powers of fertility, the sad death of one at least of the divine partners, and his joyful resurrection. Thus a religious theory was blended with a magical practice. The combination is familiar in history. Indeed, few religions have ever succeeded in wholly extricating themselves from the old trammels of magic. The inconsistency of acting on two principles, however it may vex the soul of the philosopher, rarely troubles the common man; indeed he is seldom even aware of it. His affair is to act, not to analyse the motives of his action. If mankind had always been logical and wise, history would not be a long chronicle of folly and crime.'

Frazer thus imagines to himself what it would be like to be original man confronted by the cycle of the seasons, and their uncertain clemency, and works out that he would react by trying to control them by magical rites based on his associating like things with like: similar objects or actions will produce similar effects, as that black smoke will produce rain clouds. Or things which have been in contact with one another will continue to influence one another so that lightning-struck trees provide substances which produce rain.[7] All this is worked out by *a priori* speculation, as is the next step that 'in acuter minds magic is gradually superseded by religion, which explains the succession of natural phenomena as regulated by the will, the passion, or the caprice of spiritual beings like man in kind, though vastly superior to him in power.

'But as time goes on this explanation in its turn proves to be unsatisfactory. For it assumes that the succession of natural events is not immutable, but is to some extent variable and irregular. . . .' Yet order is there to be found, and order is gradually extended: '. . . the keener minds, still pressing forward to a deeper solution of the mysteries of the universe, come to reject the religious theory of nature as inadequate, and to revert in a measure to the older standpoint of magic by postulating explicitly, what in magic had been implicitly assumed, to wit, an inflexible regularity in the order of natural events, which, if carefully observed, enables us to foresee their course with certainty and to act accordingly. In short, religion, regarded as an explanation of nature is displaced by science.' But science, though it has something in common with magic, postulates a quite different kind of order in nature.[8]

With all respect, this is all 'If-I-were-a-horse' reasoning. Frazer knew of course that all tribes must have a reasonable amount of accurate technological knowledge, or they could not have survived. Science in the sense of a deliberate search for the immutable connections between events, and the testing of already 'established' truths of this kind, is not found in tribal society— and indeed only flowered in Europe from the time of men like Bacon and Galileo, though Ancient Greeks were clearly scientists. But tribal society has an organized body of empirically verified, applied 'science'. It has magical actions and religious activity: and, equally, religious activity, and actions comparable with magic, exist into the present as we shall see. Frazer did not attempt to examine the contexts in which these different types of activity were practised and different sorts of ideas were employed, as I shall show his successors did. He postulated a theory of intellectual development by placing on a time-scale institutions which co-exist. He worked out the stages on this scale by imagining how he himself would have reasoned had he been there: first, thinking he could control nature by associating like antecedents with like after-events; by thereafter escaping from his keen-witted disillusionment into the belief that the powers were there but superior to him; and yet thereafter by escaping from his further disillusionment, this time with religion, to accepting a regularity and an immutability in nature of which man could avail himself, once he bowed to necessity.

This is, again, caricaturing Frazer's main thesis of the movement from magic through religion to science. In the course of his monumental study he lighted on illuminating themes, he pointed to significant associations, he suggested many lines of research. But he was always working out where the horse would have gone, had he been the horse. It did not—perhaps could not— occur to him that science, magic and religion may operate in quite different contexts of social relations and serve different kinds of emotional and intellectual needs. These we shall examine in a later chapter.

Frazer was not alone in reasoning thus. The other great British anthropologist of the same period, Sir Edward Tylor, tried to determine the origins of religion, which he defined as basically a belief in spiritual beings. He came to the conclusion that men must have tried to explain the differences between human beings before and after death, what happened to them when they were asleep or unconscious or in a trance, how they dreamt and saw other persons in their dreams or themselves appeared in the dreams of others. He then concluded that it is obvious that men must have seen a person as possessing a life and a phantom, in addition to a body. He went on: 'These two are evidently in close connexion with the body, the life as enabling it to feel and think and act, the phantom as being its image or second self; both, also, are perceived to be things separable from the body, the life as able to go away and leave it insensible or dead, the phantom as appearing to people at a distance from it.' Later, he argued, the beliefs would be combined: this too is an obvious step. Then men would work out that they have what Tylor calls 'the ghost-soul', a type of belief which we know ourselves and which is reported from most of the peoples of the world. This is arguing, again, 'If I were an original man, where would I have gone?'

Tylor supported this particular reconstruction skilfully, by citing piecemeal beliefs from all over the world, such as that of the Fijians, who think that a man must be awakened gradually lest he be roused before his soul has time to re-enter his body.[9] Tylor's theory is plausible enough: like Frazer he explains a whole range of facts quite logically. And the sequence of temporal origin and development may of course be correct: there is not, and never will be, any means of knowing. It is delving in what the American anthropologist A. Goldenweiser called 'a chronological vacuum'. But the facts are logically explained by putting them on an evolutionary ladder, erected out of Tylor's thought processes, and the rungs are fabricated by detaching from one another different customs and beliefs in the same community.

SURVIVALS

Sometimes it happens that the wrong kind of beliefs and practices are found in a particular society. This was explained by the subsidiary thesis of 'survival': magical thinking in Frazer's analysis survives into religious thinking. Other customs are dim forerunners of a later historical phase. None of the analyses of this type set out to relate together and show the interdependence between the customs and beliefs existing in one community at any one time. Instead the customs and beliefs are shifted about, as material products of tribal societies may be moved around in and between museum cases. Here one can show that men first swam a river with an arm across a log, then they flattened the top of the log to put goods on, then they hollowed the log a little, then they hollowed the log to get a dugout, then they added strakes to the dugout sides, then they built a boat of strakes on keel and ribs—but many peoples still scrape a hollow in the top of the keel, to connect the boat back to its origin.[10] Doubtless this is an accurate picture of the evolution of the boat from a log: and the evolution of customs and beliefs may have proceeded along the paths that Frazer, Tylor and others postulated. But besides the fact that we cannot check these theories, they were structured on pure imagining of what human thinking was like.

And they always left a great deal of associated behaviour un-explained. For example, Tylor's theory of the ghost-soul did not explain the nature of funeral rites, nor the varying attributes of the soul for different ranks in the same society or in different societies, nor the fear of death. Glancing ahead to modern anthropology, I cite how Radcliffe-Brown gave us a theory which does enable us to study these problems.

## DEATH AND THE SOCIAL PERSONALITY

Radcliffe-Brown points out[11] that two things do in fact survive a man's death. The first is the body which has to be disposed of in some way. The second is what Radcliffe-Brown calls the social personality, which is the total set of the man's relation-ships with other members of the community—that is, his position as father to children, as son to father, as husband to wife, as subject to chief, and so on. After a man has died, these relationships continue to exist: his social personality survives. In the funeral rites these relationships are adjusted to accommodate them with the fact of his death. If he is a mature adult, occupying an important position in society, his heir must be appointed to take over his place. Often the heir replaces his dead predecessor in so many respects that a social position is maintained in perpetuity through the generations: 'The King is dead, Long Live the King!' The widows may be taken in marriage by the heir, save that a man may not inherit his own mother, or they may remain married to the dead man, under what we call the 'levirate' (from 'levir', a woman's marriage to her brother-in-law, after the ancient Hebrew institution whose obligations Onan refused to fulfil), while they cohabit with some kinsman who gives them sons who are still children to the dead man.

Radcliffe-Brown's formulation of the 'origin' of the belief in a soul in terms of a person's position in society enables us to study what happens after a death. We see too why the rites vary for chiefs and commoners, men and women, adults and children, and so forth. Each of them had a different social personality, and hence it is reasonable that each should have a different form of burial, though each has the same kind of ghost-soul on Tylor's theory (but not in his descriptions of the variations). It is clear too why so many peoples believe that the soul undergoes a period when it wanders loose, in the wilds, before it is instituted among the ancestral spirits or makes a safe journey to the place of the dead. This is the period during which the survivors, the community, are adjusting themselves to the alteration in the pattern of their inter-relationships which must follow on a death. The theory also suggests why death is feared, not by the individual alone, but by society: it is an attack on the society of living men for it wrenches and dislocates their relationships with one another; and once it has gained a foothold, they fear it may not be content with a single victim. It transforms a man who was a source of satisfaction into a source of pain.

## SOCIAL FACTS

When Radcliffe-Brown began to work out his analysis around 1910, he was influenced by a school of French sociologists or anthropologists, under Émile Durkheim. Durkheim and his colleagues followed a very different line of interpretation from that of Frazer and Tylor. Frazer and Tylor (and many others) had an 'intellectualist interpretation', as it has been called by Evans-Pritchard:[12] that is, they imagined themselves as intellectual savages faced with the problem of explaining natural and human events to themselves. Durkheim argued throughout that there was a domain of 'social facts', which were peculiar and separate from psychological and biological facts; and further he contended that social facts could only be explained by reference to other social facts. He attacked various theories of society, such as that of Herbert Spencer, which attempted to derive social facts from individual personal needs and arrangements.[13] The two chief characteristics of a social fact were that it was external to the individual and it constrained his actions. That is, the individual did not invent the action or belief: it existed before he did, and he was under compulsion to accept it, or at least behave as if he did. Hence the source of social facts had to be sought outside individuals. For example, religion could not be explained by reference to individual thinking and feeling: religion was part of society. Durkheim in fact argues that God is the force of society which each individual feels pressing upon him, constraining him through what Durkheim called the collective conscience.[14] The argument that society and culture were 'super-organic', greater than any individual, was to continue for very many years. There are still many psychologists and anthropologists who in practice explain societal and cultural phenomena by reference to individual personality. Durkheim contended that this was a fundamental error, since the whole can never be explained by its parts: he compared this error with trying to find the characteristic of life in the atoms of hydrogen, oxygen, carbon and nitrogen which make up the substance of cells. Again, he stated that the hardness of bronze is not in the copper or the tin or the lead which are its ingredients, and which are soft and malleable, but in their mixture. So society is much more than the individuals who comprise it, and culture is greater than the individuals who bear it.

If we accept this view,—and it seems so obviously correct to me that I shall not justify it further—, then we automatically reject Frazer's and Tylor's type of interpretation, because it attempts to explain social and cultural facts by individual intellectual reasoning, on the 'if-I-were-a-horse' model. Radcliffe-Brown's explanation is quite different. It sees that men are born into a society and a culture which impose certain ideas and beliefs on them, including the idea of survival after death. Men do not believe in immortality—and the kind of immortality varies from society to society—because of their individual feelings or efforts of mind, but because they are taught to do so. Some anthropologists have sought the origin of the belief in man's inability to accept his own extinction. As one has put it: 'Man's hopes will hurdle death itself' (Wallis); and another wrote that in 'the conflict and chaos of death' religion 'standardizes the comforting, the saving belief' (Malinowski). Individuals may indeed in this situation get comfort and hope from the belief, but the belief transcends any individual. Its 'origin' must therefore be sought in the conditions of social life, for it is found wherever men live in society; and those conditions must explain why all societies attach such importance to the proper performance of funeral rites. The improperly buried return to trouble the living. The social importance of the belief is far greater than the comfort it gives the dying individual. This is shown by the way in which tribes who worship their ancestors give little heed to the afterlife of the spirits, but emphasize always the bonds of the spirits with their surviving descendants, and the effects of those bonds on the relationships of those descendants. The 'after-life' of the spirits is left vague, undrawn, something like life on earth, though better, and below the ground or in the sky.[15] In later chapters we shall examine the results of this shift in approach in greater detail. Meanwhile, I note that the same objections as have been levelled against the intellectualist interpretation of ritual and belief can also be brought against interpretations which refer these to the emotions of individuals—e.g. to the awe which it is alleged they must feel in the face of the immense and incomprehensible forces of nature, and so forth.[16] This mode of analysis has now disappeared from anthropology. But despite the accumulation of our knowledge about tribal societies similar *a priori* speculations about early stages of forms of organization are still found in books by eminent social and political scientists.

## THE DEVELOPMENT OF THE FAMILY

A second great field of speculation for the early anthropologists was the development of the family. Perhaps the most important study of the tribal family in that period was by an American lawyer, Lewis Morgan. Morgan had observed at firsthand the customs of the Iroquois and his book on them, published in 1851, is still a standard authority. His most significant discovery was their system of classifying kinsfolk. He found that the Iroquois used the same term towards the mother's sister as they did to mother, and correspondingly other collateral kin were classified together with close kin. Later he learnt that other Red Indian tribes had similar systems of kinship terminology, and then they were reported to him from India. He traced the distribution of this kind of system, which has many variants, widely through the world with the help of United States consuls, missionaries and others, and then set out to interpret the structure of the variants. His general thesis was that the terms of kinship used for relatives are related to other customs and particularly to forms of marriage; but that kinship terminology changes more slowly, so that a particular terminology reflects a preceding set of marriage forms. The first stage of human society he considered to be one of promiscuity, without any rule defining incest, but this stage had passed out of existence leaving no trace. The second stage was that of the 'consanguine family', based on the intermarriage of brothers and sisters, but barring that of parents and children. This too was nowhere observable, but its prior existence was demonstrated by the Hawaiian system of designating kin. In Hawaii all of the parent generation are called by a single term, with only sex distinguished; and if maternal uncles (mothers' brothers) are classified with fathers, this must be because previously all *were* fathers, in that they had free access to their sisters. Similarly, a man called all of the lower generation (all nephews and nieces) sons and daughters—because, said Morgan, all his sisters were his wives, as they were wives of his brothers; and in his own generation cousins were called brother and sister. In short, the kinship terminology survives as a kind of palaeontological record of forms of marriage.[17]

I shall not here try to summarize the elaboration of Morgan's fifteen stages of development of marriage and the family, beginning with promiscuity and ending with monogamous marriage and the family of western civilization. He incorporated this development with another evolutionary development of the technical basis of society, from savagery through various stages to grades of barbarism and on to civilization. The general thesis was taken up and set out, in a strikingly reasoned analysis, by Engels in *The Origin of the Family, Private Property and the State* (1884). Morgan's own classification of societies in the stages of technical development was guided by their forms of kinship terminology, so that it can be attacked severely: to take one striking example, he placed the highly developed Hawaiians, one of the 'very noblest of cultures devoid of the metallurgical art' (Lowie) among the lowest 'savages'. In addition, he did not examine all the kinship terms, or deal with anomalies. It is technical beyond my own brief to set out these details, which can be consulted in many books. I stress that the whole analysis is built on the presumption that men only use those terms of kinship address which are warranted by actual sexual and potential reproductive relations, save that there is a further presumption that the terminology never fits an extant marriage system, but always the preceding one.

Morgan's was only one of many similar attempts to work out the evolution of the family, and most of them depended on treating some customs as fossils surviving from the past and indicating earlier forms of society, with others as forerunners of the future. I set out one kind of model of this sort of theory. Travellers in Australia had reported that the Aborigines knew nothing of the role of men in begetting babies. These Aborigines thought that a woman conceived when the spirit of an ancestor entered her body as she passed one of a number of sacred spots. Then when a woman felt a baby stir in her as she passed one of these spots, she would ascribe it to the entry of a spirit, and her child would be linked to that spot. The Australian Aborigines

were already cast for a lowly place in the ladder of social development, so this belief fitted in well with the other class of facts
which many anthropologists besides Morgan had thrown into
a scheme of evolution. In many tribes a man inherits clan-name
or surname, property, office, from his mother's brother, and not
from his father. The child belongs dominantly to the mother's
family, not to the father's. On *a priori* grounds it was assumed,
as by Morgan, that mankind was originally promiscuous and
did not pair in marriage. Therefore no one knew who the father
of a child was; only its mother was definitely known. But the
mother's brother was known: hence his authority over the child
was socially emphasized—and hence the ignorance, or at least
the irrelevance, of the role of man as a begetter. As groups of
men began to marry groups of women, excluding outsiders,
still only the mother was known with certainty, so that the line
of the mother was dominant still. Matrilineal (as it became
known) succession must have been the earliest stage of human
society. This rule of 'mother-right', or matriliny, was broken
when individual men in one tribe began to capture women
from other tribes; the children of these captured wives were their
own and did not belong to the mothers' families. These forcible
marriages of women from outside the tribe became the pattern
for marriages inside the tribe. It was argued that the practice of
stealing brides survived in symbolic form as the reluctance which
the bride in many tribes has to show when being taken by her
husband. In some, she is ceremonially seized by her husband's
friends in a mock fight; in others, she has to weep and be enticed
with gifts through each stage of the wedding rites and consumma-
tion; even into our modern times, it is appropriate to carry her
over the threshold of the new home, as if she were a Sabine
bride. From this stage of capturing brides, as men and women
became paired in marriage or men began to take many wives,
the father got increasing control over the children: father-right
steadily ousted mother-right. In all tribes which have father-right,
the mother's relatives have some rights over the child, and these
were ascribed to customs surviving from an early stage of
mother-right. For example, among the Tsonga of Mozambique,
and many other patrilineal peoples, a man's sister's son can take
any of his uncle's property which he pleases: this is because
once he had been the rightful heir to all his uncle's property.

This kind of scheme was worked out with learned and logical arguments, sometimes based on elaborate statistics. Nevertheless it was purely conjecture. It cannot be proved or disproved. And other, opposite theories have been advanced with equally good logic. Some writers have argued that father-right must have been more fundamental than mother-right. In many animal societies one old male dominates the herd or troop, and drives away his own sons while he keeps the females, so it was argued that early human societies must have been similar. Freud deduced from his psychological investigations that in this situation somewhere the sons killed their father, were stricken with remorse, instituted the incest taboo denying the females to themselves, and from this Œdipal conflict there developed human culture.[18] Yet others have pointed out that the higher apes lived in pairs, and that was the original condition of mankind, from which they fell into group-marriage, or a man took several wives, or more rarely a woman several husbands. Arguments can be worked out to support all these schemes, and if one varies one's definition of what has survived from an earlier stage, the facts can be marshalled to support each argument. When one has worked out one's scheme, one places each tribe on the right rung of the ladder: if in a society with mother-right customs of father-right are found they indicate the beginnings of assertion of father's power; if in a society with father-right customs giving some power to the mother's family are found, these are survivals from the stage of mother-right—or the other way round. Aside from their inherent weakness, the theories are sterile, for they pose no further problems.

Modern social anthropologists approach the task of explaining this wide extension of kinship relationships in a different manner.[19] First, we have to explain why these systems should exist in tribal society but not in developed industrial societies; for Europeans also drew distant kin into closer relationships till well into the Middle Ages. We refer this correlation of extensive kinship reckoning to what I shall stress throughout as the dominant characteristic of tribal societies: they all had primary goods only, and no luxuries. That is, practically all their goods had to be consumed at once, since they had only foods which easily rotted or were eaten by insects in their simple means of storage, clothes of skin or barkcloth or other material with relatively little wear, mud and grass houses or skin tents, and so forth. In this situation, the rich man could not use his wealth to raise his standard of living markedly above his fellows. Chiefs could not build palaces, stage luxurious and selective feasts, wear jewels and costly robes. A man with a thousand head of cattle could not himself consume all their milk, meat and skins. He could only use them to attract and support dependants and thus acquire power over people. For, second, the main social investment available to a man was investment in personal relationships with others. Even into modern times we invest our wealth in gaining the right to demand goods and services from other people: but we do so through *impersonal* systems of relations, in production and in exchange with others who link us to far-flung networks of relations with very distant folk. Each family under subsistence conditions is too small to support itself, and it cannot depend on this sort of impersonal network. It acquires its helpers by calling on more distantly related kin, descendants of recently living common ancestors, and treating them as close kin. In consequence, these economic relations are direct and personal.

Men acquire their rights to call on the services of others through putting them under obligations of reciprocity, by helping them with goods and services, and usually they do so through established kinship relations, or by entering into marriage alliances with them. Even trading relations are converted into quasi-kinship relationships: in Barotseland in Northern Rhodesia (now Zambia) men begin by bartering with one another, and when they have bartered a few times they strike up a compact of friendship with general obligations of hospitality and help, until they may eventually go through a rite which makes them 'blood-brothers'. These relations of kinship and quasi-kinship enable a man to mobilize labour to assist him in major tasks and they are also insurance against disaster and shortage since he can call on his kin and his in-laws to help him when he is in need. Hunger, due to drought and flood and crop-blight or stock-epidemic, always threatens these people who are subsistence husbandmen, so that they are constantly in danger of famine. Their simple technology makes it easier to move people to food, than food to people: in times of shortage tribesmen move towards those of their relatives who have escaped disaster.

POOR AND RICH

Simple technology has a further effect. With available tools—axe, hoe and adze, spear and trap and bow-and-arrow, dugouts or canoes and fishing-nets—each man can produce little beyond what he can himself consume. Hence though the poor might work for the rich, they cannot be employed to give the rich an elaborate level of life above their own. This limitation in the economy is strikingly illustrated in a statement by David Livingstone, who himself fought the external slave-trade, about the condition of domestic slaves among the Ndebele, a Southern Rhodesian tribe of raiding warriors. He quotes with approval a missionary who had worked among these people: 'The African slave, brought by a foray to the tribe, enjoys, from the beginning, the privileges and name of a child, and looks upon his master and mistress in every respect as his new parents. He is not only nearly his master's equal, but he may, with impunity, leave his master and go wherever he likes within the boundary of the kingdom: although a bondman or a servant, his position . . . does not convey the true idea of a state of slavery; for, by care and diligence, he may soon become a master himself, and even more rich and powerful than he who led him captive.'

Of the working of the slaves, this missionary said: 'Neither the punctuality, quickness, thoroughness, nor amount of exertion is required by the African as by the European master. In Europe the difficulty is want of time; in Africa, what is to be done with it.'

There are widespread systems of trade in some areas of the tribal world, but these mostly do not take place only as direct barter. Pairs of partners are linked together in ceremonial exchange, sometimes of valuables which have symbolic worth only, though under the protection of this ceremonial exchange important useful goods, produced only in one area, may be traded; and then these may move from one ceremonial partner to another, in a quasi-kinship relationship, for hundreds of miles, as across Australia[20] or New Guinea.[21]

These economic limitations influence all forms of relations in tribal society. This appears most markedly in the situation of chiefs. Many well-authenticated records describe how African chiefs distributed the tribute which flowed in to them from their people, back among the people, either as individual gifts or in huge public feasts. At the beginning of the nineteenth century Shaka, the chief of a small tribe, conquered many other tribes to build a powerful kingdom.[22] He had tens of thousands of warriors at his command: yet, as a writer on Zulu history said, 'It is, perhaps, easier to secure increased means than a corresponding increase of capacity of enjoying them. Thus the great wealth which the spoils of fallen tribes supplied made little change in Tshaka's personal wants. His fare differed but little from that of a native of ordinary means. He knew of no choicer food than boiled beef, and the beer which was the beverage of any man successful in raising a crop of grain. His eyes were reddened by the smoke which filled the ventless hut in which he lived. He slept on a straw mat, with a wooden pillow to support his head, and a mantle made of the skins of animals to cover his body. His apparel was neither so rare nor so costly as to be beyond the means of a common man.' An English trader who lived with Shaka described how when Shaka wanted to build a new barracks for a regiment of some thousand men, he had them all march from distant forests to the site, each warrior bearing a single sapling. At the site, they danced as well as worked, and then feasted. Shaka could not put his labourers into big enterprises, though he derived great power from them.

Dr. Ian Hogbin, a professional anthropologist, virtually repeats the historian of the Zulu, when he writes that the 'possession of wealth in the Solomon Islands, as amongst ourselves, ensures prestige. But in a Native community, the same scale of comforts—or lack of them—is available for all; everyone has to spend several hours of the day at the same kind of work, all eat the same kind of dishes prepared in the same type of utensils from similar raw foods, and all sleep on the same kind of mats for beds. The house of a wealthy man may be larger it is true, and better built than that of one who is insignificant, and he may have several wives, but the difference otherwise is negligible. Reputation is accordingly enhanced not by accumulating possessions in order to use them oneself, but by giving them away.'

And here is one final example of this giving away. François Coillard, the first French missionary to the Barotse kingdom on the Upper Zambezi, considered that the chiefs exploited their people; but he described how the Barotse king distributed among the people all the cloth he obtained from a caravan of goods brought in from the West Coast, until every man around the capital had cloth fluttering from him, while the king had none. This philanthropy is basic in these systems: kings, however cruel and tyrannous, were always acclaimed as generous. Shaka's assassin and successor Dingane is said to have 'fed the vultures' with those he executed, but his praise-songs speak also of his feeding the people. It is, in some ways, the kind of American philanthropy which O.Henry satirized.

To follow the theories about tribal society on which I shall concentrate in later chapters it is essential to grasp these fundamental limiting economic conditions, for I shall refer all characteristic institutions to them. Here I suggest they account for the widespread system of classifying distant relatives as if they were close kin, though we are still left with the problem why some tribes are patrilineal, some are matrilineal, and some are omnilineal, emphasizing equally rights in all lines of descent.[23] There is too the problem, why different tribes have specific forms of terminology. We must seek the origins of both in extant social conditions.

STATUS TO CONTRACT

This account of how we now approach the problem of the kinship terminology of tribal society shows that we look not to some past form of marriage, worked out by 'if-I-were-a-horse' reasoning, but at existing technical and economic conditions to explain the present form of institutions.[24] Something of this sort of approach was already appearing during the period of Morgan, Frazer and Tylor, in the writings of a few students, who were not anthropologists, of the early history of mankind. Notable among them were Durkheim and his colleagues, sociologists rather than anthropologists. In his *De la division du travail social* (1893) Durkheim did not make a speculative reconstruction of stages, as from magic through religion to science, but demonstrated how the character of religion and ritual, and of types of law and morality, altered with the increasing division and specialization of labour. But for me personally the greatest of these men, whose book I can read as if I were conversing with a modern anthropologist, was Sir Henry Maine, whose *Ancient Law* (1861) put forward a patriarchal origin for society on the basis of Roman and Celtic and Germanic law, and his knowledge of Hindu law gained as a judge in India. Maine was a lawyer, a professor of jurisprudence at Oxford. He saw the major development of society as from a state in which its law was dominated by status, to a state in which the law was dominated by contract, a generalization which has been validated by subsequent research, and which will inform my whole analysis. And when evidence turned up to counter his evolutionary thesis that societies were originally all organized in patriarchal extended families, he acknowledged that 'the observation of savage or extremely barbarous races has brought to light forms of social organization extemely unlike that to which [I have] referred the beginnings of law, and possibly in some cases of greater antiquity'—these were reports on matrilineally organized societies, with which Maine dealt in his *Early Law and Custom* (1883). He was ready to accept new evidence, not to distort it.

The evolutionary theories I have been summarizing passed out of fashion, though of recent years a new school of evolutionism has regained strength among some American anthropologists, whose work I refer to in Chapter III. The older evolutionists were discredited partly by the demonstration of the weaknesses in their arguments, and above all by the development of much more careful methods of tracing the historical connections between different societies and the diffusion of cultural traits and material objects from one tribe to another, and from one region of the world to far-distant regions. Some of the historical theories produced were as speculative as their evolutionary predecessors, and as cavalier in handling evidence; but much important work was done in this vein. It continues to be done, under the title of ethno-history; but it has not influenced social anthropology so I leave its story aside.

### New Modes of Analysis

One of the general principles found in the classificatory system of kinship terminology is 'the identification of alternate generations'—grandparents and grandchildren are identified with one another, and united in 'hostility' to the intervening generation, which is adjacent to each of their generations. In our society, we know the effects of this identification in our belief that grandparents spoil and do not discipline their grandchildren. In some tribes, grandparents and grandchildren may call one another by the same terms as they use to brothers and sisters; or a grandfather may call his granddaughter 'my wife' and a grandmother her grandson 'my husband'. These are the kinds of terms which the evolutionists interpreted as survivals from an earlier situation in which these relatives married one another. When we find these customs in a tribe today, they are a form of joking relationship, an instituted and privileged, indeed prescribed, form of teasing. As I observed it in Northern Rhodesia, when a grandparent called a grandchild of opposite sex 'my spouse' it provoked him or her and adult onlookers to mirth, while it embarrassed the child. They explained to me: 'She [he] is my wife [husband] of the mouth only', and the idea of actual marriage was horrible to them. Radcliffe-Brown has suggested that this identification of alternate generations is related to the fact that children replace, socially, their grandparents and not their parents, with whom, indeed, they are competitors. When a man reaches the age of 20 his father will be, say, 40, and in the full bloom of mature adult life, while his grandfather, at 60, is passing out of active participation in many activities. There is competition between parent and child: it may be considered improper for a woman to continue bearing children after her eldest daughter has given birth to a child. This situation, together with the strains which arise in the parent-child relationship because the former have to discipline and train the latter into decent ways of living, introduces an element of tension and constraint in the relations of parent and child. Without these elements of strain, grandparent and grandchild are regarded as having mutual interests and are therefore identified with each another. But there is a substantial difference in age between them, and age is a basis for social differentiation: this discrepancy between two tendencies within the one relationship is handled by the pattern of joking. We shall see that joking relationships are often found in this kind of situation.

I cite this example of joking now because academically Frazer and Tylor and Morgan are as grandparents to me; and I am entitled to joke about them and their 'if-I-were-a-horse' arguments, without giving offence. I have an anthropological charter to justify my privilege. I can poke fun at their out-of-datedness, which they wear like outmoded dress. But I must also praise them for their tremendous achievement in bringing order into a mass of facts pouring in from all over the world, and for developing a large number of concepts which are still basic in our classifications: clan and moiety, exogamy and endogamy (prescribed marriage outside and inside a group), matriliny and patriliny, the logical principles of magic, and many more. Illuminating ideas light their pages. Despite all this, I find them intolerably boring to read, and even to present them I have indulged myself in caricature. What is the source of this boredom?

I am bored when I read their work because even when they select some special problem for analysis, they build the argument out of oddments of information—oddments gleaned from a variety of different books about the tribal peoples, written by observers with a variety of interests and varying degrees of understanding of what they saw and heard. In many cases this information on tribal customs came from casual travellers, who passed rapidly through a succession of native habitations and often spoke the local language inadequately or employed interpreters not very competent in the observer's home language. The notes that these travellers made were determined by the chance of what happened to be going on when they were there. They were also likely to record what struck them as interesting in itself, and as likely to be of interest to people at home. Thus the unusual, the exotic, the bizarre, even the grotesque, found their way into diaries and letters, or were extracted from these when it came to the publishing of a book. Witchcraft trials, fertility ceremonies, masked dancers, wedding ceremonies, myths—these appear to be more interesting to write about and to read about than is the daily round of agricultural tasks or the routine of domestic life. And they are far easier for the people to describe when they are questioned. I myself have found that it is much easier to get descriptions from informants of the beginning and the end of marriage—the wedding ceremony and the law of divorce—than it is to find out by questioning how married couples live together. The data on these customs, and even those on laws and political organization, were usually reproduced out of their context in the on-going process of social life. There were exceptions to this marked biasing of information among early travellers, as well as among missionaries and administrators who lived for longer periods among particular tribes: some endeavoured to get at the roots of daily domestic and political life. I have already quoted a number of these better observers. But even with most of them the bias remains. And it was on these already 'selected' facts that the early anthropologists had to draw to develop their theories.

The bias is clearly shown in what is a classic book on an African tribe, *The Life of a South African Tribe* (1913, 1927). It was written

PLATE I. Zulu Technology

*a.* Problems of storage: getting grain from a pit in the cattle-corral.

*b.* Co-wives threshing.

(see pp. 13 f.)

PLATE II. A RELATIVELY SIMPLE TECHNOLOGY

*a.* A Barotse smith shows the concentrated skill of a craftsman.

*b.* Barotse fishermen haul in a trawl net, 100 feet in diameter.

(see pp. 15 f.

by a Swiss missionary, Henri A. Junod, who resided for many years among the Tsonga (Thonga) of Mozambique. He had written about their customs and their songs and legends, but his main hobby was the study of insects. Viscount Bryce visited him and urged him that it was more interesting to study the men; and nearly twenty years later, after reading assiduously the work of the armchair anthropologists in the metropolitan countries, Junod wrote his deservedly applauded book. Junod knew the Tsonga well; but his page of contents is indicative of severe bias. This is how he records the life-cycle of a man: twenty-two pages deal with birth and infancy of which some five pages are concerned with secular matters, interlarded with taboos, while the main part is concerned with various ceremonies. Five pages follow on childhood, to be capped by twenty-six pages on rites at puberty. Marriage altogether consumes twenty-one pages, of which only six deal with secular matters; mature age and old age take seven pages; while death, with the elaboration of funeral rites, takes thirty pages—and these lead in his second volume to fifty-six pages on the ancestral spirits and their worship. This is surely out of focus; and it is in one of the best books we have on a single tribe—a book which I learnt to admire so whole-heartedly that when I first looked down from the Lebombo Mountains on to the coastal plain where Junod's Tsonga dwelt, I raised my hat in tribute to him.

The anthropologists at home do not seem to have realized that there was this bias in the books they conned for their facts. And they proceeded often to increase the bias by selecting only those facts which were directly relevant to their own problem: in the study of primitive religion and magic or of primitive mentality, they took the facts about mystical beliefs and ritual practice without weighing them adequately against secular belief and practice.[25] They assembled not only oddments for interpretation, but oddments already selected haphazardly and then culled at random. Frazer organized these oddments around his thesis of the evolution from magic through religion to science, which he had not derived from examining the facts, but had evolved out of his own mind. (Incidentally, Junod has a very careful analysis of the situations in which Tsonga reason scientifically, magically, and religiously.) Since the analysis came out of Frazer's own mind, and not out of the facts, he could do little with the facts except recapitulate them almost endlessly in support of his argument—torn out of their context, in both social and individual life, they could be strung together one after another: facts from the South Seas, from Africa and the Americas, from Asia and peasant Europe, from ancient classic civilizations and the out-of-the-way corners of modern Europe. The argument goes on, persuading by recapitulation and repetition, not by analysis. *The Golden Bough* occupies twelve fat volumes: it might have been a hundred; and it reduces with a lot of this sort of citing of facts to a single large volume.[26]

One of the most biased theories of this kind was Lévy-Bruhl's theory of primitive mentality, published in a series of books. Lévy-Bruhl was following the line of analysis established by Durkheim: viz. that the modes of thought of all peoples were 'collective representations', external and constraining to the individual. He argued that these modes of thought in 'primitive society' were mystical, governed by principles like the law of participation—things which have once been in contact with one another remain in contact with one another. It is an extremely learned, sophisticated and cogent argument, which makes excellent points. But as Evans-Pritchard points out,[27] by selecting facts showing this kind of thinking from books already biased in the same direction, Lévy-Bruhl ends with a tribal man dominated entirely by this kind of thinking. He then makes a further error, by comparing tribal man thinking in situations involving magical and religious beliefs with a European scientist reasoning in his laboratory or a philosopher in his study: he concludes that their respective modes of reasoning are very different. This error of inappropriate comparison—contrasting tribal man when dealing with witchcraft fears and magical techniques with Western man at his occasional rational enterprises—recurs repeatedly in the works of that period; and it continues among laymen to the present day.[28] It is one of the errors that modern anthropology has helped to expose.

## NEW TYPES OF DATA

It is out of this tradition that modern anthropology was born. Its birth was made possible not by the development of new theories, but by obtaining quite a different kind of data, data coming from direct careful and comprehensive observation of life in tribal society. Interpretation of this data has produced several distinct kinds of anthropology, but all of them are deeply influenced by a common factor arising out of their common heritage: an abiding interest in custom. I have indicated that our forbears worked on chance and biased facts, and that they were almost all facts about the standardized pattern of tribal life: beliefs, ritual, laws, in general, custom. These early anthropologists tried to explain custom, not human behaviour. This led to their insisting that there was some interdependence among customs. One of the main themes of this book is that the search for the systematic interdependence of customs remains a hallmark of social and other kinds of anthropology, to distinguish them from other social and mental sciences.

Tylor had travelled in Mexico and Morgan had made an excellent study of the Iroquois, but it is remarkable that none of the anthropological savants working at home thought it necessary to go into the field to collect his own data, though they considered themselves to be scientists. Indeed when William James asked Sir James Frazer about natives he had known, Frazer exclaimed, 'But Heaven forbid!'[29]

Inevitably as natural scientists rather than students of the humanities joined the ranks of anthropology they were bound to go into the field to collect their own facts instead of continuing to rely on laymen. Boas, a physicist and geographer, led the way in America with expeditions to the Eskimo and the tribes of British Columbia: he became the 'father' of a whole generation of American anthropologists. For various reasons which I shall discuss later the anthropology he fostered was not social in its bias, but cultural and historical, so the fruits of his expeditions do not concern us. From Britain, Haddon led an assortment of established scholars in an expedition to the Torres Straits region in 1898 and 1899. They were all natural scientists of different kinds, save for McDougall who was a psychologist. But their field research suffered from some of the weaknesses of the early lay recordings: they spent only a short time with each of the peoples they investigated and had short and superficial contacts with them, while they did not know the native languages and worked through interpreters. Hence they still tended to record the striking facts of custom.

It is appropriate here to discuss the influence on observation of working through interpreters. It is true, as the great American anthropologist Robert Lowie pointed out in his book about *The Crow* Red Indians (1935), that the average anthropologist cannot speak the language of the people he is studying anything like as well as an interpreter from their ranks. But interpretation is a two-way process; and the average interpreter does not speak English (or French, or other language) anything like as well as the anthropologist. Moreover the most difficult part of anthropological analysis is deciding into what technical categories of anthropological analytic concepts to fit the data: and this depends not only on knowing English, but also on being trained in anthropological theory. (Some day the converse position may arise when an African anthropologist studies the English, to analyse English life in the systems of anthropology in his own language.) Finally, to carry out anthropological fieldwork one need not know the whole language, with its whole vocabulary—among the Zulu over 50,000 words. A few thousand words will see one through ordinary questioning and enable one to follow everyday conversation, as in Europe; and one can acquire specific, more technical vocabularies—say about law, or religion—as one studies these fields of action.

With these shortcomings, the work of the Torres Straits expedition did not acquire information which by its very nature would break the bonds of existing theory. Not even the longer spells of fieldwork carried out by three members of this expedition (W. H. R. Rivers among The Todas of the Nilgiri Hills, 1906, and C. G. and B. Z. Seligman among The Veddahs of Ceylon, 1911) were able to produce a radically different kind of data, though, like those of Haddon's company, their reports were far fuller and more comprehensive than earlier records. Rivers in particular developed the careful collection of genealogies of actual people. But their work shows the bias I have described in Junod's: they still studied the societies from the outside and concentrated on custom without reference to social action.

As far as British social anthropology is concerned, the revolution occurred with the work of Radcliffe-Brown in the Andaman Islands in the Bay of Bengal during 1906–08, and of Bronislaw Malinowski in the Trobriand Islands, which lie off the south-east tip of New Guinea, at various periods between 1914 and 1918. Radcliffe-Brown has probably had a more enduring influence on the theory of social anthropology than has Malinowski. It was the latter who, almost by accident, devised a method of observation of social life and culture that produced facts which could

not be confined within the straitjackets—the Procrustean beds—
of existing theories.

Mrs. B. Z. Seligman, wife of C. G. Seligman and herself an
anthropologist of repute, tells me that they were in Sydney for
a meeting of the British Association for the Advancement of
Science when the World War I broke out in 1914. Malinowski was
an Austrian citizen and hence an enemy alien. He was in danger
of being interned by the Australian Government, but Seligman,
Rivers and other British anthropologists persuaded the Gover-
ment that since Malinowski came from the Polish part of Austria
he was really an ally. (He was resident in Britain at that time
and later was a professor in London University and became
a British citizen.) Hence the Australians agreed to 'intern'
Malinowski by allowing him to carry out field research in the
Trobriand Islands, subject only to the rule that he report his
presence regularly to the Australian administrative officers.[30]
Malinowski thus went to live among the Trobrianders, and in
time to learn their language: he not only questioned them about
their customs, but he also observed directly the process of their
community life. Thus he acquired a quite different kind of data
from his predecessors. He had invented, by chance, a new
technique and this virtually created a new series of sciences.
I consider this equivalent to the effect of Leeuwenhoek's improve-
ments on the microscope and their influence on biological
science.

This development in anthropology was inevitable. It is
fortunate that the accidental beginning should have happened
to a man of Malinowski's genius, a word I use advisedly. Perhaps,
too, he was prepared to make the most of the data he acquired
because he had already from literary sources written an analysis
of *The Family among the Australian Aborigines* (1913: in paperback, 1963), which emphasized the 'functional' interdependence
of various social institutions, and among other points insisted
that 'all the economic, social, legal and ritual customs and practices
of the Australians converge on the nodal point of family organization.' It also began to demolish the evolutionary controversy over whether the family preceded clan, or clan preceded
family, by emphasizing that the two coexist with different
spheres of activity, and thus the book disposed of theories of
group marriage.[31]

## MALINOWSKI

Malinowski wrote a series of books on different aspects of Trobriand life, which constitute the biggest single corpus of knowledge, by one man, about one tribe, which we have. In all of them he emphasizes how a quite new kind of data began to pour into his notebooks—data about how the Trobrianders lived together and operated their customs, being both constrained by these yet sometimes seeking to evade their rules. He emphasized how important it was to observe what he called 'the concrete imponderabilia' of social life. The passage in his works which exhibits most vividly for me the change in his thinking, and the change he wrought in anthropological thinking, occurs in a Riddell Lecture which he gave in 1934–35 at the University of Durham on *The Foundation of Faith and Morals* (1936). He describes there how he was recording a myth from an informant, when this informant started boasting that the myth belonged to his clan, and that he alone had the right to tell this myth.[32] Malinowski told him to stop boasting and get on with the myth. The informant kept boasting. Malinowski says it took him some months before he realized that this right of particular persons to boast that telling the myth was their privilege, constituted a most important element in it. From this he worked out that a myth might be not an intellectual response of men, puzzled by the mysteries of the world, but a 'social charter' which defined the rights and privileges of groups and persons to particular positions of social power and to particular property rights. A myth thus might validate existing social arrangements, and have to be interpreted by reference to its connection with other extant institutions of the society. He had first put forward this thesis in his lecture in honour of Frazer in 1925, and though he excluded Frazer from his attack, he was in effect demolishing the Frazerian-type of interpretation of myths propounded by men like Max Müller.[33]

In order to demolish the theories of his predecessors, their *a priori* speculations justified by stringing together isolated facts torn from their context in social life, Malinowski mobilized against them the full complexity of that context. He had recorded not just myths of origin, but the full setting of these myths: who told them and was privileged to tell them, and on what occasions and in relation to what other activities they were recounted. This kind of data could not be acquired by casual visitors or short-term fieldworkers, recording largely by questioning through interpreters, instead of observing the processes in which men co-operated and struggled within a community possessed of a particular culture.

Almost every one of Malinowski's books followed the same model. He began by setting out, say, the over-simple theories on tribal or primitive economic life put forward by earlier writers—that tribal man was ground down by the bare conditions of surviving, or alternatively that he was lazy and thriftless, living on the fruits of nature—then showing out of the complexity of his own field-material that the Trobrianders (here representing all 'savages') were involved in a complex system of production and exchange and consumption, determined by their culture, in which all elements were highly interconnected.[34] For example, the Trobrianders are involved in a cycle of exchange in which shell armbands circle in one direction, while shell necklaces circle in the opposite direction, the one being exchanged for the other. These valuables have no 'intrinsic' value or outside use: their worth comes from their role in the cycle of exchange, and the more famous of them increase in value as they are exchanged. Some valuables move thus within the Trobriand Islands: others travel long distances, and are carried by big sea-expeditions, to launch which labour has to be organized to make outriggers and prepare food. This led Malinowski to investigate the organization of labour through patterned social relationships, and the role of magic in providing safety for the voyagers and success in their *kula* trading, as the exchange of shells is called. Under the shelter of this ceremonial trade there proceeded bartering (but not between *kula*-partners) of useful goods, which are not available in every *kula* centre. He showed how prestige and social position are connected with this trade. He discusses also gardening,[35] and how men in this matrilineal society carry much of their crops to their sisters' husbands' villages to feed their sisters and children: these crops are displayed to boost the gardener's prestige. From this kind of material came other theories: in his *Crime and Custom in Savage Society* (1926) he had begun by demolishing contrasting theories that primitive man was .lawless, or that he was bound by law like an automaton, by showing that these exchanges and gifts linked people together in systems of reciprocal obligation. Similarly, in an essay on 'Magic, Science and Religion' he cited, and then demolished, the simple theories—as he saw them—of Frazer, Marett, Lang, Durkheim and others; and then proceeded to examine magic and religion in their contexts in social and individual life, and to relate them to technical knowledge. Both magic and religion, he argued, out of his observations on how they were practised, 'arise and function in situations of emotional stress: crises of life, lacunae in important pursuits, death and initiation into tribal mysteries, unhappy love and unsatisfied hate'. They are based on mythological tradition, surrounded by taboos and prescribed observances. But the end of magic lies outside its rites—it is a 'specific art for specific ends'. Religion is an affair of public affirmation, in which the end is present in the performance of the ritual itself. Both have functions, in the sense of serving man's needs in society: magic gives him confidence in situations where his empirical knowledge is limited, religious faith 'establishes, fixes and enhances all valuable mental attitudes, such as reverence for tradition, harmony with environment, courage and confidence in the struggle with difficulties and at the prospect of death'. He argues that these beliefs have immense biological value in enabling primitive man to survive.[36]

One of Malinowski's great achievements was in this way to produce a balanced all-round picture of men in tribal society. As he himself wrote in his lecture on myth: 'Our conclusions imply a new method of treating the science of folk-lore, for we have shown that it cannot be independent of ritual, of sociology, or even of material culture. Folk-tales, legends and myths must be lifted from their flat existence on paper, and placed in the three-dimensional reality of full life. As regards anthropological field-work, we are obviously demanding a new method of collecting evidence. The anthropologist must relinquish his comfortable position in the long chair of the missionary compound, Government station, or planter's bungalow, where, armed with pencil and note book and at times with a whiskey and soda, he has been accustomed to collect statements from informants, write down stories, and fill out sheets of paper with savage texts. He must go out into the villages, and see the natives at work in gardens, on the beach, in the jungle; he must sail with them to distant sandbanks and to foreign tribes, and observe them in fishing, trading, and ceremonial overseas expeditions. Information must come to him full-flavoured from his own observations of native life, and not to be squeezed out of reluctant informants as a trickle of talk.

Field-work can be done first- or second-hand even among the savages, in the middle of pile-dwellings, not far from actual cannibalism and head-hunting. Open-air anthropology, as opposed to hearsay note-taking, is hard work, but it is also great fun. Only such anthropology can give us the all-round vision of primitive man and of primitive culture. Such anthropology shows us, as regards myth, that far from being an idle mental pursuit, it is a vital ingredient of practical relation to the environment.'

Malinowski produced many specific illuminating analyses of particular institutions: in the 1920's and 1930's his findings burst like a revelation on the intellectual world, and he was invited to contribute to symposia on magic and science and religion, on language, on law. Not only students of anthropology, but also scholars in other fields, and the literary world, were enlightened by his work. His books and the books of his pupils, as well as of those anthropologists whom he influenced indirectly, are a permanent memorial to his influence. But he ran into a dead end. When his own pupils began to go into the field and pursue research by his own methods, as described above, but with his experience behind them, he was still liable to attack them as he had attacked his predecessors: he simplified and distorted what they had said, and then attacked their analytic theorizing with the complexity of his field data. Unfortunately they had data of the same type as he. For one of his major weaknesses was an inability to appreciate the full significance of another's analysis: his presentation of the arguments of Durkheim and of Sir Henry Maine are travesties of the originals. This led to a second weakness. When he wrote about tribal economics, or tribal law, his main use of the work of economists and lawyers was to set up their alleged speculations about primitive economics and law as Aunt Sallies which he could then knock down with his Trobriand coconuts: he did not try to get at the intrinsic worth in their major analyses.[37]

Malinowski appreciated that his work had helped to bring the final break-up of the investigation of a ragbag of oddments, which constituted the earlier anthropology, into different disciplines.[38] Clearly the analysis of social life was something very different from the study of man as a member of the zoological kingdom. Indeed, though in some British universities, and I believe in most in America, anthropologists are still trained in physical anthropology, in archaeology, and in the study of culture and society, it is recognized that to do research in each of these fields requires highly specialized training. Physical anthropology, investigating the structure of man and his place among the mammals, has become allied with zoology, anatomy, physiology, and other biological sciences. Psychological and cultural anthropology are related to the biological sciences and to psychology and psychiatry, and require accurate knowledge and understanding of those disciplines. But all a social anthropologist needs to know is that elaborate and well-validated research has failed to establish that there are significant differences in the biogenetic endowment of different groups of mankind—as groups. Individuals within groups may vary; but we can treat the biogenetic endowment of mankind as sufficiently equal for us to neglect specific variations as contributing to varying social organizations and their relation to culture.[39] Man is accepted as a plastic organism, whose actions and temperament are moulded by the society and culture into which he is born.

## THE BRANCHES OF ANTHROPOLOGY

If you imagine yourself as an intelligent, well-trained thinker about social life, sitting for a long period to record whatsoever goes on around you in a society you are visiting, and able as you learn the local language to pursue inquiries into what the people believe to be their ends and motives, you will appreciate the richness of the data which began to accumulate in the notebooks of anthropologists. Instead of the chance and haphazard recording of striking events and exotic customs, anthropologists accumulated stores of information on which, because of publishing restrictions, they could only draw for their books in meagre measure. It was akin to the information about the lives of their fellows which had inspired novelists, diarists, biographers and playwrights, though more comprehensive and systematic. In my concluding chapter I shall discuss the difference between the 'artistic' interpretations of these data and the interpretations of anthropologists.

These data could be analysed in several scientific frameworks. First, they could be used to work out patterns which were present in cultures, either in segments or as wholes. These patterns are there, and the search for them is a long-established line of enquiry in our own historical tradition, as studies on the spirit of the

Renaissance, or the Middle Ages, or the Victorian era, witness. Cultures show some consistency in this sense; and the analysis of this consistency became the field of cultural anthropology, strongly represented in America.[40] There is something unique about the pattern of culture of each tribe, even though we find distributed among its population the same sorts of persons as we meet in our own society.

Second, it is possible to use these data, collected by observing many different people's behaviour in a community with its own culture, to work out whether there is something common in the personalities of those people, distinctive from the personalities of members of other communities. This line of interpretation produced the cross-cultural study of personality, also strongly represented in America; and obviously its practitioners turned to psychology, psycho-analysis and psychiatry as logically cognate disciplines.[41] It has also been to these disciplines that the cultural anthropologists have looked for their fellows.

Thirdly, it was possible to concentrate on how social relationships 'hung together': the manner in which different sorts of relations between persons and groups, and within groups, influenced one another. This was the line of interpretation which produced social anthropology; and therefore social anthropologists found their colleagues among sociologists, political scientists, jurisprudents, historians and economists. They sought help in formulating their theories from these disciplines, and in turn began to influence them.

Yet, I repeat, all branches of anthropology still have in common their interest in custom—and their assumption that customs are systematically interconnected with one another. But each branch has begun to find allies in various, other disciplines. The hodge-podge investigation of oddments has broken into different specialized sciences.

Malinowski did not fully participate in this specialization of social anthropology into a separate discipline, which is the path that British anthropology, under the influence of Radcliffe-Brown, has followed. Malinowski became so involved in demolishing the stereotyped views of primitive society held by specialists in the other social sciences, that he seemed unable to turn to their empirical studies of European society for theoretical stimulation. He did not draw on economic theory to understand Trobriands economics, as Firth was to do for the Polynesian island of Tikopia (see below), nor did he draw on sociology, jurisprudence and political science as his successors later did. In the end, this blindness condemned him to theoretical sterility. His reports on his field research clearly and enlighteningly demonstrated the widely ramifying interconnections of various elements of culture and of social life. When he produced an 'abstract theory', he did so by crudely referring institutions to postulated human and social 'needs'. He saw economic organization as providing satisfaction for the needs of man for food and shelter: which indeed it does—but this is not sufficient a principle to analyse the elaborations of economic action. Again, he wrote: 'We could state that the function of the tribe as a political unit is the organization of force for policing, defence and aggression . . . the function of age-groups is the co-ordinating of physiological and anatomical characteristics as they develop in the process of growth, and their transformation into cultural categories. In occupational groups we see that the carrying out of skills, techniques, and such activities as education, law, and power, constitute the integral function of the group.' This is extraordinarily simple-minded for a brilliant mind. Besides this, he became more interested in the processes by which the individual was conditioned within a culture, and produced an extremely crude behaviouristic psychological theory, a theory which appears childish when set against the sophisticated analyses of the relation between culture and personality to which I have referred. Our debt to him remains, for he made field research by professionals into a high art, and in specific study after study he demonstrated that social and cultural facts were interconnected with one another in the present. If I can criticize him severely it is because social anthropology is a science; and a science is any discipline in which the fool of this generation can go beyond the point reached by the genius of the last generation.

Radcliffe-Brown lacked the personality which enabled Malinowski to immerse himself in the lives of the people. Malinowski did not see, as Junod did, an individual moving through a succession of rituals; he saw instead men and women growing up, marrying, living a domestic life together, maturing. But Radcliffe-Brown had immersed himself in sociological theory and had worked out a view of society as a system of regularities between the actions of persons dwelling in a physical environment and acting on it with an equipment of tools and a culture.

In his study of the Andamanese he was influenced by Durk-heimian theory in sociology, and by Shand's psychology of sentiments. He considered that social life was only possible as a moral order; and that this moral order was reflected in the sentiments of members of the community. Myths and legends then became, for example, symbolic statements typifying these sentiments, and this was their social value. Thus they contributed to maintaining the social system. Again, the social personality of the individual, whose significance in funeral rites we have already examined, was also a compound of social and collective sentiments of this kind; and rituals at changes in social position reflected the social value of the individuals and symbolically readjusted the sentiments of others to those changes. His view of society was dominated by organic, physiological parallels: the function of any custom was its role in maintaining the system as a whole. His successors were to advance this thesis considerably.

With this very brief statement on Radcliffe-Brown's early work I complete my survey of the tradition out of which modern social anthropology emerged. Both Malinowski and Radcliffe-Brown were to continue work in the modern sense for many years. I have touched only on social anthropology, since that is my own profession. I am not competent to discuss other forms of anthropology. Social anthropology is dominantly located in Britain, and secondarily in France; for many years in the United States social anthropology was poorly represented, till Radcliffe-Brown began to teach at Chicago in 1931. Since then it has spread in America, under the influence of British work and British-trained Americans. But American anthropology is dominantly psychological and cultural and historical in its emphasis. No-one has explained satisfactorily why there is this difference between the anthropology of the two continents. But the difference runs deep: leading American anthropologists have accused the British of 'selling the pass' to sociologists. Maybe this points to one reason. In America anthropology has to insist on its independence from a very powerful sociology, a subject which till recently in Britain has been on the whole neglected and despised. Secondly, I suggest that the American Red Indians who were naturally the focus of research in the United States, on the whole had had their societies severely dislocated by the Whites. Accounts of their culture were derived

from the reports of surviving individuals, rather than from observation of on-going social life. And the facts of culture, gathered in
that situation, lead naturally to a view of culture as a pattern in
itself and as influencing individuals. British anthropology was
based on observation of on-going societies: Malinowski in the
Trobriands, Firth in Tikopia, Evans-Pritchard and others in
Africa. As they saw social life in action, largely on traditional
lines, they concentrated on social relationships, and not on culture
or the individual. The historical accident of Radcliffe-Brown's
interest in Durkheim sowed theoretical seed on the tilth of data
derived from working societies. But the general anthropological
fascination with custom keeps social anthropology a discipline
distinct from sociology.

[1] This historical introduction is necessarily only a survey. There are many full histories
of anthropology to be consulted: I cite only from America Lowie's *The History of
Ethnological Theory* (1937) and from Britain Evans-Pritchard's *Social Anthropology* (1951).
Kluckhohn's *Mirror for Man* (1954) is an excellent introduction to, and case for, general
anthropology. Evans-Pritchard learnedly traces the primal forbears of social anthropology.
[2] Quoted by Kluckhohn, *Mirror for Man* (1954), p. 11.
[3] Frazer, *The Golden Bough* (1890): abridged edition (1922), p. 1.
[4] Tylor, *Primitive Culture* (1871), i, pp. 138 f.
[5] In a conversation with me.
[6] *The Golden Bough* (1890): abridged 1922, p. 324.
[7] *The Golden Bough* (1890): abridged 1922, Chapters III–V.
[8] *The Golden Bough* (1890): abridged 1922, pp. 711–12.
[9] Tylor, *Primitive Culture* (1871), i, pp. 428 *circa*.
[10] This is an evolution I was taught by the late H. A. Balfour at Oxford in 1934–35.
[11] The theory is set out in his *The Andaman Islanders* (1922).
[12] Evans-Pritchard is preparing a book setting out the situation of all these types of
interpretation, as applied to religion and magic, which I hope will shortly be published.
I have drawn on his lectures published in *The Bulletin of the Faculty of Arts of Cairo University*, 1933–34.
[13] See Durkheim *Les Règles de la Méthode Sociologique* (1895), translated as *The Rules of
Sociological Method* (1938).
[14] See Durkheim, *The Elementary Forms of Religious Life* (English translation, 1915
from French text, 1912). This example of course by brevity over-simplifies Durkheim's
argument.
[15] For an excellent account of such a situation see Fortes, *Œdipus and Job in West African
Religion* (1959).
[16] For a criticism of this kind of speculation see Malinowski, *Myth in Primitive Psychology*
(1926).
[17] Morgan, *Systems of Consanguinity and Affinity* (1871).
[18] Freud, *Totem and Tabu* (1913).
[19] See the superb essay by Radcliffe-Brown on 'The Study of Kinship Systems' in his
*Structure and Function in Primitive Society* (1952).
[20] Thomson, *Economic Structure and the Ceremonial Exchange Cycle in Arnhem Land* (1949).
[21] Malinowski, *Argonauts of the Western Pacific* (1922).
[22] For a stirring account of his career, though a romanticized view of his character,
see Ritter, *Shaka Zulu* (1955).
[23] See below, pp. 53 f.

²⁴ These scholars also produced elaborate analyses of great value, such as Tylor's 'On a Method of Investigating the Development of Institutions, applied to Laws of Marriage and Descent' (1889).

²⁵ Evans-Pritchard brings this point out well in his discussion of 'Lévy-Bruhl's theory of primitive [prelogical] mentality' (1934).

²⁶ In my 'Les Rites de Passage' I consider how Van Gennep who published a book under that title in 1909, produced an illuminating theory which was stultified by this method of proof (see M. Gluckman (editor), *Essays on the Ritual of Social Relations* (1962)).

²⁷ See footnote 25 above.

²⁸ It continually rears its head in Guy Hunter's vivid *The New Societies of Africa* (1962).

²⁹ Recounted by Evans-Pritchard, *Social Anthropology* (1951) at p. 72, from an address by Ruth Benedict.

³⁰ Firth, *Man and Culture* (1957), p. 13 does not refer to 'internment' in his account of this crisis for Malinowski.

³¹ Fortes, 'Malinowski and the Study of Kinship' in Firth (editor), *Man and Culture* (1957), p. 166. Marxists following Engels, maintain belief in a stage of group marriage.

³² I have given a fuller account of this development in Malinowski's thinking, and how he was eventually stultified by the very advances he himself made, in my essays on him in my *Order and Rebellion in Tribal Africa* (1963).

³³ Malinowski, *Myth in Primitive Psychology* (1926).

³⁴ In his *The Argonauts of the Western Pacific* (1922).

³⁵ Further analysed in his *Coral Gardens and their Magic* (1935).

³⁶ Malinowski, 'Magic, Science and Religion' (1925).

³⁷ See my fuller treatment of these weaknesses, with references to criticisms by others in *Order and Rebellion in Tribal Africa* (1963).

³⁸ This break-up was clearly stated by Evans-Pritchard in 'Anthropology and the Social Sciences' and Firth in 'Anthropology and the Study of Society' as far back as 1936 in *Further Papers on the Social Sciences: Their Relations in Theory and in Teaching* (1937: edited by J. Dugdale).

³⁹ Klineberg has summarized admirably the evidence justifying this view in his *Race Differences* (1935) and his UNESCO pamphlet on *Race and Psychology* (1951). The case for treating differences between 'races' as marginal to the problems of social anthropology is argued in M. Gluckman (editor), *Closed Systems and Open Minds* (1964).

⁴⁰ For different ways of handling these problems see Benedict, *Patterns of Culture* (1934) and *The Chrysanthemum and the Sword* (on Japan) (1946), and the various well-known books of Margaret Mead cited in the bibliography. Mead also wrote outstanding work as a social anthropologist.

⁴¹ For the kind of problems discussed in these investigations see Kardiner, *The Individual and his Society* (1929) and *The Psychological Frontiers of Society* (1945); Kluckhohn and Murray, *Personality in Nature, Society and Culture* (1949); and Sargent and Smith, *Culture and Personality* (1949).

CHAPTER II

# PROPERTY RIGHTS AND ECONOMIC ACTIVITY

### LAND TENURE: GROUP AND INDIVIDUAL RIGHTS

Widespread sharing of produce is the rule in tribal societies. Some early Western observers therefore concluded that they were 'communistic', and that individual rights in lands and other goods did not exist. There is implicit in this judgment a false antithesis between 'communistic' and 'individualistic', arising from the way in which we say that a person or a group 'owns' a piece of land or some item of property. We are speaking loosely when we use this sort of phrasing: what is owned in fact is a claim to have power to do certain things with the land or property, to possess immunities against the encroachment of others on one's rights in them, and to exercise certain privileges in respect of them. But in addition other persons may have certain rights, claims, powers, privileges and immunities in respect of the same land or property. Hence when we say that a particular group of kinsmen owns land, we are also saying that all the members of that group have claims to exercise certain rights over that land— maybe equally with one another, maybe varying with their status.[1] The incidence of rights over land varies with the technology of the tribe concerned, from those who live by hunting and collecting wild products to those who have elaborate systems of agriculture.[2] Even when, as in hunting tribes, each member of the tribe has the right to hunt freely over the extent of the tribe's territory, this reduces to a right of every individual to hunt without let and hindrance from others; and this particular right to hunt freely may exist among agriculturists whose arable land is allocated specifically to smaller groups and to individuals within the tribe. Rights of this kind can vary with the methods of exploiting the land: thus hunting with bow and spear may be free, while particular groups own rights to hold game drives or to set game-nets in particular areas.

Similar variations occur in the use of pasturage among herders. There may be areas where rights to graze stock are free, in the

36

PLATE III. Craftsmen of Central Africa

*a.* Native web, and weaver smoking the huge tobacco pipe of the country.

*b.* Blacksmith's forge and bellows of goatskin.

(both from D. and C. Livingstone, *Narrative of an Expedition to the Zambesi*, 1865)

(see pp. 15 f.)

PLATE IV. CHIEFS' PERQUISITES

Presentation at court [to Mosilikatse, king of the Ndebele] of two successful young lion hunters.
(from D. Livingstone, *Missionary Travels . . . in South Africa*, 1857)

sense that any member of the tribe may exercise such rights, while rights to use particular areas around water-holes are restricted. In Bechuanaland no man may own grazing land, which is open to all members of the tribe, but the chief in practice gives rights to men to graze their cattle in particular places and will protect them against trespassers. In that arid land the main problem is storage of water: and rights to water are granted by the chief especially when a man has sunk a water-hole.[3] In most tribes with a mixed husbandry, cattle graze freely on the crop stalks in anyone's fields, though if cattle stray into the fields before harvesting, suit for damages lies.

The position among agriculturalists is more complicated; but in Africa land-tenure laws seem to fall into a general pattern of which the Lozi tribe[4] who dwell in the great flood-plain of the Upper Zambezi River are strikingly representative. Because the river floods every year during the summer rains the people have to build their small villages on mounds in the plain which will stand above the waters. Even from these they move at the height of the flood to temporary villages on the margins of the plain. Each village on its mound is the centre of a number of pockets of arable land, scattered over the main expanse of uncultivable land in the plain and variously affected by flood-waters or by rainfall. The village is also the centre of sites suitable for fishing.

Ultimately the Lozi consider that all the land, and its products, belong to the nation through the king. Though one right of Lozi citizenship, to which all men who are accepted as subjects are entitled, is a right to building and to arable land and a right to use public lands for grazing and fishing, it is by the king's bounty that his subjects live on and by the land. Commoners think of themselves as permanently indebted to the king for the land on which they live and its wild and domesticated products which sustain them. The Lozi say this is why they gave tribute and service to the king and still give gifts. Since tribute was abolished by agreement with the British Government the king has had to purchase many of his necessities from his people, and this is the standard by which the Lozi assess their present poverty: 'Even the king bought fish today.' Sometimes people refuse payment for goods bought by the king: 'How can we take money from our father who gives us our food, for goods which are his?'

The king is thus the 'owner' of Loziland and its cattle and wild products, in the sense that he ultimately claims rights over all land. These rights entitle him to demand allegiance from anyone who wants to settle on the land; he has the power to distribute to people any land which has not been allocated by him or any of his predecessors; he has a right to ask subjects to give him land which they are using, but he cannot dispossess them; he has the right to claim any land (or other good) which has been abandoned or for which family heirs cannot be traced; he has the power to control where men are allowed to build their homes; he has the right through his appropriate councils to pass laws about the holding and use of land; and he can expropriate land for public services, subject to giving the holders other land.

To balance his rights and powers, the king is under duty to do certain things with the land. He is obliged to give every subject land to live on and land to cultivate, and he must allow every subject to fish in public waters, to hunt game and birds, to gather wild fruits, and to use the clay, iron ore, grasses, reeds, and trees with which the Lozi make their pots, utensils, mats, baskets, weapons, implements, nets and traps, furniture, huts, medicines. The king must protect all subjects against trespassers or anyone attempting to prevent them from exercising their rights. Once the king has given land for cultivation, or a fishing-site, the subject has in it rights which are protected against all comers including the king himself. Should he desire the land, either for his own use or to give to another, he must ask for it: 'The king is also a beggar.'

In practice the ruling king has not granted most of the land to its present holders: they were given their rights by his predecessors, in some cases under a tradition reaching back to legendary times. The king should not interfere with these past dispositions of land, and his own courts protect his subjects against any attempt he may make to do so. The major distribution of land is to the villages on the mounds, and it is vested in the title of each village's headman. Whenever land is given to a man he acknowledges the gift by giving the royal salute to the palace of the king, or to the king sitting in council. When a headman of a village dies and his heir is installed, the latter gives the same royal salute and to this are referred the continuing rights of his title to control the land allocated to it.

A headman thus gets from the king rights to administer this land, not to work all of it. The headman in his turn is obliged to give sufficient land, if it is available, to all heads of households in the village, including himself; and each head of a household can take his own share to cultivate but must distribute plots among all his dependants. These rights to claim some of the land attached to a village inhere in membership of the village, and Lozi insist that, by their law, if a man (or woman) leaves the village he loses his rights in the land. Nevertheless, one frequently finds people who are not resident in the village but are working its land. This they do under another law: all kinsmen, in all lines, of the main family-group of a village are entitled to make use of its wealth, provided that there is more than sufficient land for the members resident in the village. This was made clear in a case where a bad-tempered headman drove his villagers away. When his son succeeded to the headmanship he found himself head of a relatively empty village. Sons of two of his sisters who resided in other villages were working fish-dams which had been allotted to their mothers by the dead headman. The new headman sued to have them ordered either to move to reside with him or to return these dams to him. This case put the judges in a moral dilemma: for while they were reluctant to find for the headman because he was behaving ungenerously (like the dog in the manger in our fable) by wishing to expropriate from the family property kinsmen who had done no wrong to him, they appreciated that were they to find against him they would be upsetting a basic rule of land-holding—that land is vested in the headman's control as representative of the resident villagers. In a Lozi court, judgment proceeds from the most junior of the many judges to the most senior. The judges wavered in their decision: some ruled the headman was entitled to expel his kinsmen but urged him not to, while others ruled that he could not expel them. Eventually the head of the court found a brilliant solution to the dilemma: clearly the dams belonged to (expressed in Lozi by a possessive prefix to the headman's name) the headman and this law could not be varied against him because he was ungenerous; but the court could invoke its powers to discharge an unsatisfactory headman. He threatened that unless the headman were generous and allowed his nephews to use the fish-dams, the court would discharge him and find a more generous man to be headman. This case brings out clearly that rights to control the land vest not in an individual, but in the title of headmanship.[5] It emphasizes a point of great importance to which I shall later refer as basic in social-anthropological analysis: we must continually differentiate between a society as a structure of social positions (titles) and as a structure of relationships between incumbents of these positions.

This example of land-holding in a large African kingdom emphasizes firstly that in kingdoms of this kind we are not dealing with 'feudal-type' states, as is often loosely alleged. Despite their common insistence on personal allegiances between lords and underlings, which is one of the main characteristics of both a tribal and a feudal system, rights to land are quite different in the two types of state. The right of all subjects to claim sufficient land, as an inherent attribute of citizenship, marked the political systems of the Ancient Germans and Celts, and not the land-tenure system of feudalism. Under feudalism a vassal entered into a special contract with his immediate lord in which he gave service of a demarcated kind in return for control over land and those attached to it. No-one in those times could go to the king and demand land as of right, as men could do in Africa. Nor in African systems were there the means to build castles in which lords could live a different style of life from that of their under-lings. All men also carried the same simple weapons, from king to meanest soldier (spear, club, bow-and-arrow, and hide-shield). No knights superior in armour on horseback formed a class of chivalry.

Secondly, this system of land-holding was an essential part of the organization of social relations from the king downwards through the political units of villages, into the hierarchy of kinship relationships. The king may be called 'owner of the land' only as trustee or steward for the nation. He granted a primary estate of rights of administration[6] to all titles of heads of villages, including himself in his capacity as head of many villages. Each head of a village then broke his estate into secondary estates with rights of administration which he allotted to the heads of house-holds in the village, including himself. These holders of secondary estates might allocate tertiary estates of this kind to dependent heads of household, but usually secondary estates were broken up and allocated in parcels of land to be worked as arable or as fishing-sites by the holders, including the administrator of the secondary estate of administration. Thus at the bottom of the series there is an 'estate of production'. Land-holding in these tribes is thus an inherent attribute not only of citizenship, but also of each social position in the total political and kinship hierarchy.

Each parcel of land was therefore not communally owned, but was subject to a series of retreating or reversionary rights from the final user up to the king. And every one of these rights was effective. If a user of land—a holder of an estate of production—left the village, the land reverted to the holder of the secondary estate of administration of which he was a member; and if the secondary holder in turn left, his estate reverted to the primary holder of the estate of administration; and only if he, and all who might replace him, departed from the area, was the king as ultimate owner of all land entitled to claim the whole estate. All these rights are not only valid in African law, but they have also been recognized by British courts. In a Nigerian case in 1930 where land was required for public purposes, the British Privy Council held that the individual African holders were entitled to compensation, and the chiefs only to compensation for their reversionary rights. This was a major recognition of African law and showed a change of outlook from the time when the same Council held that only the Ndebele king and not individual subjects had rights in land, which hence could all accrue to the conquering British South Africa Company.

In short, if we are to understand the use of land as a unit of production in these tribal societies we have to appreciate that it is too simple to talk of them as marked by either communism or individualism. Clearly land, as it is ultimately cultivated, is worked by individuals with secure and protected rights, but representatives of their family, of their village, and of the nation have claims on the land. No superior can arbitrarily oust a junior from his holding, and the heir of each junior enters on succession into this holding. What the junior cannot do, is dispose of the land to any outsider or invite an outsider to come and use the land without consulting his superiors, up to that point in the social structure where the invitee ceases to be an outsider. That is, a junior inside a secondary estate cannot give land to a villager from outside the group which has rights in that particular estate unless he secures the approval of the secondary estate-holder; that secondary holder must consult the primary holder, the village headman, before he thus invites on to his land someone from outside the village; and a village headman must consult the king before he accepts into his village someone who is not a subject of the king. Correspondingly, a superior holder cannot force an outsider on the holder of a junior estate, without the latter agreeing.

The terminology I am using here may sound complicated, but I have adopted it for two reasons. First, there is no suitable terminology extant in European languages. Many writers use various terms from these languages, but all have connotations quite different from those involved in tribal tenure. 'Possession' is too weak a term, since it does not emphasize the strength of the rights owned by the holders of the land. 'Usufruct', defined by the Oxford English Dictionary as a 'right of enjoying the use and advantages of another's property short of destruction or waste of the substance', is often used. The dictionary definition also does not cover the strength of rights of African holders; and those who use the word, with the meaning to enjoy the fruits, similarly fail to recognize this strength. The land is not 'another's property'. Moreover, in Roman Law a grant of 'usufruct' was for use of fruits during the holder's lifetime, not transmissible to heirs, as African land-holding is. Second, since there was no suitable term available it seemed sensible to find a terminology which described the rights and duties involved and the manner in which they inhere in status itself: status as a citizen, status as a villager, and status as a dependant in a family. Each status gives rights to claim land in the appropriate estate. 'Estate' is a term deriving from status. 'Administration' and 'production' describe the rights involved at different levels of 'status'.

One term can be used for all levels of the hierarchy, since the rights and duties obtaining between adjacent holders in the series are identical: the junior must give support and respectful allegiance to the senior, who must give support and land to the junior. In addition, however, each junior holder in the series owes his duties to all seniors, and he can be expelled from all his estates up to that held by the senior whom he offends. A young man working land can be expelled from the village if he offends the headman, and from the kingdom if he offends the king sufficiently.

This system of land-holding can be worked out among almost all the tribal peoples of whom I know, though some of them, in West Africa and South-East Asia, allow pledging and sale of land, rights which are excluded in most of Negro Africa because of the ultimate reversionary rights of the chief, or the reversionary rights of the tribal community as a whole in those tribes which do not have chiefs. The hierarchy of estates may appear as a delegation of the primary estate of administration from king or paramount chief to district chiefs, then from them to sub-district chiefs, then to ward-heads, then to village headmen, as among Basuto and Zulu. It is least clearly marked where land is plentiful, as among the Bemba of Northern Rhodesia.[7] Its main effect, seen even there, is that as citizenship gives a right to claim land, so if one enters on the use of land, this founds a claim by holders of superior estates to demand one's allegiance. In tribes without chiefs the hierarchy of estates appears in the reversionary rights of the hierarchy of groups putatively linked by kinship[8] inside which smaller and smaller groups, down to the individual, nest.

## RIGHTS IN CHATTELS

We shall shortly see that tribal law emphasizes individual appropriation of produce and manufactured goods, and the dominant rights which this gives a man or woman over these. But no-one owns food or a chattel absolutely, because his kinsfolk and even outsiders may have claims upon it which he has difficulty in denying. The extreme form of a claim of this kind is seen in the Lozi institution of *kufunda*, which is defined in the standard Lozi dictionary as a 'legal theft'. *Kufunda* allowed any kinsman or kinswoman of a Lozi to take anything belonging to the latter, without exposing himself or herself to the charge of stealing which would be levied against outsiders. The Lozi attached such importance to this privilege of kinship that when their king and council signed a treaty to come under the protection of the British South Africa Company they specifically stated in it that *kufunda* was to be allowed and not to be liable to prosecution. Many years later the king ruled it to be theft, but I never heard of any-one prosecuting a kinsman for it, though I knew of families that suffered severely under the depredations of ne'er-do-wells. They accepted the depredations, even if with a lot of grumbling. Eventually one family sued in the king's court to have a man of this sort declared no longer to be a kinsman of theirs: while he was kin they felt they could not deny him this privilege; if he ceased to be a kinsman he lost the privilege. The court agreed. *Kufunda* in this large African tribe corresponds closely with what Firth calls 'forced exchanges' in the small island of Tikopia.[9] These are extreme forms of a rule which is very common, though the privilege may be restricted to particular categories of kinsfolk. In cattle-owning tribes it is almost impossible to work out who is the 'real' owner of cattle in a herd, for most cattle are also subject to claims by others for various reasons. I illustrate this situation again from the Lozi. When a Lozi girls marries as an ostensible virgin her bridegroom presents two beasts to her kin. He pays the first beast to make the girl his wife, the second is for her untouched fertility. Should he divorce her and she has not conceived, he is entitled to recover the second beast handed over with its progeny. This is therefore called 'the beast of herding': i.e. the bride's kin merely herd it for the husband until he has impregnated their 'daughter'. They have the right to hold it and to sue for it, against the world including the groom, but it is not theirs; it is still the husband's, though he cannot claim it without divorcing his wife.

The husband's obligations are discharged provided he receives her from, and gives cattle to, an apparently accredited guardian with whom she is living, whether this guardian be of her paternal or her maternal kin. Whichever side of her family receives the two beasts should give one to the other. Within each of these groups, if the recipient slaughters the beast, he should divide the meat among his kin. Different kinsmen are entitled to specific portions of the beast: the bride, for instance, gets the tongue, 'for is she not the owner of the beast since she brought it to the village?'

If a bride is not a virgin, only one beast is given. If it is killed by the person who received it, he should share the meat with the bride's kin on both sides according to fixed rules. If the beast is kept to breed, say by the father of the bride, he must give the mother's family the first and then all alternate calves. Thus he owns the beast but not all its offspring.

Courts will enforce all these claims by the bride's mother's family against the father's, or vice versa: but claims within each family are not enforceable at law; they are moral claims only, since kin should not sue one another. But any kinsman who feels he was neglected can reject responsibility if the spouses or their children run into difficulty. He will say: 'I know nothing of this marriage.'

The rules for distribution of the marriage-cattle—which I have given in simple form—show how a chattel, like land, may be subject to a cluster of rights held by different persons in terms of their relationships within the network of kinship ties. In fact their rights to claim on the marriage–cattle define their kinship relationships to the central parties. If they are not given their shares, this denies their kinship: hence they state they did not know of the marriage. The law of property is again intricately intertwined with the law of status. It means that to understand the holding of property, we must investigate the system of status relationships; and to describe the system of status relationships, we must deal constantly with relations to property.

## IDEAS OF PROPERTY AND SOCIAL SENTIMENTS

Even among ourselves this is to some extent true. To describe family relations, we have to bring in the provisions of goods and services by parents for children. If parents do not provide these they are liable to prosecution. But children no longer bear a corresponding *legal* obligation to provide goods and services for their parents, save when these are destitute, and siblings (brothers and sisters) have no such legal obligation to one another. In tribal society these obligations are strong and spread widely. A man's variegated relationships with others run through his chattels as well as his land; and the measure of how far he feels the correct sentiments in those relationships is the way he deals with his property and his produce. Anyone who feels he or she has been stinted, will conclude that the other does not feel the right sentiments of love, demanded of their relationship. This is why in tribal life persons watch, apparently greedily, what their kinsmen do with their goods; and why bitter disputes can arise over amounts which appear negligible to us—such as being over-looked in the distribution of a small pot of beer. It is not the beer that counts: the invitation to drink is a symbol of recognition of kinship.[10] The African has to eke out his distribution of his products with great skill, lest he offend some kinsman or -woman. We ourselves feel hurt in similar situations: but however our kin and friends may offend us, it is not essential for our survival that they should feel the right sentiments and recognize their obligations to us. Our living depends on a wide series of impersonal relationships in the economic and political systems.

Another crucial fact arises from this situation. Ownership cannot be absolute, for the critical thing about property is the role that it plays in a nexus of specific relationships. Hence in Africa there is no clear definition of ownership: when an African court makes a decision on a dispute over property it states that X stands in a masterful position in relation to that specific object, privilege, or person, as against some other person who is counter-claiming—i.e. the decision is made as between persons related in specific ways.

Property law in tribal society defines not so much rights of persons over things, as obligations owed between persons in respect of things. Indeed, since there is relatively little in the way of goods, the critical property rights which a man or woman enjoys are demands on other persons in virtue of control over land and chattels,—not as with ourselves, any set of persons, but persons related in specific long-standing ways with one. Correspondingly, if new relationships are being established, this is done through transfers of property, which create and define these relationships, as I have illustrated with marriage-cattle. Men similarly make payments when they enter into allegiance to a superior. Indeed gifts are given at all changes of relationships, as we give them; but in tribal society these gifts are believed to recognize and validate the new relationship of giver and recipient.

Evans-Pritchard has pointed out that the poorer a society is in material goods, the more symbolic functions these goods have to serve. In his account of the Nuer of the Sudan, a people who have few goods besides cattle, he writes: 'I risk being accused of speaking idly when I suggest that a very simple material culture narrows social ties in another way. Technology from one point of view is an oecological process: an adaptation of human behaviour to natural circumstances. From another point of view material culture may be regarded as part of social relations, for material objects are chains along which social relationships run, and the more simple is a material culture the more numerous are the relationships expressed through it. . . . Herds of cattle are nuclei around which kinship groups are clustered and the relationships between their members operate through cattle and are expressed in terms of cattle. A single small artifact may be a nexus between persons, e.g. a spear which passes from father to son by gift or inheritance is a symbol of their relationship and one of the bonds by which it is maintained. Thus people not only create their material culture and attach themselves to it, but also build up their relationships through it and see them in terms of it. As Nuer have very few kinds of material objects and very few specimens of each kind, their social value is increased by their having to serve as media of many relationships and they are, in consequence, often invested with ritual functions. Moreover social relationships instead of being diffused along many chains of material links are narrowed by the meagreness of culture to a few simple foci of interest. . . .'[11]

Material objects thus gain high symbolic value, for they stand for the range of social relationships which form the very fabric of society. And I suggest that it is in this light we must look back on the systems of ceremonial exchange I mentioned earlier and discuss more fully below. Over and above the directly utilitarian ends which these systems of exchange serve, the ceremonial goods which circulate in them may take on this high symbolic value: they represent that wider spread of peace which extends around the borders of each tribal group, and which makes it possible for that group to enjoy some possibility of pursuing its internal objectives.

Once we look at the situation of property from this point of view, we understand why a man pays cattle or other goods for a bride. He is not purchasing a woman to be a concubine or a slave: a wife's rights are very different from those of such a person. He is validating the transfer of certain rights over the bride from her kin to himself, and establishing 'friendship',— in-law relationship—, with those kin. The marriage-gifts also signify that he accepts the obligations of his status as husband, and that his own kin, who contributed to the payment, accept obligations to their new daughter- or sister-in-law and the rest of her family. We are misled if we think of a wife in this situation as a chattel of her father to dispose of as he pleases, to become a chattel to her husband. Father or husband may speak of himself as 'owner' of the woman: but this is shorthand for saying they have rights over her against each other, and accept duties towards her.

Tribal peoples often speak in this way of one person 'owning' another. Indeed I have observed in the tribes I know that their word which we translate as 'ownership' is used in all social relationships. Most commonly it is used by juniors in addressing seniors to impress on those seniors that the latter owe them obligations, as when a man begs from the king. But seniors may use it to juniors to emphasize their acceptance of those obligations. Even when a Lozi court upbraids a litigant, the judges may address him as 'My owner . . .'. They do this in order to emphasize that they are discharging an obligation to the wrongdoer by pointing out to him the error of his ways, for they speak not in anger but because the law requires them to do so. Their duty is to uphold the law, and they have this duty even to those who have offended against the law. Adults frequently call a child 'my owner' as an affectionate endearment, especially if it is fretful or hungry, to emphasize readiness to serve the child. But most strikingly the adult also uses this address when he is reprimanding the child: thus he states that he reprimands the child as a duty for he owes it the obligation of bringing it up to be a good citizen.

These forms of address emphasize that the stress of tribal law is even more on obligation than on right: the statement that person X is owner of person Y emphasizes duties as well as rights. A wife can be called 'owner of her husband' if he defaults in his obligations to her, and he will himself speak thus to her to mark his respect for her or to placate her if she is angry.

This emphasis on obligation spreads to other branches of the law, as to the law of contract, which in tribal society tends to insist that all contracts are 'of the utmost good faith'. Seller, and not buyer, must look to the quality of goods exchanged; and the concept of latent defect is applied more widely and for a longer period than with us. If a Lozi sells a cow to another and it dies some months later, he must replace it. Among some Plains Indians the 'seller' of a horse bore some responsibility if it was stolen a day or two after its purchase, or was lamed in the first race it ran for its new owner.[12] Firth says that 'the principle of *caveat emptor* would not function well in a primitive society'.[13]

## PROPERTY AND STATUS

The use of the terms 'estate of administration' and 'estate of production' in analysing land-tenure connects the situation we now find among tribes with Maine's century-old generalization that 'the movement of the progressive societies has hitherto been a movement *from Status to Contract*' (*Ancient Law*, conclusion of Chapter V, 'Primitive Societies and Ancient Law'). This generalization is among the most important which scholars have advanced to cover a sweeping movement in human history. It stresses that in the early law of Europe, as in the law of tribal society, most of the transactions in which men and women are involved, are not specific, single transactions involving the exchange of goods and services between relative strangers. Instead, men and women hold land and other property, and exchange goods and services, as members of a hierarchy of political groups and as kinsfolk or affines. People are linked in transactions with one another because of pre-existing relationships of status between them. As Maine said in another of his pregnant phrases: '. . . the separation of the Law of Persons from that of Things has no meaning in the infancy of the law, . . . the rules belonging to the two departments are inextricably mingled together, and . . . the distinctions of the later jurists are appropriate only to the later jurisprudence.' We can only describe the Law of Things, i.e. the Law of Property, in these types of society by describing also the Law of Persons, or status; and we can only discuss the law of status by talking about ways of owning rights over property. Most of the law of contract, dealing with transactions, is similarly involved in the law of status. Specific contractual relationships, for barter and loan, and the provision of services, do exist and are most important. Yet, as we saw in Chapter I, where a Barotse barters regularly with another they become 'friends' and then perhaps 'bloodbrothers'—quasi-kinsmen. Similarly, when a Barotse doctor treats a patient for a serious illness their relationship expands so that after the cure they are still 'mystically' bound together by supra-sensible bonds, and, for example, if the patient does not pay him, the doctor's medicines will renew the illness. The *kula* ceremonial exchange of shell valuables of Malinowski's Trobriand Islanders is a similar relationship, developed beyond the confines of trade: a man must try to outdo his *kula* partner in generosity, not try to get the best of a bargain.[14] Partnership of this kind involves far wider obligations of general protection and support (like Barotse 'bloodbrotherhood') even though each of the partners has not the blood of the other in his body, ritually transferred, to make him ill if he defaults in performance. When a Trobriand canoe-crew was wrecked on the island of Dobu, all were killed save one whose *kula*-partner was among the party of Dobuans who found them.

It is important to realize that even in our modern system rights of ownership are rarely unrestricted. Aside from general duties imposed by the state which compel us to have regard in our use of our property to the rights of others, restrictions arise through contractual arrangements which we make ourselves (granting leases, mortgaging, pledging, etc.) or through testamentary restraint on things we inherit or through a whole mass of regulations and byelaws defining property zones for special users, licensing vehicles for special purposes, etc. In tribal societies these restraints, and the corresponding rights, derive from status and kinship and are consequently much more closely interwoven in the social structure.

## GENEROSITY AND SHARING IN CONSUMPTION

Differentiation in control over economic resources exists in tribal society but that control must be exercised generously. This spirit of generosity is graphically illustrated in an incident reported by Llewellyn and Hoebel in their book about the 'lawways' of the Cheyenne (about 4,000 population) of the Great Plains of North America. The Spaniards brought horses to North America and these bred rapidly on the Great Plains: a number of Red Indian tribes were enabled to leave the fringing regions and take to the Plains on horseback to live off the great herds of buffalo. When an attack was about to be launched on a herd success depended on no-one beginning the hunt and scaring the buffalo before all the hunters were ready.

This rule was enforced in rotation by one of the six so-called 'Soldier Societies' in which the men were organized. No shot was supposed to be fired at a buffalo until the signal was given. The hunters on one occasion went out with the Shield Soldiers to hold them back, but as they were coming up over a long ridge down wind from the valley where the herd had been sighted by scouts, they saw two men riding in among the buffalo. A Shield Soldier chief led the men in a charge on these two violators of the rules, and Little Old Man shouted to everyone to whip them. The Soldiers shot the culprits' horses and each slashed them with his whip, while some broke their guns. The father of the two, a Dakota Indian living with the Cheyenne, rode up and upbraided them: 'Now you have done wrong. You failed to obey the law of this tribe. You went out alone and did not give the other people a chance. This is what has happened to you.'

The chiefs declared that this showed what they would do to anyone who broke their rules. The boys said nothing. Then the chiefs relented, and pointed out to their men that the boys had neither horses or weapons: 'What do you men want to do about it?'

One of the Soldiers said: 'Well, I have some extra horses. I will give one of them to them.' Another made a similar offer and a third announced: 'Well, we broke those guns they had. I have two guns. I will give them one.' All the others approved: 'Good.'

It was then noticed that five or six of the Soldiers had disobeyed the order to ride to punish the boys, and had instead gone hunting buffalo. One of the chiefs cried: 'Now we will give them a good whipping. Charge on them and whip them, but don't kill their horses.' When the slackers saw the Soldiers coming, one of them as a sign of admitted submission and error spread the fine Hudson's Bay blanket he was wearing before them on the ground. He and his friends stood behind it. The Soldiers split into two columns which slowly circled round the men. Then the Soldiers dismounted and cut the blanket into long narrow strips to wear as tail pieces at dances, and they further punished the men by cutting an ear off each of their horses.

Llewellyn and Hoebel say that 'the rehabilitation of the miscreant hunters by the very police who had despoiled them is not to be looked upon as a freak happening, for this is reported as a widespread practice of the Plains Indian police. If people had to be punished, it was done for the commonweal. Nevertheless, it ran against the generosity grain of a Plains Indian warrior to leave a fellow citizen in straitened circumstances. So long had these men, who were police of the moment, been trained in helping the poor and destitute, that after meting out punishment they meted out goods.' The lesson had been driven home: and later the lesson that no Soldier must shirk his role in enforcing the law was impressed on those who had pursued their own interests—and the buffalo.[15]

I am suggesting here that this spirit of generosity, as an admired trait in Cheyenne culture, has to be referred to the general 'economic' situation which I have emphasized was basic to the structure of all tribal societies. Given the limitations of that situation, it was impossible to use goods—even productive tools—to raise one's own standards of living, and there was no point to hoarding. As I have already quoted Hogbin on the Solomon Islands: 'Reputation is accordingly enhanced not by accumulating possessions in order to use them oneself, but by giving them away.' This is a virtue in our own civilization, and has been for millennia: but we have had available alternative uses for the use of wealth. There is virtually no choice in a tribe, so that not only are generosity and charity admired, but also there can be no flamboyant personal living as an alternative.

## CONSUMPTION PATTERNS

It has emerged that if there is any 'communism' in tribal society it is to be found in consumption, rather than in production. In fact a man may find difficulty in consuming his products on his own. Richards describes how even the Bemba Paramount Chief is unable to retain a good piece of meat for himself, to eat with his own family. His councillors will sit around him describing the meat, until for shame he is compelled to give it to them.[16] Children are trained to share in this way. Bemba 'mothers who are such lax disciplinarians in other respects, speak quite sharply to their children on this one issue'. Richards records that she saw 'a woman seize a lump of pumpkin out of a baby's hand and say in most vehement protest: "You give some to your friend, you child, you! You sit and eat alone! That is bad what you do." ' The child learns early that there are certain relatives who have a right to expect goods from him and an obligation to give to him: 'Food is something over which his older brothers and sisters have definite rights . . . he is taught that they may pounce on any delicacy that he may be eating.' Richards suggests that where our children, growing up in a society in which individual initiative is encouraged, are taught to take pride in their personal possessions, the Bemba child by contrast is taught to share with others whatever it has. I myself am not sure that the Bemba's is not also a kind of pride in possession: but it is a pride in having the thing to share and in being prepared to share it with others. I think that is what Richards implies. And this situation continues into adult life and even beyond it, where indeed it is heavily sanctioned, for Bemba fear the wrath of a person who died feeling that his rights had been denied him. Ancestral spirits expect to share in the goods of their descendants which must constantly be offered to them.

Richards also describes graphically how this sharing in consumption affects incentives to production. She points out that the economic conditions in which a Bemba woman lives 'necessitate reciprocal sharing of foodstuffs, rather than their accumulation, and extend the individual's responsibility outside her own household. Plainly, therefore, it does not pay a Bemba woman

## PLATE V. CO-OPERATIVE ACTIVITIES

*a.* House building in Tikopia. The wooden frame is erected without nails by using coconut sinnet cord for lashing. Sago-leaf thatch will be added.

*b.* Cooking with hot stones. Preparing a meal in a Tikopia earth oven.

*Photographs by Raymond Firth,* 1952

(see pp. 54 f.)

PLATE VI. DISTRIBUTION AND EXCHANGE IN THE NEW GUINEA HIGHLANDS

*a.* Two Tambul men discussing an exchange of valuables.

*b.* Distribution of pigs in compensation for a death. The chief donor counts his agnates' contributions: the recipients sit on the right.

Photographs by M. G. Meggitt

(see pp. 61 f

to have much more grain than her fellows. She would merely have to distribute it, and during the recent [in 1932] locust scourge the villagers whose gardens escaped destruction complained that they were not really better off than their fellows for "our people come and live with us or beg us for baskets of millet".' Hence it is difficult for a Bemba woman to budget, since her food is not only for the use of her own family, but has also to feed an indefinite number of relatives in a system of mutual help.

Richards therefore sums up the situation by saying that 'we are dealing with an economic system in which the accumulation of large quantities of any type of material goods was neither very possible nor considered desirable. The accumulation of food was not an end in itself for the chief or notable, but rather the means to build up a large following of people which was to him the highest aim of life.'

Yet the basis of production remained the individual garden even if others had claims on the products. In the plenty of land available to the Bemba, who planted in the ash-beds made by burning the lopped branches of trees, a man could cut a garden wherever he wished in virgin forest: but once a man cut his garden it was his. 'In fact, in the case of new garden the [Bemba] seem to believe that there is some particularly close connexion of an almost magical nature between the owner and the patch of ground he has just cleared of bush. Although a man can lend his garden to another in the second or third year, or even sell the crops on it, he should do neither of these things in the case of the first year patch.' In short, 'the system of food consumption is determined by rules of individual ownership subject to the claims of elder relatives'.

This is the kind of picture which emerges from an examination of the productive system of every tribe. On the whole, where working parties assemble to carry out some big task—clearing a garden, building a canoe or house, and so forth—they do so for individuals who feed their helpers, though these may bring their own contribution of food. Those who called the party are later expected to reciprocate in turn by working for their helpers. The produce of these working parties is owned in most respects by the individual with major rights over the garden or canoe, but subject to claims of others on the produce. The nearest to co-operative production that we find is when the technique itself demands several workers, as in the Plains Indians buffalo hunt, when some meat was given even to those who had not killed buffalo. In sea-fishing from canoes in Tikopia each of the crew and the owner ideally shared equally in the catch, without 'rent' to the canoe-owner. It is noteworthy here that the owner of the canoe may get less than members of his crew, while he cannot refuse others the use of the canoe if he himself is not fishing. In some African tribes the owner of a dam or net and the actual fishermen take the catch on alternate days. Individual appropriation of products even appears in the co-operative working of iron by smiths in the kingdom of Dahomey in West Africa, where there is considerable specialization. At any one time all members of a forge will be working on the iron of one man. The product of this labour, say hoes, will belong to the one whose iron is forged, and he will sell these hoes in the market for his personal gain. While he is disposing of these he works the iron of each of his fellow-workers in turn, until the cycle again comes round to working his iron.[17]

## THE GROUP OF PRODUCERS AND CONSUMERS: CO-OPERATION AND COMPETITION

Our discussion of African land-holding stressed how deeply involved in status relationships are rights to the basic productive resources. Despite the widely ramifying systems of trade in which some tribes are involved and the existence in places like West Africa of markets and specialist traders, people live on the land in largely self-subsistent groups, which produce nearly everything they want and consume it together. Social relationships are undifferentiated, for there is little scope for specialization. A man has few specific economic relationships, and economic relationships alone, with other men. He does his productive work with the same people with whom he lives, plays, shares good and ill fortune, rears children, celebrates weddings and mourns at funerals. Even specialists like smiths are also cultivators, and indeed so are chiefs. A man's associates are primarily his kinsfolk, though they fall into different categories which entail varying obligations. But kinship as such involves a general obligation to help and sustain one another. And, as described above, the kinship system is widely extended and many distant relatives are classed with close relatives. As a man grows up in one of these groups, there is no enterprise to draw him away from those who gave birth to him and nurtured him. What can he do elsewhere? What more rewarding labour is there for him elsewhere? More than this, there are pressures to keep him with his kinsfolk, who love him and will support him. Elsewhere he will be alone and friendless; if he is injured or killed, who will care or avenge him? Therefore men tend to remain on the land of their ancestors, so long as there is enough land, working with their kin, supporting these in quarrels. In many productive activities there must be co-operation, and this co-operation is organized through the further ramification of kinship linkages, and of relationships arising from marriages with outsiders. In this kind of economic situation we find the 'origins' of the classificatory system of kinship terminology, and not in conjectured forms of marriages, never observed, and now frowned upon.

I made the proviso in the above paragraph, 'so long as there is land'. It is obviously an important proviso. For some of these groups, through the chance operation of fertility and mortality, increase more rapidly than others. Thus pressure may build up in particular groups on the land, and some members will then have to depart—or be forced out—to seek sustenance elsewhere. In the small Polynesian island of Tikopia—less than three square miles in area—the population might rise beyond the means of the land, despite native attempts at controlling their increase. A bad year or cyclone might precipitate a crisis. The old and the infant died: or in extreme circumstances the chiefs might compel some commoners to put out into a sea whose nearest neighbouring island lay seventy miles away.[18]

Pressure on supplies, under existing conditions of technology, was always potentially severe; and it was accompanied by a high rate of infantile mortality and a short expectation of life. Many—but not all—tribal societies lived under the constant threat of famine, typified by the following wistful story told by the Nuer of the Sudan: 'Once upon a time Man's stomach led an independent life in the bush and lived on small insects roasted by the firing of the grasses, for "Man was not created with a stomach. It was created apart from him." One day Man was walking in the bush and came across Stomach there and put it in its present place that it might feed there. Although when it lived by itself it was satisfied with tiny morsels of food, it is now always hungry. No matter how much it eats it is soon craving for more.'[19] Among the Bemba, and many other tribes, there is a regular period of 'hunger-months' before the harvest comes in, when people may wander to distant relatives to seek for food.[20] People from the Middle Zambezi valley who lost their riverside crops in floods would move to their kin on the Plateau; and they sat there looking at the granaries until they were fed.[21] This general threat of shortage could be very severe among the hunters and collectors in difficult environments.[22]

Life in the tribes was by no means idyllic. In most there was a stern struggle for a living. General shortage of land[23] for one tribe might compel it to attack its neighbours to secure theirs, even though among some Australian Aborigines there was a theory that one tribe should not oust another from its area because of mystical attachments to specific ancestral spots.[24] Within tribes without governmental systems of rule—what have been called segmentary or stateless societies[25]—over-populous sections within a tribe might be compelled by the threat of hunger to try to gain control over the land of other sections which in their ideology were brothers to them, whom they should succour and help. Meggitt in a new study of the Mae Enga in an area of the New Guinea Highlands that has only recently been opened up by the Australian Government, describes the constant moral dilemmas which face groups in this situation. Necessity compels them to get more land, and if their neighbours are 'brothers' to them, they can only do so at the latter's expense. Yet it is believed that to commit this breach of fraternal obligations may bring misfortune, misfortunes defined by the cultural values of the society which stress the brotherhood of those putatively linked by patrilineal descent. It is a moral dilemma, and a grave one, even if in the end necessity prevails. There is also a moral dilemma because cultural values state that men should aid their needy kin who are related to them through women. But if you accept in kin of this kind when they plead with you, they may become more powerful in numbers than you and eventually claim that the land is rightfully theirs by the dominant rule of patrilineal origin. This dilemma may thrust itself upon a group of patrilineally related kin which has through chance of fertility and mortality become few in numbers: their weakness invites attack from their populous neighbours, who are short of land, including their own patrilineally related 'brother'-groups. On the other hand, if they try to build up their strength by inviting in men related to them through women, these may grow in strength and claim the land.[26] Tribal society is as torn between the pressures of economic interest, and even survival, and the demands of cultural and moral values as society is everywhere else.

In this way necessity may compel either individuals or sections of the largely self-subsistent settlements to leave their homes and establish themselves elsewhere. As this crisis approaches, the mother settlement may be torn by internal wrangling and dispute, sometimes reflected in charges of witchcraft and sorcery, or in divinations of ancestral spirits' wrath or other mystical retribution for offences, in order to account for the misfortunes of illness and accident and failure that are the lot of all men, and particularly of men at these low levels of technological development. Why misfortune should be attributed in this way to disturbances in social relations among the living we shall examine later.

### PRESTIGE AND INDEPENDENCE

There is a second cause for disturbances of this kind, a cause which also originates in the general economic situation. Men want not only bare subsistence: many of them also desire power, prestige and influence. Competition for these ends is severe in any society: it is more severe, and more restricted, in a largely undifferentiated society with many fewer functional occupations and special associations. Among ourselves a young man does not necessarily have to follow his father's trade and compete with his father for the latter's position, or after his father's death with his brothers for it. This is much more often the situation in tribal society. Moreover, the means to prestige and power are more restricted. On the whole, they reduce to acquiring dependants for oneself, so that one can be a 'big man'. It is possible to beget one's own dependants: this is one basis for polygyny (marrying several wives). An additional wife in an agricultural tribe is no burden since she and her children are supported by her own cultivations; and she helps produce something of a surplus in good seasons with which her husband can entertain others. Or in New Guinea she can produce the sweet potatoes to nourish pigs, the basis of wealth and prestige. But the aspirant for social influence may have to compete with his brothers, or other relatives, for control over their mutual kinsfolk in order to build up a following.

It is here that the fact that in the end agricultural land is held in an individual's 'estate of production' is important. The effect is that men (and women) produce crops on their own, even if assisted by kin and neighbours in co-operative working parties. These crops in their turn are subject to the claims of others for help and hospitality: but help and hospitality are given from an individual's store produced mainly by his own efforts. Similarly, among Bushmen hunters and collectors, although the economic life of the band in effect 'approaches a sort of communism, [it] is really based on the notion of private property. The only thing owned in common is the land. . . . All portable property is generally owned by individuals, and theft is severely punished.' People acquire the water they draw, the vegetable food they collect, and the game they kill, and though 'a man who shoots a buck or bird will cut it up, and share with the other people present . . . the dividing is done by him, and the skin, sinews, etc. belong to him to be done with as he pleases.'[27] Individual Cheyenne succoured the Dakota youths whose horses they had shot and whose guns they had broken.

There is virtue in giving aid and in dispensing hospitality: and men in these societies are moved by virtue as well as by self-interest. But virtuous performance does build up one's reputation, not only as an upright man, but also as one who can care for others. They become one's dependants. A man can thus try to win away the allegiance of kinsfolk from their common senior kinsman, in order to raise his own prestige. This produces considerable strain between them, particularly as in order to gain the prestige of headship of an independent group a man has either to oust his senior from that position, or he has to lead a dissident section to found a separate settlement.

The struggle for this kind of independence is thus deeply involved in the economic situation. The struggle is exacerbated by a variety of cultural factors. Groups of this kind tend to split along cleavages determined by, for example, closeness and distance of kinship linkages. In a patrilineal society the sons of two brothers will separate before the sons of one man, and among the latter's descendants the sons of different brothers will split apart first. In a matrilineal society, the main cleavage will be between the children of various sisters, who in a higher generation are linked by common birth from a single mother. And in these societies, because a mother's brother born of that ancestress has authority, the cleavage between the two generations and the struggle between them for leadership seem greater than in patrilineal societies, where a father appears able to continue to exercise more effectively the authority over his sons which was established during their childhood. Thus among the matrilineal Yao of Nyasaland there may develop urgent disputes between maternal uncle and uterine nephew as the former strives to retain control over his nieces and the latter to gain control over these women, who are his sisters, and their children who can build up a following. When misfortunes afflict the women and their children, these struggles for power appear in accusations by the attacking nephew that their uncle is neglecting the dependants and even that he is bewitching them.[28]

Accusations of witchcraft thus arise out of the competition between kinsfolk. They are also related to the basic economic limitation on which I am laying stress. For though a man gains prestige by his productive capacities, if he outdoes his fellows too much, they will suspect him of witchcraft. Richards reports of the Bemba, that to find one beehive with honey in the woods is luck, to find two is very good luck, to find three is witchcraft. Generally, she concludes, for a man 'to do much better than his fellows is dangerous. A man who is full when others are hungry is hardly considered to have achieved the good fortune by natural means. An occasional stroke of good luck is not resented, but to be permanently more prosperous than the rest of the village would almost certainly lead to accusations of sorcery.' And a man whose food lasts through the hungry months may be suspected of stealing by sorcery the good out of the crops in his neighbours' granaries. Here accusations of witchcraft and sorcery maintain the egalitarian basis of the society in two ways: not only is the prosperous man in danger of accusation, but he also fears the malice of witches and sorcerers among his envious fellows. In our own history accusations of witchcraft were ruled illegal when the industrial revolution began to develop.

## CEREMONIAL FEASTING AND EXCHANGE

Thus even within the limitations imposed by simple tools and egalitarian standards of consumption of primary goods, there is competition between persons in acquiring control of the means to produce goods. The competition may result from the severe pressure to have enough land on which to survive; it is caused too by the desire to acquire prestige through distributing goods to others, who then become one's dependants or partners in exchange. Beyond obtaining sustenance for himself and his family, the big man must be able to entertain, particularly by giving large feasts. Where authority is instituted in social positions which survive the death or discharge of holders, as with African chieftainships, incumbents of these positions are expected to stage these feasts and have to do so to maintain their prestige. They are also provided with the wherewithal to entertain, since the privileges of their social positions include a right to take 'tribute' from their underlings' crops, herds and kills. In one of the most famous institutions of tribal society, the *potlatch* of the Red Indians of the North-West Coast of North America, feasts of this kind by the privileged might entail vast destruction to shame competitors of equal rank.[29] For the *potlatch* was a feast given by an individual to another family, or by one family or clan to another. At these feasts, which might entail impressive gatherings, the host presented his guests with blankets, canoes, oil and other valuables. Huge quantities of precious seal oil might be burnt. The more sumptuous the presents given away and the more lavish the destruction of property, the greater the feast and the prestige accruing to the host, while the rival guest sank in public esteem correspondingly. To recover face, and regain prestige, he had to give presents in return, with interest, at a greater feast. Symbolic pieces of copper, elaborately engraved and worth hundreds or thousands of blankets, might be presented to a rival, who was even more shamed if his host broke a copper. In some of these tribes the host while giving the feast boasted of his family's prestige and its rights over property, titles and songs. These great feasts were given by tribes which lived by hunting, fishing, and collecting wild fruits, in a rich environment. But the *potlatch* flowered as an institution when the fur-trade with Whites brought in new riches.

Chiefs gave the greatest feasts since they had the requisite power to make demands on other people for help. Hence co-operation here developed in order to accumulate property so as to give it away or to destroy it, for 'rivals fight with property alone', the Kwakiutl tribe said, in order that each may 'flatten out' the other. But in addition individuals might strive to build up their own social prestige by acquiring the means to enter into this fight with property at lower levels of the system.

Individual competition to acquire prestige in this way is very acute in the Highlands of New Guinea, where many kinds of goods are exchanged: shells, bird-skins, and stone axes among them.[30] Some are useful goods which thus travel many miles from one exchange-partner to another. But the heart of any feast is the pig. And here we come to the extraordinary effect of seemingly silly taboos and customs. In some of these tribes it is taboo to eat a pig bred by yourself or a close relative, or close relatives of your spouse. MacArthur thus reports for the Kunimaipa (in an unpublished doctoral thesis at the Australian National University): 'The incentives for a man to give away pork from the pigs he kills is supported by a ban restricting the pork an individual may eat. Traditionally a person did not eat pork from pigs raised by himself or any close cognate of himself or his spouse.[31] To eat such pork was believed to entail serious consequences; a person's crops would not grow well, his pigs would not flourish and he would hunt in vain. He would become deaf, weak at the knees and short of breath, disabilities which could easily prove fatal in the event of an enemy attack. The prohibition was attributed to the use of the same growth-promoting rituals on the pigs. In addition it was believed that one's teeth fell out prematurely if one ate pork from pigs over which announcements were made for one's close cognates and affines. This, too, should be given away to people who could eat it.' A consequence of this taboo is that you have to pass on your own and relatives' pigs to someone else to eat, while you get a pig from him: and out of this compelled exchange there has developed a widely extended and ramifying set of exchanges which spread over the whole land. Indirectly men and groups of men far apart are involved in this system: directly it involves only neighbouring groups. Useful goods, produced in limited areas, may through these exchanges travel hundreds of miles to those who lack them; for while pigs are the heart of the system, they are distributed at feasts where other goods are displayed and given as gifts to pig-exchange partners. These feasts, like the feasts of the kula-exchanges described by Malinowski, thus cover a widespread system of trade in useful goods. Though men should be generous in exchanging these valuables, in practice they have an eye to the bargains they are making and expect their partners to make reciprocal returns.

The pig-exchanges achieve something beyond this. A man's prestige in his own group depends on his skill as an organizer of pig-exchanges, and on the number of partners he has in several directions and his ability to deal with them: and to manage these enterprises successfully he also has to be able to manipulate his relationships with his own people in order to obtain the means to exchange externally. He has to be able to direct the marriages of his group's men and women so that they acquire in-laws in strategic positions—for an in-law is always an exchange-partner. He has to be able to allocate his pigs and other goods so as to put others in his debt, in order that he can mobilize resources to stage a feast or dance successfully when he or his group wishes to do so. Only by showing skill in these enterprises can he become a big man; and he must also have luck, in that he gets industrious wives to nurture his pigs and to bear him children. And since certain ceremonies are prescribed by custom at particular seasons or at funerals each group has a vested interest in its big man if it is to maintain its prestige.

But since a man's prestige in his own group depends on his relations with pig-exchange partners, he as a big man has a great interest in the maintenance of sufficiently friendly relations with those partners who are big men in other groups. He is moved to oppose a state of all-out war. If war has broken out,—over land, over theft, over the rape of a woman, over vengeance for a killing—, the big man needs in the end to bring about a resumption of peaceful relations, for only if there is sufficient peace for the exchanges to go on can he maintain his prestige. Therefore we have here a mechanism,—we shall examine other similar mechanisms later—, which produces a peacemaker in the heart of each warring group.

The taboo on eating one's own pig illustrates well the sort of custom which fascinates anthropologists; and indeed why all customs are so fascinating. For we start here with what seems, as I have already said, to be a rather silly, indeed childish, super-stition, and we end with a widespread system of international trade which contributes to an international peace in which the leaders of each group have the greatest interest, in order that they be able to maintain their own positions among a very irascible and quarrelsome set of people.

Despite the fact that I was raised to condemn the conjectural historical reconstructions in which my forbears engaged, I cannot help puzzling about how a custom of this sort, with all its widespread effects, originated. We may never know the answer: yet increasing research on primates and archaeological evidence seems to suggest human society evolved not from a situation in which one family group established relations with other independent family groups, but more probably among a troop or company of manlike beings, who slowly established rules which compelled sharing.[32]

It is surely significant that this kind of ceremonial exchange is found so widely throughout the world. I have already summarized the *kula* exchange of the ring of islands off the south-east tip of New Guinea: there too a man's internal standing depended on his role in the external exchange, so that for internal prestige he had to have alliances with foreigners, which he could operate under the protection of recognizing the rules of this international trade. Bloodbrotherhood, enabling people to move in foreign lands, was similar in form through large regions of Central Africa. This form of institution is not found everywhere, of course. Among the partrilineally organized Ibo of Nigeria a man moves to trade at a distance by going to an in-law or maternal kinsman in a neighbouring group, and is passed on, under the protection of this relative, to the protection of one of the latter's relatives yet further on, and thus he progresses across the land.

## Levels and Media of Exchange

Not only are exchanges of goods between persons in particular status relationships or in ceremonial partnerships characteristic of these societies, but in addition particular types of goods tend to be associated with one another and with certain categories of social relationships. Firth's account of Tikopian 'spheres of exchange' in his *Primitive Polynesian Economy* (1939) is the clearest analysis I know of this general position. He states that there are at least three separate series of exchanges, and the goods in each of these series are not completely convertible into those of other series. Lowest is the food series, in which payments of food acknowledge small loans and services. Gifts of food, whether raw or cooked, are returned in kind, though not necessarily in the same state. The next series is the bark-cloth/sinnet-cord level, with the pandanus mat as its highest expression. These goods pay for timber, bowls, and coconut grating-stools, or specialist skill in canoe- or housebuilding, as well as damage to valuable tools and the unauthorized use of a canoe. In some circumstances they are used for ritual presentation. The third and most important series from the point of view of the utility of the goods, but not the frequency of transactions in them, includes bonito-hooks, turmeric cylinders, and canoes. Firth writes that 'the objects and services in these three series cannot be completely expressed in terms of one another, since normally they are never brought to the bar of exchange together. It is impossible to express the value of a bonito-hook in terms of a quantity of food, since no such exchange is ever made and would be regarded by the Tikopia as fantastic.'

He then presents a set of equivalences for a canoe, but stresses that these cannot be fully measured against one another. It takes two specialists, and perhaps a dozen non-specialist workers, a number of months' work with several adzes to make a canoe. Expressed as a cost of production this means a coil of sinnet cord, with perhaps bark-cloth, as payment for the raw material; bark-cloth as payment for borrowed tools; a few pandanus mats and many bark-cloths plus a number of food baskets, plus subsistence for the period of work as payment for labour and skill and management—though from this must be subtracted a quantity of food brought by the workers themselves as contributions. The exchange-value of a canoe is a bonito-hook, a coil of heavy shark cord, a bundle of bark-cloth, and food. A second value in exchange was observed by Firth, when a canoe was given to the burial party at a funeral in a chief's family, in replacement for the wooden bowl (itself shaped like a canoe) which is usually given on such occasions. This does not mean that a canoe is equivalent to a bowl in other situations: here a small canoe was given as an honorific substitute for the usual gift, and conferred prestige on the donors; and no amount of bark-cloth can be substituted in this way. Firth sums up: 'Put generally, it can be said that the social context is different in each case. The services of a burial party at the death of a chief or the son of a chief are of a complicated kind charged with high emotional significance, and though compensated for by economic goods could not be paid for only in bark-cloth and food, the types of goods by which specialist and non-specialist skill are rewarded. In other contexts again, obligations which are satisfied by bark-cloth or sinnet cannot be met simply by an increase in the amount of food handed over. Each kind of object is appropriate to a particular kind of social situation. It is as if, allowing for the obvious differences, in our society gold, silver, and copper were used as media of exchange in three series of transactions but there was no accurate means of rendering them in terms of each other' (pp. 340 f.).

Thus when we look at goods in terms of how they are exchanged against one another, we find that we have to examine their role within the specific contexts of particular status relations, just as when we looked at the rules for holding property. Under these, we saw that the social significance of goods in a tribal society is the manner in which they formed a nexus within concatenations of social relationships, where they come to symbolize the rights and duties obtaining between the parties. As the goods circulate they retain this significance, and their transfers tend to be restricted to particular levels of relationships which confine each series of goods within a sort of isolated circuit.

For this reason Firth found that Tikopia never try to relate the costs of a canoe, for example, to the exchange transactions in which it figures (e.g. as against bonito-hooks), or to establish a common measure of the labour involved. The primary value of a bonito-hook is its use as an instrument for catching bonito. Hooks are kept, however, not only by expert fishermen for this purpose, but also by other men to be used as valued property on appropriate social occasions, for they have a high value associated with their use in ritual. Yet no Tikopia accumulates bonito-hooks for commercial exchanges. Moreover, Tikopia do not make large numbers of bonito-hooks, though only turtle-shell of the required material is at all scarce. There is enough of this, however, to supply more hooks, and some is utilized for ear-rings, which rank comparatively low in the scale of utilities. To use the shell for bonito-hooks would have a much greater exchange value, and incidental labour in spare-time could be used for the tedious grinding. Seemingly the whole social context excludes additional production of hooks, and, with the Tikopia's 'lack of stimulus to ultimate acquisition', the situations in which the hooks are exchanged of themselves exclude a higher production. Goods in the bonito-hook series 'are not of great mobility in exchange', and are transferred on occasions charged with emotional significance. Food produced by every household is used to initiate or liquidate a great variety of economic and social obligations, but, except for dry and sprouting coco-nuts, it is immediately consumed. Sinnet and bark-cloth, the common articles in the middle sphere, are the 'most mobile in the Tikopia economy'. They are produced at home in each family, where they are important in many activities. But they are so frequently circulated that they may pass through many hands before they are actually consumed. They are more durable than food, but they cannot become a true medium of exchange because of the conventional limits on the transactions in which they are used. Sinnet and bark-cloth can be substituted for one another, in various transactions, though there is a greater difference in quality in different rolls of sinnet-cord than there is between pieces of bark-cloth.

In view of the circumstances we have just been examining, it is more surprising that some tribal societies have tokens of value which can be considered to approach money, rather than that most societies of this type should lack such an aid to exchange. Yet where there are such tokens, which observers have thought to be money, they still tend to function in series of exchanges, specific to particular ranges of social relations. Thus Mead considered that shells and dogs' teeth in the Admiralty Islands have 'all the requirements of a good money base'. They are rare, and they are small and portable and extremely divisible. She states that the value of every object sold or exchanged in the Admiralty Islands can be expressed in terms of dogs' teeth or shell money, and 'the idea of a common medium of exchange is perfectly clear in the native mind'. The value of this 'money' fell when dogs' teeth were imported from abroad after colonization, until the administering authority forbade this import. But dogs' teeth and shells are used in only about one quarter of all transactions. Barter is the main means of obtaining ordinary goods and no-one could go to market with dogs' teeth and buy necessities, since the seller would himself be seeking other necessities, save where a rich man wanted to build a store for social manipulation. Dogs' teeth are used in a limited series of transactions.[33]

These dogs' teeth approach money, if we follow Robertson in denoting as money 'anything which is widely accepted in payment for goods, or in discharge of other kinds of business obligation',[34] though it is clear that they only allow partial measurement of the values of various goods against one another. In other tribes of Melanesia, valuables used in some exchanges, like stone axes in New Guinea or the beads of the Palau Islands, and Trobriand *kula* armshells and necklaces, are probably better equated with jewels, if we are to seek an equivalent in our own society, These valuables are used only in limited series of exchanges, or on important social occasions, or at the organization of large-scale economic enterprises. Like *kula* valuables, those of Palau gain from their accumulation of history. Herskovits comes to a similar conclusion about the 'money-tokens' of the Californian tribes—either dentalium shells or clam-disks. Though these may be used as 'indices of value', they were primarily involved in the search for prestige and services, within patterns of social relationships. They do not seem to have entered into the subsistence economy, even where, as among the Yurok, values of subsistence produce could be expressed in terms of these valuables. The position of two series of shells circulating in Rossel Island, whose value is not expressible in terms of one another, is not clear. Interest was payable on loans of these shells, but both borrowing and repayment takes places (in Firth's words) 'within a scheme of values depending upon considerations of rank and ritual as well as ordinary advantage in exchange'.[35]

There are tribal societies where values are measured in terms of some common produce, like rice, or baskets of other grain, or areca nuts; but probably the clearest example of an approach to using money is to be found in the West African cowrie shells. This is not surprising, for considerable external trade with Europe and the Mediterranean littoral of Africa has been in existence for many centuries, and markets are considerably developed in the internal economy of the region. I have noted that here too there was also pledging and sale of land. In Dahomey and Ashanti taxing and the imposition of tolls and duties are also developed beyond the extent found in kingdoms of other regions of Africa. The most striking feature of the cowrie-shell economy is its rapid response to inflationary and deflationary pressures. This has occurred over a period of years, as more Western money came in or was reduced in quantity. In one area the pressures were seasonal: cowries altered their value in relation to French currency as demand for this currency rose in the months when taxation was due, and subsequently fell. Here there were professional money-changers and after 1914 even a money market developed. Money-changers from foreign tribes would sell notes for cowries while the franc was appreciating, when taxes were due, and with the same shells would buy back French money when the cowrie had returned to its normal value.[36] Cowries have been ousted by Western money, but survive in two spheres of activity: they are still used in small exchanges of subsistence produce and also on ritual occasions. There is some dispute whether they should be classed as money: certainly more than any other tribal medium of exchange they probably could be brought under that denotation.

## THE TRIBAL ECONOMIC SYSTEM

In his analysis of Tikopia economy, Firth considers carefully what the implications of the general situation are for constructing a scale of values for Tikopian goods, and how far such a scale might be comparable with a scale of economic values such as economists measure in our own society. More generally, he is concerned to examine whether the standard concepts of economic science can be applied to Tikopia life in so far as the people are involved in taking rational decisions to allocate scarce means to satisfy their wants. As my summary recapitulation of his discussion of exchange value shows, it is difficult to isolate specific 'economic' interrelations out of the general social context which influences men's motivations and determines how they produce, distribute and consume goods. Firth similarly shows that while Tikopia life can be analysed in terms of factors of production, organization of labour, entrepreneurship, principles of distribution and payment, and exchange and value, all of these are influenced in the same direction by the restricted field of transactions, their preponderance within established status relationships, and their setting within wider social contexts than the purely economic. It is true that Tikopia is a very small community whose members are intensively inter-related with one another; and there are other tribal societies where interest is drawn and where the profit motive has greater scope. I have used Firth's study because it seems to me to be the best in the field; and Firth suggests that even in more complex tribal economies we are still a long way from the impersonality of the market economy on which economic science has concentrated. Firth argues nevertheless that it is profitable to apply the standard techniques of economic science to the life of tribal society, and demonstrates this cogently.

PLATE VII. ECONOMIC ACTIVITY IN TIKOPIA

*a.* A Tikopia fish drive. Long-handled deep nets are used by men, and scoop nets by women and children, assembled in line over the fringing reef.

*b.* Payment to workers. Bundles of bark cloth assembled outside a Tikopia house for carriage to builders of a canoe.

*Photographs by Raymond Firth, 1952*

(see pp. 63 f.)

PLATE VIII.   THE PLAINS RED INDIANS' BUFFALO HUNT

*a.* Hunting under a masque of white wolf skins.

*b.* Horses destroyed in buffalo hunting.

(both from G. Catlin, *North American Indians*, 1857)

(see pp. 8

Unhappily, this is a relatively neglected field of social anthropology; and I must leave the problem here since Firth's argument cannot be summarized incidentally in a book directed to other purposes.

A final important characteristic of these economies is that since they lack money and highly specialized marketing procedures,[37] supply and demand do not adjust themselves to one another as they are considered to do in modern economies. Particular items and quantities of these items tend to be stabilized in exchanges against one another. Furthermore, in most tribes, during famines there can be no rise in the price of food since there is nothing against which food can be exchanged and which can itself be treasured and stored for future exploitation. This is the most graphic illustration of the extent to which general social factors control the handling of goods: for while there are people who hoard food in these conditions, against the ethical demand that they share with their fellows, they do not thereby improve their economic position though they may on the short-term increase their chances of survival. They are miserly in failing to fulfil their obligations to help their kin, and they are subject to the fear that they may be accused of witchcraft.[38] Only in a few areas were those who were starving—or short of seed—able to sell children into slavery to get help; and this occurred in areas markedly influenced by external trade contacts with more developed economies, as in West Africa and parts of Asia. This may indeed mark the point at which we must cease to talk of tribal economies.

Firth concludes that 'it will probably be agreed ... that the differences between a primitive economy and a civilized economy, as far as the "spirit" of the relationships is concerned, are quantitative rather than qualitative. To some degree the elements characteristic of Tikopia can be paralleled in modern industrial life.' I myself feel that this quantitative difference is so great that we are dealing with a quite different sort of economic situation, even though it is necessary to stress the common elements.[39]

It should be clear that these differences in the operation of the two types of economic system is not due to any difference in the character or intelligence of the peoples concerned. Differences are 'imposed' by the types of productive tools, the predominance of primary goods, and the restricted scale of the communities and their external trade connections. As a result, general social considerations are dominant over specific economic calculations, though these always enter. Nor does this mean that as these societies are absorbed into world economy, their members cannot operate in that economy in terms of its own rules. The Lozi had a more widely spread trade than the Tikopia and bartering was more important in their internal economy: but they did not pay interest on loans, had no sale or pledge of land, and generally fall into the category of a tribal economy. During the War prices of European goods on which they had become dependent rose sharply, and the prices of Lozi produce began to follow. The Lozi national council debated whether they should control the price of fish which had risen most steeply. Among the arguments raised by councillors were some which showed a sharp awareness of economic principles. One argued that they would have to fix differential prices within the kingdom because in centres near the European towns money was plentiful while at distant centres money was scarce: and prices of goods adjusted themselves to the supply of money. Others said that while there was a fall in the total supply of fish as more men left to work for Europeans with rising wages, and while demand remained high, prices were bound to rise. A third argued that control would be difficult to enforce, since a man who had a pressing need for fish for a feast would find it worth while to pay more, and generally he drew attention to the effect of a man's idea of marginal utility to him on prices in a seller's market. A fourth, following the same line, argued that an attempt to control would drive sales of fish into out-of-the-way places away from the normal centres of marketing. There can thus be acute awareness of the effect of economic pressures when radically changed conditions alter the workings of the tribal economy, even where—as among the Lozi—most transactions are still conditioned by general social, rather than specific economic, advantages.

## SUBSISTENCE AND PRESTIGE ECONOMIES

In tribal societies there is thus very limited competition between sellers in the production of goods for a market of unrelated buyers, though goods are used in competitive striving for prestige. Where a market external to the small-scale community does exist, its narrow scope inhibits any drive to increase productivity beyond a certain point. Since economic relations involving related persons are peripheral to the transactions between kin and in-laws, men look in their distribution of goods to long-term social advantages rather than to immediate bargains, and generosity is emphasized. Nevertheless, in these relations there is a code of reciprocity which in the end balances incomings and outgoings of goods and services, though this balancing may not operate between each pair of persons. He who helps his wife's brother is helped in turn by his own sister's husband. Outside of each major subsistence group there tends to be an efflorescence of ceremonial exchanges in partnerships which are assimilated to the pattern of quasi-kinship relations. The ordinary man knows most of the important techniques extant in the society, and freely transfers his labour from one productive activity to another, according to season, to the manpower of his group, and to house-hold requirements. But there is some specialization, ranging from the exercise of skills and talents to a few trades, particularly smithing, which require long training. Most specialists are however also subsistence producers even where, as in West African kingdoms, they form guilds of artisans.

Despite these limitations, clearly we must not think of these societies as solely concerned with subsistence: the search for prestige as a motivation in dealing with others is important for all their members save the humblest and poorest. In almost all of those societies which dwell in harsh environments so that they have a struggle to survive, a man gains prestige by sharing with his fellows for their sustenance the game he kills or the fish he catches. He also thus insures himself against occasions when his luck is out. As produce of whatever kind increases to satisfy more than the minimum biological needs, men acquire prestige by distributing their surpluses to their fellows in established relationships; and all those who hold high positions are compelled to do this to maintain their status. Hence we may speak of tribal economies as aiming at both subsistence, and prestige and power.

In a few societies the environment is sufficiently rich for people to compete in the production of goods far beyond the needs of subsistence, and here there may develop a competition in destruc-tion and wasteful use, as in the *potlatch* of the Red Indians of the North-west Coast of America, or in the Trobriand Islands where quantities of food are piled up and may rot. There are also a number of kingdoms, which can still be reckoned at the tribal stage, in West Africa and in Polynesia, where chiefs and their courts are able to live luxuriously and indulge in what Veblen called 'conspicuous consumption'. But generally, as quoted in Chapter I, chiefs live at a standard akin to that of commoners. Thus Firth says of Tikopia: 'To some extent chiefs and their immediate relatives require and get choicer food, build somewhat larger houses and have finer mats and ornaments. But in most of their ordinary meals they eat exactly the same provision as other people, they wear bark-cloth of the same quality and their house furniture is of the same simplicity. The interior of a chief's house is no richer in appointments, no more sumptuous than that of a commoner, though there may be more things in it.'[40]

In most tribal societies the produce flowing into the prestige economy is not always procured by additional effort, but accrues from the chance of a good season. Allan, an agriculturist, reckons that before the introduction of cash crops to Africa, men cultivated enough land to bring them in a small surplus in normal seasons—he calls this 'the normal surplus'. In very good seasons when climatic conditions were highly favourable, they had a bumper harvest for wide-scale distribution; in poor seasons they went on short commons. Allan worked this out in trying to explain why from year to year there was a very wide variation in the crop which African tribes nowadays throw on the open market. Before the creation of this external market by European occupation, the bumper seasons presumably produced large-scale feasting, while poor seasons involved mutual assistance in terms of the same set of relations. And in Southern Africa, for example, the occurrence of these variable seasons was liable to be, in the better parts, three normal years, to one good year, to one bad year.[41]

As described above, there were in many tribes considerable differences in social standing, despite the egalitarian standards of consumption. Higher social standing was associated with both greater control over productive resources and with greater claims on the labour of others. But individuals could raise their status in several ways, even if they could not enter the ranks of chiefs. Brave warriors, enterprising workers, and wise councillors could acquire goods and influence; and by their higher standing they could marry into aristocratic families. There was thus vertical social mobility. But too much mobility of this kind might be frowned on: and many societies with aristocracies had 'sumptuary' laws, which both prevented commoners from rivalling their superiors or using certain articles which were the perquisites of aristocrats. For example, African tribes distinguish between tribute which is rendered from ordinary production to the chief, and certain goods—mainly parts of animals and birds—which must be given to the chief because only he is privileged to consume them and they are forbidden to common use.

The ability of men in some societies to operate in the prestige economy depends largely on their own assiduity and energy, as in many New Guinea tribes where it is stated that men start from scratch. In other societies, the status into which a man is born considerably affects the status he can achieve in his lifetime. There is a range from the rich to the poor, even when the rich support the poor because they cannot do anything else with their wealth. And in some situations there are poor men without kin, who lack the stock or land to support themselves, and attach themselves as servants to their wealthier fellows. They tend to be treated as indigent kinsmen rather than as servants. Indeed, even in the highly stratified society of India, with its rigid ritual restrictions between castes, in the past families in the lower castes were attached to particular patrons in the upper castes from whom they received a fixed annual payment in kind in return for their services. The dependants could turn for all kinds of help to their patrons, though in general they lived in relatively miserable poverty.

Operating in the prestige economy, there are customs which constantly reduce the wealthy to the ranks of the poorer, and allow others to replace them. Among these customs are the transfer of goods at a marriage either as dowry for the bride in India or as a means of acquiring conjugal rights in Africa, as well as the provision of extravagant marriage feasts, and great expenditure and even destruction at funerals. Tribal peoples are not of course unique in doing this. But the consequence is that even in a relatively small society like Tikopia a family may have to mobilize all its resources to cope with the expenditure demanded at a sudden death: this leads to heavy outgoings even when kin help. Included in these outgoings are gifts distributed to particular categories of kin and in-laws, who will at the funerals of their own close relatives make return. Since gifts in Tikopia are constantly circulating for many reasons, and there are 'forced exchanges', it seems that a family is not rendered destitute in these circumstances. In more developed economies this may happen. Bailey lists the cost of marriages and deaths as among the causes why families in Orissa, India, spend more than their incomes permit, and enter on a process of decline in which they have to begin to sell their land. As he puts it, '. . . the imperative [to extravagance] is a social one and . . . social obligations are allowed to override economic prudence'.[42]

In Africa large outgoings of this kind take place when a family has to pay out cattle for a bride for one of its members. If the herd becomes large, the owner either gets another wife for himself or a wife for one of his sons. Temporarily, the family herd may be seriously reduced, even though in other respects the family economy is strengthened by acquiring another female member, particularly where the tribe are not pure pastoralists but also till the soil with female labour. If there are also daughters in the family, cattle will return on their marriages; if there are no daughters, the family will have to try to recoup its herd by caring for the cattle of others. In these circumstances, there is a relatively rapid fluctuation in economic resources of some families, while others have difficulty in procuring brides at all. Only the very wealthy, and particularly chiefs, have sufficient wealth in cattle to escape from these social vicissitudes.

In a number of societies which we still class as tribal, particularly in West Africa, pledging of land is allowed as well as pawning of persons into 'debt-slavery' to meet these contingencies, and to raise credit. The pawn could work off the debt. His status in the indigenous economy was protected like that of the domestic slaves discussed above: only when there were external markets for slaves from West Africa to America and from East Africa to Arabia did extensive trade in slaves develop.

## CULTURAL PATTERNS

Individuals and families and other groups may work alone or co-operate in productive activities to varying degrees among different tribes. There are even tribes in which husband and wife are considered each to produce and own goods appropriate to his or her sex independently. Landes says of this situation among the Ojibwa on the U.S.A.-Canadian border that they 'phrase an objectively co-operative economy in the most individualistic terms. The man hunts alone on his isolated trails; the wife works alone in the wigwam, with the occasional assistance of her children or elderly mother; and they [husband and wife presumably] exchange the products of their work.'[43] Among the Lamba of Northern Rhodesia a man and his wife are also regarded as independent economic units, in the sense that if a man borrows money from his wife he must repay it. To do so, he may get the money as a gift from his brother. Yet husband and wife are bound to each other in close economic co-operation. A people's cultural ideas do not necessarily reflect the objective reality. In other tribes the co-operation between husband and wife is stressed.

There is variation in the etiquette of different tribes about how a host behaves when he gives feasts or a donor when he makes gifts. In the Kwakiutl *potlatch* a man is expected to feast and present valuables to his rivals aggressively and boastingly. This is also good manners at many New Guinea ceremonial exchanges. It would be exceedingly bad manners in most African tribes to boast at one's feasts or presentations in this way. Some people even take pride in depreciating their own hospitality and gifts. Here different patterns of culturally imposed etiquette again may cover very similar objective situations.

The main part of this chapter sets out the objective framework within which goods are produced and distributed for consumption. This framework has specific limitations which place premiums on giving away goods: further examples will appear again and again below in the analyses of other societies with reference to other problems. All tribal societies are dominated by this characteristic. The Ifugao in fierce competition strive as individuals to amass goods and obtain usurious interest on loans. But a rich man may be reduced to penury by illnesses calling for sacrifice and by prescribed feasts to the village, as well as fragmentation of his estate among his children. There is objective variation in the extent to which productive activities are carried out in isolation or co-operation, and in the extent to which there is automatic or competitive distribution of goods. There is also variation in the size and character of groups involved, and whether prestige accrues to an individual or his group. The major framework everywhere is as delineated.

People's ideas about what they are doing may not accord with this reality. The etiquette with which different tribes surround a form of action common to them all may vary considerably. Some beliefs and customs will form consistent patterns with this etiquette. These are the. types of variations between societies which the cultural anthropologists seek to explain: to quote some phrasings, they are interested in the consistencies and inconsistencies in culture patterns and between emphases, themes and orientations of culture. Social anthropologists commonly take these as given, and concentrate on the role of culture in social relations (which latter also provide material for the cultural anthropologist).

An analysis of these patterns of etiquette, etc., lies outside the scope of this book. In the field of this chapter, cultural anthropologists have done considerable work. Perhaps the pioneer effort was the book on *Co-operation and Competition among Primitive Peoples* (1937) which was edited by Mead. Happily it has been republished in a paperback (1961), with a new preface and appraisal by Mead, and notes by the other contributors. It is still one of the best studies in this field, and it gives in convenient form summary accounts of the patterns orienting the behaviour of thirteen tribes in economic as well as other activities.

After surveying the material Mead and her colleagues came to the conclusion, despite difficulties of comparison which they fully recognized, 'that the Kwakiutl were grossly competitive, the Bathonga [now known as the Tsonga] were grossly co-operative, and the Eskimo and Ojibwa grossly individualistic societies'. The characteristics of the other societies studied in the book were less gross. But the investigators were able to agree on placing all thirteen (with some uncertainty over the Dakota Red Indians) on a triangle, in which the mid-point of each side is taken as the most intense development of that emphasis, while the places near the apexes stand in a more intermediate position.

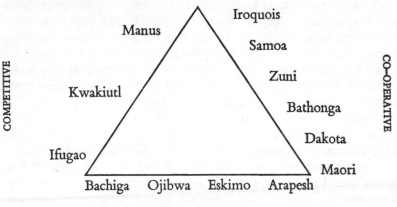

'Nevertheless, no society is exclusively competitive or exclusively co-operative. The very existence of highly competitive groups implies co-operation within the groups. Both competitive and co-operative habits must coexist within the society. There is furious competition among the Kwakiutl at one stratum of the society—among the ranking chiefs—but within the household of each chief co-operation is mandatory for the amassing of the wealth that is distributed or destroyed. Similarly among the Manus the competitive exchanges between the wealthy entrepreneurs are dependent upon a degree of co-operation within the constellation of related persons who support the leader.' Competition did not necessarily involve 'conflict' (i.e. what I call quarrelling), since it might be competition in giving away. But working with these general classifications, Mead and her colleagues searched for correlative factors.

Taking into account other societies as well as the thirteen used in this pilot research, no correlation was found with matriliny or patriliny. A low level of subsistence meant that a society consisted of very small groups, but this did not necessarily entail 'individualism'. 'Co-operativeness' in some cases seemed to increase the food supply. Nor did a particular mode of acquiring food produce a particular type of emphasis: indeed people might phrase their emphasis against the facts of the ecological situation. The amount of competition for women and goods was not consistently determined by the supply of these valuables. Finally, societies with different emphases are found in one culture area. Mead sums up: '. . . we may say that while there is an occasional correspondence between the conditions of supply, or the technological factors, or the exigencies of the environment, and the major emphases of the culture, this correspondence is the exception rather than the rule' (p. 466).

She then proceeded to a fuller discussion of the degree of political organization and other forms of social relationships. I cannot here quote this long discussion, nor is it relevant to our immediate problem. What is significant is that she found firmer connections between these major emphases and personality traits: 'strong ego development can occur in individualistic, competitive, or co-operative societies'.

'. . . The social conception of success and the structural framework into which individual success is fitted are more determinative than the state of technology or the plentifulness of food.'

'There is a correspondence between: a major emphasis upon competition, a social structure which depends upon the initiative of the individual, a valuation of property for individual ends, a single scale of success and a strong development of the ego.'

'There is a correspondence between: a major emphasis upon co-operation, a social structure which does not depend upon individual initiative or the exercise of power over persons, a faith in an ordered universe, a weak emphasis upon rising in status, and a high degree of security for the individual.'

Some of these associations seem to be inherent in the definition of individualism, co-operativeness, and competitiveness. Others led to further fruitful research on the relation of personality and culture, and modes of character formation. Later research is discussed in Mead's new 1961 appraisal, together with independent developments in the same and related fields. These are not directly relevant to the problems here analysed. I quote this book for its importance, but stress that cultural anthropology had begun to diverge from social anthropology, which is the emphasis of my book.

[1] Hoebel's *The Law of Primitive Man* (1954) discusses the importance of keeping clear the different kinds of rights and immunities enjoyed by persons; he follows the elaborate terminology of the American jurist Hohfeld. For brevity, I use 'rights' with its several meanings. Hoebel's book also describes the maintenance of law in several societies at different stages of political development.

[2] Forde discusses well the range of these societies in *Habitat, Economy and Society* (1934). Herskovits, *Economic Anthropology* (1952), considers rights in land and property under different types of technology.

[3] Schapera, *Native Land Tenure in the Bechuanaland Protectorate* (1943).

[4] My essay on 'The Lozi of Barotseland in North-Western Rhodesia' in Colson and Gluckman (editors), *Seven Tribes of British Central Africa* (1951) describes this African kingdom. (The book as a whole gives a view of a variety of African tribes.) See also the chapter on land-tenure in Gluckman, *The Ideas in Barotse Jurisprudence* (1965). More generally on Africa consult Biebuyck, *African Agrarian Systems* (1963); and Goodenough, *Property, Kin and Community in Truk* (1951).

[5] This case is described in full in my *The Judicial Process among the Barotse of Northern Rhodesia* (1955), pp. 178–87.

[6] See Sheddick, *Land Tenure in Basutoland* (1956) for a final working out of this terminology, which I advanced in *Essays on Lozi Land and Royal Property* (1943) and used in my essays cited in footnote 4 of this chapter.

[7] See Richards, *Land, Labour and Diet in Northern Rhodesia* (1939), on the Bemba.

[8] See below, p. 271.

[9] *Primitive Polynesian Economy* (1939), pp. 316 f.

[10] I cite a number of Lozi disputes to illustrate this situation in my *Judicial Process among the Barotse* (1955), and deal with the role of property in *The Ideas in Barotse Jurisprudence* (1965). See also Firth, *Primitive Polynesian Economy* (1939), pp. 322 f.

[11] *The Nuer* (1940), p. 89. But note that Howell in his *Manual of Nuer Law* (1954), p. 194, records that 'disputes over small items of property never appear before the courts' of Nuer Government-sponsored chiefs, which have been established by the Sudan Government.

[12] Cited Herskovits, *Economic Anthropology* (1952), p. 205.

[13] Firth, *Primitive Polynesian Economy* (1939), p. 349.

[14] To cite another example, so too with 'trading partners' among some Eskimo. Spencer, *The North Alaskan Eskimo* (1959), p. 169.

[15] *The Cheyenne Way* (1941), pp. 111–12: an exciting analysis of how law and order flourished and flowered in this tribe.

[16] This account of the Bemba is taken from Richards, *Land, Labour and Diet in Northern Rhodesia* (1939).

[17] The limited nature of co-operative working and the emphasis on individual appropriation is brought out in Herskovits' culling of examples in *Economic Anthropology* (1952), pp. 99 f. He describes the smiths in *Dahomey* (1938), I, pp. 75–76. For a good analysis of the facts in one tribe see Firth, *Primitive Polynesian Economy* (1939).

[18] Firth, *We the Tikopia* (1936). Firth revisited this island in 1952–53, and in a second book, *Social Change in Tikopia* (1959) he describes how he and his colleague, Mr. J. Spillius, aided the islanders, whose numbers had increased greatly, to cope with the devastating effects of a cyclone on food supply. They used two-way radio to secure the help of the Administration, hundreds of miles away.

[19] Evans-Pritchard, *The Nuer* (1940), p. 83.

[20] Richards, footnote 7 of this chapter.

[21] Colson, *Marriage and the Family among the Plateau Tonga of Northern Rhodesia* (1958).

[22] Thomas, *The Harmless People* (1959) on Bushmen; Steward, *Basin Plateau Aboriginal Socio-Political Groups* (1938); Meggitt, *Desert People* (1962).

[23] The critical density of population even for some agricultural tribes was as low as 6 per square mile: over that density they were short of land. For pastoralists and hunters it was even lower. See Allan, *The African Husbandman* (1965), for the problems involved in making these calculations.

[24] Warner, *A Black Civilization* (1937).

[25] Fortes and Evans-Pritchard (editors), 'Introduction' to *African Political Systems* (1940).

[26] Meggitt, *The Lineage System of the Mae Enga* (1965). In this connection on another New Guinea tribe, see Brookfield and Brown, *Struggle for Land* (1963). Lewis, *A Pastoral Democracy* (1961), touches on a similar dilemma among the Somali.

[27] Schapera, *The Khoisan Peoples of South Africa* (1930), p. 127.

[28] For an excellent analysis see Mitchell, *The Yao Village* (1956).

[29] There is a vivid description of the *potlatch* in Chapter VI of Benedict's *Patterns of Culture* (1934). Goldman describes the institution of the Alkatcho Carrier of British Columbia in Linton's *Acculturation in Seven American Tribes* (1940): I cite this authority because the book makes available accounts of a variety of Red Indian cultures. An excellent modern study is Codere, *Fighting with Property* (1950), which gives full references. I recommend also for the reaction of a *potlatching* tribe to its new situation, Colson, *The Makah Indians* (1953).

[30] There are several good studies here, such as Reay, *The Kuma* (1959).

[31] But MacArthur's footnote suggests that the taboo disappears when 'international' peace is established by an outside power, though pig-exchange persists: 'This applied equally to women. The prohibitions are no longer observed. During the mass emigration from the Kunimaipa to the Bubu valley the Kunimaipa learned from their kinsmen in the Bubu that eating pork from pigs raised by oneself and one's kin did not lead to the consequences predicted by their ancestors. The inhabitants of the Bubu are said to have abandoned the old custom after observing the practices of Europeans. Nowadays, the Kunimaipa are willing to eat pork from pigs raised by their relatives, though a few baulk at eating pork from their own pigs.'

[32] It seems that the primitive (in the real sense of the word, since all living races are modern men) manlike Australopithecines and their kindred species in Africa lived in companies. Le Gros Clark in his 1961 Presidential Address to the British Association for the Advancement of Science argued that thus 'culture' could have originated. Important work on monkeys and baboons has supported this line of analysis: see Tax (editor), *Horizons in Anthropology* (1964).

[33] Mead, 'Melanesian Middlemen', *Natural History* XXX (1930), pp. 115–30, cited in Herskovits, *Economic Anthropology* (1952), pp. 255–57. Herskovits also summarizes accounts of similar valuables discussed below.

[34] Robertson, *Money* (1922), p. 2.

[35] *Primitive Polynesian Economy* (1939), pp. 306–7.

[36] Labouret, *Les Tribus de Rameau Lobi* (1931), pp. 362–63, cited in Herskovits, *Economic Anthropology* (1952), pp. 247 f.

[37] Since the manuscript of this book was completed, Bohannan and Dalton have edited a book on *Markets in Africa* (1962).

[38] See below, pp. 221 f.

[39] Firth, *Primitive Polynesian Economy* (1939), p. 355. On this problem it is illuminating to read the review of F. M. Knight, an economist, of Herskovits' *Economic Anthropology* and Herskovits' reply. Both are reprinted at the end of later editions of Herskovits' book.

[40] *Primitive Polynesian Economy* (1939), p. 34.

[41] Allan, *The African Husbandman* (1965).

[42] Bailey, *Caste and the Economic Frontier* (1957), pp. 58 f.; Barton, *Ifugao Law* (1919).

[43] In Mead, *Co-operation and Competition among Primitive Peoples* (1937), p. 91.

# CHAPTER III

# STATELESS SOCIETIES AND THE MAINTENANCE OF ORDER

## POLITICAL DEVELOPMENT AND EVOLUTION

In the previous chapter I queried whether we should continue to speak of a 'tribal society' when we encounter systems of production which are highly diversified, and in which specific types of economic relationships are differentiated sharply from other kinds of social ties. This situation is accompanied by much specialization in labour on other bases than a division of tasks between the sexes and the generations. Markets are established for more than the bartering of basic necessities, and become important centres in a whole system of impersonal exchanges. Land is also subject to exchange against other goods, and can be held by title of purchase, while it is subject to lease, pledging and mortgaging. Contracts of sale, hire and loan to strangers, as well as service and agency, are important in the economy, even if there is no general theory of contract. A form of money is the standard medium of exchange.

In setting out these characteristics I have with difficulty avoided stating that societies embodying them developed out of tribal societies, lest I become embroiled in controversies about the occurrence of a single evolutionary development for each tribal-type society into a differentiated society. We can contrast the two types of society without considering this developmental problem. But it is certain that the tribal-type antedated the differentiated society in the whole march of human history. It does not follow that in all regions of the world every society has passed through a steady course of development from one to the other stage. This major development has occurred in a limited number of areas, involving particular societies, which have then spread their influence, by trade and conquest, until tribal-type societies became involved in their economic and political systems. In the last century the highly differentiated relations of Western industrial society have been extended to most of the world's tribal societies. During that period the members of those tribes have found themselves involved in the productive systems and the exchanges of the Western world, and under the rule of its powers. In the past, the developed polities and economies of China, India, Egypt, Greece, Rome, and other states have similarly absorbed tribal societies, and lifted them into their exchange economies.

There are many theories to account for why these complications should have developed in particular areas at particular periods. One suggestion—which has been criticized—is that major developments of this kind occurred in alluvial flood valleys, which were both highly productive and which required the development of complex irrigation works and control of those works.[1] Again, clearly as inter-regional exchange grew the entrepôts, both on sea-trading routes and along caravan trails overland, were favourably sited for development, since not only did they develop economic power but also men from varied cultures met there and interchanged ideas with one another.[2] I cannot here tell the story of this development, and of how these more complex economies and polities expanded into tribal areas[3] where people for long might continue encysted within their unspecialized systems of relations. It would require another book. And since we are dealing with a quite different kind of social system once these major developments have taken place, my analysis is confined to the tribal societies, with simple tools, lack of luxuries, and restricted trade, both internal and external. These limitations, as we have seen, set limits on the economic divergences which could be established between 'classes', and between rulers and subjects. Hence in confining ourselves to tribal societies we are dealing with political systems in which the struggle for power and prestige might be acute, but it was fought along lines of territorial and genealogical cleavages, and not between differently endowed economic groups. The study of the tribal situation is intricate enough to be a special field. It also produces propositions which can give useful insight into more complex polities.

Even within the limitations I have set for tribal societies, there is a good range in types of political system, from the small bands of hunters, like Bushmen or Australian Aborigines or some Plains Red Indians, to organized kingdoms with considerable rank differentiation, as among the Maoris and Hawaiians, and particularly African states like those of the Zulu, the Lozi, the Baganda, the Kongo, to take some scattered examples. Even bigger states are found in West Africa, in Dahomey and Ashanti or among the Northern Nigerian Emirates, but these are at least on the verge of ceasing to be classifiable as tribal states. The Mayan and Inca states seem definitely to have passed that verge.

It is possible to range the political systems of tribes along a scale of morphological development, beginning with the small hunting-band, all of whose members are related to one another by blood or marriage and who accept the leadership of one or more of their senior members. There are larger bands composed of more people. Then we find fairly large tribes organized in an elaborate framework of 'kinship' groups, or sets of age-mates, before we come to chiefdoms with some instituted authority and governmental organization, and finally to quite large-scale kingdoms. In doing this, we make the assumption that tribes which have governmental apparatus with authority of the type we find in our own societies are different in basic structure from those that lack this apparatus; and this may well be true in general terms. But we shall see that this does not necessarily mean that the states have a more complicated social organization. Furthermore, if we make some arrangement of morphological development in these terms, we cannot be sure that one has evolved out of the other in the general sweep of human history.

I do not mean only that we have historical records which show that in Europe and Asia and Africa large states have broken up into their component sections. In addition, we cannot be sure that if mankind everywhere was first organized in hunting-bands, no section could move from that type of polity straight to well-organized statehood without passing through intervening stages. It does seem probable, however, that there has been a general development in this direction, and that it has accompanied, or been accompanied by, the domestication of stock in a few places, and primarily by agriculture. Few hunters and fishers have well-structured chieftainship: perhaps the *potlatching* North-west Coast Red Indians, in their rich environment, are the most notable example. Normally, outside of North America before the coming of the Whites, the hunting and fishing people have been steadily pushed into the less accessible regions by their pastoral and cultivating neighbours: the Bushmen into the mountains and arid regions of Southern Africa, the Pygmies into the forests, the Negritoes and many Indian 'Aboriginals' into the jungles.

And though the pure pastoralists have been predatory raiders who have swept over agricultural societies on many occasions, the pastoralists in general have also been steadily ousted from those areas favourable for cultivation—areas, indeed, which are often not suitable for stock. This too looks like a general trend in history.

The crude kind of social evolutionism which I have discussed in the first chapter fell into disfavour; but a new school of anthropologists emphasizing evolutionary development in a much more sophisticated manner and using far better data on the tribal peoples has emerged in the United States under the leadership of Leslie A. White.[4] Their general argument is that the evolution of human society is to be *generally* correlated with increasing control over energy, stated in a series of laws of the type, 'culture advances as the proportion of nonhuman energy to human energy increases' (White). But in addition to putting forward propositions to cover the main general evolutionary development, these scholars have also written a series of studies which attempt to interpret variations in the organization of tribes in particular regions in similar terms.[5] I draw attention to their work, but shall not present it here: for my purpose is to show the kind of functional interdependencies which social anthropologists have sought to establish within political systems.

The extent to which instituted authority within a 'governmental' type of polity occurs is not simply associated with either total size of the political community or with density of population. That is, we know of relatively small communities which have chieftainship, like Tikopia. But it is true that authority in these chiefdoms is seldom powerful and tyrannical. The true 'tyrant', as against the temporary bully, is more likely to emerge in fairly large states. Again, there are situations in which considerable populations are organized in what they feel to be a political unit, without instituted leadership, as among the Nuer in Sudan where a single tribe can number up to 45,000 souls. But probably there is a top limit to the population which can be organized as a political unit without governmental apparatus. More surprisingly, some of the most densely populated parts of Africa, like the Tiv in Nigeria or the Bantu Kavirondo peoples near Lake Victoria (over 200 and over 70 to the square mile respectively) lack chiefly institutions, while peoples like the

Bemba and Zulu, estimated to be under four to the square mile, had powerful chieftainships.[6]

To some extent, the answer to this problem may be that the governmental organization which we find in states at these levels of economic development has an inherent instability which continually leads to its breakdown, so that the difference between tribes organized under chiefs, and those which lack chiefs, is not as great as it appears to be. The present and the next chapter are mainly concerned to elucidate this suggestion.

It appears that even the simplest hunting-band regards itself as the possessor of a given territory, even if the boundaries are not always clearly defined. This was true of Australian Aborigines, and of Eskimos and American Indians: and Schapera has recently brought out how strongly this statement applies to Bushmen and Bergdama in South Africa.[7] He shows that each of their communities claims exclusive rights to a given territory, as well as the right to manage its affairs independently of external control. The members range widely over their territory in the eternal quest for food,[8] some families moving off in different directions, then linking up with others, then reuniting with some of their closest relatives again.

Though most of a band are thus in some way kin or in-laws to one another, unrelated persons can join. Schapera therefore criticizes one of Maine's most famous dicta in *Ancient Law*, where he wrote: 'All ancient societies regarded themselves as having proceeded from one original stock, and even laboured under the incapacity for comprehending any reason except this for their holding together in political union. The history of political ideas begins, in fact, with the assumption that kinship in blood is the sole possible ground of community in political functions; nor is there any of those subversions of feeling, which we term emphatically revolutions, so startling and so complete as the change which is accomplished when some other principle— such as that, for instance, of *local contiguity*—establishes itself for the first time as the basis of common political action. . . . The idea that a number of persons should exercise political rights in common simply because they happened to live within the same topographical limits was utterly strange and monstrous to primitive antiquity.' Schapera cites examples of hunters and pastoralists to whom this does not apply: for they absorb people of alien stock and base their association on territorial ties. Maine's statement is undoubtedly misleading. But he makes clear elsewhere in the book that in classical Greece 'strangers' could join a political state; and he was aware of the various devices by which they did so, including the manufacture of genealogical links, a process satirized in Greek comedy. He meant to imply that the revolution occurs (as he saw it) when the fact of settlement in a territory was enough to give citizenship, without establishing kinship by adoption or marriage, or by some fictitious genealogical link. The alteration comes when a kinship idiom to express political association is no longer demanded: as we have already seen, the kinship idiom of tribal society in practice covers relationships directed towards various purposes.

## The Hunting Band

A hunting band in most cases is small and compact, seldom having more than a hundred members, and they live together either continuously or for the better seasons of the year. Where the band occupies a harsh environment, as hunters often do, it cannot grow in size because the resources are insufficient, and population growth may be deliberately restricted. Bushmen and Eskimo both practised infanticide and the pious killing (Eskimo) or abandonment (Bushmen) of feeble old people because there was not enough food for all, and continual roaming made it difficult to move the helpless. Food and hunger dominated life.[9]

Some hunters have leaders who are called 'chiefs' in the literature, but outside of the North-west Coast Indians this term probably gives too grandiloquent an idea of their position. For example, Schapera writes that 'the Bushmen or Bergdama chief . . . has no judicial functions or organized penal powers; his main duties are to direct the migrations and subsistence activities of his people and to perform certain ceremonies for their welfare'. There is no subordinate hierarchy of officials, since the 'chief' can discuss matters with all the men with whom he is involved as they sit round the fire. But there is succession to office, a 'chief' being succeeded by brother or son, with age or ability taken into account. There are no installation ceremonies. The Bergdama 'chief' has certain privileges: he is treated with respect, he usually has more than one wife, he can pick the best skins and ornaments for himself and his family, and he receives tribute of the best meat, of honey, and of tobacco. Special ceremonies attach to the life crises of himself and his family. The Bushman 'chief' has far fewer notable marks of his status.

Since the Bushman 'chief' is a leader, and not a ruler, redress against a wrongdoer has to be procured by self-help. A thief, an adulterer, or the murderer of a near kinsman may be attacked and killed; and it seems that such an incident may lead to an unlimited vendetta in which killings continue. These vendettas may also occur between neighbouring bands, though these inter-marry and meet to trade. Trespass by a stranger on a band's territory is resented and repulsed, and among some Bushmen groups a stronger band could in the past dispossess a weaker of its territory, though it is reported of other groups that the victors did not deprive the vanquished of their land or even occupy it 'lest harm and disaster overtake them'.[10]

The Bushmen and Bergdama are representative of the very small band in which there is little instituted authority and social relationships within bands are mainly relatively close ties of kinship. The Eskimo[11] are similarly organized. Here there seems to be little development of special associational links, outside of the family matrix, and cross-ties between groups are established mainly by intermarriage and trading partnerships.[12] Spouses by customary law have to be sought from outside the circle of near relatives, and this produces a basis for friendly relationships, though it does not exclude the vendetta following on the fact that self-help and -protection are the main mechanism for enforcing rights. Nevertheless these bands had codes of law, and presumably on the whole these were observed. The vendetta operated against the occasional defaulter. And in tribes of this kind there operated also a series of other sanctions to bring people into line, like the Eskimo singing-duel, in which he who felt himself to be wronged could challenge his alleged wrongdoer to a competition in verbal castigation. Hoebel considers that ' "right" is immaterial to the singing or its outcome (though the singer who can pile up scurrilous accusations of more or less truth against his opponent has an advantage in fact)'. But un-fortunately information on how the Eskimo who actually chal-lenge one another to these duels are related is lacking so it is difficult to analyse the social implication of this process.[13]

Once the number of a band exceeds a couple of hundred, the social organization tends to become much more complicated. This emerges in the variation of the social systems of Plains Red

Indian groups.[14] The Comanche, who probably had the largest herds of horses of all these Indians, had a common tongue and culture, and there does not appear to have been warring between their several autonomous bands, though there were no overall Comanche political institutions. These bands ranged in size from small camps of extended families up to bands of several hundreds of persons. People could move between bands. Bands functioned as units during the period of the great buffalo hunts. At other times they broke up into smaller groups of relatives, each with a permanent leader in the form of some outstanding man of ability and influence. When the band assembled, several leaders were accepted as 'the peace chiefs' of the band. Peace chiefs had little instituted power: their main duty was to decide when and whither to move camp. They had to be kind, generous and wise, self-effacing, able to act as arbiters and to influence people to adjust differences, though seemingly they should not thrust themselves into situations where quarrels were probable, since Hoebel notes that they are not recorded as appearing in the major disputes narrated to him. Perhaps it would have been unsuitable for them to compromise their position and dignity by attempting to intervene in situations they were not sure they could control. (A Lozi prince, despite the power of Lozi political organization, thus justified to me his refusal to try to control a crowd at a dance: he said he would be punished if he placed himself in a position where his status would be overlooked by commoners out of control.)

There was no hereditary succession to these leaders, but sons tended to succeed their fathers. These peace chiefs did not lead the Comanche on their raids: a raid was led by any warrior with the initiative to organize one and the influence to obtain followers. A man secured his rights by outfacing his wrongdoer, who was however constrained when in the wrong ultimately to make redress, lest the accuser's kin be drawn in while his own kin refuse to support him; and a weak man might call in a champion-at-law to force his suit upon the wrongdoer. The Comanche did not have the unlimited vendetta: in theory at least a blood-revenge killing should not have been avenged.

The political system of the Cheyenne, who numbered about four thousand in total, was far more complicated. During the winter months, because of meagre food resources the Cheyenne scattered over the countryside in widely separated camps, under headmen who were natural leaders. In the summer months they assembled together, in order to perform great tribal rituals. Each band came marching in, singing and whooping, to take up its position at a traditional point in the camp-circle. Here the tribe was ruled partly by a council of chiefs and partly by the Soldier Societies. The chiefs numbered forty-four, and were appointed for a definite tenure of office. Every ten years the chiefs were renewed, each chief appointing a successor from his own band, but who should not be his son. This is not surprising since the Cheyenne were matrilineal, and a man often joined the band of his wife's kin. Each band therefore contained men from several matrilineal clans, except for the Dog Soldier band whose position is discussed below.

Among the forty-four chiefs, there were five superior priest-chiefs. All these chiefs were under duty to care for the widow and the orphan and to be peacemakers: 'the dignity of a chief did not permit him to take part in any quarrel; he might not take personal vengeance for an offence committed against himself; to do so would result in loss of influence.'[15] Thus we have a pattern demanded of generosity, self-restraint, wisdom, sternness when required, and above all integrity. The council had executive and judicial authority: it alone could make peace and it exiled murderers, and in turn could end that exile when it considered that the offender had expiated his offence. And among the Cheyenne murder of a fellow-tribesman was a grave sin which polluted the sacred Medicine Arrows of the tribe, so that these had to be elaborately renewed. Meanwhile the tribe's enterprises were adversely affected in every way, while the viscera of the murderer 'rotted' and emanated a noisome odour repugnant to the beasts of the prairie. Myths validated these beliefs.

Individual chiefs served as mediators in other disputes and they directed the movements of the camp.

We have already met the other arm of Cheyenne government, the Soldier Societies, or military associations, as they have been called. Their membership included all fighting-men. Most significantly, except for one society which was composed of a single band, five of the societies drew their membership from the various bands into which the tribe broke up for the winter, as well as from the various clans. Theoretically the Soldier Societies were under the authority of the chiefs' council, but they developed an autonomy in power of their own. Here the Cheyenne organization exemplifies two principles of political organization of radical importance everywhere. First, it shows that social cohesion develops as men who are allied in terms of one customary rule of association (band-membership) are grouped under a different rule (soldier-society membership) with others who have a different allegiance under the first rule.[16] That membership of the Soldier Societies cut across band-allegiance, helped break down the autonomy and isolation of each band as against the tribal entity. It is perhaps significant—those who have studied the Cheyenne have not as far as I know discussed this point—that some suspicion was entertained by others against the tribal loyalty of the Dog Soldiers, who were composed of members of a single band. This band was formed shortly before the Cheyenne came under American rule: it largely married within itself so that it had few cross-linkages into the rest of the tribe or its other Soldier Societies. '. . . [In] two great crisis situations Dog Soldier chiefs were forbidden to have contact with American officials lest they make unauthorized and unwanted yet binding decisions. Bull Bear, in 1863, was restrained from meeting in treaty council with the American Commissioners. More spectacularly, the Cheyennes threatened to kill Tangle Hair, head chief of the Dog Soldiers, in 1873 when Captain Wessels offered to release him and his family from the freezing and starving confinement to which Dull Knife's band was being subjected in the Fort Robinson barracks.' The Cheyenne were determined to die rather than capitulate to the Government's demand that they return to Oklahoma whence they had fled, and they feared that Tangle Hair if given freedom would order them to capitulate.[17]

Second, the Soldier Societies, though theoretically exercising a delegated authority, in practice developed an autonomous power of their own, as all subordinates tend to do. We have seen how the Soldiers controlled the great hunts; and I wish I had the space to reproduce some of the vivid descriptions provided by Llewellyn and Hoebel in their book on *The Cheyenne Way* of how the Soldiers acted and developed as police and judicial officers. They searched for certain types of wrongdoers and compelled redress or meted out punishment, intervened on occasion in familial disputes, and when confronted with new kinds of disputes made 'judicial law'.

A third principle of great social importance is also present in Cheyenne political organization: this is the role of mystical symbols in signifying the ultimate common interests of a tribe. The Medicine Arrows are clearly such a symbol, and their significance and influence on tribal well-being are raised beyond questioning by the myth which validates their eternal existence. Another important symbol was the Holy Hat lodge. This lodge was a sanctuary for anyone, even an enemy horse-stealer, who if he found refuge there was given safe-conduct out of Cheyenne territory. The wife of the lodge-keeper is reputed on one occasion to have used the circle of her arms, symbolic of the circular lodge, and the stick on which the Hat hung, to succour a girl whose brother-in-law, whom she had refused to marry, was unjustifiably going to hand her over to a Soldier Society to rape— unjustifiably, because only a husband had the right to do this to an unfaithful wife. The manner in which objects charged with 'supernatural' power symbolize and operate to maintain ultimate group values recurs constantly in tribal political systems. Indeed, the Cheyenne assembled as a tribe, not only to hunt the buffalo (which they might have done more successfully in bands), but also in order to perform ceremonies, including the decennial renewal of chiefs, ceremonies which they believed to be connected with the welfare of all of them. But the combination of bands was helpful in their fights with other tribes on the hunting-grounds and for better winter-quarters in the protected spots of the great prairies.

CROSS-CUTTING TIES AMONG THE TONGA

These three principles of organization are well illustrated by the Plateau Tonga of Northern Rhodesia.[18] They live to the west of the Zambezi river escarpment, and in historic times they were severely raided and pillaged by stronger tribes organized in kingdoms some hundreds of miles from them. This situation lasted virtually till the 1890's when British protection was extended to them, through the British South Africa Company. What sort of society do we find after the severe hammering they received from other tribes?

The Tonga are scarcely distinguishable as a tribe: indeed it is not always clear to whom the name should be applied. In all directions they shade into peoples, possessing similar cultures, but called by other names; and the boundaries at which people call themselves by other tribal appellations, and are called thus by outsiders, vary considerably. There were no chiefs: when the British came they set up 120 local leaders as chiefs, for perhaps 60,000 people—i.e. one chief per 500 people. The number of these chiefs has been reduced by stages to fourteen.

Yet there has always been a Tonga 'society'; and to appreciate what this society is, we have to look at a whole series of groups and relationships.

Tongaland is a typical piece of Africa, possessed on the whole of poor soils, with pockets of fertile soil. Beyond the search for soils of some fertility, and free from waterlogging, groups were not tied to particular areas of land, and hence considerable movement was possible.

The Tonga live in small villages which used to be widely scattered in the hope of escaping raids. They still live in villages, for several reasons, including obedience to a Government rule requiring that all men live in villages comprising at least ten taxpayers. In some areas it is not easy to distinguish the boundaries of villages, since the huts of two villages are mingled together; but people know to which headman they theoretically owe allegiance. The headman has little power, and members of a village are not responsible for one another in difficulties. But at certain rituals they assemble as groups of fellow-villagers. For many purposes, small clusters of closely related persons within the village are more important: they build their huts together and co-operate in diverse activities. A large village consists of several such clusters, whose important people are usually related to the headman.

The village itself moves frequently, as is common in Africa under agricultural systems where the soils and the techniques do not allow permanent agriculture. There has also been much shifting of Tonga since 1904, to make place for European farms along the railway line which cuts through Northern Rhodesia, and Tonga move within the Tonga Reserved areas to get near the line of rail in order to market maize, eggs, and other products.

Within the village, there is also movement of clusters and of individuals for many reasons. Sanitary needs—to get away from insects—and rotting huts compel some moves. Other moves are to get new land. Some moves arise from social factors, such as the maturing of young people, and marriages. New friendships may induce people to move, or they flee from quarrels between villagers and within clusters: it may be difficult to be friendly with everyone in a largish group all the time. In the course of these moves, a cluster, if it numbered ten taxpayers, could set up as an independent village. Individuals move so frequently that when Colson made her survey, only 36 per cent of the men and 20 per cent of the women were living in their natal villages; and she thus measured a minimum of mobility, because, as she notes, these had not lived there all their lives. Some had previously resided in two, three and even four villages in the course of their as yet uncompleted lives.

This high geographical movement of villages, clusters and individuals, is made in terms of several types of social relations. Land rights, where the population does not press heavily beyond the land's capacity, are permissive. A man can just take up vacant land where he can find it. A man who first settled in a particular local area retains a little prestige from this, but he cannot stop others following him. Hence in any area there exists a very variegated pattern of links between headmen, and between them and their villagers.

Single men and single women may move. In general, women more often (63 per cent) move on marriage to live with their husbands, than husbands move (37 per cent) to their wives' villages, though as we shall see the main succession to social position and inheritance of property are in the female line.

Villages average 22 huts and each is occupied by related families. A man can only be independent if he is head of a family household, and he can also only establish contact with the spirits of his own kin-groups if he has a wife to brew beer that he can offer to them. Again, out of this seemingly simple ritual rule we shall find there develops a widespread network of ties—like the ties developing out of the New Guinea taboo on eating one's own pig. Among the Tonga this rule compels relations between each family and larger and more enduring groups.

Every Tonga belongs to a group of matrilineally related kin— i.e. they are related through females. This group is called the *mukowa* (as the clan is), but I shall use this Tonga term henceforth to describe the smaller groups. Tonga also belong to one of fourteen clans, again by matrilineal descent. All members of a *mukowa* therefore must be members of the same clan; but not all members of clan are in the same *mukowa*. The *mukowa* functions as a unit while the members of a clan never meet together. But men and women of the same clan cannot marry one another: *a fortiori*, a man and a woman in the same *mukowa* cannot marry. Hence a marriage sets up a link between two *mukowa*.

The children of a marriage belong primarily to their mother's *mukowa*: but their father's *mukowa* also has important rights over and duties to them. When a marriage begins to settle down and is regarded as stable, the house is dedicated to certain spirits who look after its welfare. The first shrine established is to the husband's spirits, and this shrine is primarily responsible for the welfare of the family and its dependants living in that hut. The main spirit concerned, selected by divination, may be that of the husband's father, if he is dead; and we must note that since a man belongs to his mother's *mukowa*, his father is of a different *mukowa* from his. As a person can only make offerings to the spirits of his or her own *mukowa*, this means that the husband cannot himself offer to the spirit which cares for his house and children. He can do so if the presiding spirit is of his mother's *mukowa*. Otherwise he must get a member of his father's *mukowa* to make the offering of beer, though his wife brews it. A member of the wife's *mukowa* must offer to their spirits at the shrine of the doorway.

Thus a man must be married to be ritually independent in the sense of having a shrine at which he can approach the spirits that control his destiny: if his wife dies, or they are divorced, he loses this privilege. An unmarried man is in religious beliefs incomplete, while a woman can make offerings from the beer she brews.

The family household is a group of great importance, since in it children are born and reared, and its members co-operate in productive activities and consume the produce together. But in it there is a meeting of the interests of a whole series of groups: (1) the husband and his *mukowa* own the hut, and his *mukowa* fellows will inherit its goods when he dies. They should visit the household's members when they are ill, should come to mourn at deaths, should help with the marriage-payments of its members and with paying the husband's fines and damages, should purify his wife if he dies and find another man to inherit his position—and only marriage, be it noted, enables him to establish an inheritable position. In the past, his *mukowa* also helped him to enforce his claims and avenged wrongs done to him. (2) The wife's *mukowa* performed the same duties for her, and for her children who belonged to them, not to their husband's *mukowa*. (3) The *mukowa* of the husband's father's mother and also of the wife's father's mother, to neither of which they belonged, also had important duties. This extension of duties might proceed to the husband's father's father's mother's *mukowa* and the wife's father's father's mother's *mukowa*.

Each household is thus the focus of the interests of at least four *mukowa*. Since members of the same clan and *mukowa* cannot marry one another, nor can two women from the same *mukowa* marry two sons of the same father or paternal parallel cousins (sons of two brothers), nor can two men of the same *mukowa* marry two closely related women from one *mukowa*, an immensely complicated network of alliances and mutual dependence is established by the linked interests of all the *mukowa* in the many households of any neighbourhood—and beyond it. The rules forbidding marriage are even more complicated than those I have set out: the network is therefore in reality that much more complicated. Intermarriage between the *mukowa*, which has to be spread widely by the rules prohibiting marriage, thus compels a wide spread of links of this kind; and so long as people believe that their fortunes and misfortunes, and those of their children, depend on the spirits of various groups, they are forced into relationships of dependence with a whole series of these groups.

The internal structure of each *mukowa* facilitates this spread. In many societies, the members of a kinship group have their positions relative to one another fixed by genealogical reckoning, which in recent generations is probably pretty accurate. When we find a group of this kind, we call it a *lineage*.[19] A genealogy of this kind ranks persons as closer and more distant kin, but even peoples like the Nuer, who have a system like this, resist the implied loss of close kinship as people move further away, by calling, e.g. the father's son (by a different mother) 'my mother's son', and a father's brother's son, 'my father's son'—much as in England we call all cousins, 'my cousin', without specifying degrees. Nevertheless, in the end genealogical reckoning does force people to recognize closeness and distance of kinship. This situation does not arise among the Tonga, who do not keep a genealogical reckoning. It is exceedingly bad manners to emphasize distance of blood-relationship between members of a single *mukowa*—even if you know that distance and even though you recognize that a full-brother is more likely to help you than a

distant *mukowa* mate who theoretically is under the same obligation to you.

In result, any individual who can establish a claim of any kind
to be a member of the *mukowa*, can be absorbed and treated as if
he or she were a close relative, through uterine links, of all other
members. A man establishes this claim by practical activity, such
as helping at funerals, contributing to the marriage-payments
made by men of the *mukowa*, helping pay fines and damages—
and in the end he will be helped in turn and share in the *mukowa's*
marriage-payments coming in from the mating of its women
and in inheritances of the property of members which is distributed
at their deaths.

Other rules are consistent with this pattern. It is a general rule
that in lineage systems, with their genealogical reckoning, cattle
coming in for the women marrying out are distributed among the
women's male kin according to nearness of relationship. Among
the Zulu and many other tribes the bride's own brother gets the
main part of the cattle, and uses them to obtain a bride for himself. The Tonga taboo this strongly. You cannot take cattle of a
woman of the same generation as yourself or of a woman two
generations away: you can only take the cattle of a woman of
the first or third generation below your own. More than this,
if a man drinks milk from the cattle of his sister's marriage he
will fall ill. His father, or mother's brother, who obtain these
cattle, and with whom he may be living, has therefore to send
these cattle to others to herd, lest his dependants be imperilled.
And since a man cannot marry with his sister's cattle, he must get
cattle to marry elsewhere: so, like the taboo on eating one's own
pig, this taboo forces a whole series of links on people with those
more distantly related than their own close kin. A man must
have a wide spread of kin. This taboo is further consistent with
the whole structure of the *mukowa*: and it enables people to attach
themselves to a *mukowa* when they move, by fulfilling the obligations of membership. In the past, membership of some *mukowa*
was essential for a man since it alone protected him from attack;
nowadays it is extremely useful, though the British Government
provides ward over person and property.

In addition to the *mukowa*, the Tonga have their fourteen clans,
also matrilineal. As stated above, a clan never meets as a group.
Nor does it own land, and it has no group rituals. Yet the Tonga
insist that clans are the most important groups they have and they

cannot conceive of a society without clans. They believe that Europeans have clans but with their usual chicanery conceal this from Africans. The Tonga say, 'The clan is our flag'. We may well ask why they so regard it when it never assembles as a group, and has no property and no ritual.

Tonga told a missionary early in this century that 'God gave us clans so that we could marry properly', for clans set the clearest taboo on intermarriage of members. Besides this, a man should not enslave a fellow of his clan, and he is under some obligation to help him or her. But dominantly the Tonga emphasize the rule of exogamy, and we have seen how this is a primary mechanism for spinning the network of alliances between groups. There are many other important aspects of clan-membership. You can edge your way into a *mukowa* of your clan-name, wheresoever you wander, even outside the borders of Tongaland, for the clans stretch beyond these. In the several moves which Tonga make, wherever they go, even if they change membership of the secularly and spiritually protective *mukowa*, they carry clan-membership with them. It is persistent and enduring, and theoretically cannot be changed: it is the most enduring element in Tonga society. *Mukowa* can break up, die, realign with others, reform; villages can disappear: people with a limited number of clan-names are always there.

## TONGA JOKING-RELATIONSHIPS

Beyond this, Tonga clans are interlinked in joking-relationships, some of whose forms we discussed in Chapter I. We have seen that this is a relationship which combines friendship and antagonism, the pretence of hostility with real friendliness. Tonga have joking relationships of this kind between grandparents and grandchildren, between cross-cousins (children of a brother and a sister), and between in-laws of the same generation. Most of these involve pleasantries with sexual innuendoes, and, save between grandparents and grandchildren, some horseplay and 'petting'. The grandparents may, as among the Lozi, joke to their grandchildren: 'You are my wife'; 'My wife, get water for me'. In addition, members of certain paired clans are allowed—indeed required—to joke with and abuse one another, and these jokes are different from those made between pairs of relatives.

Each clan is associated with certain animals, insects, and natural phenomena: and each clan has two or more partners who joke with it about the antagonism between their associated animals, etc. Thus a Muhyamba clansman explained:

(i) we are ants and we joke with the bees, for they make honey and we eat it;

(ii) we are hyaenas and we joke with lions, who kill the meat which we eat;

(iii) we are hyaenas and we joke with the goats because we steal them;

(iv) we are hyaenas and we joke with the hares because we both are tricksters.[20]

These may seem very poor jokes indeed. But it is essential to note that they are a prescribed, compelled form of behaviour. As E. L. Peters has said of the behaviour of young men's groups in rural Wales,[21] they establish a pattern of permitted joking and disrespect which validates the apparently more biting jokes listed below, and beyond that the castigatory duties which joking partners undertake.

The more biting jokes are of this pattern:

(i) 'Your mother is dead,' answered perhaps with, 'So is yours.'

(ii) 'Your mother's brother is dead.'

(iii) 'You are a sorcerer: you are killing people.'

Tonga stress the importance of the whole web of joking relationships between the clans, for in practice each clan is linked with a number of other clans. Each clan can call on its clan-joking partners in a number of specific situations:

(i) to shame a person who has incurred community dis-approval, which is something that fellow-members of a *mukowa* cannot themselves do, since they are under obligation to help him—for fellow-members of a *mukowa* are, *a fortiori*, members of the same clan;

(ii) to shame those who are guilty of incestuous actions or desire to marry in breach of exogamous rules—that is, to protect the politically essential rules compelling marriage outside of established groups and networks of relationships;

(iii) to upbraid a man who is wasting his property—which fellow-clansmen and kinsmen cannot do, since they have claims on that property, and if they protested against the waste they would be expressing the wish to inherit from the owner, which implies a wish that he may die;

(iv) to shame would-be suicides—who, I suggest, may be thought to be driven to this action by difficulties with their kinsmen.

Joking-clan partners also have certain duties:

(i) they have to purify from the ill omen of a collapsed granary, with its implied loss of food;

(ii) they bury suicides and lepers (*quaere*: those whose bodies rot in life?);

(iii) they clown at funerals to cheer up the surviving kin, and ask why they grieve since they killed the deceased with sorcery— thus expressing a fear among the kin that one of their number in fact did so;

(iv) in an emergency, if a required relative is not available for a ceremony, a clan-joker can substitute for any kinsman or kins- woman;

(v) when a man is out of food, he can go to his clan-joker to beg for help.

If we survey these duties, we see that the clan-jokers are con- cerned with morality, with care for property, with food, with maintaining the rules of exogamy that spin the network of kin- ship ties, with symbolizing all kinship, with preserving life, with burial of the ill-omened dead, and with urging life despite death. In Tonga society the observance of these rules and adherence to these values cannot be urged by *mukowa* and other kin lest they be suspected of denying their will to assist, or asserting a wish that the delinquent die in order that they may take his property: 'strangers' undertake these duties, and they do so through a joking- relationship which proclaims a social interest in what a man does, while it emphasizes that those stating this interest are not them- selves directly concerned in the relationships, of persons and property, involved. The social interest in life, in property, in morality, in kinship, and in intermarriage of 'enemies', is thus attached to the only enduring groups of Tonga society. Hence the clans stand for an ultimate social morality, through the system which interlinks many clans as clan-jokers; and one set of values of social life is embodied in these enduring groups.

And the 'strangers' enforce these values on people in the prescribed formula of joking which has been established as a standard relationship through the pattern of seemingly silly joking.

Two important principles of organization are involved here. First, we have looked at the elements of conjunction and disjunction, of common interest and divergent interest, which give the typical setting of joking and teasing. In joking relationships between pairs of persons, each may be privileged in the midst of his joking to reprimand his partner. A wife's brother stands in this relationship to his sister's husband among the Cheyenne. Since they are a matrilineal people, responsibility for the woman's welfare is divided between her husband and her brother; and the brothers-in-law can abuse each other for default in duties to her, in their stream of privileged joking.[22] Among the Tonga this kind of joking between clans has important political consequences, both by giving many more friends to all men and by providing privileged arbiters of morals in a society without political authorities. This moral element must not be overlooked. It appears again among the Tallensi of Ghana, whose social system is too complicated to be presented here.[23] Briefly, every locally centred Tallensi clan is divided into lineages, each of which is permanently connected with lineages in other clans, to produce an over-lapping series of ties of friendship, focused in grades of land- and ancestral-shrines. Beyond a certain point, for each clan, there comes an end to the range of friends, and here there are clans who are friends of one's friends but also friends of one's enemies. These are 'clan-jokers'. Fortes at a solemn funeral sacrifice saw two young men steal meat from the victim and run away waving it above their heads. Elders were angry, till they recognized who had done this: then they laughed and wrestled to get the meat back. This is a typical joking situation, manifesting the opposed elements: without rights to participate in the sacrifice, the jokers steal of it, as an uterine nephew, outside of the agnatic line but closely related by descent from it, among the patriarchal Mozambique Tsonga also steals from sacrifices to his mother's brother's ancestors.

But what is significant for us about the Tallensi situation, is that in the next ring of clans—who are almost your enemies—some of them are the people who can exercise the strongest 'moral coercion' (Fortes) over you. You dare not refuse anything they ask, lest your whole line of descent perish. Hence if a man gives up hope from grief and falls into despair, these are the people who urge him to rouse himself—and he cannot refuse lest ill from ancestral wrath afflict not only him but also all his line. These people are those on the very fringe of one's social relations, seemingly on the verge of moral relations. The Tallensi parallel emphasizes the strong moral element in the Tonga clan-joking relationship—and the fact that it is connected with Tonga ideas about the fundamental values of human life and social existence. In Tongaland these ultimate moral values are connected with the enduring groups, the clans, in which membership is derived from the very process of being born to a mother—an obvious enough fact, but one basic to patrilineal as well as to matrilineal systems of kinship, since men can only produce heirs through their wives.[24]

Secondly, in both these situations the person who emphasizes these values is *a stranger*, someone from outside of the normal run of activity in which a man engages. I use 'stranger' here to cover persons who are outside the particular type of relationships involved in a specific situation. Here again we are dealing with a very common occurrence, frequently institutionalized: the manner in which 'strangers' are called in, or enter, to solve internal crises in the life of a group. Frankenberg has written an analysis of the communal life of a Welsh village which brings out vividly how 'strangers' and also 'foreigners', who are complete outsiders, are thus manipulated by the villagers.[25] As the villagers run a series of recreational activities, which symbolize their communal unity in competition with other villages, they encounter a series of crises over failures, over positions of prestige and influence, and over quarrels arising from other situations. When factions emerge which wish to pursue different courses of action, the final decision which drives one party out of the recreation is put into the mouth of a stranger, who is then blamed for spoiling an otherwise harmonious village. Or so they believe. The roles of lawyers, arbitrators, and others in modern life are sometimes similar: they can propose courses of action in the interest of an organization or group, which if proposed by an 'insider' would be rejected by others as self-interested. And I have always been impressed with the insight of Hugh de Selincourt who wrote a novel about *The Cricket Match* between two rival villages, in which a leader had to be found who could hold together gentry and labourers and shopkeepers. He selected

Paul Gauvinier: '. . . God knows where Paul Gauvinier came from or what he was. . . . He was irritatingly difficult to place. The modern artist, vocal in paint or words or music of ill-temper and distortion, found him crude and healthy and athletic. The sportsman felt he was a queer artist chap; the village people thought him a gentleman, the gentry were not quite sure— was he a gentleman? There were no two stools between which the poor fellow did not fall. He wasn't quite English; no, and he wasn't quite French.'

In tribal organization, this role of the stranger as mediator is frequently institutionalized. The process becomes more significant when previously hostile tribes have had to unite against foreign domination. Then some outsider, not occupying a role of authority in established systems, arises as a prophet, backed with supernatural powers, to unite the previously warring groups. This has happened in several areas of Africa: among the Nuer, among the tribes of the Cape Province of South Africa, in East and Central Africa. Similar movements have occurred in other parts of the tribal world under colonization: they fall outside my present brief, but many are referred to in Worsley's *The Trumpet Shall Sound: A Study of 'Cargo' Cults in Melanesia* (1957). From our own history we know this kind of phenomenon well: we have only to recall how Joan of Arc, not only a peasant but also a woman, managed to unite the squabbling noblemen of 'France' against the English.

## THE JESTER

It is probably in some such light that we should analyse the manner in which the court jester operated as a privileged arbiter of morals, given licence to gibe at king and courtiers, or lord of the manor. Jesters were usually men of low class—sometimes on the Continent of Europe they were priests—who clearly moved out of their usual estate. Normally they were entitled to mock at anyone in the midst of their tales and jokes, and even in some countries to play practical jokes on their betters, perhaps by spilling food on them. Seemingly those who were gibed at or maybe rebuked for faults could not protest. In Shakespeare's *King Lear* and other of his plays the jesters mix with their fooling acute commentaries on the foolishness and foibles of their employers, and even on their evil-doings; reminders of mortality and religious duty were set in a stream of witticisms. These dramatic representations do seem to reflect the actual situation of many of these court-jesters. If we look on the relation of jester and employer as a kind of joking relationship, it is possible to suggest that here there was a standardized pattern of fooling and smart repartee, aimed at amusing the employer, and at which he could not take offence. After all, was not it for this purpose that he employed the jester? Then if the jester mingled into these baseless gibes pointed rebukes, still cast in obscuring witty form, to draw attention to tyrannies and oppressions, any protest from the employer would show that he recognized the point of the attack, and in a sense he would be admitting his fault. For it was the job of the jester to gibe. In a system where it was difficult for others to rebuke the head of a political unit, we might have here an institutionalized joker, operating at the highest point of the unit (where the Tonga clans in their linked joking stand)— a joker able to express feelings of outraged morality. Biographies of jesters of monarchs show that they often in this way obtained great influence, as the jesters of Henry VIII, Elizabeth I, and James I, did over those rulers. Of Will Tarleton, jester to Elizabeth I, his biographer said that his jests did her more good than the medicines of all her physicians, and the sermons of her chaplains. Great courtiers had to seek access to the Queen through this man who did not fear to tell her the truth.[26]

Jesters of this kind were also attached to many African monarchs. They were frequently dwarfs, and other oddities; and their duties included besides the playing of jokes, the singing of the praises of their rulers. Jordan writes of these praise-singers: 'But it must not be thought that these bards were mere flatterers. While they drew attention mainly to the good and praiseworthy, they also had licence to make sharp criticisms of the habits of their subjects [the chiefs]. It is here that the bard found greatest scope for his wit.

'Dingane, murderer and successor of Shaka (creator of the Zulu nation), was mean and greedy, always having a ready excuse to "eat up" the cattle of his wealthy subjects:

> He is the needy offspring of Mpikazi,
> with eye forever cast on the people's herds;
> his cattle are gathered like honey-combs,
> found and seized wherever he goes.'

Their respective praise-singers rebuked the Bomvana chief Luhadi for licentiousness, and the Thembu chief Ngangelizwe for tyrannical doings which drove away his subjects to other lands. Jordan states too that the modern Xhosa poet, Mqhayi, used the praise-song form to praise Great Britain when the Prince of Wales in 1925 visited South Africa, by being sarcastic about all it had promised the Bantu (Africans of South Africa) and then left them without.[27]

I add another example from the Barotse. When the flood rose and fell in their flood-plain habitat, the king moved with his court from a capital in the plain to one on its margin, and then back. The journey back was made down a canal, the journey out over the flood-waters. The king's barge was paddled by great princes and councillors, and in it his bandsmen, who as we shall see were sanctuaries for alleged wrongdoers, played his xylophone and beat his drums. The drummers were privileged to throw into the water (to be picked up by the fleet of dugouts) any of these great men who had offended them and their sense of justice during the past year. I was told (for no-one was thrown overboard when I made the voyage), that they seized particularly on those magnates who had stinted the bandsmen of gifts of food.

RITUAL VALUE OF THE LAND

After this excursus to examine the implications of joking relationships, I turn to another area of Tonga relations. A tribe is obviously dependent on its land, and its land either is itself the focus of shrines and ritual or it is associated with the principal ritual symbols of the tribe. Among the Cheyenne murder con-taminated the Sacred Medicine Arrows, but also 'a pall fell over the Cheyenne tribe. There could be no success in war; there would be no bountifulness in available food. "Game shunned the territory; it made the tribe lonesome." So pronounced Spotted Elk; so assent all Cheyenne.'[28] The ritualization of land is partly in relation to the manner in which land produces sustenance, and partly in relation to the fact that men's social relations are markedly influenced by their distribution on the land. All relationships have a territorial dimension, and hence this enters into the moral structure of a tribe. Moreover, land and its products are the focus both of general tribal interests and of competition between individual tribesmen. For the prosperity of all depends on the land as a whole being fertile and providing game, while individuals compete for rights over particular pieces of land and over particular game roaming on it. This competitive element within the general wish for prosperity emerges in beliefs such as those of the Bemba who hold that he who obtains too much bounty is a witch. The fundamental conflict between general and individual interests is related to the ritual of the land:[29] in Chapter V we shall see that situations of conflicts of this type are typically those in which ritual appears to be instituted.

The Tonga similarly have rituals of the land. Close relationships develop between the Tonga living in neighbourhoods inhabited by a few hundred people. There is a feeling that there should be peace among them. They have to stage rituals to purify the soil after a slaying in a neighbourhood, or after the death of a stranger, whose kin must pay compensation. They mourn deaths among their own folk together. They also combine to pray for rain, and to celebrate first fruits and harvest, at certain shrines, which I shall call land-shrines.[30] There are a very large number of these shrines, each of which holds sway over a few square miles of land inhabited by four to five villages. A couple of shrines have widespread reputations, but there is no hierarchy of shrines. The rituals for rain are enacted for two or three days in a year, during which a ritual peace is imposed in the name of the shrine: the *mukowa* lose their rights to exact compensation for offences during this period. In some districts, the ritual peace is opened by a period of ritual licence—like joking an exhibition of privileged aggression arising from contrary elements in relationships—during which no offence save murder is held culpable. In other districts compensation for offences committed in the period of ritual peace had to be paid to the shrine or to the community through its elders, instead of to the injured person and his kin. At the biggest shrine the ground is covered with hoe-blades paid by those who fought or committed adultery or stole during this period. Nowadays this ritual peace has been absorbed in the *pax Britannica*.

All the inhabitants of a cult area had to attend the rituals. Thus once a year a man had to co-operate with his neighbours to avoid drought, flooding rains and lightning, famine, epidemic or other pestilence: neighbourhoods thus had to co-operate and avoid feuding for the common good on which individual prosperity depended. And rituals might have to be performed at other times, lest ill befall, on occasions when a shrine was desecrated: people are still fined for desecration. If feuding within a neighbourhood became too severe for the rituals to be performed, one section had to move out. On the other hand, members of one cult-community would fight another whose members treated their shrines with disrespect, even though the shrines themselves are simple natural objects, like trees or holes in the ground, or small untended huts in little groves.

The spirits of these shrines are connected with Leza, God, who has power over all things, and hence the spirits have power over rain. A land-shrine spirit is either that of the former first settler in an area, or a spirit which possesses a 'prophet'. Often the possessing spirit is a foreigner—the stranger again responsible for general good; but sometimes it is the spirit of a dead member of the neighbourhood. As a land-shrine spirit it is known by a different term from that which describes it as a spirit affecting its individual kin: in its land-shrine role it afflicts with general disasters, and not with misfortunes to individuals, save those who violate the shrines. Thus land-shrine spirits bring general drought, general crop failure and not poor harvest in one man's field, general epidemics and not individual illness. Land-shrine spirits, through their 'prophets', oppose innovations; but on occasion they have been laughed at, as when one said people should not build brick houses. When a prophet is possessed, if the spirit has not already got a shrine, the people are called to build one and annual ceremonies are performed at it. If it seems effective, its cult will prosper. The prophet's *mukowa* will provide a priest on his or her death.

I need not describe the simple ritual in detail. Beer is offered with dancing and singing of rain-songs as the congregation goes from house to house asking for rain. The site of the shrine is cleaned and if it is a hut, this is repaired. The people eat a communion meal, while the leader prays for rain and good crops and health, and points out to the spirit that they had done what they were ordered to do and were 'still living in the way you showed us'. Similar rites are repeated. All the people in a neighbourhood, and not only those of the *mukowa* which owns the shrine, must join in, because the rain falls on all their fields.

The shrines have short histories: most of them are cults established by men and women still remembered by those living when Colson was carrying out her study (1946–51). Since the cult itself is unlikely to be of recent origin, we must assume that shrines are mortal, and that save in exceptional circumstances most in the end lose their congregations while new shrines are established for new congregations. It seems probable that this process is related to the dispersal of congregations, in the past by war and epidemic, now by the exhaustion of fields and the search for better opportunities elsewhere. Shifts in social relations, already discussed, over relatively short periods alter localized concatenations of alignments and leadership. New men arise to represent these changes and their emergence eclipses old shrines, for these new men clamour for the chance to control the destinies of rain, famine and pestilence. Thus each shrine influences the lives of the Tonga, but does not tie them to one area to build a permanent congregation. Colson suggests that in the few areas where a few shrines have proliferated to form an interlinked chain, this followed on British recognition of the priests (the 'rainmakers') as chiefs. In these places the shrines centre now on instituted authority, where in the past there was only a personal leadership from a man who continued to manifest an interest in local affairs after his death. We must remember that this was a difficult kind of leadership to maintain, since it required that a man rise above the pull and the pressure of his own demanding *mukowa* and other close kin, to hold together a set of persons related by very varied ties.

Colson concludes that these shrines, like a sea-anchor, slowed the drift of people, without stopping it; but that nevertheless they were the foci of small communities, recognizing the rudiments of a community law. Modern chiefs, created by the British, have tried to use these shrines as props to their foreign authority.

THE NETWORK OF SOCIAL TIES

The Tonga thus present an intricate network of social ties, established on quite different principles, so that men who are opposed to each other under one rule, are allied with each other under another rule. Nor have I given all the rules. Ties of trade, and particularly ties established by men's placing their cattle with others for herding, complicate the network of interdependence. (Tonga do this to spread herds against risks of disease, and in the past raids, and so that their kin cannot exercise claims on cattle, for a man gives away his own cattle to others to herd and himself herds for yet others. His kin may not know which are his own beasts.)

Colson demonstrates the effects of this interweaving of ties in an analysis of the events which followed on a murder in the district where she was working.[31] A man of the Eland clan killed a man of the Lion clan. The murderer was arrested by the British authorities and sent to gaol: but the Lions broke off all relations with the Elands who lived nearby. Eland men in Lion villages, and Lion men in Eland villages, told Colson that in the past they would have fled home: as it was, the Lions ostracized their Eland fellow-villagers. Eland women living with Lion husbands among the husbands' kin were subject to insults and threats—which upset their husbands. A prominent local leader intervened. The Elands proffered compensation through joint in-laws of themselves and the Lions; peace was made, and blood-cattle were promised to compensate for the homicide. The Elands were slow in paying. Eventually a son of an Eland woman by a Lion man fell ill and died; the diviner said that the murdered man's spirit had killed the child because the cattle had not been paid. The women began again to exercise pressure on male kin to settle the matter. The dispersal of the *mukowa* vengeance-group through several villages, and the marriages of its women with men of other vengeance-groups, produced divisions in the ranks of each group, and exerted pressure for settlement. The death of a child, related to both vengeance-groups, a death which custom ascribed to the vengeful spirit, shows how mystical sanctions bring pressure on the members of the group in the wrong to meet their dues.

Colson's full exposition of this case demonstrates that despite the absence of instituted authorities who can compel settlement of disputes, the Tonga cannot mobilize in permanently hostile factions. Each offence mobilizes different groups concerned in that case and that case alone, but the general turmoil which results affects also those not connected with that offence. That is, permanent bad relations are possible only where the hostile groups do not have kinsmen living together in some other local groups, and where these hostile groups are not linked together in the network of kinship and marriage ties to the same other *mukowa*. At this distance—since in local regions there is considerable intermarriage and inter-movement—clashes are not likely; where clashes occur in smaller regions, the cross-cut of ties brings pressures for settlement.

## CONFLICTS OF LOYALTIES

The great American anthropologist Kroeber recognized the importance of this conflict of loyalties in his study of *Zuni Kin and Clan* (1917): 'It is impossible to proceed far into the complexities of the social and religious organization of the Zuni without being impressed with the perception that this community is as solidly welded and cross tied as it is intricately ramified. However far one form of division be followed, it branches off by innumerable contacts into others, without ever absorbing these. Four or five different planes of systematization cross cut each other and thus preserve for the whole society an integrity that would be speedily lost if the planes merged and thereby inclined to encourage segregation and fission. The clans, the fraternities, the priesthoods, the kivas, in a measure the gaming parties, are all dividing agencies. If they coincided the rifts in the social structure would be deep; by countering each other, they cause segmentations which produce an almost marvellous complexity, but can never break the national entity apart.'

Kroeber spoke of dividing agencies, where I say 'conflicts of loyalties', of affiliation, of duty, of right, or of organizing principle. I repeat from the 'Introduction', that I stipulate that I thus restrict 'conflict' to refer to oppositions compelled by the very structure of social organization. I know that 'conflict' in everyday use can describe surface disturbances of social life. I consider here is a field of study which will only be worked successfully if we specialize different words from the riches of English to refer to different levels of phenomena. Otherwise it is not clear what we are talking about, and we cannot progress in our analyses. For surface disturbances of social life, depending on their nature, we can use competition, dispute, argument, quarrel, strife, dissension, contention, fight, etc. I like to reserve 'struggle' for events with deeper and more fundamental roots, and 'conflict' for discrepancies at the heart of the system. But I reserve 'conflict' for the relation between discrepancies that sets in train processes which produce alterations in the personnel of social positions, but not alterations in the pattern of positions. I prefer the already established term 'contradiction' for those relations between discrepant principles and processes in the social structure which must inevitably lead to radical change in the pattern. Conversely, I stipulate that 'co-operation, affiliation, association, ties, bonds', refer to surface links between persons or combined activities; 'solidarity' to a more deeply rooted interlinking; and 'cohesion' to the underlying principles of structure that give unity to the system of a social field.

Like Zuni society, Tonga society is complicatedly integrated within itself. This integration, and the power of control which other persons and groups have over the individual, arise from his roles in a whole series of different overlapping systems of relationships. If he seeks to act in terms of one set of obligations, he is faced by counter-demands in other sets. The entanglement of obligations leads to attempts to seek an equitable settlement in terms of a moral code—which is mystically validated by spiritual powers. Possibly the system would not work without this mystical validation: the New Guinea taboo on eating your own pig or that of a close relative compels you in the end to give it to others and to seek pigs from them. Again, among the Nuer, who also lack instituted chiefs, a man's principal interests lie in his patrilineal lineage: but the curse he most fears is that of his mother's brother, a member (perforce under exogamous rules) of another patrilineal lineage. The maternal uncle can bless his nephew, and his curse 'is believed to be among the worst, if not the worst, a Nuer can receive, for, unlike the father, a maternal uncle may curse a youth's cattle, as well as his crops and fishing and hunting, if he is disobedient or refuses a request or in some other way offends him. The curse may also prevent the nephew from begetting male children.'[32] In Tongaland it may be the husband's father's spirit—a member of neither spouse's *mukowa*—who oversees their house: thus frequently ritual and mystical power is strongest where there is least secular power. In these tribes which lack governmental apparatus—and in many who have this—the role of ritual and religion, and of mystical beliefs, including those in witchcraft, emerges as enforcing respect for social ties which have no sanction of force to support them. Inevitably, many people pursue their own interests without acknowledging their obligations: since misfortune is the lot of all men, and will be that particularly of those who through failure to meet their obligations lose the support of persons to whom these are due, their fate will in the end justify faith in these beliefs.

I have had to analyse Tonga social organization in detail, though still over-simplifying, to show how societies, and smaller social groups, derive their integration from the divided allegiances of their members. Out of the interweaving of relationships, all established by custom and validated by mystical beliefs, emerges what social cohesion there is around the *mukowa*, the clans with their joking partners, and the ephemeral rain-shrines which give fixed points of reference. In most tribes, there are some localized nuclei of people whose common residence gives them common interests, symbolized by ritualization of the land, but each nucleus is unable to command the whole-hearted allegiance of all its members, because various of these members are related in different ways to persons in other nuclei. Fortes similarly concludes that among the Tallensi 'there was never any danger of wars or smaller fights breaking the society up into a number of anarchic fragments. They were inhibited from doing so by the countervailing influence of the strong social ties between traditionally hostile groups. Indeed their very occurrence stimulated the reassertion of the overriding common interests of the society and the reaffirmation of the bonds of unity between the factions.'[33]

This division of allegiances is a general aspect of all social life: a society can be kept going by force alone, as during an occupation, but if conquerors are to reach a position of stability they must institute relationships with the subjected which cut across the division between them, and which divide the subjected. Extreme *apartheid*, now being attempted in South Africa, demands the use of more and more force. *Divide et impera* is a principle of social cohesion, not only a Macchiavellian tactic.

It is essential to grasp this principle if we are to understand how social groups maintain themselves. More particularly we require it to interpret how rules of self-help and vengeance operated without constantly disturbing social life. In early Europe the duty to take vengeance, and the risk of having vengeance inflicted by a murdered man's relatives, fell on the *sib* or kindred, which seems to have been a circle of kin traced from the individual through all lines up to seven or eight degrees. It is clear that such a set of people, in any closely settled neighbourhood, might quite probably contain relatives of murderer and victim. The great mediaeval historian, Marc Bloch, considered this situation and stressed that the circle of relatives would change every generation, so that though 'the duties were rigorous . . . the group was too unstable to serve as a basis for the whole social structure'. He goes on to point out that, 'Worse still, when two families clashed it might very well be that the same individual belonged to both—

to one of them through his father and to the other through his mother. How was he to choose between them? Wisely, Beaumanoir's choice is to side with the nearest relative, and if the degrees are equal, to stand aloof. Doubtless in practice the decision was often dictated by personal preference.'[34] Bloch here wrote as if the choice was limited to selecting between joining in the duty of taking vengeance, or to resisting those doing so, or standing aloof; and this conclusion might very well emerge from looking at statements of the 'law'. Hence his use of the phrase 'worse still', to cover the clash of duties, is significant. For in fact if the wish be to avoid armed conflict, it is 'better still': once enough people are involved in this conflict of loyalties, they can exert pressure towards peaceful settlement and compensation, since they have an interest in the restoration of harmonious relations between the members of the two kindreds. Doubtless many offences were compounded under this kind of pressure, and therefore they did not get into the records or legends on which historians perforce work.

The anthropologists who have studied this kind of situation clearly have an advantage over the historian of the dark ages, since they were able to observe the pressures making for settlement of disputes—though of course not always succeeding. Nevertheless when I read Bloch, and some other historians of the period, I wonder whether they make sufficient allowance for what is unlikely to be recorded or remembered, as against what passes into folk history, or allow enough for the form in which events enter that history. The vendetta that results from unsuccessful compromise is more likely to be remembered than disputes which are settled. For example, early anthropologists reported that in East African tribes practising vengeance no attention was paid to the events surrounding a killing. Blood demanded blood, and that was that. The German anthropologist, Thurnwald, thus said that a Kikuyu who hurled a spear through a lion which had pinned another man to the ground, would be held responsible for murder because his spear went through the lion and his comrade. This clearly was the law: was it so rigidly applied? When Peristiany studied the Pokot of East Africa, it seems that the best account of a feud which he could collect began when a member of the Hawk clan in a fight against a neighbouring tribe missed his enemy with an arrow and killed a member of the Dove clan. They were resident in different but not widely separated federations of villages. The Doves made an armed demonstration against all Hawks living in the murderer's village. The prominent elders in the federation feared that the dispute might spread and persuaded the Dove elders accompanying the warriors to submit to their arbitration. The resident members of each clan exerted pressure on members of both parties to agree to a compromise: the murderer to pay compensation, the near kin of the murdered to claim only reasonable compensation, and not an extravagant one, lest one day they too be under extravagant demands. Finally the Hawks, though outraged by the claim, handed over to the Doves a hut full of goats with a calf attached to each of its two doors. In the next generation a Hawk was killed by falling from a Dove's tree which he had climbed to get honey: the Hawks failed to secure the damages they had paid years ago. In the third (the present) generation two Dove brothers were accused of committing adultery with wives of Hawks, and again the Hawks demanded a hut of goats and two calves.[35] Peristiany does not make this point, but I suggest that it is significant that this is the vendetta apparently best remembered. The outrage was that the Doves demanded such high compensation, neglecting that the 'murder' occurred in a fight against common foes, which should have induced them to accept much less compensation. Other circumstances, further back in history, may indeed have made the deceased's kin so intransigent.

We have continually to remember that recitals of actual vendettas may put the whole working of the doctrine of self-help and vengeance out of perspective, so that the picture which emerges is what Pollock and Maitland wrote about Anglo-Saxon times in their great *History of English Law*: 'Personal injury was in the first place the cause of feud, or private war, between the kindreds of the wrongdoer and of the person wronged'; while the *Shorter Cambridge Mediaeval History* states that feud (vendetta) 'produced a state of incessant warfare in the community, and divided the kindred themselves when the injury was committed by one member against another of the same group'.[36] Yet the structure of the vengeance groups themselves suggests that some of the processes we have examined among the Tonga were at work to produce settlement. It is significant that Bloch noted that 'among . . . feuds, the chronicles especially have recorded the conflicts of the great noble families . . .', and that '. . . interminable quarrels arising from often futile causes set the hostile houses at each other's throats'. He does not seem to have drawn the conclusion that perhaps among the common people and lesser nobles feud was in fact rarely waged, for he insisted that '. . . at every level of society the same customs prevailed'. Only, according to him, by as late as the thirteenth century when the nobility had finally become an hereditary body, did it tend to reserve for itself, as a mark of honour, any recourse to arms, while at the same time princes and judges became interested in maintaining the peace.

I venture to suggest that this analysis overlooks the pressures of countervailing relationships. It seems that the group which resided and worked together was some form of patriarchal joint family, while the vengeance group was the quite differently constituted sib which I have described above. Each man, with only his full-brothers and full-sisters, was the centre of his own sib; and every individual was a member of the sibs of many other people. Presumably in a long-settled district, where there had been much intermarrying, almost everyone would have been a member of most neighbours' sibs. In this situation there must have been many peace-seekers. At least this is the situation among the Kalingas of the Philippines, whose vengeance-group is similarly organized.[37]

Bloch stated that feuds were waged often over 'futile causes'. It is possible that if men spring to arms over futile causes, deeper causes provoke them. Barton, a missionary who studied the Kalingas, reported a fight between two villages in which several men were killed, because one village refused to admit that the other's hunting dogs had chased a wild pig to them so that they were able to kill it—though Kalingas acknowledge that the party whose dogs start a pig are entitled to the pig whoever kills it. These two villages, it turns out later in the book, were in a permanent state of hostility—a real state of feud—starting with a quarrel about ownership of land. Quarrels of this or similar kind may well have underlain apparently futile feuds in the early Middle Ages. They could have been waged between noble houses—and even commoners—at a distance.

In this connection, it is important to note that under the rule of self-help a man can gain his rights by thrusting his claims into the relationships between persons heavily obligated to one another. Fortes thus reports that a Tallensi creditor in the old days could raid the livestock of any clansman of his debtor, but not those of a neighbour of his debtor who belonged to a different clan. In the latter case a reprisal raid was launched. In the former case the victim demanded compensation from his own clansman, the original debtor; and Fortes says he knew of men who pawned a child or sold him into slavery to redeem this obligation to a clansman, and prevent the event becoming a source of trouble inside the clan. Fortes concludes that 'it is not the clan but the debtor himself who is responsible for his debt. Self-help is a technique for putting pressure on a debtor through the mechanisms of clan and lineage cohesion.'[38] One wonders if the creditor seized on a clansman of the debtor related to him through some uterine link.

Colson gives a similar picture of self-help among the Tonga. If a man from *mukowa* A stole goods or killed a man from *mukowa* B his people were held responsible. If they did not pay immediately, men of B would go to a village where people of A lived and wait at the waterhole to seize women from the village. A then had to mobilize its wealth to pay without more ado before the women's heads were shaved so that they could be sold as slaves. This thrust the dispute into the offender's village, because it is unlikely that only women of *mukowa* A had been seized, since wives came from many *mukowa*. Several *mukowa* would then be set against A.[39]

The study of these stateless societies may thus give a model for interpreting the surviving fragments of evidence about our own historical past. This study also focuses attention on to principles which operate in all forms of groups, ranging from modern states to business organizations, schools, universities, and recreational societies. The more members of these groups are associated with one another through a variety of ties, linking different sets of persons, the less can factional dispute and intrigue destroy the general consensus of major group membership. This is not to argue that all conflicts of loyalty are 'good', which is not my problem: I draw attention to the effects of divisive allegiances on morale and on ability to adjust and control disputes.[40] They cannot exclude disputes, nor inevitably settle them. When a group comes to a situation where it ceases to be successful in pursuing its aims, it will in the end break up; and when constituent groups of a tribe run into such problems as an acute shortage of land, they may, as we saw for the Mae Enga, turn forcefully against those to whom they are by custom heavily obligated.

## LEADERS

A problem which requires further investigation in this type of society is the role of the 'big men' and leaders. To aid this analysis we probably require to specialize more carefully than we have done in the past the manner in which we apply words like 'chief' to tribal leaders. Is it appropriate to call the Bushman's band's head a 'chief', and then to apply this word also to the head of a tribe who can order a man's execution? Again, David Livingstone spoke of Monze, the most famous of the Tonga rainmakers, as 'the chief of all the Batongas of this area'; but when the hunter Selous was attacked in the village next to Monze's he sought protection there: 'Monzi and his men . . . were friendly, I could see, but the old man was in a state of great alarm when he heard how my rifle had been stolen and my life attempted at the next village. "You must leave my village immediately", he exclaimed; "they will follow you up and kill you. Be off!" He filled my pockets with ground nuts, and sent me out of his town, with three of his men, at once.' This suggests very little chiefly power.

Clearly we require here to specialize a series of words out of the wealth of English to denote different kinds of tribal leaders, with varying types of authority. We can set out these leaders in terms of a range of increasing authority, without implying that one type of leader has necessarily developed out of the preceding type in the series or that those with most authority have passed through the whole series. The situation is somewhat complicated by the fact that secular authority does not necessarily coincide with ritual authority: a priest or magician may exercise considerable influence alongside a headman or a chieftain, sometimes supporting him, sometimes acting against him.

Probably the simplest type of authority is that of the elder, or patriarch, the most senior and able kinsman in an inter-related band. This defines the Bushman and the Bergdama leader, though some specific cultural privileges and prestige attach to the latter's position. Elders of a number of groups of this kind may co-operate in giving joint leadership and direction, as among the Pokot above. Radcliffe-Brown considers that the 'embryonic' form of public legal action is found when a number of elders may declare a man to be 'a bad lot' and order his execution:[41] his own kinsmen may be required to carry out this execution so that a blood-feud is not provoked, as among the Eskimo when a man becomes a habitual killer.[42] Here the community is acting to control a persistent wrongdoer, and action is instigated by those who in virtue of their kinship positions can speak on behalf of the constituent groupings of kin in the community.

A different kind of leadership is seen in the 'big man' of many tribes of New Guinea and other parts of Melanesia. This man may use his kinship relationships and marital alliances, to build up his position and influence, but he depends on his industry, his enterprise, and his skill in exchanges to get followers in his own community and strategic partners in other communities. It may be also that these 'big men'—the sorts of local leaders who also emerged among the Tonga—happen to occupy crucial positions in a number of the systems of social relationships such as we have been analysing among Tonga and Cheyenne. If a man does this, presumably he is able to manipulate many people to build his own local prestige and even exercise a little authority, while he can establish important external linkages with other important men in other communities. For it is not suggested that cross-cutting ties, either among Tonga or among Tallensi, spread evenly across the land. There are points where the ties are knitted together more tightly. Such a point may be fixed by geographical or ecological facts. Thus Tallensi society focuses on the relatively fertile Tong Hills. Correspondingly, topographical barriers may break the spread of ties, as large rivers or marshes and stretches of uninhabited bush do among the Nuer. And within areas of land thus determined, particular individuals, to whom are linked many others so that they exercise considerable social power, or even individuals of dominant personality, may provide centres of social action for longish periods.

In some societies, like those of several New Guinea tribes (or indeed among the Tonga), most big men built up ephemeral prestige.[43] The position of Monze had remained of importance at least as a land-shrine priesthood for some eighty years or more before the British recognized him as chief. Other leaders have lost their influence, or it has evaporated after their death. Similarly in New Guinea a man who has emerged as a local leader by the luck of his wives' fertility and the numbers of his kin and their in-laws, as well as by his industry and his astuteness in the system of exchanges, may as he grows older and loses his capacity to work and to travel find that he slips back into an unimportant old age. Yet even in tribes where this is the rule, there are suggestions that a few positions in the system of inter-tribal exchange are so crucial, lying as they do on roads of trade, that when their incumbents die, some relative succeeds to the position and its associated partnerships in exchange. These problems require further investigation.

This succession to a position of key importance in the network of social relationships, both within a community and in its dealings with outside communities, is frequently found: it has been described throughout Africa, where Richards named the process 'positional inheritance'. It is a form of the 'universal succession' which was an important institution in ancient Rome. Maine wrote that a universal succession is a succession to a *universitas juris*, which is 'a collection of rights and duties united by the single circumstance of their having belonged at one time to some one person. It is, as it were, the legal clothing of some given individual.' Under universal succession one man is then invested with the legal clothing of another, becoming at the same moment subject to all his liabilities and entitled to all his rights. As described in Chapter I, when a man dies his 'social personality' (Radcliffe-Brown) survives to continue to affect the inter-relationships among his survivors. These relationships have to be readjusted to accommodate the fact of his death: and this may be done by dispersing his rights and duties in different sets of relationships among various heirs, and by appointing others to his official positions. Or there may be competition for these. When most of his positions devolve on a main heir, we have universal succession or positional inheritance. Where this rule operates, the position itself survives the death of a series of incumbents. This is the situation with a corporation sole in English law, 'an individual, being a member of a series of individuals, who is invested with the qualities of a Corporation . . . the King or the Parson of a Parish [are] instances of Corporations sole. The capacity or office is here considered apart from the particular person who from time to time may occupy it, and, this capacity being perpetual, the series of individuals who fill it are clothed with the leading attribute of Corporations—Perpetuity' (Maine).[44] Once a position begins to acquire this attribute, we have an institutionalization of prestige and influence, if not of forceful authority, which accrues to each new incumbent.

The logic of the situation, and hints I find in chance statements about some of the societies whose competitive politics in cere-monial exchange have been described by observers as a struggle between individual men for a power and influence that disappear or are dispersed at their deaths, persuade me that some of the positions which these men attain are corporations sole. They occupy such key positions, that neither their own groups, nor their trading-partners, can afford to let the particular network of exchanges drawn together in the positions collapse. I throw out this suggestion to those studying societies of this type. I emphasize its possibilities by drawing attention to the fact that in his descrip-tion of the ring of *kula* exchanges Malinowski stressed the indivi-dual character of the partnerships, but out of Malinowski's own material a young anthropologist has been able to show how a dead man's partners in exchange assemble for a distribution, in which the 'proceedings serve, in effect, to pull together the *kula* links of the dead man for the last time in his own name, and establish them afresh for his successor . . . '.[45]

In Melanesia, positional inheritance through varied lines has been clearly described where the position is that of a headman of a village. It is this type of headman, and the temporary 'big man', who are likely to become the bully. These big men are more liable to become bullies where the imposition of colonial rule has given them powers which were not inherent in their offices traditionally. Hogbin has described graphically how such a bully exploited his fellow-villagers by manipulating both the Japanese and the Australian authorities during and after the Second World War. By accusing his villagers of collaboration and treason, and though himself a collaborator with the Japanese establishing his fealty with the Australians, he was able to bring down unmerited punishments on their heads, degrade them before him, and extort dues from them. Eventually his machinations were exposed by an anthropologist, then a member of the Military Administra-tion.[46] It is significant that this abuse of the power conferred by a colonial power is more often reported throughout the world of these petty officers, than it is of the powerful chiefs with a tradition of ruling. Hence it is these Government 'warrant chiefs' who tend to become the first targets of their fellows during risings. The removal of the sanctions on their influence and power, which we shall examine in the next chapter, seems often to rouse a barely bridled cupidity and lust for power.

With this example we move to instituted authority. But before making that step, I draw final attention to the importance of corporations sole in stateless societies. Among the Tallensi, for instance, the major set of political relationships consists of a complicated series of linkages between ritual offices, held by the heads of lineages and clans. In the interests of all Tallensi they have to perform religious ceremonies at shrines for which they are individually responsible, but these shrines are so interlinked that on important occasions sacrifice at one cannot be successful unless sacrifice is also made at all the others.[47] Besides the Tonga type of society, there are stateless societies which have permanent nuclei of social positions, about which the whole series of social relationships are organized.

Finally the corporation sole is found in the position of the chief and the king, and in the relation of this position to other political offices. In some tribal systems, these positions may be related to one another through what Cunnison has called 'perpetual kinship'. For example, if a man leads his followers out of a village where the headman was his mother's brother, the headmanship of the new village is perpetually sister's son to the headmanship of the old village; and however new incumbents of these positions are related to one another in reality, they will consider themselves as mother's brother vis-à-vis sister's son.[48] (In some respects this perpetual kinship obtains between Tallensi shrines.) Kinship thus expresses certain forms of relationship between headmen and the villages they represent, and the idiom of this relationship influences their political actions. Among the Luapula Lunda of Northern Rhodesia, studied by Cunnison, this perpetual kinship obtains also between the king, the corporation sole representing the conquering tribe, and the chiefs of conquered tribes into whose families he later married. I cite this example here, because Cunnison has investigated further the influence of this situation on the Lunda's ideas of history. Since the positions are corporations sole, the present incumbent is logically identified with each of his predecessors: and when he describes what any predecessor did, he does so in the first person and the present tense, even though the events with which he is concerned happened many decades or even a couple of centuries earlier. In this situation it is immensely difficult to work out the time-scale of events. Genealogies also become shortened, since the sisters (in this matrilineal tribe) of past holders are sisters to the position, and it is impossible to distinguish from which particular holder in which particular generation one of these sisters founded a line of descendants, unless there are external checks. If similar processes operate in societies, like those of the recently opened New Guinea Highlands where there are no such external checks, the existence of corporations sole among the 'big men' may easily be overlooked, since present incumbents may not always distinguish the achievements of their predecessors from their own.

[1] Wittfogel, *Oriental Despotism* (1957).

[2] On the importance of markets see Polanyi and others, *Trade and Market in the Early Empires* (1957).

[3] For an excellent account in India see Bailey, *Caste and the Economic Frontier* (1957).

[4] *The Evolution of Culture: The Development of Civilization to the Fall of Rome* (1959); *The Science of Culture* (1949). See also Steward, *Theory of Culture Change* (1955), and Sahlins and Service, *Evolution and Culture* (1960).

[5] Sahlins, *Social Stratification in Polynesia* (1958).

[6] Fortes and Evans-Pritchard (editors), 'Introduction' to *African Political Systems* (1940).

[7] *Government and Politics in Tribal Societies* (1956).

[8] I have already referred to the graphic description by Thomas of this eternal quest in *The Harmless People* (1959).

[9] For good accounts of other hunters, see Holmberg, *Nomads of the Long Bow, the Siriono of Eastern Bolivia* (1950), Lévi-Strauss, *A World on the Wane* (Brazil) (1961), and Warner, *A Black Civilization* (Australia) (1937). There are many others, of course.

[10] Schapera, *The Khoisan Peoples of South Africa* (1930), pp. 149 f.

[11] For a good summary account of the 'law-ways' of the Eskimo see Hoebel, *The Law of Primitive Man* (1954), Chapter V.

[12] See below, pp. 308 f.

[13] I attempt an analysis of the singing-duel below, at pp. 303 f.

[14] Chapter VI in Hoebel's *The Law of Primitive Man* (1954) compares three of these groups.

[15] Hoebel, p. 145, quoting from Grinnell's *The Cheyenne Indians: Their History and Way of Life* (1923). The same character is demanded of a councillor in the large Barotse state (population 300,000). A Lozi councillor should never use force, which a policeman may do: see 'The Case of the Violent Councillor' in my *Judicial Process among the Barotse* (1955), pp. 83–90.

[16] I have elaborated on the importance of this principle in my *Custom and Conflict in Africa* (1955).

[17] Hoebel, *The Law of Primitive Man* (1954), pp. 149–56.

[18] Colson, *The Plateau Tonga of Northern Rhodesia: Social and Religious Studies* (1962). See also her essay in Colson and Gluckman (editors), *Seven Tribes of British Central Africa* (1951).

[19] For an analysis of a society of this type see Evans-Pritchard, *The Nuer* (1940), summarized in Chapter I of my *Custom and Conflict in Africa* (1955) where I try to bring out the principles I am discussing among the Tonga.

[20] The hare and the hyaena (or jackal or fox) are the tricksters of many cultures.

[21] In a discussion at Manchester, on which he will shortly publish a paper.

[22] See Hoebel, *The Cheyennes* (1960), p. 28.

[23] Fortes, *The Dynamics of Clanship among the Tallensi* (1945): reviewed appreciatively in Chapter I of my *Order and Rebellion in Tribal Africa* (1963).

[24] See below, pp. 223 f.

[25] *Village on the Border* (1957).

[26] I have not had time to consult sources, but Welsford's book on *The Fool* (1935) has enough to support this suggestion, made to me by A. L. Epstein (pp. 59, 77, 81, 170, 202–4, 208, 317)

[27] Jordan, 'Towards an African Literature' (1957), vol. 2, no. 1, pp. 104–5.

[28] Llewellyn and Hoebel, *The Cheyenne Way* (1941), p. 133.

[29] See the 'Introduction' of Fortes and Evans-Pritchard (editors), to *African Political Systems* (1940). For a fuller discussion, see Fortes, *The Dynamics of Clanship among the Tallensi* (1945).

[30] Colson calls them 'rain-shrines' since the main ritual at them is a solicitation for rain, but I consider that 'land-shrines' covers more appropriately their wider function. Note that in this region rains break in October and cease by April: there is one sowing and one harvest season.

[31] *The Plateau Tonga of Northern Rhodesia* (1962) Chapter IV: 'Social Control and Vengeance in Plateau Tonga Society'.

[32] Evans-Pritchard, *Kinship and Marriage among the Nuer* (1951), pp. 164–65.

[33] Fortes, *The Dynamics of Clanship among the Tallensi* (1945), p. 242. Note that he says 'inhibited', not 'prevented'.

[34] Bloch, *Feudal Society*, translated from the French, (1961), at p. 138.

[35] Peristiany, 'Pokot Sanctions and Structure' (1954).

[36] Vol. 1, pp. 128–9.

[37] Barton, *The Kalingas* (1949).

[38] Fortes, *The Dynamics of Clanship among the Tallensi* (1945), p. 245.

[39] In *Seven Tribes of British Central Africa* (1951), pp. 134–5.

[40] For examples in small groups see Homans, *The Human Group* (1952). On the general theory see Simmel, *Conflict and the Web of Group-Affiliations* (1955) and Coser, *The Functions of Social Conflict* (1956).

[41] 'Preface' to Fortes and Evans-Pritchard (editors), *African Political Systems* (1940), p. xv.

[42] Hoebel, *The Law of Primitive Man* (1954), pp. 88 f.

[43] See e.g. Reay, *The Kuma* (1959); Meggitt, *The Lineage System of the Mae Enga* (1964); Pospisil, *Kapauka Papuans and Their Law* (1958), on the New Guinea mainland. Oliver has an excellent account of 'Leadership' in Part III of his *A Solomon Island Society* (1955).

[44] *Ancient Law* (1861), Chapter VI.

[45] Uberoi, *Politics of the Kula Ring* (1962), p. 107.

[46] Hogbin, *Transformation Scene* (1951).

[47] Fortes, *The Dynamics of Clanship among the Tallensi* (1945), summarized in Chapter I of my *Order and Rebellion in Tribal Africa* (1963).

[48] Cunnison, *The Luapula Peoples of Northern Rhodesia* (1959). For a similar analysis of another matrilineal people, see Mitchell, *The Yao Village* (1956), and on a patrilineal people Watson, *Tribal Cohesion in a Money Economy* (1958).

# CHAPTER IV

# THE STATE AND CIVIL STRIFE

## RANGES OF AUTHORITY: ANUAK

There are many tribes constituted like the Tonga, though the details of their organization vary considerably. In other tribes, often neighbour to the former type and dwelling in similar environments, there exists chieftainship endowed traditionally with authoritative power to judge on disputes, to execute judgments and other decisions, and to mobilize labour and armies under sanction of punishment. When we move to consider political systems in which this authority exists we are dealing with more straightforward methods of maintaining public order, but we shall meet also with some of the networks of relations and mechanisms discussed in the previous chapter

Chiefs in the tribal world range considerably in power and influence from the heads of small tribes to the kings of nations numbering some hundreds of thousands of people. There is also great variation in their secular and ritual powers. I examine the bases of their rule, and the checks upon their authority, by analysing a number of chieftainships in Africa. I set them out in a series, ranging from leaders with mainly symbolic functions and little secular power, to powerful secular kings, in order to bring out the underlying facts which affect the structure of states. Again I do not intend to imply that the later described societies in the series have developed out of the earlier described ones, or that they have passed through each of the stages in the series.

I begin with the position of leaders—they can hardly be called chiefs—among the Anuak who live on both sides of the Ethiopian-Sudan border. Since they live in difficult terrain and since those in difficulties with the Sudan Government could escape across the border, their polities, marked by constant civil wars and rebellions, were observed in almost indigenous working order.[1]

The north-western villages are inhabited each by between 200 and 300 people. These villages are isolated from one another in a savannah country which floods during the single rainy season, and they used to be stockaded against forays by foreign tribes and other Anuak. As the people are agriculturists who cannot keep many cattle because of tsetse fly, needs for pasturage do not bring villages into contact. There is wide travel by Anuak to trade in order to get goods required for marriage-payments, but otherwise Lienhardt considers that each family could produce its own subsistence. Villages may have been formed in the past as units of mutual defence.

The focus of each village is the court of its headman, who is a member of the principal patrilineal sub-clan in the village which may include fragments of other sub-clans. The headman's huts are little better than those of his villagers, but the numerous posts of his homestead's fence are decorated and are surmounted by the skulls of beasts he has killed to feast his people and by trophies of large game he has distributed. He holds certain emblems of which the most important are beads and drums which belong to the village, and not to the headman of the time. He is approached with obeisances and other signs of respect, and a special vocabulary is used in relation to him and his property. Thus he has a 'court', and the villagers take pride in this court. While the headman himself has not power to punish a man who neglects these courtesies, if he is popular his supporters will fine the wrongdoer—but they appropriate the fine for their own feasting.

This is characteristic of how Anuak deal with their headman. He is obliged to feast them and provide for them. While he is headman, the villagers—and particularly the company of young men whom he tries to recruit about himself as all rich men do—cultivate fields for him and attend on his homestead. But if he exhausts his property they desert him, for 'the Anuak are quite ruthless in their treatment of past benefactors, once the immediate gratification of their desire for feasting and display can no longer be provided. . . . Further, in the provision of bounty, it is the recipients and not the benefactor who are thought to render the greater honour. . . . The prestige which a great man receives on account of his generosity is of more value to him than the material goods which he is bound lavishly to dispense in order to obtain it' (Lienhardt). He would lose favour even more quickly if he were mean, eating his food himself and using his beads to marry more wives instead of feeding his villagers and aiding them to obtain wives, for, as Anuak told Evans-Pritchard, 'After all what did we make him headman for except to eat from him?'

When a headman is stripped of the wherewithal to maintain his court, at least a faction in the village will arise to 'ostracise' him (as Lienhardt puts it) and to install in his place one of his kinsmen, who must be son to a previous headman, but not to the incumbent since son does not oust father. This rule compels a rotation of the headmanship between branches of the entitled family. If the rebels are successful—and it may require a fight to expel him if he retains support of some villagers—the ousted headman retires probably to the village of his maternal kin where he has maintained a separate set of gardens, in order to prepare himself for another attempt on the headmanship. The villagers take over the fruits of the garden they have cultivated for him, and possibly also batten on the grain and other wealth which the new incumbent brings from *his* maternal village.

A headman may lose support in other ways. If he tries to insinuate himself into favour, he demeans himself and makes the village contemptible in the eyes of other villages; if he tries to domineer, he alienates people. The golden mean of composed spiritedness is difficult to attain, since individuals will vary in their judgments on him according to their interests in any situation. Moreover, while he has no power to compel disputants to accept his adjudication, his people expect him to throw his influence on the just side of a claim, and this will alienate the other side. Whatever he does, some will think he favours his uterine kin and friends at their expense. 'A headman is bound at some time to make enemies even in the course of making friends', writes Lienhardt. The dissatisfied withdraw from the court, or even the village, while the opposition faction builds up.

Finally, the headman himself has assumed his position against the wishes of supporters of other claimants, or in a 'rebellion' to ostracize a previous incumbent: and he must favour his supporters while trying to win the support of his opponents. Inevitably he raises an opposition to himself. The situation is exacerbated because factional struggles are endemic in each village, and each faction (it seems that not more than two dominate the village at any one time)[2] concentrates its intrigues on securing the headmanship for its own candidate.

While the headman cannot compel villagers to obey him, a kind of order does emanate from his court. Anuak themselves state that protracted hostilities in a village would completely disrupt its life: and while the village accepts a particular headman he and other neutrals can, for instance, persuade the killer of a fellow-villager to offer compensation and the victim's kin to accept it. When there is no headman this kind of order does not exist: therefore 'killing in a rebellion is compensated for by killing in a rebellion'. Nor is compensation payable for killing at certain wild and 'orgiastic' dances held by villagers away from the headman's court. These dances symbolize the contrast of the order at the court itself: since at the court around the drums of headmanship are staged dances in which headmen and people mime the struggles and conflicts in which they are involved—a feature of ceremonial and ritual we shall later discuss—without this breakdown of control.

The villagers thus derive many satisfactions from a headman's court: feasting, display for themselves and their village's prestige, and the deployment of some order in their lives. We can understand why they value highly their privilege of ostracizing headmen, even though sometimes it leads to fights in which friends and neighbours may kill one another. They believe that no-one should be in office for a very long time; and unless there are no other claimants, only a man of exceptional wealth and talent could achieve a reign of more than a few years.

Our information is less full on why claimants intrigue for the headmanship, even after being ostracized, since the strains of office are great and eventually it leads to impoverishment. Presumably they want the prestige and they grow up with ambition instilled in them. Perhaps too it would be publicly shameful for them to abstain and they are pressed into the struggle by their fellows, for Evans-Pritchard states that a rebellion may occur without any jealousy between the claimants themselves, and be 'the outcome of competition between factions in the village rather than of rivalry between individual members of the headman line'.

Lienhardt considers that the rebellions express in action the opposition between the factions of the village and prevent the 'complete fusion' of the constituent sub-clans under the 'oligarchic' or 'autocratic' domination of the headman's line, while the temporary acceptance of a new headman prevents complete break-up: indeed if no agreement can be reached, this may occur. What is also stressed by the reports cited is that since Anuak households could apparently maintain themselves in isolation, they are in fact kept together in the constant struggle[3] to support their own contender for the headmanship. Their interest in the headmanship (like the rivalry in organizing recreations in the Welsh village referred to above) may absorb disputes within their own ranks, including those between and within the 'alien' groups in the village, whose number is said to increase the incidence of these rebellions. What is certain is that the headmanship is a symbolic and active focus of the unity of segments and people within the village, even if it be a unity of incessant intrigue and 'civil war'.

Strikingly, no party emerges which aims to destroy the headmanship as an institution, nor do other sub-clans in the village claim that they be entitled to provide the headman. In these circumstances, what we know of other African cultures would lead us to expect that the headmanship would include power to use ritual to ensure general fertility and prosperity, and that the headman's line alone would be privileged to do this because of its ancestral title. Evans-Pritchard[4] implies that where the headman is of the original line of the village he has not these functions, though the account is not quite clear on this point. What is stated, is that where a line from outside the village, possibly members of a now-commoner clan descended from one of the early 'kings' of South-eastern Anuakland or a noble of the 'kingly' clan (see below) has ousted the traditional line, a descendant of the traditional line has slight ritual functions as 'father of the land'. He is believed to make the soil fertile, fish abundant, and rain in season, though Anuak do not place much faith in the efficacy of his prayers during drought. He can also bless individuals by 'his earth'. More importantly, when a village moves to one of its several sites, he goes ahead and sacrifices a sheep or goat, 'so that no dissensions or other calamities may happen in the village built on "his earth" '. Where the headman's line is traditional to the village, 'the earth is said to belong to the headman alone and there is no Father of the Land'.

This separation of secular 'authority' from priestly office in connection with the Earth held by autochthones is frequent in Africa. It operates to some extent in the Tonga land-shrine cults, and has high importance in West Africa, for example among the Tallensi, where an elaborate cult of the Earth is maintained by autochthones not only for themselves but also for the prosperity of a group of incomers who hold such secular authority as exists.[5] Even in more powerful states the earliest inhabitants may be believed to have special powers over the earth and its fruits.

In south-eastern Anuakland commoner headmen have been displaced steadily, and are still being displaced, by members of a noble clan[6] who apparently came from outside Anuakland. The nobles married commoner women whose sons were reared in their maternal villages where they might gain a footing. Or villagers unable to agree on a candidate for their headmanship, or with no claimant to put against an 'unsatisfactory' headman, might invite in a noble to solve their difficulties. Evans-Pritchard observed how nobles thus extended their influence outwards from their main centre. The noble replaced the headman as the symbol of unity of the village, was invested with the village emblems, held the drums, and was the centre of a court, which had more pomp than an ordinary headman's since special etiquette surrounded all nobles. But 'his real power . . . [was] probably less than that of a headman in most commoner villages'. Indeed a person entitled to be headman might exercise more influence than the noble until, as has happened in two districts, the villagers handed over land-rights to their noble.[7]

The ruling noble had to distribute his wealth and strive to keep his court working, but once a village had installed a noble, it could not eject him by force. If, when the people showed him he was no longer wanted, he did not leave voluntarily, they had to invite another noble to attack him.

Nobles, whether permanently or temporarily installed, struggled for possession of a number of royal emblems. These are now reduced to five bead necklaces, four spears, two stools, a spear-rest, and some drums. Possession of the emblems made a noble what Evans-Pritchard calls 'king', though there is no Anuak term to distinguish him from other nobles. A noble could only compete for this 'kingship' if a holder placed a particular necklace on his neck, a privilege for which he paid: if he was not invested, he lost noble rank.

Nobles led their villages in fights to win the emblems. Transmission of the emblems, and succession to 'kingship', was marked by bloodshed, since originally no noble was powerful enough to hold the emblems permanently. Then came a series of peaceful as well as bloody transmissions. Around 1900 one man acquired rifles from Ethiopia and retained the emblems for a long period, during which he was subject to attack only by two others, similarly armed. The seeds of any further development of power out of this situation were crushed when the British in 1921 began to control the transmission, though as late as the Second World War one noble, unlike his fellows, sided with the Italians in hopes of gaining the emblems.[8]

Nobles recognized that there were 'rules of the game' necessary to maintain this circulating kingship. The holders of the emblems, even the petty tyrant with rifles, invested others, creating their own privileged enemies and potential assassins. Moreover, in the middle period it became more and more the practice for the holder of the emblems either voluntarily to surrender the emblems to a rival, if a close kinsman, after having possessed them for a year or two, or to hand them over to a defeated claimant, while remaining himself content with the honour of victory. Defeated claimants were no longer slain. If the holder was defeated, he had to flee and abandon the emblems where they could be found.

In these struggles each claimant depended on the willingness of his villagers—often his maternal kin—to fight for him in attack, and the holder relied on his villagers not to desert him. Each village fought the others to get the emblems for 'its noble', and thereby gain in prestige. All the villages participated in the 'kingship' through the class of nobles in whom the people took pride, and to whom they were related by uterine ties; and the villages were thus involved in an inter-village polity through the recognition of the symbolic value of the kingship over a wide area, though a major aspect of this polity was a state of chronic civil war. The 'kingship' stood above any of its incumbents: even rivals for it obeyed its rules, nobles were driven by ambition and their kin to aspire to it, and it symbolized a kind of Anuak unity.

The king had little authority in his own village, and he and his villagers gained little of secular advantage from the 'kingship'. If the king raided other villages, his was itself exposed to raids. Raids for material goods were largely made on foreign tribes. Even the three nobles with rifles were each leader of only a small coalition of villages. The then 'king' was ruler in his own village, had control over adjacent villages, and exercised an influence, largely by force of arms, over a yet wider area. He had personal authority only in his own village, and no administrative machine.

Evans-Pritchard calls the Anuak kingship 'ritual' though the 'king' performed no ritual for the welfare of land and people.

The trees which grew about the graves of dead kings were sacred,[9] as were some other trees at which 'God' was supplicated. People used to visit the trees on the graves of nobles as well as kings to seek their aid in difficulties; and recently invested kings were required to sacrifice at one such grove, which presumably no-one from outside the royal clan could do. Evans-Pritchard was told that in a great drought or other misfortune a local noble would sacrifice at a dead king's grave. Hence the king as such had little ritual duty, though the standing of the whole noble clan was validated in this cult. Therefore I consider it better to speak here of a 'symbolic or ceremonial kingship' rather than a 'ritual kingship', in order to emphasize the mystical powers of a kingship like that of the Shilluk, confrères of the Anuak, which I now examine. Like the Anuak, Shilluk kingship was striven for in recurrent civil wars rooted in the territorial dispersal of the population, but its high ritual power enabled it to unite 110,000 people in a nation.

## The Shilluk Symbolic Kingship

The Shilluk[10] settlements are strung mainly along the west bank of the Nile in the Sudan. They are a sedentary agricultural people, possessing about one head of cattle to each four of the population. They dwell in hamlets occupied by 1–50 homesteads, each the residence of a small patrilineal lineage. The head of a hamlet is selected by lineal descent and approved by the king's bestowing on him a robe of honour. He sits on the council of a 'settlement' composed of a group of hamlets, with, it is said, a population ranging from less than 100 to more than 600 adult males. There are said to be about 100 settlements: but it appears that either the sizes of settlements or the size of the nation (110,000 souls) must be stated in terms of the wrong units.

Each settlement has a chief, who inherits his position and is also confirmed by the king. The chief is selected from the dominant lineage of the settlement, and if this is not the lineage of the first settlers, their descendants have some prestige as owners of the soil.

The Shilluk feel themselves to be a nation under the leadership of their king, but he has little control of their secular life. He has no power to allocate land or to compel disputes to be submitted to his adjudication, nor can he issue orders on other matters. If he intervenes in a quarrel, he does so as peacemaker, or by throwing his own levies and men of nearby settlements on one side rather than the other. The chiefs of settlements and hamlet-heads are not king's officers in an administrative organization: each was rooted in his own segment whose unity and independence he symbolized. Combinations of settlements for war in the past were formed independently under their own leaders.

Though the king can exercise important influence in major disputes, his main role is sacerdotal. He represents the great leader of the Shilluk in their heroic age—Nyikang, who with supernatural powers conquered Shillukland and divided it among the lineages of his followers. Nyikang has lived through a line of thirty-one kings (1948): in them he personifies the unchanging polity and moral order which centres in the kingship, to which his companion conquering lineages still have ritual duties. The myth justifies and hallows present alignments of property, influence, and power.[11]

The kingship particularly is hallowed by its association with Nyikang, who is the medium between God and men. He 'enters' each king at installation, so that Shilluk say 'Nyikang is the king, but the king is not Nyikang'. Hence the graves of dead kings—formerly their capitals—become shrines of Nyikang whose ritual power is distributed through the land. Ceremonies are performed at those shrines for rain, at harvest, and in times of sickness and pestilence. The kingship is identified with the general interests of all Shilluk: fertility of men, cattle, crops and some wild beasts, and in the past success in war. The kingship is thus greater than its incumbents. The king has to observe taboos and ritual to protect the kingship, and if he becomes ill, weak, senile, or otherwise unworthy, theoretically he should be killed 'to save the kingship and the whole Shilluk people'. But while he rules he is Nyikang, so that when he died Shilluk said 'there is no land'. (Among the Lozi, the phrase is: 'When the king dies, the land falls into a coma'.)

The relation between kingship and king is manifested in the ritual of installation. Under Anglo-Egyptian rule, a few days after a king has died his successor, chosen from among sons of kings, is elected by two chiefs of settlements to the north and south of the capital near the centre of the long narrow kingdom. As these chiefs have ritual duties, the country is divided into two ceremonial halves. They have to secure the support of the country for their nominee, which they do by consulting twelve important chiefs and the two chiefs of the northern and southern marches of the kingdom. The new king should come from the opposite half of the land to that of his precedessor. Then the whole country should participate in his investiture. Different settlements and groups of people have specific roles in this ceremony or must supply important regalia and other appurtenances. The effigies of Nyikang and his son are brought from a shrine in the north, backed by an army. As they march south they are treated with reverence, for Nyikang's spirit has left the dead king to re-enter the effigy, which now is Nyikang. This army meets in mock combat the king-select who is supported by an army of the south: and the army of the effigy captures the heir from out of a block of his clan and his own personal followers and takes him to the capital. 'The kingship captures the king.' Nyikang's effigy is placed on the royal stool, then removed; and the heir sits on the throne and trembles as Nyikang 'enters' him. A second mock battle is fought between the new king and the army of the effigy, over a newly married bride of the king, who is provided by a certain clan. Nyikang claims her on the grounds that she was married with cattle of the royal herd and therefore she is wife to Nyikang who owns those cattle. Now the king captures the girl and Nyikang has to make peace with him: the king receives homage and exhortations to rule well from the chiefs, while the effigy of Nyikang no longer contests his authority, and a few weeks later returns with the effigy of his son to the shrine in the north.

The symbolism is clear. Nyikang, the symbol of Shilluk unity, with his power to affect national prosperity, is the kingmaker. The king is forcibly separated from his own relatives and lieges to be placed at the head of the nation, above sectional loyalties. Invested with Nyikang's power he is able to seize his royal bride and to receive the homage of all chiefs.

But each son of the king was born outside the capital, since pregnant queens were sent away to bear their children, generally to their natal settlements. Each potential claimant was reared by a settlement chief, who was often his mother's brother. Since the polygamous kings married queens from many settlements, princes were spread over the land, and various settlements became identified each with a prince whom it would support in his claim for the throne. Ties of maternal origin intersected the territorial

*1*. The visitors approach.

*b*. A common relative in-law stands between the hostile parties.

*photographs by M. G. Meggitt*

(see pp. 109 f.)

PLATE X. A Chiefly Welcome

First visit of N'Dumba Tembo (a chieftain of a small 'Angolo' with his bandsmen).
(from H. Capello and R. Ivens, *Benguella to the Territory of the Yacca*, 1882)

dispersion of settlements by linking some of them at one time, and all through successive generations, with the kingship to which 'their' sister's son could aspire. But in recent decades a convention, at least, has developed that different royal lines take it in turn to provide the king; and it is the custom for the reigning king to raise a scion of a rival line as his probable successor. This custom is connected with the dichotomy of the kingdom into northern and southern halves, between which selection should also alternate. The kingship is made to circulate between representatives of the different parts of the kingdom. The establishment of a fixed capital is also new: in the more distant past kings ruled from the settlements where they had been reared—to become after their deaths cenotaphs of Nyikang—so that the kingship and its court moved through the land.

Since in Shilluk theory a king's physical powers influenced national prosperity, the king was held responsible for what we would call 'natural' disasters, and rebellion against him was warranted in the national interest. As Evans-Pritchard says, these 'were not revolutions but rebellions against the king in the name of kingship'. Rebellion was justified because the king had failed to uphold the kingship. But in practice rebellion was probably waged by a prince as leader of a discontented faction, and particularly as leader of his part of the kingdom. Hence Evans-Pritchard believes that few kings were killed according to prescribed ritual rules when their physical powers waned. Nor does he accept that the furtive manner in which a king was *required* to act—prowling about his capital at night, like the priest of Nemi with whose nocturnal ward I opened this book—proves that kings lived in constant fear of assassination. He considers rather that kings met violent deaths at the hands of rebellious factions.

The civil war was then fought for the kingship in the idiom that a particular king had desecrated its sacredness. Evans-Pritchard concludes that the office is sacred because its incumbent king symbolizes a unity above sectional divisions, 'and this is only possible if his office is raised to a mystical plane. It is the kingship and not the king who is divine,' though the king is temporarily invested with that divinity. Since the individual king comes from a particular section of the nation, there is a contradiction, inherent in one man occupying that position, 'between dogma and social facts, in a sense between office and person, . . . and this contradiction is solved by customary regicide'. The basis for this contradiction is the dispersal of the kingdom's population in widespread localities, each of which has particularist sentiments. As each becomes associated with a prince through maternal ties, these sentiments are expressed through dynastic rivalries. But all Shilluk have a deep and abiding interest in the kingship of Nyikang, which can influence their welfare: hence in the past they fought for that kingship, and not for independence from it. Evans-Pritchard suggests that the development of this kingship into what Frazer called 'the divine king' is likely in a system 'in which the political segments are parts of a loosely organized structure without governmental functions', though the ritual and symbolic values of kingship do not disappear even where there is a higher degree of centralized administration.

I would add that there is a further contradiction inherent in a kingship and all positions of authority: that between the high ideals of office and the inherent frailties of men dealing with their fellows. We have seen that it was impossible for the Anuak headman to have, in the eyes of all his villagers, that composed spiritedness demanded of him. All officials must fail in the eyes of some.[12] Among the Shilluk this appears strongly in the belief that natural disasters were due to the king's frailties. These beliefs 'force' civil wars on the nation and keep its segments (as among the south-eastern Anuak) involved in incessant struggle with one another for possession of the sacred kingship of Nyikang.

Two of the Shilluk arrangements around kingship are found in more strongly organized states. First, the dichotomy of the kingdom into two counterpoised halves exists also in the Lozi kingdom (discussed below) which also is sited in a long narrow river-valley. This has two capitals, fairly near one another at the centre, one ruling the north, one the south. The junior, southern capital, ruled at most periods by a princess, duplicates the northern, and both had to collaborate constitutionally to take national decisions. Each was a sanctuary from the other.[13] The institution of a woman, princess or queen-mother, apart from such a territorial dochotomy, as a second ruler—and sanctuary—to the king is common: it has been vividly described among the Swazi of South Africa[14] and is found in many African kingdoms.

Second, the circulation of the kingship through different houses or dynasties is also a common device for distributing and balancing power, of particular importance in the strongly organized Muslim Emirates of Northern Nigeria. Among the Nupe the Emirate rotates through three houses, and with it all important offices of state. A learned noble here told Nadel that primogeniture which in the past worked because there was powerful magic behind the king's authority, was seen through bitter experience not to work after the Fulani conquest: 'For the Fulani dynasty, which came to power as a large group, composed of jealous relatives and partisans, a divided succession was the only solution. The country too, he added, could only benefit from such a balance of power.'[15] If we reflect on how maternal and marital alliances under monogamy embittered mediaeval politics round the kingship, it is easy to appreciate how much more complex such struggles could be in polygamous societies.

## AUTHORITATIVE CHIEFTAINSHIP

The Anuak and Shilluk polities show other principles of organization which appear in the structure of some tribal states under chiefs who were considered to have the authority to demand the right to forbid internal fighting and to compel submission to their adjudication, and who had at their command officials and bodies of troops to enforce their decisions. All these states were based on a husbandry, in crops and/or cattle, supplemented by hunting and collecting, which required a widespread dispersal of the population. Even where a chief controlled the state through his own administrators, he usually ruled by having officers to represent him in the various areas of the state—what I shall refer to as 'counties'. He had to delegate power. In many African tribes, each chief in practice at succession found an existing distribution of power, in which counties were already headed by traditional, often hereditary, leaders, to whom their subjects recognized an allegiance independent of the allegiance which they granted to the chief himself. A chief might reduce the power of these county chieftains by placing members of his own family among, or above, them: this gave power against him not only to commoner chieftains, but now also to 'princes' who had claims to his chiefship itself. Often the chief himself was not responsible for creating his potential rivals in this way: his ruling father or grandfather by custom was required to place the sons of his important queens (who were numerous under polygamy) in various parts of the tribal territory, with their own followers.

Though theoretically they were subordinate to the main heir, and in one way the latter's state officials, in other respects they became leaders of autonomous blocks of followers who would fight for them against the chief in an attempt to seize the throne from him. Each of these royal contenders received particular support also from his own maternal kin and relatives-in-law, whose power around the 'throne' depended on their personal ties with the ruling chief, as well as on their position in the total political structure. Since weapons were simple, and possessed by each warrior, each county chieftain and royal head of followers had a personal army which he could use to support him in struggles with the chief.

Hence the kinds of struggles around the throne which marked Shilluk polity are found even where an authoritative chieftainship has developed. The limitations of the economy—both the simple tools and the absence of luxuries which would have enabled aristocrats of all types to live as a different class from their subjects—prevented any horizontal stratification developing across the kingdom. The subjects, either directly or through their intervening leaders, gave tribute to the chief and worked his fields for him; but as we have seen he could only re-distribute this tribute to them as individuals and in feasts and ceremonies, enhancing his power but not cutting himself off from them. In most of these states (I shall examine exceptions later) there was no substantial differentiation in the types of products exchanged between the various territorial segments of the nation to establish an integrating economic system which would keep the segments bound together in mutual advantage. Communications were not well developed: paths had to be traversed on foot and rivers by paddled dugout canoes, and once a state covered any size of territory, news to the centre travelled slowly and royal levies could not be moved rapidly.

In these circumstances, it is not surprising that many of these states were constantly splitting up, with segments setting themselves up as independent political communities. The history of all the tribes of Southern Africa until the beginning of the nineteenth century, and of many thereafter till European rule was established, is marked by the proliferation of new tribes with their own chiefs.[16] Here the record is well documented, because of long contact with Europeans who have provided checks on indigenous traditions. The situation seems similar in other parts of Africa, where the corroborating documentation is not as satisfactory.[17] The rate of proliferation of new tribes in Southern Africa seems to have been most rapid, possibly because here the Bantu tribes, even though they arrived there many centuries ago, were still migrating and expanding in a relatively thinly populated country.

As each segment was equipped for economic independence it could move off if it could find vacant land, whether it was led by a commoner or a 'prince' of the chief's family. But it is striking how often these divisions were preceded by a struggle for the chieftainship itself; and how it was these struggles which precipitated the hiving off of a segment which lost the battle for the established position. This position was hallowed by its association with the chiefly line's ancestral spirits, who not only conferred prestige on the present incumbent of the throne but also were held partly responsible for the prosperity of the tribe as a whole. Important regalia and emblems, some embodying parts of the bodies of dead chiefs, as well as the graves of those chiefs, focused the loyalties of subjects and stirred the ambitions of the chiefly family. Nevertheless, the head of a segment, once independent, himself became a ritual leader, appealing to his own ancestors, who had been held responsible previously for his own district when he was subordinate.

This determination to try to acquire the main chieftainship appears as a strong abiding loyalty towards it in the sentiments of the people. Here, as among the Anuak and the Shilluk, we are observing a process of rebellion as distinguished from a process of revolution. I am here specializing these words so that 'rebellion' covers an attempt to oust the incumbents of offices of power or influence without attempting to alter the nature of those offices or the claims of particular types of persons to be their incumbents: I use 'revolution' to cover attempts to alter the offices themselves, or to install quite different types of persons in them.[18] I know of no instance in South Africa where the structure of the polity was altered after a revolt, or where anyone but a member of the chiefly family was installed as chief. Hence in these revolts a contender for the throne could lead his followers in an attack on his reigning kinsman without casting in hazard the system of chieftainship itself or even the title of his own family to that chieftainship. It meant, too, that the ruling chief feared rivals from among his own paternal uncles, brothers and cousins (since these were patrilineal societies): he did not fear revolutionaries. But he had to watch carefully how he dealt with his subordinate chieftains, for those he offended might throw in their lot, and their private armies, with one of these princely rivals against him.

Beyond this, the chief had to deal carefully with his commoner subjects. If he acted tyrannously, these might turn to one of his kinsmen, who promised to rule more benevolently. Not all chiefs acted with this wisdom: but the sanction of armed rebellion by the people, though led by members of the royal family, was always present. A number of separate processes thus combined to produce rebellion: dynastic struggles for power in the chiefly family; the self-assertion of segments of the tribe in attachment to their own prince; the struggle for power around the throne of commoner chieftains of counties, and particularly the support of the maternal kin and in-laws of particular princes; the reaction of the people to a particular chief's mode of rule.

When a large part of the population supported a rebel prince against his reigning kinsman because the latter was a tyrant, they were defending the chiefship against an incumbent who had broken the values of that office. These rebellions were fought to defend the office, and not to attack it. And since a series of 'natural' disasters might be ascribed to the unworthiness of the incumbent, here too, as among the Shilluk, mystical beliefs in validating rebellion against a 'desecrator' increased the tempo of civil war. This idiom was applied also in situations where one prince attacked another, either before or after accession, on the grounds that he was the true heir, and not the other. For a usurper had no right to the throne. In this respect the rules of succession also thrust civil wars upon tribes. For under the succession law of most tribes, no man was clearly designated as heir to the throne. There was sometimes a rule which stated (as among Shilluk) that any of the descendants of a chief might aspire to the position, or be selected for it. In other tribes there was a series of rules which designated different possible heirs. Even in the South African tribes where the general rule stated that the heir was son to his predecessor's principal wife, uncertainty was created because under different rules different wives were indicated as the principal one. This obscurity was further complicated because a chief might select on personal grounds one wife and her sons for favour, against a wife who had better claims on the position. Hence at any one time there were likely to be several claimants to the throne, each of whom could establish a valid claim. The rules of succession themselves contributed to produce civil wars.[19]

In several South African tribes the heir was supposed to be born by a wife married after a man had become chief, perhaps late in his life, and hence the heir might be a minor when his father died. Then one of his father's brothers or one of his own elder half-brothers might act as regent; and in Africa, as in Europe, regents were not always prepared to abandon power when their wards reached maturity. In fact it was not easy for them to do this. For in these small-scale societies any man with the appropriate status became a centre of power and intrigue, whether or not he wished to, as was shown recently by the unhappy position of the punctilious Tshekedi, regent for Seretse of the Bamangwato. Even the good regent who faithfully discharged his obligation has been suspected of intriguing and attacked by his own ward, either for alleged abuse of his trust or for alleged later intriguing.

For each man of importance had his own army, as we have seen, and he could not retire into individual privacy. Intriguing factions and his own faction might push him into activity, or be suspected of doing so. And only he was liable to accusation of treason, and not his followers. In these systems men had mediated allegiance through intermediate lords to their chief, and were obliged to support these intermediate lords in revolt. Though they might be slain in the heat of battle or pursuit after a defeat, they were not liable thereafter to rightful prosecution. This is the law of treason late into the history of Europe. Marc Bloch gives an example as typical of feudal society: 'When Hugh Capet [king of 'France'] retook Melun in 991, the viscount, who had defended the fortress against him, was hanged together with his wife, and this was certainly not so much because he had rebelled against his king as because he had at the same time committed the atrocious crime of breaking his fealty to the count, his immediate lord, who was in the royal camp. On the other hand, Hugh's own followers demanded that he should pardon the knights who had defended the castle. As vassals of the viscount, had they by taking part in his revolt done otherwise than display their "virtue"—as the chronicler puts it—meaning their loyalty to their feudal obligations, which took precedence over their loyalty to the state?'[20]

We see then that the struggles for the chieftainship by various contenders were not mere expressions of dynastic rivalries and ambitions, but were related to the distribution of the population in dispersed counties, a distribution itself compelled by the requirements and limitations of their husbandry. In the absence of a good system of communications and interdependent economic interests each county developed its own autonomy, and loyalty to its leader, who was both its representative to the ruler, and the ruler's officer. If royal this leader would compete for the chieftainship, which was of highest value: if a commoner, the leader would seek power through supporting a particular member of the royal family. Each leader had his own troops to support him, for every man owned the simple weapons available. Discrepancies within the law of succession raised a number of rightful claimants, and the law of treason penalized these claimants and not their followers. There is a high internal consistency between the various principles involved in political systems of this type.

A rebellion did not produce a fundamentally different kind of political structure, and the birth of new tribes out of old tribes increased the number of independent units similarly constituted. New tribes acknowledged their relationship to the old, sometimes in terms of the perpetual kinship which I described at the end of the previous chapter. The original tribe, headed by the senior house of the dynasty, retained its pride of ancestry; and among the several tribes of Bechuanaland this is still exhibited in the right of the Hurutshe chief, though his tribe is one of the smallest, to precede his fellows in the eating of first fruits.

This prestige of the chieftainship, and the sentiments of the people about it as well as the power it offers to claimants, helps explain why struggles went on for its possession and not simply struggles for independence. In addition, the series of cross-linkings which cut across the territorial division contributed to preventing incessant rebellion. The chief and his kinsmen and subordinate officers were related to one another by diverse ties of kinship, as also were commoners. Putting out cattle to be herded established another set of links. In some tribes, county heads secured their followers through territorial allegiance: while members of the royal family had followers attached to them who were distributed through various counties. Finally, among many of the tribes the men (and sometimes the women) were organized in regiments of age-mates which mobilized only on the orders of the chief, for war and for labour. Divided loyalties are significant in these chiefdoms as in the stateless societies. And as segments were divided against one another, the chief could often mobilize more allies than there were rebels.

But there is a more important unifying principle. I have approached the analysis of these states from an examination of civil disorder, in order to emphasize two points. First, we have seen that those Anuak villages which competed for the kingship and the Shilluk settlements were united in a kind of recurrent civil war, which resolved the conflict between the centripetal tendencies of unity and the centrifugal effects of territorial dispersion. To understand the structure of tribal society—or indeed of any society—it is essential to grasp that conflicts of organizing principles, expressed in disputes and quarrels, are not merely disruptive breakdowns in social organization but are attributes of society itself. Secondly, these are at work even within systems of authority. The institution of chiefship did not get rid of these factors in social life or the struggles that resulted from them.

It did produce important differences. Political life might still contain competition for prestige and power over people, and control over resources. But decisions were taken about public matters like war by an organized series of councils, while authoritative judgments were made on disputes in courts to which litigants and witnesses could be summoned to give evidence; and both sets of decisions were enforced by 'police' and troops at the order of the chief and his officers. These might also order the investigation of offences both against individuals and against laws of the tribe: a code of criminal law existed. All subjects therefore gained in security *vis-à-vis* their fellows from the stronger political order, though they might be more liable to tyrannous oppression by those in authority. They had to pay imposts of various kinds to their various superiors, but they shared in the distribution of wealth from the chief, even though he and his court were supported largely by the work of their subjects. This continually working administrative machine, and the organization of the tribe through it, countered the fissiparous tendencies discussed above. In South Africa, and in many other tribes of this type, all members of the tribe participated in the work of the machine, since they were entitled to attend and speak at meetings of councils at various levels or organization, whether these meetings were to deliberate on hunting and war or to judge on disputes.

Rebellions were recurrent, emerging from the very structure of the state, but they were not continual. Unfortunately we have not the data to work out whether they occurred in some regularity, after allowance has been made for the chance operation of human fertility and death, and of external events. I suspect that the tempo of rebellions was influenced by the maturing of young men into full adulthood, who then found their path to power obstructed in the undifferentiated society by their seniors; but it is now impossible, probably, to demonstrate this. One of the tribes which I have myself studied is the Zulu, and their traditional history has been superbly recorded by Father A. T. Bryant, a Catholic missionary. I tried from this history to work out the proportions of peaceful and disputed accessions to chieftainships, and the proportion of peaceful splitting of tribes to those resulting from war. It was impossible to make the computation, or to set them in a time-scale, because of the distortion of genealogies which was considered in the last chapter.

KINGSHIP

I have been describing relatively small chieftainships, in which the subjects numbered 20,000 at most, and often probably less, but a number of states which embraced well over 100,000 people existed in Africa. Since the Shilluk were 110,000 in number, we know that a state of this size can still retain its unity with only a ritual kingship, depending for its authoritative interventions on the king's ability to mobilize other segments in his support against the recalcitrant. The shape of the Shilluk homeland, with the relative fertility of the Nile's banks, probably contributed to their continued unity. The history of other states of this size, particularly during their formative years, has been marked by the formation of independent political units.[21] Presumably there is some limit to the size of area and population which can be ruled on the technical basis I have described, Some of the largest of the African states, like the Congo Lunda, sent out armies to conquer semi-independent kingdoms for their commanders.

Once these larger states are well established, the prestige of the kingship (as it may now be called rather than chieftainship) grows. Its ceremonial and ritual are more important. Competition for the possession becomes keener, between princes and their supporting county chieftains and followers. The growth of state power is insufficient to counter the conflicts arising from the widespread distribution of population and power: but the constituent segments are more likely to battle to win the kingship for their leaders, before defeat may drive them into submission or independence. Among Zulu, Swazi, Bemba, Ankole, Ganda, Lunda, and other large states, rebellion persists in the form described above, with little division into new independent units striking deep into the heart of the kingdom.[22]

Nevertheless on the longest consideration there is an apparent instability deep-rooted in these states; though the unifying influence of the kingship may keep the segments united for many years, the state was likely in the end to break up. This has happened for various reasons to formerly great states, like the Karanga empire in Southern Rhodesia, both from external attack and from internal dissension.

I suggest that if we knew enough of the history of Africa it would show the constant temporary emergence of states of this type out of pressure of population on the land, or the sudden arrival of a band of conquering migrants, and the establishment of kingship which was acceptable to all subjects. Since the kingdom's segments were not dependent upon one another for specialized production of various goods, after periods whose limits I cannot fix, the state would fall apart, and there would be left many small chieftainships. Force at the centre, and ritual supremacy, seem to me insufficient to give permanent internal stability to such a state. Regions of Africa have probably displayed what can be called an oscillating equilibrium between a large state holding together a while and a number of smaller states. In some respects this is akin to the picture which Leach draws of *The Political Systems of Highland Burma* (1954), where, among the Kachin, lineages claiming prestige through first settling an area, and giving their daughters in marriage to others, achieve a certain aristocracy, which then breaks down into an egalitarian equality, till another group of aristocrats emerges for some other reason based on cultural precedence. Only at salt and jade mines, and at important points on trade routes, do chiefs establish a more permanent authority. Similarly, I believe that wherever a state in Africa has had a longer and more permanent history, it will be found that this is based on some special kind of external trade, or on the internal differentiation within the nation. For example, the Lozi who have probably dominated for centuries the region marked on maps as Barotseland, live in a great flood-plain which produces goods that are different from the products of all the surrounding woodlands. Barter-trade was therefore between the plain and all its surrounding areas, and not between those areas. When the Lozi conquered the whole region, their king received tribute from all the areas of his realm, and as he re-distributed this tribute he became the clearing-house in a wide-spread and mutually satisfactory exchange of goods.[23] I am not suggesting that the position of this flood-plain in relation to the surrounding region would necessarily produce a state dominated from that plain: we know now of many systems of ceremonial trade which achieve important exchanges. But once a state was established there, it had a stability arising from its position at the heart of the network of exchanges.

### ADMINISTRATIVE COMPLICATIONS: LOZI

The Lozi state's stability was additionally related to its apparatus of administration. The flood-plain itself, which lay at the heart of the state, was only divided into rival territorial segments for a relatively short period, when a prince ruled as king at the northern, senior capital, and another prince at the southern capital. As a result of the internecine fighting which developed, the Lozi established a convention that the southern ruler should be a princess who could not claim the kingship.

The king (and this princess) ruled through three councils consisting of a large number of commoners who were appointed to, were promoted between, and could be discharged from, a set of titles of varying seniority and power. One set of councillors— the most influential—sat on the right of the king in full council. Another set sat on his left, and they have usually been called in English 'stewards', because they were particularly in charge of the king's property and tribute. But the councillors-of-the-right also controlled these, and the stewards in council exercised the same functions of state as their fellows on-the-right; they advised and decided on matters of national interest, both secular and ecclesiastical, they acted as judges, they led troops in war, and they mobilized labour. Princes and husbands of princesses also had the right to sit in council, though in a separate block; and they too exercised these functions.

These officials of all three kinds operated in the capital itself, and did not go out to rule their own districts, for districts were not the administrative divisions or the military divisions of the nation, which numbered towards 300,000. Lozi administrative divisions were formed by attaching men, scattered about the kingdom, to organized sets of councillors, from all three blocks. Attachments were so arranged that not all the same people were fellows to one another in their three series of attachments.

Among the Zulu, Swazi, Bemba and many other peoples the king's councils included trusted officials who had influence but lacked the power derived by princes and great chieftains from the backing of their own bodies of followers, organized in territorial administrative divisions, which enabled them decisively to control the course of national politics. In Loziland the personal followers of a prince or councillor were relatively few, though important for his rise in influence: his administrative followers were widely scattered and assembled only for the king's works and wars, so that they did not develop an internal autonomy and loyalty *vis-à-vis* the state. Hence these administrative divisions did not rise in support of their officials in revolt against the king.

Nevertheless these councillors could check and control the king. Delegation of authority always creates power against him who delegates. The Lozi say that when the king appointed his chief councillor to rule for him, he made that councillor 'another kind of king' who could control him. For the chief councillor now represented the people against the king, as well as the king to the people. This situation, working through all the councils, affected political action, for councillors wielded influence widely outside their offices. Hence councillors out of favour, or jealous of one another, or hostile to the king's policy, or objecting to tyrannous rule by the king, could try to rouse people to revolt, in *ad hoc* bands. Here commoner councillors had to find a prince to lead the revolt: rebellions were as elsewhere fought in the name of the royal family's claim to the kingship. These rebellions were rarer among the Lozi than in South Africa, where territorial segmentation produced struggles for power between counties with organized loyalty to chieftains, but rebellions still threatened the unwise king.

Lozi councillors were rewarded during their tenure of office because almost every title had attached to it a village or villages, and estates of arable land and fishing sites, of great value in the flood-plain where much of the land was useless. If an official was promoted from one post to another, he abandoned the emoluments of the first office and took up those of the second: if he were discharged, he lost the emoluments. Theoretically, competition for all offices and for promotion between them depended on merit. Hence Colson regards these Lozi appointive officers of the state as '. . . the beginnings of bureaucratic government . . .'.[24] But, she adds, '. . . in the general simplicity of the government purposes there was little chance for specialized offices to arise. The public organization was not differentiated into separate bureaux, and the power of officials was held in check by the fact that they could be replaced by one another.'

Colson speaks only of 'the beginnings of bureaucratic government' because she emphasizes that Lozi councillors were not bureaucrats in any modern sense: they were far more akin to the county chieftains of South African Bantu, or to European feudal nobles, despite their lack of private armies. They exercised general, and not specialized, political power. It may have been the specific conditions of the Lozi flood-plain[25] which compelled the scattering of people during the flood-season out of one set of villages to another set variously dispersed, that prevented the establishment of territorial segments whose leaders with their armies could dominate national politics. But now that I am here analysing the whole series of African states, I am also struck by the reported size of Lozi capitals in former times. They reached up to 10,000 people, far beyond the size of the Zulu capital, say, where regiments of warriors were quartered. All the councillors at the capital had their own gardens and fishing-sites. They were still subsistence producers. There was a wide-scale distribution of tribute among the people: each party bringing goods of one kind were rewarded with goods of another kind. But some tribute was culled to support the kingship and the large court. Here was the main part of political activity around the kingship. No aggrieved or ambitious councillor could retire to a country estate peopled by his private army. If he wished to rebel, he had to recruit warriors where he could find them. And he had to tempt or persuade—one rebellious councillor even forced— a prince to be his candidate for the throne. Dynastic struggles for power were fostered by royal polygamy and the breeding of many sons of kings. Any prince born after his father ascended the throne, by any woman instituted in one of the several queens' titles, was eligible. The ambitions of the princes interacted with the intrigues of councillors, and with the reaction of the populace to the manner of rule of the extant king, to foster constant revolt.

The possible effect of the large population in the Lozi capital must be distinguished from the situation among the Tswana (Bechuana). Most Tswana tribes were concentrated in 'towns', which among the Bamangwato reached 20,000 in size. These towns were not 'capitals'. Virtually the whole tribe resided in such a town, which was surrounded by a ring of garden-land with cattle-posts farther out still. Relatively few of the tribesmen lived outside the town.

### Politics of the Capital: Buganda[26]

The political situation is altered when there is horizontal stratification of the population, based not only on a conquest by invaders but also on the establishment of two quite different styles of life between rulers and ruled. These are found in some of the kingdoms of Ruanda-Urundi and Uganda, and of West Africa. The rigidity of social stratification varies greatly in both regions; and I can summarize only some examples out of the large number which have been analysed by anthropologists.

A number of the kingdoms in the general region around Lake Victoria have been created—probably in fact as well as in tradition—by pastoral peoples acquiring domination over agriculturists. In Buganda[27] these different elements of population have become 'amalgamated', while in Bunyoro[28] there is no 'rigid caste-like discrimination' based on origins, though there are important status divisions. Ankole in Uganda, and Ruanda, are among the kingdoms which exhibit these 'caste-like distinctions'. In Ankole the distinction was so strong that the former agriculturists were forbidden to herd cattle.[29]

The country Buganda, whose people are called Baganda, was a protectorate of one nation within the formerly British protectorate of Uganda.[30] Its polity is in many respects similar to that of the Lozi. But the cleavage between king and court in the capital (10,000 population) and people, was much greater. Nevertheless there was not yet a complete horizontal stratification with radical differences in style of life barring intermarriage between aristocrats and commoners. Commoners still had free access to land and lived with kinsmen. This situation was altered when, owing to a misunderstanding of Sir Harry Johnston's, the British treaty of protection established a class of landlords with estates whose inhabitants became tenants.

Until that time, the history of Buganda was dominated by an attempt of an incoming conqueror and his successors to protect their own power against the officials and chiefs they had to recognize, or had themselves created, in order to rule the nation. The first king of the present royal house according to tradition was invited by clan-chiefs to overthrow a tyrannous ruler of his own dynasty. He united the existing six clans under himself and then re-granted to them their estates of land. But he also created fifteen new clans and granted estates of land to them. Members of the clans were to some extent dispersed. In addition, he established a number of chiefs having territorial jurisdiction, perhaps over demarcated counties: succession to some of these chiefships was hereditary, to others not. Many generations later, again according to tradition, a king reduced the power of the indigenous clan chiefs, as well as of certain important hereditary chiefships. A much later king established his favourites in a new type of 'military' chieftainship, again with estates and followers, and these posts were definitely not inheritable. Each new king thereafter established at least one of these posts. I call these officials 'military chiefs' to bring out that while in civil matters each fell under the county chief in whose jurisdiction he lay, he mobilized his troops independently of that county chief. The 'military' chiefs were the king's men, to balance the power of the county chiefs. Finally, a king late in the nineteenth century established his own company of distinguished warriors and armed them with guns. A later king enticed all men with guns into similar companies. These warriors were given estates dispersed through the country, and they were freed from the jurisdiction of the local county chiefs. Thus at various stages kings made new types of authority to counter the power of already instituted authorities. Furthermore among the Baganda, as among the Lozi, king and not chief himself approved each chief's subordinates, so these were not bound in allegiance to the chief: among the Zulu, subordinates were approved by the county chief and not the king.

Some of these county chiefs had important advisory or judicial positions around the kingship at the capital, and others had ritual duties. The court was here very large, and filled with powerful officials who did not rule counties but had estates of land and

PLATE XI. DRUMS OF STATE

*a.* The Barotse national drums, representing the commoners, travel in the state barge, paddled by magnates, as the king moves from dry-season to flood-season capital.

*b.* The drums of a Barotse princess ruling in a capital—these drums are sanctuaries for the oppressed.

(see p. 144)

PLATE XII.  ROYAL BAND

Reception at Sepo's [Holub received by Sepo, the Barotse king; note the king's bandsmen].
(from E. Holub, *Seven Years in South Africa*, 1881)

people attached to their offices. Besides the Chief Councillor, there were officials with special duties. As among the Lozi, the king could appoint, promote and discharge officials, so that Colson reckons they too have 'the beginnings of bureaucratic government'.

The Baganda were conquering more and more territory when the British arrived: they even built good roads to aid their armies and civil administration. They gained wealth from these conquests, and this wealth was increased because Buganda lay as an entrepôt between the incoming Arab traders and the further hinterland. The core of the nation, around the capital, seems to have participated in this access of wealth. Hence it does not seem to me that we have here a deep horizontal cleavage across the nation, as in Ruanda, despite the rich life of the court and the reduction in power of the clan chiefs (the *bataka*).

According to an unpublished manuscript by Southwold, of the thirty-three kings whom the traditional history records as having reigned up to the establishment of the British Protectorate in 1894, fourteen came to the throne through rebellion. When Baganda retail their history they cite some other unsuccessful rebellions and abortive conspiracies. Some conclusions can be drawn about how and why a rebellion was organized and prosecuted, and about the place of rebellions in the political process.

During the periods covered by the first ten and last four generations of the royal house, it was rare for two men of the same generation to rule, and rebellions were correspondingly infrequent. During the middle period of eight generations (and nineteen kings) kings were commonly succeeded by their brothers, and ten of the fourteen successful rebellions occurred. There is a clear and almost regular pattern: a younger brother of the king would rebel, and later there would be a rebellion by a prince of the next generation who perhaps saw his own chance of succession postponed by his uncle's rebellion.

In order to make a rebellion it was necessary to have a prince to put upon the throne: indeed a proverb says 'Without a prince the Baganda do not rebel'. All princes whose father or father's father had been king were eligible for the throne; and since kings were polygamous, the number of eligible princes was large. Later kings, however, were so successful in butchering their potential rivals that the group of eligible princes was twice almost extinguished. But a prince could rarely depose the king without assistance; and since he could place little trust in the other princes, who were also rivals for the throne, he would normally be allied to commoners, and especially the powerful commoners, the chiefs.

There were three factors which led to rebellions: unpopularity of the reigning king, either among the nation generally or at least among some of the chiefs; the ambition of a faction of chiefs to seize the reins of power by placing their own nominee on the throne; and the ambition of a prince to gain the throne for himself. Obviously two or all of these factors were likely to be at work together; but in specific cases history as told by Baganda usually lays greater emphasis on one or other of them.

Some rebellions are described as the work of a rebel prince and his personal followers alone. In others the initiative was taken by chiefs, and the prince they enthroned was not involved until the rebellion was well developed or completed (in fact in one of the most recent the prince was enthroned against his will). Others again are represented as the result of a conspiracy between prince and chiefs.

Though sometimes the deposed king is described as bad and unpopular, this may perhaps be merely the victors' propaganda (as in English history Richard III may have been slandered by the followers of Henry VII). In only one case is it plain that popular revulsion against the king was a major factor; this rebellion, which the Baganda themselves regard as unique, can truly be described as a national revolt. Significantly, this was also the one case where the vacant throne was offered not to a prince but to the leading commoner, who had been made blood-brother to a prince. He said he was a commoner, and declined in favour of his royal blood-brother.

Sometimes a rebellion was made simply by murdering the king, and for this the prince alone, or a small group of conspirators, would suffice. Six rebellions fall into this category, if we include two where a prince is said to have killed the king by sorcery, and one where the king abdicated (but was not killed) because his brother was making sorcery against him. In the other eight cases it was necessary to fight a battle against the king, and hence the rebels had had to assemble an army.

Sometimes Baganda history states that the rebel prince assembled the army himself. In one relatively recent case the prince established himself in an inaccessible area and made it known that he was recruiting soldiers; by the time the king took alarm, the prince had assembled an army large enough to defeat the royal forces. But, because administration in Buganda was efficient, because the kings had a special department charged with spying out rebellions, and because princes were normally kept under close watch, this can hardly have been a common strategy. Since speed was essential the most effective strategy for rebels was to take over part of the governmental machine, by winning the support of chiefs and their followers.

The Baganda say that the core of a rebel faction (or of a faction loyal to the king personally) was the relationship between a prince and one or more chiefs who were his mother's brothers (though, as with other African peoples, this might sometimes mean simply mother's clansmen). Since the prince could not trust his rival paternal kinsmen, he naturally looked to his maternal kinsmen, who as commoners could not become king themselves. And they had solid reasons for supporting him, since the maternal relatives of a king had many prerogatives and advantages. The details given of several rebellions and conspiracies clearly exemplify this. The rebellious unit in these revolts was a prince plus his mother's clansmen, and these were scattered over the land. Note that a dispersed unit of this kind cannot easily secede from the nation, and similarly also it tended to make the rapid mobilizing of an army difficult. This led to other types of alliances, and perhaps a need for mercenaries. Since a king could not marry into his mother's clan, the accumulation of other allies was also hindered.

But there is more to it than this, since some of the rebel chiefs were definitely not mother's clansmen of the prince they supported. We can only guess what other bonds served to join chief to chief, and chief to prince, in making a conspiracy; probably, as in more developed states, the factions which strove for political power were coalitions held together largely by the fact that to carry weight a man must join either one side or else the other. One thing is quite clear: the opposed factions were not regularly based on territorial divisions of the nation, as they were among the Shilluk and South African tribes. A county chief, for example, might be a leading rebel, while one of his sub-chiefs was a loyal defender of the king.

When rebellion issued in a battle, the prince and chiefs who were leaders needed also common men to fight for them—though perhaps not very many, as the king did not keep a standing army around the capital. Since a chief could not count on the support of his subordinate sub-chiefs, presumably he could not count either on the men whom he was entitled to lead into battle in the king's name. Nowhere in the history is it suggested that a county or other administrative division fought as a unit in rebellion; on the contrary, it is implied that the rebels had to recruit a force specially for the purpose. One rebellion, which was still in living memory when the history was written down, had been brewing for a long time. The rebels, who included several important chiefs, failed to suborn a princess to help them murder the king. They then arranged to rendezvous some distance from the capital, but were there arrested by a local chief, obviously before they had gathered an army.

This is understandable, in the light of the administrative system and social structure of Buganda. Few chiefs, and as we have seen increasingly few, were hereditary. Most chiefs were appointed by the king, and were frequently transferred from post to post. And they were obliged to spend most of their time in attendance on the king at the capital. It was therefore unlikely that a chief could sufficiently attach himself to the people whom he governed for them to put loyalty to him above their loyalty to the king. Besides, partly as a result of this kind of chiefship, the common people did not feel strongly bound to live with their clansmen, or at places hallowed by the graves of their ancestors, but rather moved freely about from one end of the country to the other. Consequently, though a chief might perhaps expect the support of his clansmen, he was not likely to find very many of them living together in one area. Perhaps the armies which fought for rebels were largely composed of their clansmen; but these did not represent any local section of the kingdom.

Nearly half of the successful rebellions were palace conspiracies to murder the king; with but one exception, the rest seem to have been accomplished by rather small-scale battles in which the mass of the people were not involved. Rebellions were therefore in effect a speeding up of succession. Yet undoubtedly rebellions were a means by which political rivalries and conflicts among the important people, the princes and chiefs, were expressed and resolved. The common people were not involved, because their bonds to particular chiefs and princes were generally much weaker than their loyalty to the throne and the nation. The machinery of government was not closely bound to the people at every point, but was to some extent a world of its own with its own internal conflicts in which the people did not participate.

Although the population of the capital must have run to tens of thousands, there is no sign that a city mob took any part in rebellions, as it may have done in some West African states. This is doubtless because very stern measures were taken to control the population of the capital. Periodically, and especially at times of political dissension, or when there were large numbers of rowdy men abroad in the streets, the royal executioners were sent out to ambush the streets of the capital and to seize and kill all persons who could not give a good explanation of their presence. Those arrested had not necessarily committed any crime: they are described as people who had no employment in the capital, and included innocent peasants who were bringing in food. The specialist servants of the king—his musicians, cooks, potters, etc.—who wore uniform or badges as evidence of their employment, were exempt; so too were chiefs, and the retainers and kinsmen under their protection. It is therefore not surprising that the common people went in fear of their lives in the streets of the capital, and if they had to go there hastened home again as soon as their business was completed. Since the occasions for such purges amount to a description of the circumstances in which insurrection might have been feared, Dr. Southwold and I suggest that their purpose may have been to forestall mob action, and to ensure that only persons firmly under the control of the king and his chiefs could stay in the capital.

The preceding history illustrates also how relationships and small groups survive through conditions of change, and how difficult it is for rulers (as for revolutionaries) completely to eliminate past arrangements. The traditional clan-chiefs (*bataka*) of Buganda have persisted in their claims to land and power, up to the present; and because loyalty to clan-membership persists, the ideology of *bataka* has in recent times been on occasion a rallying point for popular discontent. A conqueror can 'abolish' institutions by decree: these institutions may well reassert themselves as centres of dissidence. Or old types of leaders and elite work their way into new positions of privilege and power. Social development proceeds not only by new forms of organization replacing old forms, but also by multiplication and diversification, in which the old survives alongside and possibly duplicates the new, though often with changed functions.

### HORIZONTAL STRATIFICATION: RUANDA[31]

There were three categories of people in the kingdom of Ruanda. The population numbered towards 2,000,000 of whom around 85 per cent were Hutu who are tillers of the soil. It seems that they ousted the Twa, pygmoid hunters (under 1 per cent), partly by felling and clearing the forests where these hunted, many centuries ago. Also centuries ago Tutsi herdsmen (around 15 per cent of the population now), much taller and lighter than Hutu, came with their cattle and were welcomed by the Hutu as guests. Steadily guests ousted hosts. Then the Tutsi seized control of an area from which they conquered outwards, till their king ruled a territory of broken hills 100 by 140 miles in extent. In this kingdom the Tutsi formed a dominant layer (Maquet and others call it a 'caste'), which lived partly off the Hutu, with whom intermarriage was disliked but allowed. The Twa also served the Tutsi, as hunters and in other occupations, but neither Tutsi nor Hutu would intermarry with them.

Pressure on land in the kingdom was severe, with a present density of 235 per square mile. There have been many famines due to drought and locusts; and in addition fertility of the land has been falling as Hutu cleared bush to make arable which Tutsi converted into pasturage.[32]

The king with his queen-mother maintained an elaborate court, both in the central capital and at provincial capitals where he placed queens, drawn from many Tutsi clans, and concubines. He was regarded as divine and connected with God, and the strength of the nation was associated with his own strength. He observed taboos lest the country suffer. But though he is described as supreme judge and legislator, and ordered major wars, he apparently did not maintain a permanent council for these purposes, as the Lozi or Zulu did. He was however theoretically responsible for appointing three sets of chiefs who administered the country in different sets of ties: he did not, as we shall see, try to co-ordinate their work, but indeed preferred them to be at loggerheads.

Subjects dwelling in a neighbourhood were responsible through a nominated head of one of the local lineages (whose appointment

they could reject) to a 'hill-chief'. There were a few Hutu, and
fewer Twa, among these hill-chiefs. The hill-chief was appointed
by an army-chief (see below): but in the division of the kingdom
into districts comprising several hills, each hill-chief was responsible to a 'land-chief' for tribute of agricultural produce and labour
going forward from Hutu to the local royal capital, and thence
to the main capital, while he was responsible to a 'cattle-chief'
for dues going forward from Tutsi herders. These higher chiefs—
of the land and of cattle—were mainly Tutsi, with an occasional
Hutu. Each of these types of chiefs kept a jealous eye on the
doings of his opposite number within the same district (note that
the hill-chief was appointed by neither of them). Often sons
succeeded their fathers in these posts by the king's permission,
but the king could appoint 'outsiders'. The land-chief judged
land-disputes, while other cases went to the army-chiefs whose
subjects were dispersed through all the districts, so that members
of any district belonged to several armies.

The military structure was very complicated. There were
several armies in the kingdom, for each king was supposed to form
a new army. Shortly after his coronation the king summoned
to his capital the sons of his Tutsi clients who had not yet received
a military training. They formed a company, which was trained
in military skills, dancing, history, the composing of poetry and
skilful debating, and in maintaining composure in the face of all
trials. Four or five companies of this sort formed the fighting
nucleus of the army, to which were attached as auxiliaries Hutu
and Twa lineages, and perhaps some Tutsi lineages, drawn from
previously formed armies, and resident over the whole country.
(It is worth noting here the similarity of these attachments to the
Lozi divisions, and also to the system by which Zulu warriors
were attached to princes, whose followers were spread over many
counties).[33] Armies, to which attachment was hereditary unless
changed by royal decree or permission, cut across territorial
dispersion. Armies had their own cattle, herded by warriors, and
their members looked to their army-chiefs not only as leaders in
war, but also as judges and protectors, and supporters in disputes
with other commoners and lords. Some armies guarded the
frontiers: all might raid, or combine to conquer, neighbouring
territory.

Finally, most Hutu, as well as poor Tutsi, were attached as
clients to rich Tutsi, perhaps themselves attached to even more

powerful Tutsi patrons: but clientage did not ascend to one's patron's patron automatically, as feudal ties tended to do in Europe. Most big chiefs, and many other Tutsi, were clients of the king. The client gave service and supplies to his patron, and received in return cattle to live off and protection against the exactions of other powerful persons. The relationship was difficult for a client to break, but he could transfer himself to a new patron, though probably with some loss; and he could ask his army-chief to protect him against unwarranted ill treatment by his patron.

Maquet compares the three layers with 'castes', because membership was fixed by birth, despite the rise to Tutsihood of a few Hutu; because intermarriage was restricted; because they followed different occupations. He sees the main problem of the Tutsi conquerors to have been how to maintain their domination over the Hutu, though their numbers were between 1 : 10 and 1 : 8 and though they lacked technical superiority of the kind later European conquerors had. Cattle gave prestige and power, based only on cultural values, and presumably the Hutu could have tried to break the Tutsi monopoly of military skills, since the same weapons were available to them. Yet the Tutsi depended on the crops and labour of the Hutu, whose surplus production to support these overlords was not 'very big'. Since the Tutsi lived at a higher level than the others, they required more produce than their proportion in the population. While seeking some balance here, they had to maintain a caste society and yet promote national cohesion, exploit yet protect the lower strata, delegate power to subordinate authorities and yet maintain a centralized and absolute rule. Maquet considers that these problems were solved at least till land deterioration struck at the whole basis of the state. But Frankenberg cites the evidence of the numerous famines and the consequent deaths of Hutu to conclude that the balance of Tutsi demands, on land and goods and labour, against Hutu needs, did not result in what Maquet later was to call 'moderate and intelligent exploitation'.

Maquet suggests that several processes maintained the political, if not the economic, equilibrium. The king's divinity and ritual power were acknowledged by most subjects. No clear-cut groupings based on residence existed to develop a cohesion hostile to this monarchy. He argues strongly—as I have above— that 'through several structures, subjects were much more efficiently bound among themselves and to their rulers than in a unique hierarchy . . . even if one link was broken, the subject did not escape from his superior chiefs'. Exactions on the peasants were kept in bounds by the fact that they could appeal to a chief in one of the various hierarchies to protect them against exploitation by a chief in another, or a man could appeal to his patron, and vice versa. Finally, this 'plurality of structure' was a very effective means by which the central government maintained power through misunderstanding, hostility and jealousy among the subordinate chiefs. They could not unite against the king. Even one of the armies on the frontier could not assail the king: its troops' allegiances were interwoven with those of troops in other armies, who would combine under the king to oppose such a move.

No other dynasty has seized the throne in traditional history, but there were attacks on the king by other princes claiming the throne. For the heir was selected in secret conclave from among the sons of the king, with preference given to a younger, and hence physically powerful, son, that he might communicate this strength to the nation. His name was only announced after his father's death, and as other sons and their mothers might not agree with the choice, says Maquet, 'there was often a period of unrest, even of civil war, before the new *mwami* (king) became an effective ruler'.[34] Unfortunately details of how people of the various strata enrolled themselves in these dynastic struggles are not clear. These seem not to have swung most of the nation into action, as Zulu or Bemba, or even Lozi, civil wars did. They were primarily dynastic struggles, with the competitors apparently supported by their maternal kin and their own clients.

More significantly, Frankenberg suggests that there was a religious cult, that of Nyabingi, led periodically by possessed prophets, which represented in some aspects a struggle of the Hutu against Tutsi domination—a phenomenon not found in the kingdoms I have so far discussed. German, followed by Belgian, rule restrained this development. When Ruanda-Urundi in 1961 was on the verge of independence Hutu and Tutsi began to kill one another in large numbers, in an incipient struggle for future control: the Tutsi for continuing domination, the Hutu for independence from this.[35] This type of clash between rulers and subjects has not been reported from South African or Rhodesian kingdoms, though new types of leaders after independence have attempted to restrict the power of chieftainship: I suggest it arises in Ruanda because that nation contained a horizontal division based on occupation and varying consumption patterns, with less re-distribution of tribute from rulers to subjects. The division of the society from the dynasty of rulers through subordinates into the ranks of commoners is no longer dominant. Nevertheless, the system of husbandry with its accompanying distribution of population, the poor communications, the simple weapons and the personal basis of power, with the still limited economic integration of the parts of the nation, resulted in civil strife being endemic.

CITIES, BUREAUCRATS AND MOBS: WEST AFRICA

In some West African states, which had long been in extensive contact with other regions of Africa and Eurasia through direct trade and which had also been enriched by the slave-trade fed by successful conquest, government was yet more complex than in Ruanda and Buganda. They had large-sized capitals (50,000 plus people) with elaborate courts supported at relatively high standards of living by tribute and tax and slave-labour. Members of the court-aristocracy were sent out into the provinces to rule their people, including such indigenous leaders as existed. Specialist artisans in 'guilds' produced not only utilities but also luxuries in gold, silver, leather, cloth, iron and wood. Bureaux of officials with specialized functions looked after the different functions of the state. I feel it is no longer appropriate to class these states as having tribal political systems, even though many of the processes of dynastic struggle are still found in them and even though the mass of the people still live otherwise in tribal-type conditions. It is necessary to justify this judgment, for the difference will be shown below to be associated with a radical change in the form of state rituals.

I begin with a brief summary of the structure of Dahomey.[36] According to Herskovits, it contained before French conquest a relatively small population of between 200,000 and 300,000 people. Nevertheless, Dahomey shows greater development of bureaucratic control of national activity than any other state south of the Sahara. In it cowries, as elsewhere in West Africa, provided a form of money allowing the accumulation of storable wealth. A census was taken, and there were mnemonic counters for the keeping of elaborate records in order to levy taxes. Records were checked because three sets of officials, including wives of the king, heard all business. Markets were controlled and transactions taxed by the state, which also dictated general economic policy in deciding what food crops each district should grow, as well as the output of other goods such as salt, iron implements, pepper, ginger.

Herskovits divides Dahomey into four 'socio-economic classes', between which there was some mobility—more indeed than in Ruanda. Rule on the whole was concentrated in the hands of those descended from the highest class, though according to Herskovits' account this rule of the theoretically absolute monarch was tempered by a benevolent paternalism outside of matters affecting his dues. This ruling courtly class was large and had to be supported on these dues. It was also polygynous so that kings had many sons, from whom the heir to the throne was selected. Intrigues, in which the queens took a lead, over the selection were rife, and historical records vouch that 'a new King was compelled to make good his position, . . . hotly contested by one of his brothers'. But only one king 'successfully disputed the throne with a brother who had taken it over. In this case, however, Gezo deposed a ruler who because of great cruelty was thoroughly hated by his subjects.'

Details on how the nation aligned itself in these contests are difficult to work out. But it seems that there were no segments backing contenders: they were supported by favoured great men, and the fate of unsuccessful conspirators was enslavement or death.

Nadel's classic study of the Nupe state in Nigeria, published under the title *A Black Byzantium* (1942),[37] deals with political organization from the village upwards. I am here concerned with the court established by Fulani Muslim conquerors in about 1820. In an internecine war between Nupe princes of an earlier dynasty, one sought Fulani aid and then became afraid of the Fulani, who fled to other Fulani at Ilorin. The Nupe king already had cavalry: he is reputed to have attacked Ilorin with 4,000 horsemen and 10,000 foot soldiers, but his army was allegedly routed by magic. The Fulani seized Nupe.

Warfare was endemic in the next decades. The indigenous Nupe revolted against the Fulani, who expanded the kingdom. Eventually a son of the first conqueror, who had claimed only Muslim spiritual leadership, obtained the sacred regalia of the ancient Nupe dynasty and was established as king. Fratricidal wars now broke out inside the Fulani ruling family. In addition, there was a revolt by one of the king's 'mercenary generals' from Bornu who ruled the kingdom for a period before being defeated by a Fulani combined operation. Now followed a peaceful period except for border raids and 'punitive expeditions against recalcitrant vassal tribes'. The Niger Company supported some of these tribes and the king was defeated.

It will be clear why Nadel called Nupe *A Black Byzantium*. We have moved far from the simple rebellious cycle of South African tribes where each prince has his own following. Here are revolting tribes and even a mercenary general, as in Ancient Rome. Both warlike and peaceful expansion were dictated by the wish to tap sources for slaves and close the trade routes to other states. The first European explorers found the Fulani Nupe capital rich in cattle from the north, horses, camels, and ostriches, and the markets full of precious goods from North Africa as well as other regions of West Africa. Southern conquests attempted to control the routes to the coast where slaving-ships put in. 'The splendour of court life of Nupe meant work and income for thousands, incessant production in the workshops of the craftsmen, and rich business for the merchants. Beautifully built houses to live in; gorgeous gowns, horses, saddles, arms, to be given as presents to courtiers and members of the household; food and drink, music and dances, for the great feasts celebrated at court, these were (and still are) the daily needs of the royal household.' The craftsmen were organized in guilds. The nobility was organized in complex ranks of titles with special duties. Trade and tax as well as raids supported this wealth.

A further development was the high status of court slaves, who were also ranked. Indeed, towards the end of Fulani Nupe independence, slaves ousted princes and nobility from the most responsible state offices. These slaves were bound to the king, and had not outside allegiances. Nadel sees them poised against 'the rise of a powerful, dangerously independent feudal nobility'. These nobles held their 'fiefs' from the kings. But their contributions to the royal army, around the nucleus of the royal body-guard, consisted of 'levies of slaves, volunteers, and mercenary soldiers'. The cavalry was important, armed with cotton-wool armour and sword and shields, as well as spears.

It is not possible here to describe the complex administrative system or the organization of allotting estates to nobles. As in

Buganda, nobles moved through what Nadel calls 'fiefs'. 'But the connection of fief with rank, involving as it did a change of fief with every promotion, did not allow the mutual attachment between the feudal lord and his subjects to grow really strong and permanent—too strong and permanent for the safety of the king and the unity of the state. To balance the danger that might arise from a too firmly entrenched feudal lord, the kingdom had to risk the other danger of maladministration and discontent among the people of the fiefs.' Here are more strongly marked the themes Maquet described in Ruanda; and here too we find patronage and clientship operating to add strength to patrons and to give protection to the client in exchange for loss of freedom.

Political struggles take on a very different character. Subjugated tribes rebel. Once even, all the peasants in one region refused to pay tribute and were only defeated on their march a few miles from the capital. Nevertheless the true revolutionary situation has not yet emerged: 'Kings have been deposed and exiled; they have to fight and intrigue for their power; they are subject to the openly working balance of power.' The result is that there is not 'the identification of the person of the king with the unity of the society', such as is found in mystical beliefs of Shilluk and Swazi. 'Loyalty to a personal king [of Nupe] is factional; solidarity and loyalty on a national scale rallies round the throne and round the abstract principle of kingship rather than round the actual king.'

Nadel describes many other 'binding forces in the kingdom'. One was a system evolved by the royal dynasty to restrain the effects of struggles among them. Only three of the seven sons of the first conqueror founded houses, and these now succeed to the throne in strict rotation. Nadel remarks: 'One of my most enlightened informants, a very learned man and himself a member of the royal nobility, defended the present form of succession against the old primogeniture on these grounds: the old system could work in ancient Nupe, when there was a powerful *kuti* (magic) behind the *Etsu's* [Emir's] authority. For the Fulani dynasty, which came into power as a large group, composed of jealous relatives and partisans, a divided succession was the only solution. The country too, he added, could only benefit from such balance of power.' We can see that his historical vision was limited. Fighting for the throne was persistent in ancient Nupe. The rule of rotating succession through two or more houses is found in chieftainships very weak in temporal power as far away from Nupe as Southern Rhodesia, and it obtains in many tribes among commoners.

In Nupe the tripartite division affects the whole organization of the court. Every privilege and possession is fitted into it. Members of the three houses move through important titles with each succession. Land round the capital is divided into three, one section for each house. The capital is also thus divided. Every king during his reign tries to increase the power of his house. But if he oppresses the masses they may turn to his successor. There is a balance, but it is 'precarious', and 'is written in rivalries, feuds, intrigues, and revolts, which threaten the peace of the country and tear Bida into rival factions'. And out of this situation, to show yet another parallel to ancient Rome, or to London in medieval times, emerges the power of the city mob.[38] Nadel does not elaborate this point: I infer it from a single sentence (p. 120) separated widely from his analysis of revolts.

M. G. Smith's study of *Government in Zazzau* (1960), another Nigerian state conquered by Fulani, shows much the same central picture as Nadel's account of Nupe. Here, too, are cavalry with 'armour', grades of nobility with promotion between titles, and (until British intervention) succession through a number of royal houses. Clientship offered protection. But slaves seem here, in contrast with the Nupe, to have lost office to royal office-holders. The system was marked by the 'systematic dispersal of fiefs attached to any single office, which deprived fiefs of military importance and reduced the opportunities for independent military adventures by individual fief-holders or groups'. Smith's discussion of revolts is brief because they are irrelevant to his main theme; he therefore only cites lists to show that competition for political power was acute. These revolts exhibit both attempts at assassination by members of the royal family, as well as essays on the throne by outsiders. None of these revolts, according to his records, swung devoted supporters of a fief-holder behind him against the king.

Neither Nadel nor Smith was primarily interested in the same problems as I am dealing with here: I have compiled my abbreviated analysis from very comprehensive studies which were directed at different problems, and which tended to regard revolts as outbreaks on the public peace, not as inevitable in this kind of economy. For highly developed as their economies were when compared with those of South and Central African states, they were still based on subsistence farming with some guilds of craftsmen. Raids and slaving, and not the internal economy, produced much of the wealth. We are a long way from that differentiation of the economy which appears to eliminate the dynastic struggle as the focus of political intrigue, and which accompanies a clear rule of succession denoting one heir. Hence politics are still dominated by rebellion in the royal family; but now there is the added kind of revolt, that of subject tribes for independence. Since revolts were in some sense regarded by Nadel and Smith as aberrant, rather than endemic, features of the polity, the information on how support was mobilized is thin. It may have been difficult to obtain.

I have followed them in using the word 'fief', though I hesitate over its applicability with its implications of feudalism, a term which Nadel used. For these systems were not feudal in terms of rights to land. Most of the villagers were seemingly able to obtain land by right, possibly because it was 'plentiful'. Strangers coming into a village area were given land by the chief responsible. But this giving of land did not establish a hierarchy of ties through a series of lords, up to the king, in the feudal pattern. 'Fiefs' were tribute-farms, rather than estates which established sets of mutual rights and duties between lords and lieges. These West African states were tribute-organizing states, in which much use was made of the labour of slaves. The ancient Mediterranean states are better parallels, as the title of Nadel's book implies. But they also show some parallels with the working of feudal political systems as a whole. They are quite different from the territorially segmented states considered in the earlier sections of this chapter.

## THE TRIBAL STATE AND BEYOND

This chapter has dealt with the influence of technology on the distribution of population and the relation between rulers and subjects in a series of African states. Even in those states where centralized administration is relatively strong, and there is some degree of social stratification, these are insufficient to counter the divisive effects of sectional interests in the absence of a complex economic interdependence of regions. As all men possess effective weapons, contestants can raise private armies to support their essays at power. There are accredited leaders to head revolts against tyrannical rule. Civil war is further precipitated by complicated, variable, and flexible rules of succession, which produce several claimants to the throne. Sometimes beliefs which ascribe national misfortunes to the king's ritual unworthiness increase the tempo of revolts. In the less developed economies people support their own prince, for these revolts are rebellions to defend the kingship against the unfit or usurping incumbent. The kingship is of high symbolic value and may be endowed with mystical powers affecting general welfare. While revolts change the ruling personnel, they may yet, for some period, keep segments fighting for the throne and thus within the state.[39] Tendencies to fissure are inhibited also by a plurality of intersecting systems of allegiance.

That is, frequent revolts seem to occur where the parts of a kingdom are not bound into the centre and to one another by a diversified economic system, in which various provinces come to depend on one another, and in which specialized occupations and more luxurious wealth produce horizontal stratification sufficiently strong to reduce territorial divisiveness. But there can be considerable development of stratification without eliminating dynastic struggles due to the existence of many claimants for the throne. The mass of peasants in these states are not so closely identified with particular princes that they swing into action on their behalf, except against the worst tyrants, though in some of the big towns the populace may form mobs, like the city-mob of Rome, for whose support factions of the elite compete.

The high worth of the kingship as a focus of struggle between princes, and its role in the balance between and among them and 'barons', continued late into European as well as Asian history, as, e.g., the Wars of the Roses show. The kingship serves to unify a state of a kind[40]—what Southall calls 'a segmentary state'. Only a closely interwoven network of economic dependence finally eliminates dynastic struggles; and as this develops I suspect that rules of succession begin to define one legitimate heir, so that there are no contenders for the monarchy, which focuses national unity. Competition then becomes restricted to offices around the monarch, and if revolt breaks out it may be against the monarchy itself, and not against the unworthiness of the incumbent or his advisers (as it was even in the Peasants Rising of 1381 in England). Revolution may occur, as well as rebellion.[41]

PLATE XIII.   BAROTSE ROYAL POWER

*a.* The fleet assembles to move the king out of the floods to his dry-season capital.

*b.* The king's power mobilizes men to haul nets attached to floating trays up a river.

(see pp. 144 f.)

PLATE XIV. Zulu Ceremonial

*a.* A local chief's regiments assemble to greet the lineal descendant of the great Zulu kings.

*b.* Representatives of the bride's party at a Zulu wedding ritually abuse the bridegroom's party.

All political structures embody two systems of action: an administrative system in which decisions are taken, rights protected and dues exacted, and a system of competition for power.[42] The offices of the administrative system become prizes of power in the competition, and there is struggle for privileges of administration, such as jurisdiction, or the power to take dues from taxes.

Rebellion in most of these African states has therefore to be examined as a process of 'repetitive change', since after it occurs there is no alteration in the structure of authoritative offices or the character of the personnel who hold them. But changes of this kind are, of course, repetitive only over a limited period of time, and they may lead in the end to more definite changes of pattern. However, so long as the basic economy and technology remain constant, these changes of pattern are limited. Even if a state splits, and a new state is established, the latter duplicates its parent-state.

In some senses, however, 'repetitive rebellions' are present even in social systems which contain the possible seeds of revolution: and repetitive processes may operate through drastic revolutions. The study of Africa gives us insight into our own history, and our present and future state.

In addition, these African states exhibit vividly two other important attributes of all administrative structures, since these attributes are standardized in customs and mystical beliefs. First, they show the effects of the multiple and therefore divided allegiances of individuals on the total system of relations. Second, they show that every administrative official is affected by these divided loyalties: he represents the interests of superior authority to his subordinates, and at the same time against that authority he represents the interest of his subordinates, as well as their interests in competition with like and unlike social units of equivalent status. Conflicts of interest are thus focused in one office. These conflicts are most marked in the offices which lie at the bottom of the administrative hierarchy. In indigenous African organization, this is the headman of a group of villagers or kinsmen, who rules them for the state, but is deeply involved in their web of relationships. Under colonial rule the chief occupied a similar position vis-à-vis the European administrator: the chief was one of his people as the administrator could never be, but he was a junior official of the administrator. In our own society typical figures in this situation are foreman, charge-hand and shop-steward in industry, non-commissioned officers in the armed forces, and prefect or monitor in schools. The conflict of authority and representation in these positions is stereotyped in many beliefs and legends.[43]

Why then, if the technology and economy were marked by such strong fissiparous tendencies, did any states emerge in Africa? There is no one factor which can account for this development. Some migrating tribes did not develop chieftainship (e.g. the Nuer): others did (e.g. early South African tribes). Some kind of chieftainship, even without much secular power, may develop by the entry of peaceful invaders (e.g. Anuak, Shilluk, Alur), or incomers may reach an unauthoritative adjustment with the autochtones (e.g. Tallensi). Some anthropologists have suggested that clientage gives followers who enable a man to become a chief. Populations of heterogeneous origin usually are organized in states; but again not always. A larger development of external trade often,[44] but again not always (Yao), produces a large unified state. Many states are undoubtedly derived from some form of conquest, but each state has a unique history, though we can isolate several factors which contribute to the development of chieftainship and kingship. Once established, they were highly valued: but their incumbents were always beset by the endemic threat of revolt.

[1] The following account is compiled from Evans-Pritchard's report of a survey he made on a hard march through Anuakland in 1935 when the people were at loggerheads with the Government: *The Political System of the Anuak of the Anglo-Egyptian Sudan* (1940). He followed this with a record of observations made while he was leading Anuak guerillas against the Italians during the War: 'Further observations on the Political System of the Anuak' (1947). Evans-Pritchard in both reports emphasizes the need for fuller investigations: a reader can only marvel at the remarkable analysis he achieved in such difficult conditions. Lienhardt later made this fuller investigation and has published preliminary articles: 'Nilotic Kings and their Mothers' Kin' (1955) and 'Anuak Village Headmen' (1957, 1958).

[2] It is worth referring here to an analysis of the two-party system of the Swat Pathans, by Barth in *Political Leadership among the Swat Pathans* (1959). In a later article he argues from the theory of games that strategic choices keep persons in the orbit of one of the two factions ('Segmentary Opposition and the Theory of Games', 1959).

[3] Evans-Pritchard cites many rebellions, and Lienhardt (1958) describes an interconnected series in detail.

[4] Evans-Pritchard, *Political System of the Anuak* (1940), pp. 48–50; 'Further Observations on the ... Anuak' (1947), pp. 84 f.

[5] Fortes, *Dynamics of Clanship among the Tallensi* (1945), pp. 98 f.; my review of it in *Order and Rebellion in Tribal Africa* (1963).

[6] Evans-Pritchard, *Political System of the Anuak* (1945), pp. 76 f., and Lienhardt, 'Nilotic Kings and their Mothers' Kin' (1955), pp. 36 f., discuss the myths of origin of this clan. Evans-Pritchard's two reports deal with the political relations involving these nobles.

[7] Evans-Pritchard, 'Further Observations on the Anuak' (1947), pp. 74 f.

[8] From Evans-Pritchard, *The Political System of the Anuak* (1945), pp. 51 f., 89–90. Evans-Pritchard describes the historical developments of this system more fully.

[9] Evans-Pritchard, *The Political System of the Anuak* (1945), pp. 70 f. The graves of all nobles are treated with respect.

[10] I draw on Evans-Pritchard's brilliant Frazer Lecture of 1948, *The Divine Kingship of the Shilluk of the Nilotic Sudan* (1948, 1962) in which he re-analyses what others have written about these people. Later articles are Lienhardt's 'The Shilluk of the Upper Nile' (1954) which describes Shilluk cosmological ideas, and 'Nilotic Kings and their Mothers' Kin' (1955).

[11] On this role of myth see Malinowski, *Myth in Primitive Psychology* (1926, 1948), cited above p. 26.

[12] See Gluckman, 'The Frailty of Authority' in *Custom and Conflict in Africa* (1955).

[13] Gluckman, 'The Lozi of Barotseland' (1951).

[14] Kuper, *An African Aristocracy* (1947).

[15] Nadel, *A Black Byzantium* (1942), pp. 88–9. See also Smith, *Government in Zazzau* (1960), pp. 104 f.

[16] Schapera, *Government and Politics in Tribal Societies* (1956).

[17] See the excellent studies by A. W. Southall of *Alur Society* in Uganda (1953), and by Watson of the Mambwe of N. Rhodesia (*Tribal Cohesion in a Money Economy*, 1958).

[18] Sahlins (*Social Stratification in Polynesia*, 1958, pp. 42, 50–1, 146, 193) shows the similarity of the Polynesian situation. Where royal dynasties were ousted, the victors sometimes assumed secular chieftainship, while the original royal lines became sacred chiefs.

[19] I cite examples in detail in my *Order and Rebellion in Tribal Africa* (1963): also of the law of treason, discussed in the next paragraph. This law is more fully discussed in my *The Ideas in Barotse Jurisprudence* (1965).

[20] Bloch, *Feudal Society* (1961), p. 233.

[21] Barnes, *Politics in a Changing Society* (1954).

[22] See my *Order and Rebellion in Tribal Africa* (1963) on Zulu, Swazi and Bemba; various essays in Fortes and Evans-Pritchard (editors), *African Political Systems*; Kuper, *An African Aristocracy* (1947) on Swazi.

[23] Gluckman, 'The Lozi of Barotseland in N.W. Rhodesia' (1951). This 'clearing-house' distribution of tribute is described in contemporary records.

[24] Colson, 'The Role of Bureaucratic Norms in African Political Structures' (1958).

[25] Gluckman, 'The Lozi of Barotseland' (1951).

[26] A recent book, Gutkind's *The Royal Capital of Buganda* (1963), summarizes historical records on it and discusses its modern situation.

[27] Note that Buganda, occupied by Baganda, is a nation within the formerly British Protectorate of Uganda (L. P. Mair, *An African People in the Twentieth Century*, 1934).

[28] Beattie, *Bunyoro* (1960).

[29] Oberg, 'The Kingdom of Ankole in Uganda' (1940).

[30] I follow the analysis of Southwold, *Bureaucracy and Chiefship in Buganda* (1960), and he has kindly aided me by supplying further data and analysis in an unpublished manuscript written especially for this book. I largely follow his own wording.

[31] I draw on Maquet, *The Premise of Inequality in Ruanda* (1961), and also on an unpublished thesis written by Dr. R. J. Frankenberg at Manchester University, in which he analysed (before the publication of Maquet's book) most of the available material on Ruanda.

[32] Frankenberg emphasizes this process strongly.

[33] Gluckman, 'The Kingdom of the Zulu of South Africa' (1940), and Chapter II of *Custom and Conflict in Africa* (1955).

[34] Accession wars are reported among all the kingdoms of the region. In Buganda there were mechanisms to check them.

[35] London *Times*, Sept. 9th, 1961. And in 1964 there has been large-scale killing of Tutsi by Hutu.

[36] Herskovits, *Dahomey* (1939).

[37] It would be too complicated for me to discuss the famous kingdom of Ashanti because it presents certain anomalies arising from its federal structure. The founding of judicial jurisdiction of chiefs and kings required that litigants take an oath, so that they could be tried for blasphemy (cf. the Ancient Roman *legis actio per sacramentum*). Ashanti has a standardized procedure for 'destooling' (dethroning) chiefs (Rattray, *Ashanti Law and Constitution*, 1929).

[38] On 'The City Mob' see Hobsbawm, *Primitive Rebels* (1959). Cohn, *The Pursuit of the Millenium* (1957), discusses the role of the city mob, and its threats to authority, in mediaeval salvationist movements (especially at pp. 28 ff.).

[39] See Fallers, *Bantu Bureaucracy* (c. 1956), pp. 130–43.

[40] See Chapter XXXI of Bloch, *Feudal Society* (1961).

[41] I discuss more fully this development, and how and perhaps why it became 'treason' to wage war on the king of England for the first time in 1352, in Chapter II of my *Ideas in Barotse Jurisprudence* (1965).

[42] See e.g. Smith, *Government in Zazzau* (1960), and Southall, *Alur Society* (c. 1956), pp. 242 f.

[43] I have not space to set out this situation fully, but see my *Custom and Conflict in Africa* (1955), Chapter II, and *Order and Rebellion in Tribal Africa* (1963). An excellent study of this situation is Mitchell, *The Yao Village* (1956).

[44] Wilson, G., *The Constitution of Ngonde* (1939).

# CHAPTER V

# DISPUTE AND SETTLEMENT

## LEGISLATION AND ADAPTATION

In all states of the type discussed in the last chapter there was adjudication, legislation, and the taking of executive decisions in the interests of the state. As far as one can tell from what has been written about the stateless societies, their leaders depend so much on their traditional positions that they do not and cannot legislate in any formal sense, but they must take administrative decisions to regulate the group's affairs. Unfortunately no anthropologist has recorded in detail the discussion and implementation of such decisions. The anthropologists have concentrated on the forms of groups, such as those discussed in previous chapters. Nor have there been adequate accounts of the actual process of administration and legislation in states with one notable exception: Schapera's *Tribal Legislation among the Tswana of the Bechuanaland Protectorate* (1943).[1] How exceptional the study is, is shown by the fact that I can find the word 'legislation' in the index of only one of the standard English books on African states on which I have been relying.[2] Schapera tried to discuss his Tswana material in the light of data from all records on legislation in other South African tribes, and he discovered merely brief statements to show that all their chiefs legislate, in council, and a few examples of particular laws they enacted. Hence we have to rely almost entirely on his analysis of the Tswana.

Historical records vouch that chiefs have traditionally had power to legislate. Until the coming of Europeans there were few occasions to demand legislative action to deal with new situations, save when chiefs like Shaka of the Zulu, or Moshesh of the Basuto, or the Buganda king, created new states and had to work out a new form of political organization to cope with increased size or to organize their new army.[3] From South Africa, with its long occupation by Europeans, we have a few examples of early legislation. A Xhosa chief ruled that the marriage cattle were not recoverable after the death of a wife, and allegedly a Fingo chief's power to order girls to sleep with young men was abolished (see Schapera). Zulu told me that their third king allowed a widow, who disliked cohabiting with a kinsman of her husband, to whom she remained married under the leviratic custom, to live with any man she pleased; but the king still ruled that her children should continue to belong to her dead husband. The man with whom she lived was to be entitled to one beast from the marriage cattle of the girls he begot. Schapera describes how one Tswana chief reduced, and even abolished, the payment of marriage-cattle after his people had lost most of their cattle in Ndebele raids, while another chief reinstituted its payment after the effect of these raids had been mitigated.

A Tswana chief first discussed[4] any proposed legislation in a small council of his confidential advisers. In theory he should then have referred it to a more formal and wider council of all the heads of wards in his town. Thereafter it was proper to refer the proposed 'statutes' to an assembly of all the tribe's men, any of whom could express an opinion. Some chiefs on occasion did not consult the ward-heads, or did consult these but not the popular assembly. In some cases, faced with a problem, the chief would consult the popular assembly without putting any proposal before it. Schapera illustrates this last procedure by describing how a chief asked his assembled tribesmen whether it was right that widows and daughters inherited nothing from husbands and fathers respectively: the men agreed that they should have rights to inherit. He also cites a discussion in another tribe about the control or abolition of beer-drinking.

The chief expressed his decision on the debate, in the light of opinions expressed, as the enactment of a law. He was wise if he followed the majority opinion, but it was rare for the assembly to reject the chief's proposals, though instances are recorded. Unpopular measures established by many chiefs have been ignored and even resisted, though the British Government's presence has helped to prevent splits arising out of intrigues provoked by the enforcement of such measures.[5] Even a strong-minded autocrat like Kgama of the Ngwato feared—or perhaps said he feared as an excuse—to impose a tax for education when asked by a British officer to do so, lest he split his tribe. Yet he had by personal edict, against what he assumed to be the wishes of his tribe, abolished initiation ceremonies for boys and girls, had prohibited beer-drinking, and had enforced observance of the Sabbath. Other chiefs also issued edicts in this way, without consulting their public councils as required by constitutional law. Schapera surveys the evidence available, and he shows that no chief used his powers in this way to increase his own privileges, but on the contrary chiefs in some instances abolished their privileges. I add that in many other tribes among the main laws issued by chiefs, have been those affirming their privileges. All the legislation cited was at least ostensibly in the interest of the tribe, even if some was dictated by a particular view of the demands of Christianity.

Schapera sorts the actual laws passed under several heads, according to whether they reaffirmed or prohibited or modified traditional usages, or whether they introduced or prohibited or modified new practices. His general conclusion is that the chiefs have made a substantial effort through legislation—and through judicial decision[6]—to deal with changes in tribal life since Europeans have come to the country. Mostly they have done so by abolishing or modifying traditional usages regarded as incompatible with the new situation: only occasionally have chiefs by legislation introduced new usages. British authorities' legislation has had widespread effects, but tribal legislation has been negligible as an instrument of change when compared with the effects of such 'social forces' as labour migration, money and trade with Europeans, presence of the British administration, and Christian evangelism.

New laws have sometimes recognized these changes. I would myself suggest that in this respect the Tswana legislators do not show much less acumen or powers in designing adjustment than legislators in most other states, if we take into account the comparatively small development of commercial life in each tribe. The main new social and economic relations of tribesmen are with Europeans. As most tribesmen earn their living by migrating to work in the Union of South Africa, chiefs have no power to legislate on matters affecting these men who are then out of their jurisdiction. Moreover, the system of labour migration, as we shall see in Chapter VII, enables tribal and family life to continue in organized systems of relations in such a way that little direct legislation is required to control them.

Schapera was also struck by the fact that the Tswana and Basuto[7] seem to have legislated more than tribes in the Union of South Africa. He suggests that this may have been due to the

British policy of 'indirect rule' under which chiefs and their councils were endowed with legislative powers. But Barnes has shown that the Ngoni chiefs under indirect rule on Northern Rhodesia often preferred to legislate judicially: since there was no written record of their law, they could state as traditional usage what was in fact new.

Clearly there has been wide variation in the extent to which chiefs have used legislation to help their own adjustment, and that of their people, to new situations. Schapera even found wide variation in the extent and subjects of legislation among the eight Tswana tribes, though often one or more chiefs were inspired by a fellow's example to introduce a particular statute. In the history of each tribe there has also been considerable variation. He poses several possibilities: '(a) the situations giving rise to [some] such laws were peculiar to the tribes in question; (b) the chiefs of such tribes may have been individually susceptible to influences that other chiefs resisted; (c) a chief may have acted on his own impulses without being necessarily influenced by immediate pressure either from extraneous sources or from developments within the tribe. To decide which of such factors was the dominant motive for legislation calls for a detailed study of tribal history and the biographies of the chiefs.' As Schapera says, few such studies have been made in Southern Africa, and I have shown that they are lacking also on other parts of Africa. As the new nationalistic regimes in Africa are likely, for a time at least, to be more antagonistic to chieftainship than the European powers were, it may well be too late to get information on these points, which have been so sadly disregarded by us anthropologists. It is only fair to add that while the public debate on proposed legislation is easy to observe, the manner in which new legislation is formulated, and the intrigues it provokes, are often secret in the extreme and hard to observe. Nevertheless, this has been a much neglected subject: and we need considerably more data before we can attempt that comparative generalization which Schapera stresses to be as necessary as the detailed study of single tribes.

## STUDYING THE SETTLEMENT OF DISPUTES

Far more attention has been devoted by anthropologists to the settlement of disputes. Even in this field it is only in the last twenty-five years that anthropologists have begun to publish detailed records of the course of disputes from their origin to their attempted settlement, and of the course of events that followed upon this attempt. We have been very short on 'case-law'. For example, the record by Colson (cited above) of what happened after a murder among the Rhodesian Tonga is the first—and still the best—description of such a set of events in an African stateless society. But while all other scholars of this type of African society have focused attention on the problem of the adjustment of disputes, only Bohannan[8] has so far given us a full account of a number of what Llewellyn and Hoebel call 'trouble-cases'.

There are a number of excellent analyses of these 'trouble-cases' among North American Indians, including Llewellyn and Hoebel's on the Cheyenne and Hoebel's on the Comanche. The Cheyenne probably should be classed among states, despite their small population, as should the Kiowa and the Zuni whose law has been analysed by Richardson, and by Watson Smith and Roberts respectively,[9] even though all these tribes allowed individuals far more scope for self-help and vengeance than was allowed in African states. The study of Naskapi law[10] is clearly of a stateless band.

Students of these societies labour under the difficulty that the 'colonizing' powers have suppressed indigenous modes of self-help and have made unnecessary full dependence on the pressure by 'public opinion' and cross-linkages towards settlement, through establishing systems of organized authority, including their own dominant power. Hence the cases on which these anthropologists have to rely are often partial records from the past by contemporary untrained observers or the recollections of disputes by aged informants. These do not give full details, and they are particularly weak on the concatenation of social relationships that have influenced the course of events. The anthropologists who are investigating the tribes of the highlands of New Guinea, as these are being opened up, are beginning to produce studies of adjustment, and of failure to adjust disputes leading to strife.[11] Here the lead was set by Malinowski's book on *Crime and Custom in Savage Society* (the Trobriands) in 1926. Finally, while Barton, in his classic books on the Kalingas and Ifugao of the Philippines, makes very good analyses of the body of rules of the tribe and illustrates these with records of cases,[12]

I do not think he deals adequately with processes of, and pressures towards, settlement.

The 'colonizing' powers have changed far less the modes of adjustment of disputes under African chieftainships, though they have limited the types of criminal cases which courts may try. They have virtually eliminated the blatant public use of ordeals and divinatory techniques in the assessment of charges of witchcraft or sorcery, or in the determination of guilt in 'not-proven' accusations. Finally, they have restricted the use of tortures and of certain modes of punishment and arbitrary action. Hence anthropologists studying these states had a better opportunity than had their fellows investigating the stateless societies to provide detailed records on the judicial process which would illustrate how this worked in earlier days. Few have done so: indeed, I think my own book on *The Judicial Process among the Barotse* (1955) is still the only one to present accounts for an African state of 'trouble-cases' of the full type for which Llewellyn and Hoebel pleaded as far back as 1941.

It is striking that anthropologists have neglected to such an extent to provide details on the activities of political officers and, if I may personify for once, the activities of political institutions. They have written in general terms, with a few short illustrations, about powers of legislation without analysing procedures by which particular pieces of legislation were effected; about administration without analysing the taking and executing of particular decisions; and about law without analysing the attempt to adjust particular disputes. Nor have they analysed adequately the effects of particular actions of these types on the continuing interaction of the persons concerned. Though I had recorded among the Lozi in 1940 and 1942 important court decisions on disputes threatening to disrupt certain villages, when I made a brief visit to Loziland in 1947 I stupidly did not realize that I should visit those villages before all else to try to assess how the court's decisions had influenced the relations between the villagers. Happily younger anthropologists have begun to pursue 'cases' in this way.[13]

If one tries to understand why anthropologists have not provided these records, there are probably several answers. In the first place, this kind of neglect has characterized all the social sciences. The so-called 'case-study' of how lobbies and pressure-groups and public opinion operate to influence the process of legislation, or of administration, has only of recent decades become important in the development of political science, of social administration, and I think also of economics. Even in the field of jurisprudence, where the study of decided cases is the core of the subject, analysis is confined to counsels' public statements and judges' judgments: there has been, as far as I know, little empirical investigation of the origins of types of disputes; how they are processed by lawyers and public officials; how judges and juries react to them in the light of their social positions; and how court-decisions influence the subsequent life of the disputants. Many sociologically minded jurisprudents have, of course, emphasized the importance of these problems;[14] but observations on these aspects of social control are difficult to make since, like intrigues and the activities of pressure-groups, they perforce are secret and confidential. Even if observations are made, publication of facts and analysis runs risks of suits for libel and prosecution for contempt of court. Rumour among sociologists has it that the attempt of an American university to 'wire' a jury room to get data for analysis was declared by a Congressional Committee, rightly or wrongly, to be un-American and against public interest.

'Case-studies' of the working of small groups, such as factory workshops, hospitals, schools, universities, gangs of youths, sets of immigrants, villages, particular elite groups, etc., have also become a focus of sociological inquiry in the last thirty years. These investigations have illuminated the internal interdependence of activities, sentiments, customs and norms, and leadership within these groups.[15]

Studies of this kind are also liable to be derided by other students of society or personality as scientifically invalid, since they may not be 'typical' and conclusions drawn from them lack that ostensible confirmation which figures summarizing single and associated aspects of large numbers of 'cases' appears to give. This accusation has been levelled by many psychologists, on top of other criticisms, at psycho-analysis, whose practice and theory have always been dominated by intensive investigation of individual cases. Quantitative and statistical analysis are important tools of analysis, but they are tools only. As Homans has put it, 'Let us make the important quantitative, and not the quantitative important'. Indeed, Sir Arthur Eddington pointed out on the other side that numerical correlations often conceal problems.

The problems they may conceal are the mechanisms operating to produce the numerical connections between similar aspects in many cases; and it is with the mechanisms by which laws are enacted, decisions are taken and executed, and disputes are adjusted, that I am here concerned. Here, specifically, a detailed analysis of one good 'case' at least is essential for understanding, however atypical it may be. I myself consider that thorough analysis of all the complications of a number of individual personalities has been and is essential to the advance of psychological theory. Let me make clear that in supporting one method of research, I do not decry others. Each method has its relevance and its values, but also its limitations.

Social anthropologists are thus not unique among social scientists in contenting themselves with generalized statements about these kinds of activities, while devoting their attention to the structure of the system in which the activities are carried out. On top of this analysis of social structure, they explained only the rules of the game, without analysing how the game was played. I must say at once that I believe this to have been an inevitable stage in the development of social anthropology, and of our knowledge of the tribal peoples. Faced by a truly enormous variety of tribes, living in diverse environmental situations, organized in a complexity of forms of social groupings which I have not even been able to begin to indicate here, and each in some ways possessing an unique culture, we had to provide a systematic morphology of the forms of tribal society and the patterns of its cultures. Our achievement here has been considerable. Anthropological monographs in the last forty years have advanced knowledge of tribal politics, economics, domestic relations, ritual and religion, and law, until the study of this field is a specialized, academic discipline in itself. Since these studies have raised general theoretical issues about the nature of social life and culture, the various branches of anthropology have been accepted as making a distinctive contribution within the social and human sciences, and have been deployed on peasant and modern industrial societies. In addition, the studies of tribal life by anthropologists helped to eliminate among most educated people the idea of tribal society as mere savagery.

Despite the great wealth of data which Malinowski's methods of research brought into social anthropology, his books and those of his successors were still written at the level of custom. This is, of course, an over-simplification. But it states a general position fairly accurately. Malinowski and the next generation of anthropologists—in which I am proud to include myself—made a large number of observations on how tribal peoples actually behaved, listened to cases and quarrels and obtained commentaries on all these incidents, as well as collecting genealogies, censuses, budgets, texts on customs and rituals, and answers to 'cases stated'. An anthropologist returned from the field with so much data that his major problem was how to pare it down for publication; and this problem has become more grievous as publishing costs have risen and so many anthropologists are at work that no one can keep up with what is written in the subject. Problems of presentation therefore combined with theoretical interests to restrict the amount of data about particular persons or sets of relations which found their way into anthropological books. The tendency was to write in terms of general statements and then from a mass of examples select the apt and appropriate to illustrate specific customs, principles of organization, social relationships, etc. Hence I call this 'the method of apt and isolated illustration'. Each 'case' was selected for its appropriateness at a particular point in the argument; and 'cases' coming close together in the argument might be derived from the actions or words of quite different groups or individuals. There was no regularly established connection between the series of incidents in cases cited at different points in the analysis. I have already quoted how in Barton's book on the Kalingas, the incident in which one village 'stole' the wild-pig, which another village was pursuing, becomes intelligible when we work out that the villages were already at feud over a dispute about land. Barton used his illustrations aptly to outline the culture, the customs and the organization of Kalinga society. He did not use cases to analyse what has been called 'the on-going process of social life', within a social organization, equipped with a particular set of customs and beliefs.

Anthropologists of my generation did use cases in more complex ways. Many studies began by taking a single situation and examining its internal structure in terms of the interdependence of the roles of the participants. They then traced the roles of these participants in other situations, and related the customs and beliefs involved in those varied situations to one another, to illustrate the tribal culture, structure and ethos. A notable example of this type of exposition was Bateson's *Naven* (1936). The *naven* is a ceremony of the Iatmul of New Guinea in which a boy's mother's classificatory brothers, at important events in their nephew's life such as his initiation, or killing his first pig, or any important other first achievement, dress as women, dirty themselves, and in other ways make a laughing stock of themselves. The first achievement of girls may also be occasions for *naven* ceremonies. Bateson uses this ceremony as an entry-point into the whole society and its cultural, social and ethological structure.

Fortes similarly used the great Harvest Festivals of the Tallensi to open an analysis of the system of interlinked ritual dependences of their clans, as Colson used a murder among the Tonga to illustrate their varied networks of relationships.[16] Few anthropologists traced a series of events through the history of particular groups. Even biographical studies of particular tribesmen were subject to this limitation. One notable exception was Hogbin's *Transformation Scene* (1951) which analysed the career, in its social setting, of a bullying New Guinea 'big man' over a long period.

I have given a sketch of these modes of using 'case' material because I believe they partly explain why there are so few studies of legislative, administrative and judicial action: during the course of the ensuing analysis we shall see how younger anthropologists are developing new techniques of dealing with 'cases'.[17] But there is yet another reason, in my opinion, why there has been this neglect of these types of action. Anthropologists, like jurists, have been too deeply interested in discussing whether 'law' exists in the stateless societies, and what is the relation of 'law' to 'custom' both in these societies and in states. I attempt now to clarify this problem.

## WHAT IS LAW?—THE TERMINOLOGICAL PROBLEM

Many volumes have been written on this subject, and it may seem a sweeping impertinence if I say, somewhat categorically, that much of this controversy has arisen from arguments about the word 'law', apparently based on the assumption that it must have one meaning, and one meaning only. But the contrary is obviously true. Indeed, in any language most words which refer to important social phenomena—as 'law' obviously does—are likely to have several referents and to cover a wide range of meanings. We should therefore expect that the English word 'law', and other related words, will not have a single precise meaning. If jurisprudence is full of controversy centring on how 'law' should be defined, the terminological disputes are increased when tribal societies, with their very different cultures, are investigated. Since our own words for 'law' and related phenomena are already loaded with meaning—indeed many ambiguous meanings —students of tribal societies run into difficulties as soon as they try to apply these words to activities in other cultures. Yet, on the other hand, how can we think or write outside our own language? Must we develop a special technical language?— which some confuse with jargon, though that is something quite different, being a flabby and flaccid style of writing. Or should we, as some anthropologists have argued and practised, conclude that it is misleading to try to discuss tribal law in the principal concepts of Western jurisprudence, and instead produce pages peppered with vernacular terms? This problem is therefore a general problem in all social science. I have mentioned it in discussing chiefs and kings. Obviously it applies to discussions of 'class'. I try to clarify the use of words like 'law' to focus attention on the several ranges of problems which have been obscured by arguments over definitions. I hope also that in doing this I may establish a model to indicate how other barren terminological disputes may be avoided.

I begin with the predicament of a writer who gave an unusual definition of law. In 1930, Mr. Justice Jerome Frank of the American Bench wrote a provocative and iconoclastic attack on what he called 'the myth of the certainty of law'.[18] He argued that in trial courts many things besides the rules of law affected how judges, and even more juries, converted the raw material of evidence into facts-in-law. Economic interests, religious values, social and individual prejudices, and even the judge's or a juryman's digestive state and particular dislike of witnesses' idiosyncracies, or their susceptibility to counsel's arguments, might influence the course of a suit. Hence decisions of these courts cannot be predicted with assurance, and law is highly uncertain. He concluded that the certainty of law is a myth which deceives nearly all judges as well as the public, and that judges are partly a substitute for the omnipotent omniscient father-figure of early childhood. Eighteen years later, in the preface to a sixth edition of his book, he said: '. . . I seriously blundered when I offered my own definition of the word law. Since that word drips with ambiguity, there were at least a dozen defensible definitions. To add one more was vanity. Worse, I found myself promptly assailed by other Law-definers who, in turn, differed with one another. A more futile time-consuming contest is scarcely imaginable. Accordingly, I promptly backed out of that silly word battle' by publishing an article to say that 'in any future writing . . . I would, when possible, shun the use of the word Law' (at p. vi).

Frank's original definition exposes the seeds of dispute: 'For any particular lay person the law, with respect to any particular set of facts, is a decision of a court with respect to those facts so far as that decision affects that particular person' (at p. 47). This is the process commonly called 'going to law', and hence Frank was perhaps justified etymologically in defining the word thus. We should note that he specifically said this was what law is 'for any particular lay person', and that (at p. 47) it was not the lawyer's usual definition. He protested in this later preface that several critics had complained that he 'cynically sneered at legal rules, considered them unreal and useless', because he 'stressed the effects of many non-rule ingredients in the making of court decisions'. He countered that this was as absurd as arguing: 'if a man says there is hydrogen as well as oxygen in water, discussing both, surely he cannot be charged with denigrating the oxygen or with saying that it is unreal or useless'. To avoid this mis-interpretation in future, he therefore asked readers to understand that when he used the word 'law', he was writing about '(1) specific court decisions, (2) how little they are predictable and uniform, (3) the process by which they are made, and (4) how far, in the interests of justice to citizens, that process can and should be improved' (at p. vi). It seems to me that Frank may be fairly criticized if he underestimated the effect of legal rules and pro-cedures on decisions in trials, but not for his use of the word 'law'. However, though he was perhaps justified etymologically in applying the word 'law' as he did, he might have avoided the 'silly word battle' and the 'futile time-consuming contest' had he made happier use of the riches of English. Thus he could have spoken of 'going to law' as 'litigation' and of court decisions as 'adjudication': then if he said adjudication is affected by many things besides the rules of law and hence litigation is uncertain, argument might have proceeded about his analysis, and not about his use of the word 'law'.

If we are to write in English about the sociology of law, 'it is [as] important', Stone insisted, 'for social analysis, as . . . for

PLATE XV. ROYAL TROOPS

King of Buganda reviewing Colonel Congo's regiment.
(from J. H. Speke, *Journal of the Discovery of the Sources of the Nile*, 1863)

(see pp. 147 f.)

PLATE XVI.   ROYAL ENTERTAINMENT

King Mtesa of Buganda holding a levée, the royal drums in background.
(from J. H. Speke, *Journal of the Discovery of the Sources of the Nile*, 1863)

(see pp. 154 f.)

logical analysis, to keep distinct the various meanings of the word "law" '.[19] Failure to do so can lead to fruitless disputation; and the literature on tribal law is full of this. Radcliffe-Brown and others have defined 'law' on occasion by the sanctions behind it, basing themselves on one of Roscoe Pound's remarks, that law is 'social control through the systematic application of the force of politically organized society'.[20] Further, if 'politically organized' implies the existence of courts, then there are societies without law.[21] Thus Evans-Pritchard stated that 'in the strict sense of the word, the Nuer have no law'. Yet in another work on them published in the same year he spoke of Nuer law and of legal relations, and he described how people might recognize that justice lay on the other side in a dispute.[22] His pupil Howell (an administrative officer) followed him here in his *Manual of Nuer Law* (1954), stating that 'on this strict definition, the Nuer had no law . . .'. He adds immediately: '. . . but it is clear that in a less exact sense they were not lawless', and he states that he therefore uses the term law 'rather loosely'.

Many jurisprudents have followed the same line of analysis. Thus Seagle concludes, in a penetrating study of the historical development of law, 'that the test of law in the strict sense is the same for both primitive and civilized communities: namely the existence of courts'.[23] Note how these scholars emphasize the phrase 'in the strict sense'.

Other writers have broadened the scope of forceful sanctions as demarcating 'law'. Radcliffe-Brown did this later in his career.[24] And Llewellyn and Hoebel in their analysis of *The Cheyenne Way* of social control, and other books, speak of law and order having teeth. Hoebel puts it: 'The law has teeth . . . that can bite if need be. . . .' But it must be legitimated biting. Hence he says that '. . . for working purposes law may be defined in these terms: A social norm is legal [note the transition from 'law' to 'legal'] if its neglect or infraction is regularly met, in threat or in fact, by the application of physical force by an individual or group possessing the socially recognized privilege of so acting'.[25]

Malinowski, in a first famous definition of 'civil law', in his book *Crime and Custom in Savage Society* (1926), brought in other sanctions, those of reciprocity and publicity, but he also stressed the fact that law is 'a body of binding obligations, regarded as a right by one party and acknowledged as a duty by the other'.[26]

This part of his definition alone has been stated to be law, for example by Vinogradoff[27] and recently by Goodhart.[28] Elias follows them in his learned study of *The Nature of African Customary Law* where at the end of a chapter, entitled 'What is Law?', 'with some trepidation' he 'ventures' to suggest that the 'law of a given community is the body of rules which are recognized as obligatory by its members'.[29] We have just seen how differently Hoebel concluded a chapter, also entitled 'What is Law?'

It would be tedious to give further definitions or to show how often a scholar having defined 'law' in one way, proceeds to use it in other ways, or has recourse to other words like 'legal' or 'penal sanctions'. Stone's magisterial study of *The Province and Function of Law* considers these problems through eight hundred pages of incisive argument. On my counting, the *Concise Oxford English Dictionary* gives thirteen definitions. No-one can fairly be criticized if he uses the word in one sense rather than another. As Frank said, a dozen defensible definitions of law can be given—defensible etymologically, and probably in terms of the facts. There is no 'strict sense' of the word 'law'. Personally, I sympathize with Elias in his feeling that it is awkward to say that a society which in practice has a large number of rules to define right conduct, and whose members mostly observe these rules and are penalized if they do not, nevertheless has 'no law' because it lacks instituted courts. Logically and etymologically this can be justified. I would prefer to say they have 'law', but lack 'legal institutions'; or even, since Radcliffe-Brown and Hoebel and others have already applied 'legal' to any forceful sanctions, that they lack 'forensic' institutions.

It seems obvious to me that to deal with these problems we should take advantage of the riches of the English language, and specialize a range of words to cover the different types of facts and the problems involved in this field of 'law'. Each of these words indeed, like 'law' itself, may be ambiguous; but by agreement and convention we should be able to achieve this specialization. Then we shall be able to proceed with our analysis of the facts to which we have agreed to apply the words.

I do not here suggest such a scheme, for I have set out my own proposals elsewhere.[30] I am stressing only the crucial importance of the first step, accepting the multiplicity of meanings of words of this kind and then stabilizing a series or hierarchy of words to discuss the phenomena of social control. This step is crucial and surprisingly difficult. Anthropology has been full of debate on the difference between Radcliffe-Brown's and Malinowski's theories of law. In practice the only difference was that Malinowski applied the word to one set of facts, and Radcliffe-Brown to another. Fortunately Stone and other jurists have urged that we undertake this task of specializing words by convention.

I would here add only that my reading of others, and my own attempts to tackle problems in these fields, incline me to suggest that we continue to use the word 'law' itself loosely, as Howell was compelled to do in order to deal with Nuer life. We need then to find other words—possibly the Latin 'corpus juris'—to cover the body of obligatory rules on which Elias based his definition, while using 'legal', 'forensic' and 'penal' to cover the various kinds of sanctions.

American and British scholars have written about tribal law in English, eked out by some Latin in tribute to the Roman juristic genius, which is part of their heritage and their language. This assumption has been questioned. At least two important studies of African tribal law query whether we can translate adequately the concepts, procedures, and rules of one culture into the concepts of another culture. One scholar, Bohannan,[31] argues that our own jurisprudential vocabulary is what he calls a 'folk-system', and that it is illegitimate to raise a particular folk-system to the status of an 'analytical system'. If he were correct, we would have to be 'cultural solipsists', unable to compare and generalize widely—unless we were to develop a whole new independent language without national home. I shall try to show in the course of discussing various problems in the study of tribal law, how stultifying Bohannan's suggestion is.

## ADJUDICATION AND MEDIATION

Frank's predicament shows us how essential it is to separate our problems through the use of distinctive words. I begin my survey by taking his major problem—what I have suggested we call the process of adjudication, rather than law. This is the process by which, in African tribes with courts, judges take and assess the evidence, examine what they regard as the facts, and come to a decision in favour of one party rather than another. Epstein[32] and I have tried to analyse this situation by comparing it with the models of the judicial process erected by jurists in Europe and America. We considered that this comparison enabled us to relate similarities and differences in the processes of trial in these varied societies so as to bring out how judicial aims and reasoning were related to other elements in social life; and I take this to be the anthropologist's task. This procedure, with its insistence on comparison, clearly is dangerous. But let us look at what happens if we insist on the uniqueness of each society's culture, as, for example, Krige did in his study in South Africa of Lovedu judicial arrangements. In his book on their culture, *The Realm of a Rain-Queen* (1943),[33] which he wrote with his wife, he begins his discussion thus: 'The genius of the Lovedu political system is its network of reciprocities; the genius of the legal system is the procedure of reconciliations and compromises; and both the political and legal systems reflect the main emphases and purposes of the culture. *Khoro* [court] proceedings, the full-dress trials of the Lovedu, stand out conspicuously among the various judicial arrangements, some of which we may be inclined to call quasi-judicial, but in reality none of our legal terms are appropriate. Their *khoro* is court-like, but it is not a court in our sense of the term; their law is law-like, not the equivalent of our law.' In an earlier article he had put this view more forcibly: 'In one social environment it [law] is like a fish adapted to a submarine existence, in another like a bird fitted for an aerial life. To judge the effectiveness of fins as if they were organs of flight is as mistaken as to regard Native Law in terms of our legal conceptions. . . . Native Law cast in our moulds loses its shape and its plasticity, and hardens to inflexible steel.' Krige then stresses, against the formality of our courts, the kitchen-like atmosphere of Lovedu village-courts.

I find it difficult to assess this analysis, because Krige nowhere describes in adequate detail the whole process by which Lovedu *khoro*, though only court-like, listens to the parties in dispute and achieves its aim, which is stated to be 'friendly readjustment'. The only case he cites in detail, in fact, involves readjustment by separation rather than friendly reconciliation. Clearly, as I shall show, there are important differences between these Lovedu courts and ours. But even if we follow Krige's analogy, one may be the fins of a fish and the other the wings of a bird, yet both fins and wings are organs, with some similarities of structure, which propel a body through a fluid on some similar principles.

The poetical style of writing, allied with the belief in uniqueness of Lovedu culture, have thus obscured the issues: we are not given adequate evidence to assess either similarities or differences in procedure.

Bohannan, in his *Justice and Judgment among the Tiv* (1957), does not use analogies of this kind, and gives better evidence, but he states Krige's view more explicitly in analysing the lowest grade of courts established by the British among the Tiv of Nigeria. His main emphasis is that 'the *mbatarev* [elders] suggest a settlement, and the litigants must concur if the case is to be considered thoroughly successful' (p. 61). I draw attention to his use of the adverb, '*thoroughly* successful'. For while he stresses several times that a good judge does not force a decision on the parties but gets them to concur if he can, he cites several cases where in the end judges did lay down decisions against a recalcitrant litigant. Nevertheless he concludes that 'the importance of such concurrence by the litigants cannot be over-emphasized. . . . Tiv *jir* [courts], then, discover a solution to a dispute which is in accordance with the *inja* [given in the glossary as *custom*] of the Tiv, and in which all the parties concerned in the *jir* [case] concur. This is comparable to, but vastly different from, the fact that Western courts make a decision in accordance with the facts of the case and with the "law", and have the authority to enforce that decision. It is very difficult to discuss the acts and values of either system in the words and concepts and language of the other' (at pp. 64–5).

Bohannan has here moved to totally illegitimate conclusions. Whatever the Tiv may say is the ideal ending of a case, when litigants do not concur their judges lay down a verdict; and it is clear that Tiv judges must take some decision, even if (as with Lovedu judges) it is a decision to postpone a ruling in the hope that the parties will reach accord on their own. Meanwhile, whatever happens about enforcement, his cases show in detail that the judges take evidence and assess it in terms of a series of well-known rules, which are 'universal' and 'permanent' (at p. 55). We can in fact discuss the process of reasoning of Tiv judges—and I suspect Lovedu judges—in the same terms as are used by Western jurists to analyse our own judicial process: the use of witnesses, preferably independent, for proof even if there be more faith in oaths than we have;[34] the formulation of different types of evidence; the check on behaviour of reasonable conformity with customary modes of action (at p. 25); and the application in cases of the rule that privileges and powers must be reasonably exercised (at p. 25). In short, I would undertake to analyse the processes of reasoning of Lovedu and Tiv judges in English to illuminate the general problem of how men of alleged impartiality sit on the evidence and through cross-examination assess it in terms of social rules, to illustrate both similarity and differences. And if I knew Lovedu and Tiv, I believe I could explain to these peoples the outline of how Western judges reason, even if they could not always agree with the logic of decisions based on premisses different from their own—such as the prejudice of English judges against using girls in exchange-marriages, which Tiv think quite moral. It would, of course, be easier to describe Lovedu and Tiv judicial processes in English, than the English process in Lovedu or Tiv, because of the elaboration and refinement of our jurisprudential vocabulary.

To insist on cultural uniqueness obscures, in this case, the analysis of judicial reasoning. In reality, one observes a complex integral process which includes specific cultural elements and about which the people think in ideal terms. Furthermore, the analysis of judicial reasoning involves considering the types of social relations out of which dispute has emerged. Among Lovedu and Tiv, where most transactions take place between closely related persons, usually kinsmen or in-laws, if these sue each other the problems raised for judges must be different from those set judges who are trying cases involving persons linked only by contract or tort, the common situation in Europe or America. Where closely related persons are involved, as among the Tiv, the judges may well try to adjust their dispute so that they should be able to resume their friendly relationship and it is a substantial advantage if all concur in the adjudication. This has been demonstrated often enough. Hence what we are shown is not that it is impossible to discuss African procedures and values in English, but that if we want to understand African courts, we have to take into account the social relations on which they operate. In fact, Bohannan's cases show that Tiv judges are more anxious to get the litigants' concurrence in cases involving blood-kin, than in cases involving strangers, or even in-laws whose relationship is about to break. I found this to be the situation also in Barotseland. Correspondingly, what Krige is arguing, is that a South African court might fail to take account of this situation in laying down a legal judgment in a Lovedu case. But that is a different matter from saying that we cannot translate from one culture to the other.

Furthermore, those who stress these differences are taking a very narrow view of the institutions which exist in the West for settling disputes. It may be true that in cases of tort and contract and crime Western judges lay down decisions irrespective of what the litigants think, though I dare say that even then the judges hope that their arguments on the facts and on the law, and the moral issues, are so cogent that the losing party is compelled to acknowledge justice, and the wrongdoer to feel his guilt. It may be true that when divorce cases come to court Western judges usually find either that there are grounds for divorce or there are not, without trying to reconcile the spouses. But anyone who has followed the actions of judges in divorce cases, or other family disputes, knows that a judge may intervene to suggest that the whole matter were better settled between the parties with their lawyers' help. A judge may even take this line in a commercial case. And outside of the courts themselves, many settlements, in which both parties have to concur, are arranged by lawyers or arbitrators, who are among our social mechanisms for adjusting disputes.[35] Presumably Marriage Guidance Councillors work on disputing parties as Lovedu and Tiv judges do, without authority to lay down decisions or enforce verdicts. These are the commonest situations in our society where closely related persons are at odds. The setting up of Works Councils and industrial conciliation tribunals shows a parallel development in the industrial field. Here also long-term relations are involved, which cannot be settled by the authoritative verdict of a court. Comparison must always be made across cultures with appropriate institutions; and a double comparison may be required. For, in the end, though the methods of tribal courts resemble in some respect those of councillors in our own society, they approximate more to the methods of our courts. They are authoritative.

The accurate treatment of similarity, and the correct emphasis on difference, are possible if we set our problems in stages. We can first look at the assessment of evidence on facts against norms of action, whether these be what may be called rules of law or customary practices. There will be certain similarities arising from what are probably universal elements in any judge's or arbitrator's task. But we have then still to examine the differences.

Clearly many of these arise from the fact that most tribal cases involve disputes between closely related persons, enmeshed in an intricate network of relationships with others to whom they both are related, whereas most English and American cases involve persons who are strangers to each other outside of a single linking relationship. There is thus commensurability. We have not been misled by the apparent uniqueness of two cultures. On the contrary, we advance our analysis through understanding the inter-relations which make these cultures what they are.

A third stage is reached if we introduce the variable, how does the existence of enforcing mechanisms influence the process of judicial reasoning? *A priori*, we should expect that where a judge is backed by powers of enforcement, he may feel that he can shorten the process of listening to the evidence and coming to a decision, while the judge who is not thus supported, may be more patient. I am not sure that this is what happens in practice in tribal societies. Certainly Barotse judges, who are armed with enforcing powers, insist that every litigant must be allowed to speak fully. The situation is dominated by the hope that the parties can be reconciled, and hence must speak out fully. Unfortunately, we have very few detailed texts on trials by tribal judges.

We also lack good texts on how mediators and arbitrators work in Africa. Wilson says that among the Nyakyusa of Tanganyika two parties may agree to the appointment of an independent person to hear their dispute, and the case is argued before him. His verdict stands only if accepted by both parties.[36] This sort of general statement is not very useful for detailed analysis and comparison. It is important that the range of authority of these adjusters of disputes, who are not judges, and of their procedures, be made clear. Fortunately evidence from outside Africa is better. As cited above, Hoebel describes how an aggrieved, but weak, Comanche can call on a brave man to press his suit against an alleged injurer: 'The intervening champion was acting as a legal champion. He made no pretence of judging the case or of mediating.' He was not an arbitrator. He forced the defendant to pay as the plaintiff would have done had he had power and strength.[37] In the one case cited, the champion-at-law helped a weakling whose wife had been stolen: would he have done so if the issue were not clear, since by Comanche rules an injured party can mass his kin and friends to assist him press his claims, while the wrongdoer cannot mass his own supporters in his defence? And is the status of wrongdoer always clear?

Another type of intervention is exemplified among the Yurok of California. Force was a Yurok's principal method of securing redress. Nevertheless the parties to a dispute each appointed unrelated persons from different communities, who took evidence from them and 'other available sources', conferred among themselves and with the parties about the relevant law, and laid down a verdict. This could be evaded by the loser, but there were strong pressures on him to abide by it.[38] Hence these Yurok go-betweens are almost judicial arbitrators, like those in our own system.

On the other hand the role of the Ifugao 'go-between', as Barton calls him, is different: 'To the end of peaceful settlement he exhausts every art of Ifugao diplomacy. He wheedles, coaxes, flatters, threatens, drives, scolds, insinuates. He beats down the demands of the plaintiff or prosecution, and bolsters up the proposals of the defendants until a point is reached at which the parties may compromise.' If either party will not listen, he may threaten symbolically to throw his armed support on the other side; and since he must be unrelated to the others, this may apparently be decisive.[39] Nevertheless, I would regard him as a conciliator, rather than an arbitrator.

Among the Nuer a person called 'man of the earth' can stop two disputing parties from fighting by hoeing up the ground between them. Furthermore, a murderer can seek sanctuary with him, and he can try to compel the victim's kin to agree to a compromise and to accept blood-cattle in place of vengeance by threatening to curse them by the earth on which they dwell. There is no suggestion that he listens to and weighs evidence,[40] so that he is best described as a ritual mediator.

If we distinguish the champion-at-law, the intermediary, the negotiator, the mediator, the conciliator, and the arbitrator[41] on a scale of augmenting authoritativeness, we would clarify our problems by focusing attention on the ranges of social pressure which back their actions. Secondly, we would make clear how far they call for evidence and cross-examine; and this is surely always essential in the analysis of law. Thirdly, and most importantly, we would examine in which several ranges of relationships between parties the different procedures are effective, or ineffective, both within single societies and comparatively.

I suggest that even a proto-judicial process is found only when evidence is examined and assessed, as among the Yurok. What then are we to say of the procedures by which a community decides to get rid of what Radcliffe-Brown called 'a bad lot', and Llewellyn and Hoebel 'the status of the finally intolerable'— the recidivist who constantly thieves, rapes or murders? Here there was apparently action on the basis of well-established knowledge, known to the elders of the community, without an actual trial. This procedure seems widespread in societies without organized courts and chiefs. Usually, as among Eskimo, the consent of the villain's kin must be secured in order to exclude blood-revenge. This is definitely a proto-judicial process, involving rational discussion of the case in the light of sensory evidence. Hoebel says that in this kind of [small (?)] community 'the question of evidence in disputes does not raise a great problem; sufficient information seems usually to be at hand'. He adds that 'when fact is not known . . . resort may be had to divination, but apparently only when an element of sin enters, . . . or . . . death through sorcery'.[42] He apparently classes all these operations as 'legal'. But the process by which both parties, or the accused in 'criminal' suits, are confronted with evidence, and are themselves heard and cross-examined, influences decisively both the development of political structure and the pattern of social relations. Therefore it seems wiser to separate procedures terminologically, and to confine 'legal'—or 'forensic'—to procedures in courts. Even divination in cases of sin or sorcery in courts is used differently from the way it is used among the people involved, as I shall show below.

A fortiori, therefore, I would not classify such institutions as the Eskimo song-contest under the rubric of 'legal' as Hoebel tentatively does. He notes, as cited, that when an aggrieved person challenges his injurer to an exchange of insulting songs, ' "right is immaterial" . . . (though the singer who can pile up scurrilous accusations of more or less truth against his opponent had an advantage in fact)'. Later there is a reconciling exchange of gifts and a feast. This sort of procedure has to be compared with processes of social control in small groups in our own society, such as the 'slanging-match', which may also end in a reconciling drink, rather than with courts. If we call the 'slanging-match' legal, what word can we use for procedures in court? (As I have suggested, we might specialize the word 'forensic' for these.)

I yield to no one in my admiration of Llewellyn and Hoebel's studies of specific tribes' law, but in classifying all procedures of settlement together they seem to me to confuse issues. Above all, the emphasis is taken off analysis of the whole concatenation of relationships between persons in which particular procedures of control operate. The data on the Eskimo are not Hoebel's: but he does not raise the problem, between what kinds of persons are song-contests used?

Bohannan describes such a contest—'drumming the scandal'—among the Tiv.[43] Under their rules, allegations in the song that are capable of human performance must be true. If they are not, a suit for slander lies. But if not—in this contest one party chanted that the other 'changed himself into a pig at night and made it unsafe for every sow in the countryside'—there are no grounds for such a suit. Bohannan's record of the originating dispute is not very full. The defendant was secondary marriage guardian of the wife of the plaintiff's son, and 'had been guilty of some rather high-handed tactics that caused the marriage to fall through'. The defendant had then refused to act as intermediary to get the plaintiff's marriage-payment refunded, and they had 'exchanged angry words'. The plaintiff then made up a taunting song which he and his relatives sang at night so that the defendant, whose home was just over a quarter of a mile away, could hear. Singing and then counter-singing continued for three weeks until the 'chief' appointed by the British moved the contest into his court, lest it provoke a fight for which he be held responsible. There it was judged (in Solomonic wisdom) that the plaintiff won his suit (on grounds which are not reported) while the defendant won the singing-contest.

Bohannan says he was told by the 'chief' and the defendant's 'song-maker . . . that in the old days "drumming the scandal" was a favourite method of settling disputes, and almost always led to fighting. Whoever won the fight won the dispute.' Unfortunately he discusses it only as a 'method of settling disputes', without identifying to what types of dispute in what types of relationships it was appropriate. Of its very nature it could only be used against a neighbour. In Tivland 83 per cent of men dwell with their patrilineal kin near other similar kin: hence it seems likely that a man 'drummed the scandal' if he felt he had been wronged by a partilineal kinsman. In the case cited the plantiff was Torgindi of Mbayar lineage and the defendant

Mtswen of Mbagishi lineage. Early in Bohannan's book (at p. 14) a genealogy relating these lineages through putative patrilineal descent is given as:

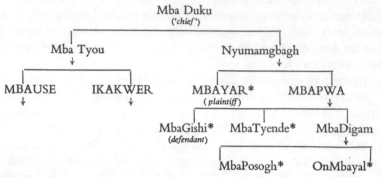

*Note.*—Lineages in capitals provide elders on the court. Lineages with asterisks have tax-collectors.

In an article by Mrs. L. Bohannan on genealogies as charters of present organization among the Tiv, she says that 'Mbayar is in size equivalent to any of the component segments of Mbapwa, Mbayar's sibling segment. Most people cite Mbayar as a child of Pwa rather than as a sibling segment. Some say that the elders who in the past told the administration that Yar was Pwa's brother were mistaken, but that it isn't worth-while doing anything about it. Other elders say that Yar was born the brother of Pwa but in size has "become the child of Pwa".' We are not told which interested elders said what. There is thus some uncertainty about the relative positions and the patrilineal descent of these two lineages. And it seems that members of these two lineages can marry one another, since the dispute is over a woman for whose marriage the defendant is responsible. Dr. and Mrs. Bohannan state that there is considerable variation in the genealogical distance at which patrilineally related groups can intermarry, but that 'the major exogamic group, . . . is generally a large lineage of some eight to ten generations in depth and with a population of some 8,000 people'. The population of all MbaDuku (see genealogy above) is about 10,000 people. It includes many lineages besides those of the litigants. One wonders if these two lineages have only recently begun to intermarry. They appear in one other case in Bohannan's book on Tiv law (at p. 25). Here a youth of agnatic lineage MbaYar took five chickens from his mother's lineage in MbaGishi, under the custom allowing privilege of this kind to a sister's son. His mother's brother sued to have a declaration that this was excessive and unreasonable, and the youth was told to repay two chickens.

I have gone into this case in some detail to demonstrate that the operation of this sort of redressive procedure cannot be evaluated without an analysis of the inter-relationship of the parties. The data I have tried to piece together suggest that the drumming of a scandal among the Tiv *may* be appropriate in a particular set of relationships, and not in all. In the one case cited, the evidence is that the disputants belong to lineages whose relative relationship is unclear and who may be entering on the stage where they intermarry—which may also be the stage where they fight with lethal weapons. Closely related lineages fight with clubs or stones; less closely related lineages fight with bows and arrows which are not poisoned, and they shoot into the air, trying only to scare one another. But between segments of some eight to ten generations in depth—the same depth as those which are cited as likely to intermarry—'the possibility of war is admitted, as is the use of poisoned arrows and Dane guns [muskets] and the attempt to kill one another in fighting'.[44]

I am guessing here—perhaps wildly. But there are indications in the data that the litigants in this case belong to lineages on the fringe of a particular kind of patrilineal relationship, beyond which parties cease to regard themselves as 'close brothers'. They are near to murderous feuding. Naturally one begins to wonder whether we are here confronted with another ambiguous relationship in which a 'joking-pattern' is employed to draw public attention to a breach of moral duty, which cannot be dealt with by other redressive institutions, either because there are none, or because straight litigation is excluded by other moral rules. And the drumming contest may be the escape from fighting with arms. The defendant's song-maker who pictured the plaintiff as a lusty pig, told Bohannan that 'he had thought of some much worse things to suggest that it was in Torgindi's [the plaintiff's] nature to do, if it were only humanly possible, but that [the defendant] had stopped him saying that all he wanted to do was to win the contest, not to "spoil Torgindi's heart" permanently. They were, after all, neighbours.' This suggests both a close relationship to be restored later, and the existence of rules restraining the parties' ridicule, but not that of the song-maker, who came from a distance. After the 'chief' settled the matter, he ordered the song-makers of both parties to stay away for a longish period. One song-maker commented to Bohannan some months later 'that chiefs and District Officers spoil all the fun'.

Alternatively one wonders if the song alleging promiscuity by the plaintiff—that he was a pig who rendered the countryside unsafe for sows—was a scathing, indirect reference to the fact that his son had pressed a suit to marry a distant kinswoman, like an animal forgetting the rules of proper mating. At the court hearing the defendant's party waved figurines of the plaintiff and his wife 'in a somewhat compromising position' (p. 143). Contests of this kind have to be connected with contexts of social relations.

Joking and ridiculing are thus appropriate in particular types of relationships as sanctions on wrongdoing. These relationships, as shown above, are likely to be those with an element of ambiguity. Ridiculing when relationships are close, cuts too near the bone. Complete strangers—unless brought into an institutionalized joking-relationship—can only insult one. What was the relationship between the Eskimo challengers at a singing-contest? They had surely to be related, since the contest ended in reconciling feast and exchange of gifts.

How 'joking relationships' are used to penalize wrongdoers is well illustrated from the Crow Red Indians (and the Hidatsa). The Crow are organized in matrilineal clans: a man belongs to his mother's clan. But he must treat with respect all the members of his father's own, i.e. maternal, clan. Since men of one clan marry into all the other clans of the tribe, the sons of these men of the father's clan are scattered through the tribe. Radcliffe-Brown associated respect and privileged joking as alternative possibilities in this type of relationship. A man therefore has a joking-relationship with sons of the father's clan (and certain linked clans) outside his own clan: he may make offensive remarks about them and must receive in good part such remarks by them. These joking relatives, in this pattern of abuse, may call public attention to one another's shortcomings. When a Crow 'has committed some reprehensible deed, e.g. married a clan mate, or shown jealousy, it was not the function of his fellow clansmen but of his [joking relatives] to reprove him or make fun of him. They would spread the news of his wrongdoing and throw it in the offender's teeth and he was obliged to take all this in good part as the prerogative of the [joking-relatives].' This ridiculing extended to ignorance of technical procedures, poor sportsmanship, improper marriage, cowardice, and apparently anything that was socially reprehensible.[45] Note that these jokers were closely, but indirectly, related through their common paternal descent from one clan. As members of different matrilineal clans they were not mutually involved in the system of intra-clan obligations. The right to punish by ridicule is tied to the most permanent groups of the Crow, as among the Tonga.

A further important procedure is suggested by this Tiv case. Is the use of the word 'scandal' in 'drumming the scandal' chance, or significant? Does it indicate that the defendant's behaviour did not found a suit in court, but was only morally reprehensible? And did the plaintiff 'drum the scandal' to focus public attention on this scandalous behaviour? A Lozi may commit an offence against a kinsman, or particularly an in-law, in order to get the latter to bring suit in court against him, so that the court may then be made aware of the other's neglect of moral duties. For example if a man's wife neglects his kin, he cannot sue her, as she can sue him for divorce if he neglects her kin. He can divorce her freely, but may not wish to do so. In this situation, I recorded cases where the wronged husband snatched food from his visiting father-in-law, who then left in high dudgeon. Placatory gifts were sent by the husband after him; but the wife sued for divorce. She was refused her suit and publicly rebuked for her failings. The court also ordered that the husband was entitled to the return of his placatory gifts; but he refused these, saying he wished to emphasize that he had no quarrel with his father-in-law.[46]

One is reminded of how a Cheyenne father shot his own horse in the presence of the Soldier Society braves who had been prepared en masse to rape his daughter, who was however saved by the Holy Hat Keeper's wife.[47] Similarly, Radcliffe-Brown describes how if two Andamanese of the same camp quarrel, one may work himself into a rage in which he destroys his own property and those of innocent bystanders, as well as of his enemy. This destruction may proceed in some tribes as far as suicide.[48]

This kind of action in a society without organized courts brings the moral defaulter up against public opinion, or some influential person. In the end, the Tiv singing-contest was brought before the 'chief' appointed by the British, himself an elder of the larger lineage embracing the lineages of both parties: the test of the singing-contest included a trial of the default. The 'chief' said he acted to avoid a fight. Fear of 'breach of the peace' has been frequently a procedural device to found and strengthen jurisdiction both where authority is weak and where the offence at issue is not subject to effective sanction. The social-anthropological analysis of its operation demands that we return always to the problem of relating procedures to the social relations within which they operate.

## THE PROBLEM OF ENFORCEMENT

Variations in the sanctioning mechanisms of a society may thus influence the judicial process or the process of mediation, even if these have their own logic of reasoning. Analysis of the sanctions themselves, of modes of enforcing right conduct, should be carried out separately. Enforcement is technically, with us, a problem of political science rather than jurisprudence: and there is good reason for this division of labour. At least, I find that many anthropologists who analyse social order in societies without courts, with a determination to find there processes akin to those of societies which have courts, run into difficulty. This determination hinges on the use of the word 'law' to mean 'social control through the systematic application of the force of politically organized society'.[49] These societies may well have rules of right conduct enforced by regular procedures: in this sense of the word, they undoubtedly do have 'law'. But procedures of enforcement where there are no courts differ radically from enforcement through courts, even if both types of process are associated with what may be called the political organization. Tiv and Eskimo song-contests are something quite different from a forensic contest. Studies of how courts were introduced into tribes which lacked these institutions emphasize this strongly.

Nadel in an impressive book (1947) on *The Nuba* tribes in the southern Sudan analysed the very great variation in their organizations and cultures. He concludes the book with a discussion of the present and future position of Nuba law. He stresses 'the interdependence of law and political institutions', though he does not restrict political institutions to organized government with courts. He argues that even in a society without courts the purpose of both law and political organization is to 'direct and canalize the use of force'. Law is what is enforced, custom is what is not enforced. The essence of his problem then becomes to define the occurrence of 'force' in the Nuba tribes, so that he can distinguish their law under the restricting rubric he has accepted. This leads to a long and involved argument to show that certain departures from norms among the Nuba in fact provoked a forceful reaction, approved publicly, and hence to assert that these norms can legitimately be called 'law'. The modes of enforcement vary considerably, as well as the range of persons involved in them; and the attempt to classify some offences as 'law' and some modes of enforcement as 'legal' as if they were akin to courts, becomes casuistical. Part of the reason for this analysis seems to be a wish, in advising the Government, to dignify some rules as fitting for enforcement by the new courts. But we learn that in practice these courts do not follow Nadel's rule, drawn from their traditional past: for while 'the number of traditional "laws" ' was small, 'the trend in the Nuba tribes is towards treating all social customs (customs bearing on social relationship) as legitimate, enforceable laws' (p. 507). Howell reports the same situation in the courts established by the Sudan Government in Nuerland. Nadel deplores this tendency, saying: 'Far be it from us to foster legal totalitarianism' (p. 508). This reaction, while it may be morally justified, prevents his analysing why new courts act thus.

It may be that wherever courts become established, they will tend to enforce customs, breaches of which in themselves did not provoke in the past a forceful reaction. This may be, as shown below, because these breaches point to more radical defaulting from demands of right conduct. Nadel might have pursued this problem had he not been too concerned to demonstrate that the Nuba had possessed 'laws' in the restricted sense he set himself.

Furthermore, he would then have looked in detail at the problem of how far these courts use what he mentions in passing as 'rational evidence.' He refers to this twice only, once in saying that all systems cannot depend entirely on it so that oaths and some ordeals must be recognized by Government, and once as a pious hope that it will develop. We do not know if the newly established courts take evidence at all. We hear only, again in passing, that the people approved of the elimination of 'the former contest of strength, whose issue was always uncertain, and often unjust'

(p. 506). Nuba seem to have some feeling for proof and right. Similarly, Howell, starting with the same definition of law for the Nuer, tells us that judges in their new courts tend to side with litigants in terms of traditional group loyalties. He does not describe the position of independent judges, if there are some, or how any of these various judges get at the facts to bias them in favour of their own party. Maybe the courts take no evidence. If so, this should be stated explicitly, for then Nuer courts are not courts at all, but negotiations between disputing parties under the (then) *pax Britannica et Aegyptica*. There seems to be some process of taking evidence, determining proof, and assessing liability in these Nuer courts: Howell gives much incidental evidence to the point. For example, we are told that the court is 'taking as a criterion what a reasonable Nuer may be expected to do in certain circumstances', and this surely requires evidence of what the parties have done.[50] These points are central to the operation of courts, and they are not stated clearly in these two analyses because the authors are caught in one definition of 'law' which obscures this problem.

## LAW AND CUSTOM

The tradition of defining 'law' as what courts will enforce has thus logically produced an attempt to isolate enforcing mechanisms in societies that lack courts, and to define as 'law' any rule or obligation to which these apply. This tendency accompanies an attempt to differentiate law from custom, as if they have to be quite separate categories. Nadel's discussion cited above is dominated by this attempt.

Schapera[51] has given us a full list of the Tswana terms which describe their rules of conduct: *popêgô* or *maitseô* (manners, etiquette, polite usages); *letsô* or *moetlô* (custom, traditional usage); *tlwaêlo* (habitual practice); *moila* (taboo); and *tshwanno* or *tshwanelo* (duty, obligation). But the Tswana refer to their rules of conduct collectively as *mekgwa* and *melao* (singular forms, *mokgwa*, *molao*). *Mokgwa* in general applies to what we would term 'manner, way, fashion; habit, usage, wont; custom, traditional usage', and always in the plural form to 'manners, etiquette, polite usages'. *Molao*, again, may be used to refer to a single 'law or ordinance,' to 'the law' as a whole, or more rarely to an 'order or command of the Chief'. Normally, the Tswana do not distinguish between these two terms when they apply them, but if pressed the Twsana will sometimes say that 'one can be punished for a breach of *molao*, but not for breach of a *mokgwa*'.

This use of more than one word to cover the same rules, and of one word to cover more than one type of rule, is not due to inability on the Tswana's part to differentiate between types of rules. Our own words similarly serve multiple purposes. '*Custom*' in the *Concise Oxford Dictionary* is given as both 'usual practice' and as 'established usage having the force of law', aside from meaning duty on imports. One of the many meanings of 'law' is 'body of enacted or customary rules recognized by a community as binding'.

Among both Tswana and ourselves abstract words referring to important elements of social life are liable to have multiple meanings. And the more important the element, the more probably will several words refer to it, or various of its aspects. One professor of jurisprudence has complained that the most fundamental legal terms are *least* precise in meaning. We should expect this. The range of meanings of these words may offend some philosophers and lawyers: it offers a challenge to anthropology and to sociology. Individuals in society seek to achieve their own ends by manipulating their social as well as their physical environment. How do they manipulate the multiple meaning of words? For our present problem, what do Tswana and Anglo-American judges do about, and with, the multiple meanings of words applicable to forms of right and wrong conduct? Has the fact that in English we have to work with the one word 'law', while Latin has *jus* and *lex*, French has *droit* and *loi*, German has *recht* and *gesetz*, Italian has *diritto* and *legge*, been 'responsible for much that is inadequate and untrue in the juridical theory of English writers', as Salmond claims in his *Jurisprudence*? What are the effects on Lozi judicial reasoning of their possessing one word to define a right and duty?[52]

In my study of *The Judicial Process among the Barotse* (1955, at p. 195) I show that the judges begin by saying that a litigant is in the 'right', therefore he has the 'right' in the case, therefore he has a 'right' to, say, a piece of land. The slide from one imprecise meaning to the other was sometimes difficult for the outsider to observe; the judges did not seem to be aware of it. Therefore it is possible that Tswana judges similarly shift the range of application of *mokgwa*, which is a rule of conduct rather less enforceable in courts than a *molao*, according to their assessment of the merits of the action. A judge may in this way hold that a particular rule of conduct or even a piece of etiquette is an 'established usage having the force of law', to quote the Concise dictionary: i.e. this *mokgwa* is a *molao*. In another case, on the merits he can reverse this decision, this *molao* was only a *mokgwa*. I put this in the past tense, for it largely in this way that Barotse judges dealt with changing standards of right behaviour and expressed modern opinion's disapproval of old customs.

When I recorded how Lozi judges worked thus, I found that the decision on what rules to enforce was only part of the judges' problem. As often, also, the judges in deciding on the merits of a case examined all the actions of the parties, and wherever they found departures from established usage—from custom—they became suspicious that the deviating person had committed more serious breaches of rightdoing. Conformity to relatively unimportant custom was thus enforced, not because nonconformity was itself wrongful, but indirectly, since nonconformity was taken as evidence of major wrongdoing. And in a tribal society there are far more standardized usages of this type than in our own. As Fortes says, in another context, 'a great deal of . . . kinship custom is specific. In ceremonial situations different categories of kin often behave in prescribed ways which sharply distinguish them from one another'—and, indeed, such prescriptions mark their behaviour in everyday situations. Departure from these customary ways of acting may point to more serious default.[53]

It may well be that it is in this sense that the trend in the newly established Nuba courts is 'towards treating all social customs (customs bearing on social relationships) as legitimate, enforceable laws: exogamous rules have found a place in the new matrimonial law, and disputes over bride-price or inheritance, even over the customary, half obligatory, gifts between friends and relations, are all now causes of law suits. This is true also of petty quarrels, or offences against kinship etiquette, such as the lack of respect towards a father-in-law.'[54] Newly fledged powers may like to try their wings. Equally, a people unused to authoritative defence of their privileges may compel this trial. Yet we have seen that each gift and each act of respect in these societies demonstrates that the performer has the right sentiments towards one. Suit on default is in fact an action to defend the whole relationship.

This being so, classifying rules as 'custom' until they are enforced by courts, when they become 'law', seems to obscure a vital problem in the judicial process. It is surely significant that 'custom' is not distinguished in this way from law considered as 'decisions of a court' in developed jurisprudence, though ostensibly our relationships are not so beset with specific customs. With us, law in one meaning is a body of enacted or customary rules: in the judicial process, custom is one of the sources of judicial decision. Statutes, precedent, equity (morality), and legislation are the usually named other sources: and I would add at least the necessities of natural law, since judges take judicial notice of these, even if they have to be proved.

But I consider that 'custom' as a source of judicial decision plays a much greater role in our litigation—and therefore forms a greater part of the body of the law—than is commonly stated. As in Africa, so among ourselves, established current usage constantly enters into trial and adjudication when the crux of many cases is reached. What is mental cruelty of spouse to spouse to justify divorce? What is circumstantial proof of adultery? What is reasonable care? These and many other questions are answered in terms of certain standards, posed in the form: 'Was that action reasonable or not?' And those standards must be 'customary', in the sense of current practice. A husband's behaviour to his wife in 1960 may be judged to be cruel, where in 1860 it would merely have been severe. But no statute has changed that definition. Friendship between a spouse and a person of opposite sex nowadays allows them to be together alone, without suggesting adultery. Reasonable care in driving a car is defined by constantly changing standards.

In anthropology defining 'law' as 'court-enforced custom' has the further disadvantage that, as we have seen, it provokes barren dispute about whether or not the Nuba have 'law'—when they are certainly not 'lawless'. Howell declared that the Nuer in the strict sense 'had no law . . . but it is clear that in a less exact sense they were not lawless'. This is surely a futile outcome of a problem of definition.

Perhaps anthropologists have been led into this kind of problem because colonial legislation has recognized tribal 'law and custom', which seems to imply that the two words cover different categories of rules. It is now clear, I hope, that it is more fruitful to accept that in one meaning 'law' is a body of binding rules and includes 'custom'. The restriction of 'law' to judicial decisions in courts—litigation and adjudication, i.e. going to law—elevates another meaning of the word to an unwarranted imperium. All societies have bodies of accepted rules: in this sense they all have law. Some have courts, to apply this law: they have what we may call 'forensic' institutions. But most obligations even in these societies are observed without forensic compulsion: other sanctions, positive and negative, are effective. Other societies lack forensic institutions: in them conformity is induced by various rewards and sanctioned by what Nadel has called the 'intrinsic penalties' of social relationships themselves. These sanctions are supported by champions-at-law, negotiators, mediators, conciliators, and arbitrators, none of whom are judges. If we specialize our terms, we clarify our problems.

### 'INTRINSIC PENALTIES'

It is much easier to analyse how a person or group reacts to breach of obligation than it is to determine why so much of social life proceeds without breach. In practice, most people abide by the code of law and morality of their society. Clearly many are reared to accept this code and internalize it as the conscience. They feel uncomfortable if they default. Some may fear the reaction which a breach provokes. Why an individual for emotional and intellectual reasons conforms to the code and discharges his obligations is a problem for psychologists. My task is to outline the social setting of conformity.[55]

Malinowski studied in the Trobriands a society without courts, and he used his data to attack two opposed ideas about tribal peoples. The first was that the individual tribesman is completely dominated by the group and obeys the commands and customs of the community with, to quote Malinowski, 'slavish, fascinated, passive obedience.' This, he says, had superseded the view that 'the "savage" is really savage, that he follows what little law he has but fitfully and loosely'. So 'hypertrophy of rules rather than lawlessness' became accepted as the characteristic of tribal life.

Malinowski shows that in the Trobriands there was an order in social relations to which people conformed, and that they were penalized for default. He describes the widely ramifying systems of give-and-take between kinsmen and in several sets of ceremonial exchanges, and shows how since 'largesse is a matter of honour and praise, the average native will strain all his resources to be lavish in his measure. He knows, moreover, that any excess in zeal or generosity is bound sooner or later to be rewarded' (at p. 31). This is the picture sketched in Chapter II of this book. But Malinowski also stresses that 'the free and easy way in which all transactions are done, the good manners which pervade all and cover any hitches or maladjustments, make it difficult for the superficial observer to see the keen self-interest and watchful reckoning which runs through it all' (at pp. 26-7). Moreover, 'whenever the native can evade his obligations without the loss of prestige, or without the prospective loss of gain, he does so, exactly as a civilized business man would do' (at p. 30).

Malinowski gave us a pioneer account of social life as an uneasy balance between the demands of social commitments to others and the drives of individual self-gratification. He showed moreover that this gratification is largely achieved by meeting commitments. But he drew attention also to what Llewellyn and Hoebel later called the 'range of permissible leeway, and the range of actively protected leeway' in a man's and a society's conduct. So Malinowski wrote that when a man 'acts as informant to a field-anthropologist, it costs him nothing to retail the Ideal of the law. His sentiments, his propensities, his bias, his self-indulgences as well as his tolerance of others' lapses, he reserves for his behaviour in real life. And even then, though he acts thus, he would be unwilling to admit often even to himself, that he ever acts below the standard of the law. The other side, the natural, impulsive code of conduct, the evasions, the compromises and non-legal usages are revealed only to the field-worker, who observes native life directly, registers facts at such close quarters with his "material" as to understand not only their language and their statements, but also the hidden motives of behaviour, and the hardly ever formulated spontaneous line of conduct' (at pp. 120-1). I do not know of a finer exposition of this view of social life than *Crime and Custom in Savage Society*, written though it was 38 years ago, and short though it is.

Malinowski reports a series of situations, in which clear wrong-doers were allowed to get away with their offences, and other situations in which redress was taken against wrongdoers. He shows how in this matrilineal society a chief favoured his own son unwarrantably. Then dramatically the chief's nephews, his rightful heirs, drove the son away after one of them had been in a fracas with him and had been imprisoned. The son left: his father was deeply grieved and resentful, and his mother died of grief. His chief antagonist divorced his wife who belonged to the same sub-clan as the son. 'There was a deep rift in the whole social life of Kiriwina.' In other situations actual wrongdoers carry on their misdemeanours till publicly exposed; then they may commit suicide by throwing themselves from a tree, to mobilize public opinion against the exposer. Or a person wronged may do this. Suicides for these reasons are reported also from the Cheyenne and other peoples.

Malinowski thus dealt with many processes of control and tolerance of wrongdoing. But the attention of his critics has focused on the part of his book in which he argued that 'the rules of law stand out from the rest in that they are felt and regarded as the obligations of one person and the rightful claims of another' (at p. 54). Each party's claim is another's liability: one's liability today becomes a claim tomorrow. Malinowski showed the balancing of reciprocal obligations, in a complex cluster o claims and liabilities, between owner and crew of canoes, in rights to harvests, in claims for ritual services on kin and in-laws at mortuary and other rites, and in yet other situations. Above all, he established the importance of reciprocity by analysing how inland people exchanged vegetable products for fish with the coastal peoples in set partnerships. 'This arrangement is primarily an economic one. It has also a ceremonial aspect, for the exchange has to be done according to an elaborate ritual. But there is also the legal side, a system of mutual obligations which forces the fisherman to repay whenever he has received a gift from his inland partner, and vice versa. Neither partner can refuse, neither may stint his return gift, neither should delay' (at p. 22). And each community depends on the products of the other for its own feasts, at which the hosts acquire internal prestige.

On this basis Malinowski concluded that ' "civil law," the positive law governing all the phases of tribal life, consists then of a body of binding obligations, regarded as a right by one party and acknowledged as a duty by the other, kept in force by a specific mechanism of reciprocity and publicity inherent in the structure of their society. These rules of civil law are elastic and possess a certain latitude. They offer not only penalties for failure, but also premiums for an overdose of fulfilment. . . . It scarcely needs to be added that "law" and "legal phenomena" . . . in

[this] part of Melanesia, do not consist in any independent institutions. Law represents rather an aspect of their tribal life, one side of their social structure, than any independent, self-contained social arrangements. Law dwells not in a special system of decrees, which foresee and define possible forms of non-fulfilment and provide appropriate barriers and remedies. Law is the specific result of the configuration of obligations, which makes it impossible for the native to shirk his responsibility without suffering for it in the future' (at pp. 58-9).

Social anthropology is a discipline which so far has established a number of what can be called 'laws' (in another sense of the term)—propositions which state invariable interdependencies between discrete types of events. These are at a fairly low level of abstraction. But they are 'scientific laws'. Some are obvious, others not so obvious, and yet others so paradoxical that they appear to run counter to commonsense. The skill of an anthropologist lies in his ability to apply these propositions to complex social situations, selecting from among them and weighing their application. Hence the strength of the subject still resides in the monographic analysis of particular systems of relationship. It is therefore a tragedy for us that many people—anthropologists and others—seem unable to read a whole book in order to assess the total analysis, but seize on, and seek to demolish, isolated statements.

In this instance, it was Malinowski's isolated definition of 'civil law' which fired the critics' indignation. To take but one instance, Seagle in his admirable *The Quest for Law* (1941, at pp. 31-3) involved Malinowski's stress on reciprocity as an intrinsic sanction in relationships, with the definition of custom. He even remarks sarcastically that Malinowski was 'singularly fortunate in selecting the locale for his theory' because the Trobriand 'economic system was based on a dual division of labour'—the exchange between inland and coastal villages. This, of course, is only a fraction of the ground Malinowski covered.

Here the seed of misunderstanding was planted by Malinowski's application of the word 'law' in his attempt to define for a society without courts the mechanisms of social control which operate positively to induce people to fulfil their obligations. I consider that he was justified etymologically in calling these rules 'law', and perhaps also the sanctions, if he so wished. But the adjective in 'civil law' confused the issue by dragging in a technical distinction in jurisprudence. He also confused the issue by using his data, which produced this definition, to attack the views of Maine and others who were dealing with quite different problems. I consider that Malinowski's very application of the word 'law' here led to much of the criticism levelled against him. If we substitute 'social rules and social control' for 'law' in his work no one can doubt its value or stimulus.

Malinowski was concerned largely with what we may call, following Nadel, the 'intrinsic sanctions' of social relationships. These sanctions, both rewarding and punitive, are embedded in the social relationships themselves. Malinowski himself said: 'Law and order arise out of the very processes which they govern.'[56] Homans in his analysis of small groups cites this statement with approval. He follows this with a quotation from Mary Parker Follett who compares social control with 'the self-regulating, self-directing character of an organism as a whole', as analysed by some biologists, psychologists and philosophers. The emphasis is on 'control through effective integration'. Homans himself then makes explicit how this control operates in small groups where an individual departs from obedience to the norms of the group. He is punished either openly or by the withdrawal of his fellows' interaction with him, by ridicule, and so forth.[57]

The principal lesson which Malinowski's analysis taught, was that social control in the most general sense—'law' as he called it—can only be understood within an analysis of the relationships under sanction. This is what I tried to indicate must be our method of studying song-contests. And it is in this field that many social anthropologists have made notable contributions in investigating a wide variety of social arrangements, both of domestic life and of special associations. Clearly I cannot even summarize a few of these studies here: they have to be read in full.

In the course of these analyses the anthropologists have illuminated the significance of such institutions as the payment of cattle or other goods for a wife, ceremonial exchange, reaction to chiefly misrule: these are a few examples taken from my preceding pages. Here indeed has been the main work of anthropology. Its practitioners have also compiled the rules of conduct which may be said to make up the laws and customs of particular tribes: but valuable though these handbooks are, they do not themselves give insight into the structure of social relations they help maintain. It is like trying to give a view of married life by publishing a list of the forensic rules and approved usages which devolve on spouses, supplemented by a list of common breaches of this code.

## THE NOTION OF RIGHT AND RIGHTDOING

Malinowski insisted on the extent to which self-interest moved a man to fulfil his obligations. He did not thereby deny that a man enjoys doing what he and his fellows feel to be right. Recognition of the rightness and wrongfulness of particular sides in a dispute is an essential part of social life everywhere.

The Nuba did not like the contest of strength to decide disputes, since its 'issue was always uncertain, and often unjust'. Among the Comanche, a plaintiff was compelled by public opinion to prosecute his own suit and he might be 'killed in carrying out his social obligations to prosecute. Small comfort in that,' adds Hoebel. But there was some attempt to equalize right and justice. 'The aggrieved was allowed the privilege, apparently not customarily granted the defendant, of marshalling his kin and friends to aid him in seeking restitution. In many instances these partisans took over complete responsibility of negotiations. In other cases, the aggrieved accompanied them on their mission, but refrained from entering the bargaining activities. In no single specific case did the defendant take recourse to similar reinforcements. It does not seem to have been his privilege.' But 'the "rightness" of the aggrieved party's case was a strong operative factor when it came to gathering his group. To participate in such a group if petitioned was a kinship responsibility, though not an obligation. It was rather reciprocity' which pressed a man to attend: he might in his turn need help.[58] But sense of 'rightness' also clearly operated.

Evans-Pritchard writes of the feuding Nuer in similar terms: 'The Nuer has a keen sense of personal dignity and rights. The notion of right, *cuong*, is strong. It is recognized that a man ought to obtain redress for certain wrongs. This is not a contradiction of the statement that threat of violence is the main sanction for payment of compensation, but is in accord with it, for a man's kinsmen will support him only if he is right. It is doubtless true that if a man is weak it is unlikely that his being in the right will enable him to obtain satisfaction, but if he is in the right he will have the support of his kin and his opponent will not, and to resort to violence or to meet it the support of one's kin and the approval of one's community are necessary. One may say that if a man has right on his side and, in virtue of that, the support of his kinsmen, and they are prepared to use force, he stands a good chance of obtaining what is due to him so long as the parties to the dispute live near one another.

'When we speak of a man being in the right we do not suggest that disputes are mostly a clear issue between right and wrong. Indeed, it would be correct to say that, usually, both parties are to some extent right and that the only question which arises is, who has the greater right? To state the matter in a different way: A Nuer dispute is usually a balance of wrongs, for a man does not, except in sexual matters, wantonly commit an act of aggression. He does not steal a man's cow, club him, or withhold his bride-cattle in divorce, unless he has some score to settle. Consequently it is very rare for a man to deny the damage he has caused. He seeks to justify it, so that a settlement is an adjustment between rival claims. I have been told by an officer with wide experience of Africans that Nuer defendants are remarkable in that they very seldom lie in cases brought before Government tribunals. They have no need to, since they are only anxious to justify the damage they have caused by showing that it is retaliation for damage the plaintiff has inflicted earlier.'[59] Many cases in all societies are a balance of rights and wrongs. And people always, like the Nuer, in erecting a defence to a claim state that defence in terms of 'rightness'.

In my study of the Barotse judicial process (especially at pp. 49 f.) I showed how this sense of 'rightness' operates in courts so that if the parties and witnesses lie, they cast their lies in such a form that they will appear to have acted not only reasonably, but indeed uprightly. They work with the same norms as the judges. This enables the judges to attack them in cross-examination and probe out the weaknesses in their stories wherever they have deviated from the norms and usages intrinsic to their relationships with one another. Secondly, by examining a series of cases I have been able to show that the judges after listening to the evidence form a decision that 'right' lies on one side rather than the other. They come to a conclusion on the merits of the case. Thereafter they try to state the law so that it supports the judgment on 'rightness'.

## TRIBAL IDEAS ABOUT LAW: THE COMPARATIVE PROBLEM

I pass now to yet another field of jurisprudential problems, the analysis of the ideas of tribal jurisprudence. Here again we are faced with the problem of translation; and again I take issue with Bohannan. Bohannan begins by insisting, rightly, that we describe accurately a people's own ideas, what he calls their 'folk-system'. But I would argue that he goes too far when he urges (fortunately neither obstinately nor consistently in practice) that (at p. 69): '. . . the cardinal error of ethnographic and social analysis . . . [is] raising folk-systems like "the law", designed for social action in one's own system, to the status of an analytical system, and then trying to organize the raw social data from other societies into its categories. I have also,' he says, 'tried to avoid the equivalent error of raising the folk systems of the Romans or the Trobriand Islanders to the level of such a filing system for data which may not fit them.'

It seems odd to me to put Roman law, enriched by international commerce and connections, and by the doctrines of the law of nations and natural law, on a par with Trobriand law, as a 'folk system'. But we must examine primarily the conclusion which seems to imply that we cannot use English concepts to write about any tribe's law. Nor can we use, apparently, the concepts of any other tribe.

Bohannan's treatment (pp. 102 f.) of the Tiv concept of debt illustrates where his doctrine leads. He explains that the Tiv word translated as 'debt' (*injô*), 'covers a wider range of phenomena and social relations than the English word "debt" usually does'. You are in debt if you borrow and do not repay, if you herd stock for your kinsman, if your animal damages your neighbour's crops, if you marry a woman from another group without return, and presumably if you assault another, while the phrase 'flesh debts' is important in the necrophagous beliefs of Tiv about witch-craft. In addition, 'many personal relationships are expressed in terms of debt'. Hence Bohannan states that: 'Rather than fit Tiv cases into European categories like tort, contract, property rights, etc., thus hiding the most important thing about them, I have organized the cases in such a way as to illustrate the Tiv notion of debt or *injô*, while allowing us to make the finer distinctions outlined . . .' in considering marriage cases. In his conclusion (at p. 212) he says even more emphatically that though 'we found it possible to say that Tiv "have" actions which resemble tort, contract, or the like . . . were we to do merely that, we should miss the organizing concept which contains several English categories. This categorizing concept is debt. . . . Many torts have debt aspects; most contracts have debt aspects. Tiv "classify" on the notion of debt, as it were, not on the notion of "tort" or "contract".' So far so good, and most interesting. But Bohannan goes on to argue that 'it is not for us to say that Tiv do not understand tort or contract; neither is it for Tiv to say that the English do not understand debt. We must realize that the same general type of material can be classified in several ways. It is, in the long run, the folk classifications that are important to social anthropologists, not the "presence" of torts or contracts which are both folk and analytical concepts in other society.'

This last step is astonishing. Should we not try to understand why the Tiv fail to distinguish as explicitly as later English law does between torts and contract and property suits, and instead think of the relationships established by all transactions and all trespasses on the privileges of others, as 'debt'? I am sure we should and can. Certainly it seems significant that Leach should have stated that the Kachins, in Burma, subsume many relations under the head of 'debt'. Leach writes: 'Almost any kind of legal obligation between two Kachins is likely to be described as a debt. . . . [There is a] close correspondence between the Kachin concept of debts and the anthropologist's concept of social structure. . . .'[60] Dr. Emrys Peters informs me that Bedouin in Cyrenaica similarly use 'debt' to cover wide ranges of social situations. This is true also of the Barotse whom I studied, and it is implied in reports of some other African peoples. It may be true of people like Kalingas and Ifugao who have contracts and torts, but whose ideas about these are not reported. We have clearly here not a problem of Tiv concepts alone, but the general question why at least some peoples at simple levels of technology and commerce subsume under 'debt' the relationships which at more complex levels of technology and commerce are distinguished as contract and tort.[61]

Even at these levels the distinction between 'contract' and 'tort' is a refinement which is of importance in professional legal circles and in courts. In ordinary social life we use 'debt', particularly in the form of 'indebted', as well as 'owe' and 'ought', to define all social obligations. In Latin, *debere* is used 'of general obligation', while *debitum* covers 'obligation' and duty' as well as 'debt'. We could describe the whole of American or British social structure in terms of 'obligations', and hence of 'indebtedness'. The difference in ordinary life between societies can be exaggerated. I even venture to affirm that both Tiv and Kachin have words for 'agreement' and for 'injury', which are the roots of 'contract' and 'tort': all Bantu peoples in Africa and the Bedouin have such words. The distinction between these foundations of dispute, and the differing legal consequences which flow from it, are largely the fruits of a specialized profession of jurists equipped with writing.

Yet the development of this elaborate jurisprudential distinction between contract and tort accompanied a considerable development in political structure and commercial life. Seagle points out that 'even Roman classical jurisprudence . . . never developed general theories of liability in tort and contract', as later jurisprudence was to do.[62] The problem of why in less complex economies all suits tend to be suits for 'debt' is a real one.

Therefore when an anthropologist has set out as clearly as he can the classifications of the tribe he is studying, he has merely taken the first step. Thereafter these classifications have to be related to the types of social bonds which characterize this tribe. This inevitably involves comparative analysis, with translation of concepts from one culture to another. Since the Romans never evolved the kind of elaborate theory of contract and tort that modern Western law has evolved, the categories of modern law are likely to be more developed and refined than those available to the Romans, great jurists though they were. *A fortiori*, these modern categories will be more refined than the categories used by Tiv jurists—and they do have their jurists. This seems to be the pragmatic reason why we can talk about almost all Tiv law in English, but not about these aspects of English law in Tiv. It is possible for us to discuss the Tiv failure to distinguish obligations arising from contractual and tortious relationships—and I would add status relationships—with our more elaborate distinctions, while we could not discuss these more elaborate English distinctions in Tiv, since according to Bohannan it lacks the necessary words. And provided we watch with due care how we apply English concepts, we can do so without injustice to what actually goes on in Tiv life, of which Tiv thought may be an inadequate and sometimes incorrect reflection.

We might indeed find that even current English jurisprudential vocabulary is not refined enough: for finer and more accurate distinction we may have to specialize extant words, or invent new words or phrases. I can only note here that Hohfeld thought we must break up the basic concepts of 'right' and 'duty' into eight constituents for clear analysis, and Hoebel has suggested we adopt this refinement in anthropological recording.[63] Of course a Tiv anthropologist might legitimately try to handle English law in Tiv without these distinctions—if he could. Modern Hebrew has taken over the English words for tort and contract, since these refined concepts were not known in ancient Israelite times.

The classification by a number of tribal peoples of claims in contract, in tort, and over property, all as 'debt' thus points the way to a further problem. In Chapter II of this book I cited Maine's statements that the movement of progressive societies has hitherto been from status to contract, and that the Law of Persons is not separated from the Law of Things 'in the infancy of law'. I showed too how property rights become distinguishing attributes of status relations. We saw further that some transfer of property is necessary not only to mark changes in status, but also is essential to establish a valid contract. Seagle concludes his discussion of the 'great savagery of early law towards debtors' under contracts, by saying that 'they had sinned against the great God of Property, not of Contract. The Hittite Code and ancient Chinese law imposed blood penalties for what we should regard as mere breaches of contract.'[64]

The Tiv are not unique, but on the contrary exemplify well a general condition of tribal law. The same condition is found in much more complex technological systems, and lasts on until contract flowers with the great expansion of commerce.

I myself would push the sin of the defaulter further back than Seagle does: the offence is against the God of Status, as well as Property. Bohannan's data seem to me to show that among the Tiv committing a tort, or entering on a contract, are brought together in that they are conceived to set up a status relationship between the parties, on the image of the most significant relationships of Tiv society—permanent status relations. The process of this expansion I described in Chapter II above. In these relations the indigenous categories emphasize the elements of 'ownership' of rights and 'indebtedness' on obligations involved—i.e. the debt. To sum up, Tiv concentrate on 'debt' because they think of

PLATE XVII. JUDICIAL ACTION

*a.* A Zulu district head delivers judgment.

*b.* The Barotse court in the capital, looking over the steward's section, across the throne dais, towards the councillors.

(see pp. 154 f.)

PLATE XVIII. SOCIAL CONTROL AMONG THE TIV

*a.* A Tiv man about to be in contempt of court.

*b.* Members of a Tiv Lineage gather at the chief's place to 'drum the scandal'.

*Photographs by P. J. Bohannan*

(see pp. 191

the property element which arises out of tort and contract as establishing the relation which has to be adjusted between the parties. Hence 'damages' awarded in court are called 'debt' by the Tiv (and by other African tribes).

Modern social anthropology has concentrated on the monographic analysis of particular societies, and there has been a strong reaction against the crude comparative methods used in the evolutionary theories of the late nineteenth century. But Radcliffe-Brown, who was one of the leaders of that reaction, always insisted that we must work both comparatively and with a developmental morphology. Hoebel has shown how illuminating and effective this can be in the study of tribal law. We cannot understand any African tribe's law in isolation, as a unique expression of the culture of one people, though descriptively it may indeed have a few unique elements or a few unique combinations of common elements. To understand a particular tribe's law we must see it in a comparative frame: and the main outlines of that frame have been drawn by Maine and many other jurists. When we contrast any tribal society with modern society we are also working with a distinction the implications of which have been elaborated by many sociologists and anthropologists: the difference between Durkheim's mechanical and organic solidarities, Tönnies' *gemeinschaft* and *gesellschaft*, von Wiese's sacred and secular societies, Weber's traditional and bureaucratic societies, Stalin's patriarchal and industrial societies, Redfield's folk-society and urban civilization. We neglect the comparative mode of analysis on which they, in these varied terms, reached consensus, at our peril.

There is thus involved here an important problem in the sociology of knowledge: why a particular people have certain ideas about law, government, enforcement, debt, contract and agreement, injury and wrong. We have to try to show the connection between these ideas and other elements in social relations.

Each society may have its own 'jural postulates', as Kohler named them: i.e. tendencies and presuppositions arising from its complex of physical, psychological and socio-economic conditions and the movements which arise from these conditions. But where socio-economic conditions are similar, many postulates will be shared.[65] Hoebel bases his analyses of the systems of law of five tribes on their jural postulates: he does not stress sufficiently the common elements in all tribal systems.[66]

[1] See also his *Government and Politics in Tribal Societies* (1956). He also discusses the problem of legislation about specific topics in his books about Tswana married life, land tenure, labour migration, and in his *A Handbook of Tswana Law and Custom* (1938).

[2] In Barnes, *Politics in a Changing Society* (1954). The subject has been dealt with in general terms in a number of articles. I give examples of legislation, but do not discuss its process, among the Lozi in *Judicial Process among the Barotse* (1955).

[3] Schapera gives examples for the Tswana in his *Tribal Legislation* (1943), p. 7.

[4] Lozi legislation had to be discussed separately in a complex series of councils: see my 'The Lozi of Barotseland' (1951).

[5] See my accounts of the manner in which the presence of the British helped prevent the deposition of a Lozi king attempting to prohibit drinking of beer (*Judicial Process among the Barotse*, 1955, p. 88).

[6] See also on this point my *Judicial Process among the Barotse* (1955).

[7] Ashton, *The Basuto* (1952). These tribes dwell in British Protectorates.

[8] Bohannan, *Justice and Judgment among the Tiv* (of Nigeria) (1957). Since this manuscript was completed, Gulliver has published a fine series of cases among the agricultural Masai of Tanganyika (*Social Control in an African Society*, 1963).

[9] Richardson, *Law and Status among the Kiowa Indians* (1940), which is used by Hoebel in *The Law of Primitive Man* (1954).

[10] Lips, *Naskapi Law: Law and Order in a Hunting Society* (1947).

[11] Pospisil's *Kapauka Papuans and Their Law* (1958) is an account of a people not yet administered by the Dutch in Western New Guinea. The disputes cited are illuminating, but they are too briefly reported for the type of analysis I am considering. Berndt has analysed a number of disputes in *Excess and Restraint: Social Control among a New Guinea Mountain People* (1962).

[12] *The Kalingas* (1949); *Ifugao Law* (1919).

[13] See also below, pp. 235 f.

[14] Among recent writers, I cite only Stone, *The Function and Province of Law* (1947) and Seagle, *The Quest for Law* (1941). Llewellyn has also done so, and with Hoebel makes much of this point in *The Cheyenne Way* (1941).

[15] Homans, *The Human Group* (1950), presents and analyses a number of such studies, including Firth's study of Tikopia kinship relationships. Readers entering on this field for the first time will find W. F. Whyte's *Street Corner Society* (1943) particularly fascinating.

[16] See above, p. 108.

[17] Schapera gives a good account of administrative decisions with the background but not the course of deliberations in *The Political Annals of a Tswana Tribe* (1947).

[18] *Law and the Modern Mind* (1930). I am aware that since Frank wrote much has been written on these topics: but I can best introduce this topic to those who do not know this literature by citing Frank. The whole topic in so far as it has affected social anthropology is discussed in my *Judicial Process among the Barotse* (1955).

[19] Stone, *The Province and Function of Law* (1947), p. 662.

[20] A. R. Radcliffe-Brown, 'Primitive Law' in *Structure and Function in Primitive Society* (1952), at p. 212. Hoebel, *Three Studies in African Law* (1961), pp. 423–4, says the 'attribution of such a working definition of law to Pound does injustice' to Pound; and he traces the taking over of Radcliffe-Brown's statement by other anthropologists. Pound said this, but it certainly gives an unfairly narrow idea of the breadth of his view of 'law'.

[21] I do not consider that either Pound or Radcliffe-Brown implied this, but Radcliffe-Brown did state that societies without courts might be considered to have no law. See Malinowski's comment in his 'Introduction' to Hogbin, *Law and Order in Polynesia* (1934), p. xxiii.

[22] Evans-Pritchard, 'The Nuer of the Southern Sudan' in *African Political Systems* (1940), pp. 293–6; contrast *The Nuer* (1940), pp. 160–5, 168.

[23] Seagle, *The Quest for Law* (1941), p. 34.

[24] See, e.g., what he says about 'the rule of law' in his 'Preface' to *African Political Systems* (1940).

[25] See also Hoebel, *The Law of Primitive Man* (1954), pp. 27–8.

[26] *Crime and Custom in Savage Society* (1926), at p. 58.

[27] *Common-sense in Law* (1913), p. 59.

[28] Goodhart, 'The Importance of a Definition of Law' (1951).

[29] Elias, *The Nature of African Customary Law* (1956).

[30] In *The Judicial Process among the Barotse* (1955).

[31] *Justice and Judgment among the Tiv* (1957).

[32] *Juridical Techniques and the Judicial Process* (1954).

[33] See also his 'Some Aspects of Lovedu Judicial Arrangements' (1939).

[34] Since Tiv believe false swearing may bring down mystical punishment, while false evidence after oath or affirmation is necessary with ourselves principally to found prosecution for perjury.

[35] Points emphasized by Llewellyn and Hoebel, *The Cheyenne Way* (1941), p. 60, and by Seagle, *The Quest for Law* (1941).

[36] 'Introduction to Nyakyusa Law' (1937). The texts at the end of *Good Company* (1951), a book by his wife on this tribe, directed to a different problem, are not detailed enough to help.

[37] *Political Organisation and Law-ways of the Comanche Indians* (1940), pp. 62 f.

[38] After Hoebel, *Law of Primitive Man* (1954), pp. 24 f., 51 f.

[39] *Ifugao Law* (1919), p. 94.

[40] Evans-Pritchard, *The Nuer* (1940) : summarized in Chapter I of my *Custom and Conflict in Africa* (1955). See also Howell, *Manual of Nuer Law* (1954), p. 28.

[41] Cf. the range of words used by Llewellyn and Hoebel to describe functionaries of settlement (*The Cheyenne Way*, 1941) and Seagle's insistence on the difference between adjudication and arbitration (*The Quest for Law*, 1941, p. 61).

[42] *Law of Primitive Man* (1954), pp. 51–2.

[43] *Justice and Judgment among the Tiv* (1957), pp. 142 f.

[44] Some of these citations are from L. and P. Bohannan, *The Tiv of Central Nigeria* (1953).

[45] Provinse, 'The Underlying Sanctions of Plains Indian Culture' (1937), citing from R. H. Lowie's *Social Life of the Crow Indians* (1912).

[46] Gluckman, *The Judicial Process among the Barotse* (1955), p. 79.

[47] See above, p. 91.

[48] See above, p. 204.

[49] See above, p. 181.

[50] *Manual of Nuer Law* (1954), pp. 231, 227.

[51] *Handbook of Tswana Law and Custom* (1938), p. 35 f. The terms among the Lozi are similar, since their homeland was once conquered by a group speaking a related language (see my *Judicial Process among the Barotse*, 1955, Chapter IV).

[52] One of these Lozi words for a right-duty is *swanelo*. cf Schapera's citation of Tswana *tshwanelo*=duty, obligation—and also right.

[53] I myself have the fullest discussion among anthropologists on this problem in my book on the Barotse judicial process (summarized in 'The Reasonable Man in Barotse Law' in my *Order and Rebellion in Tribal Africa*, 1963). Bohannan gives the multiple meanings of Tiv words and defines them acutely, but does not discuss this problem.

[54] Nadel, *The Nuba* (1947), pp. 507–8.

[55] I draw here largely on Malinowski's *Crime and Custom in Savage Society* (1926) and on Homans' *The Human Group* (1951), Chapter XI. Homans acknowledges his own debt to Malinowski.

[56] *Crime and Custom in Savage Society* (1926), p. 126.

[57] Homans, *The Human Group* (1950), pp. 288 f.

[58] *Political Organisation and Law-ways of the Comanche* (1940), pp. 60–1.

[59] *The Nuer* (1940), pp. 117–18.

[60] *Political Systems of Highland Burma* (1954), pp. 144, 154.

[61] I discuss this problem at greater length in my *The Ideas in Barotse Jurisprudence* (1965), Chapter VIII.

[62] *The Quest for Law* (1947), p. 152.

[63] Hoebel, *The Law of Primitive Man* (1954), Chapter IV, where other references are given. Stone, *The Province and Function of Law* (1947), has a full discussion of Hohfeld's conceptions (Chapter V).

[64] *The Quest for Law* (1941), p. 256.

[65] See Stone, *The Province and Function of Law* (1947), pp. 336 f., cited by Hoebel in *The Law of Primitive Man* (1954), p. 6.

[66] In his *The Law of Primitive Man* (1954).

# CHAPTER VI

# MYSTICAL DISTURBANCE AND RITUAL ADJUSTMENT

## MYSTICAL AGENTS AND SOCIAL CONTROL: (1) WITCHES AND SORCERERS

Among the important mechanisms of control and adjustment in tribes are mystical beliefs of various kinds. I here follow Evans-Pritchard who contrasted 'mystical' beliefs as occurring in operations which are out of sensory observation and control, with 'empirical' beliefs which state knowledge of operations in which every step is under sensory observation and control.

These 'mystical' beliefs are of many kinds. The Cheyenne Sacred Medicine Arrows are immediately contaminated by a murder inside the tribe. This contamination itself affects the well-being of the tribe. The would-be husband of his sister-in-law, whom he planned to hand over to his Soldier Society, was, like his fellow-braves, frightened by the prospect of desecrating the Holy Hat. Important ritual objects can thus directly control believers. And objects of this kind, as well as shrines, in many tribes are sanctuaries for the wrongfully accused, and sometimes even for wrongdoers and enemies, just like the Cheyenne Holy Hat. Through large areas of Africa drums are symbols of authority, as among Anuak and Shilluk. An accused Lozi who was threatened with severe punishment was succoured if he could get to the royal drums or drummers, and this sanctuary extended to defeated enemies in battle. These beliefs were spread over much of Central Africa. Lozi royal graves, and other objects and officials related to the kingship, are also sanctuaries from the threats of commoner councillors.

However, though kings themselves were considered to be full of mystical power, this did not protect them against assassination or rebellion. On the contrary, these beliefs exacerbated the dangers to them, if they were held to have failed in their ritual worth or duties. It was the kingship, not the king, that was hedged with divinity. A particular king could desecrate that divinity. Yet royal blood partook of that divinity; and the shedding of the blood of royal princes was considered to be mystically dangerous, so that if they were executed it was by strangling, stifling, drowning, starving or burning. And a man who killed a rebellious prince, or an attacked king, was punished by the master he had thus served.

I cannot here enter into the widespread sanctioning of all types of social relationships by mystical beliefs. This would only be possible in an analysis of the relationships themselves. *A fortiori,* I cannot examine the many aspects of these phenomena which have been analysed by anthropologists. Even if I restrict myself to their role in social control, I have to exclude the manner in which they are part of the fabric of social structure itself. Some parts of this problem have been touched on in the preceding analysis, as, for example, the manner in which myth is a charter of existing arrangements. Ritual ceremonies and magical performances are sometimes so woven into economic activities that they in effect organize and control the timing and the work itself.

In the space I have available to me, I propose therefore to look at how beliefs in certain mystical agents as the causes of misfortune are related to the processes of social control discussed in the previous chapter. These mystical agents are mainly witches and sorcerers, and ancestral and other spirits.

Evans-Pritchard, in his fascinating study of *Witchcraft, Oracles and Magic among the Azande of the Anglo-Egyptian Sudan* (1937),[1] made explicit how these beliefs act as a theory of causation. Briefly, it may be asked of every unfortunate happening: 'how did it happen?' and 'why did it happen?'. The difference between these questions is made clear by one of Evans-Pritchard's examples. If an elephant tramples on and crushes a hunter, the Azande see how he was killed, in terms of the might and weight of the elephant which crushes a man. But Azande also ask, why did this elephant and not another elephant kill this hunter and not another hunter, on this occasion and not another occasion? Or, to take another example, Azande seek shade in the heat of a tropical day by sitting under their granaries which are built above the ground on poles. Termites eat through these supports, and the weight of the granary brings it down, perhaps to crush the people sitting in its shade. Azande see that it is the termites that destroy the supports, and that the weight of a granary crushes a man as the weight of an elephant does. But they ask again, why did the granary fall at the particular moment when those particular people were sitting under it? Azande answer these 'why's' by saying that a witch malevolently caused that elephant to kill that hunter on that occasion, or that granary to fall just at the moment when those people were sitting in its shade.

Azande observe clearly and generalize about the empirical 'how's' of misfortunes: a heavy weight crushes a man. Wild beasts attack hunters. But they also try to explain what has been called 'the particularity' of misfortunes—why particular persons suffer them. Here beliefs in witchcraft enter. Similarly, beliefs in witchcraft explain why one man's crops fail and not another's, why a man falls ill when he has previously been well and his fellows are still well, why a small wound festers instead of healing, why a poisonous snake bites a man so that he dies. Among the Azande the belief is also used to explain why particular warriors and not others, are killed by particular enemies, in battle. Clearly those slain were killed by enemy spears: but an internal enemy, the witch, has caused this particular death. And this witch is held responsible in internal tribal relations.

These beliefs—or similar ones—are not found among tribal peoples because of any biogenetic difference between them and ourselves. It is only a brief 300 years since legislation outlawed accusations of witchcraft in England. Some 150 years ago there was the outbreak of accusation in Massachusetts. Chapter II related the beliefs to the economic relations of tribal society: seemingly the full flowering of the industrial revolution was required to eliminate them. Only then do people ascribe their particular misfortunes to the operation of chance, when scientific, empirical explanations have had their say.

Thus when an Azande suffers a misfortune, his society's beliefs, with which he has been reared, offer him a responsible agent in the form of a witch. He seeks the particular witch responsible for his immediate misfortunes by consulting oracles or a diviner or witch-detective (a better term than witch-doctor). These modes of seeking for the witch bring out that beliefs in witchcraft are a theory of morality as well as a theory of particular causation. When the sufferer consults an oracle he thinks of people who have cause to wish him harm and puts their names to the oracle. A typical oracle consists in giving a substance, collected and prepared with many taboos, to chickens while asking questions, such as whether a particular person is the witch you are seeking. The chicken dies or vomits the substance to answer 'yes' or 'no' to the question. The substance, used widely in Africa, is probably a strychnine which is 'haphazard' in its effects, since the operator cannot determine what quantity of the substance will be lethal or will be vomited.

A man might, if accused, claim the right to take the oracle-substance himself, or have it administered to his son, to test the validity of the accusation. In other tribes, it was more common for the oracle-substance to be thus given to suspected witches or evildoers. I quote here an account from David Livingstone's record of this institution, for the pungency of his conclusion. He described it in Chapter XXX of his *Missionary Travels and Researches in South Africa* (1857). 'As we came away from Monina's village, a witch-doctor, who had been sent for, arrived, and all Monina's wives went forth into the fields that morning fasting. There they would be compelled to drink an infusion of a plant named "goho", which is used as an ordeal. This ceremony is called "muavi". . . . When a man suspects any of his wives have bewitched him, he sends for the witch-doctor, and all the wives go forth into the field, and remain fasting till that person has made an infusion of the plant. They all drink it, each one holding up her hand to heaven in attestation of her innocency. Those who vomit it are considered innocent, while those whom it purges are pronounced guilty, and put to death by burning. The innocent return to their homes, and slaughter a cock as thank-offering to their guardian spirits.' Livingstone says all tribes of the Zambezi had the ordeal. The Barotse administered medicine to a cock or a dog. He comments: 'I happened to mention to my own men the water-test for witches formerly in use in Scotland: the supposed witch, being bound hand and foot, was thrown into a pond; if she floated, she was considered guilty, taken out, and burned; but if she sank and was drowned, she was pronounced innocent. The wisdom of my ancestors,' he concludes, 'excited as much wonder in their minds, as their custom did in mine.'

In the Azande chicken-oracle procedure, the consultant puts to the test the names of several personal enemies. Hence in the end a man who, he believes, has cause to wish him ill, will be indicated as the witch. Now early observers had noted that a man almost always accused a personal enemy of bewitching him. They therefore concluded that the whole business was fraudulent.

Evans-Pritchard demonstrated that this alleged fraudulence was essential to the reasonableness and credibility of the system of beliefs.

An Azande witch is a person with a certain black substance in his intestines, which can be seen after an autopsy. (It is probably a passing state of digestion.) A man may not be aware that he possesses this substance, which is the power of witchcraft. Even if he has this power it will remain 'cool' inside him unless he entertains vicious feelings against a fellow. But if he hates another, feels anger against him, or is envious of him, grudging him good fortune and resenting his success, the witchcraft becomes 'hot'. Its 'soul' will leave the witch's body and consume the internal organs of the other to make him ill, or cause him other misfortune. The power of witchcraft is believed by Azande to be inherited in the patrilineal line, so a man is not himself responsible for possessing this power. But if he is a good man it will harm no one. Vicious feelings set witchcraft to work. This is why a sufferer seeks among his personal enemies for the witch who has caused his misfortune.    Azande beliefs in witchcraft are a theory of morality, and they condemn the same vicious feelings that we regard as sinful.

Witchcraft beliefs condemn these vicious feelings even more severely than we do. For while vicious feelings alone are not punishable in our courts, in witchcraft beliefs these vicious feelings are endowed with a mystical power, by virtue of which they can, without the knowledge or will of their bearer, cause misfortune to others, who can seek redress. But witchcraft cannot be used to account for one's own moral offences or palpable lack of skill.

The morality which is implicit in witchcraft beliefs is shown even more clearly if we look at Azande beliefs in 'sorcery', which Evans-Pritchard distinguishes from 'witchcraft'.[2] A witch's ill feelings are endowed with power to harm others by the substance in his belly. But a man may wish another harm without possessing this substance. Then he can only harm his enemy either directly and openly, or by resorting to sorcery, which involves the deliberate decision to use noxious magic. This is, of course, a belief: it is not certain that anyone in fact uses sorcery.

Sorcery is used by Azande to account for sudden illnesses and deaths. Witchcraft takes longer to achieve its object. Sorcery may account for cases in which the corpse of an alleged witch on autopsy discloses no sign of witchcraft substance, though I do not remember Evans-Pritchard making this point in his very full and careful analysis of how beliefs in witchcraft, oracles and magic accommodate and absorb the evidence that appears to show them to be invalid. He shows there, among other things, how experiences of this kind are explained as due to breach of taboo in preparing the oracle-substance which makes a false detection. Each apparent failure is thus rationalized in terms of other mystical beliefs. Thus the whole system is bolstered by what outsiders may see as contradicting evidence.

Among the Azande, if a sufferer's oracles say that a particular man, X, is causing him harm, he sends an intermediary with the wing of the chicken that died to X's name, to X. X is then constrained by good manners to blow water over the wing, while he states that he was ignorant of causing harm and if he has been doing so, he hereby 'cools' his witchcraft. The formula is effective, even if the accused does not accept the charge as valid. If a death is in question, the verdict of the dead person's kin's oracles must be confirmed by the chief's oracles: the accused used to pay damages. After the Anglo-Egyptian Government forbade accusations, the deceased's kin made vengeance-magic to punish the witch; and as people died in the neighbourhood, the oracle was asked if each was the guilty witch, till an affirmative answer was obtained.

In one form or another, this pattern of beliefs and similar techniques of divination has been analysed through most of the tribes of the world. Some peoples do not as clearly separate sorcery and witchcraft. Among others, such as Nyakyusa or Tiv, there is a single power which the possessor, when secularly powerful, can use for social advantage, to defend his fellows against witches and to procure good for the community, or he can use the power for evil gain.[3]

In Chapter II, I set out the general conditions in which beliefs of this kind operate. Witchcraft beliefs condemn the unduly prosperous: the Bemba who finds three beehives in the woods is a witch. For another aspect of witchcraft beliefs is that a witch is believed to be able mystically to filch from his fellows, so that he has better crops than they have, catches more fish, kills more game. These beliefs are related to the basic egalitarianism of the economy. The beliefs tend to maintain the standard. For he who is too prosperous will fear the envy—and the witchcraft—of his fellows, while they will suspect him of witchcraft.

The beliefs also sanction the general code of morality, by putting pressure on individuals to control their feelings—or at least to avoid showing vicious feeling openly. For if you show anger, or hatred, or jealousy, against a man, and he then suffers a misfortune, you may be accused of bewitching him.[4] Correspondingly, it behoves you to act well to your fellows, lest you provoke them to bewitch you.

Witchcraft beliefs, however, do not operate in all social relationships. Among the Azande accusations are excluded from among the group of patrilineal kinsmen who have to avenge one another's death. The belief in the patrilineal inheritance of witchcraft is presumably connected with this duty. An Azande commoner does not accuse nobles, not only because he is afraid to, but also because their behaviour to one another is determined by notions of status. Men do not accuse women. But witchcraft is believed only to operate over short distances, and men accuse their neighbours: for 'people are most likely to quarrel with those with whom they come into closest contact, when the contact is not softened by sentiments of kinship or is not buffered by distinctions of age, sex and class' (Evans-Pritchard on Azande only, in his book at pp. 104–5).

Subsequent research in Africa has confirmed Evans-Pritchard's analysis of the logic of witchcraft beliefs, and the situations in which they operate. Great variation has been found in the categories of persons accused in various tribes. For example, most of the tribes of Rhodesia and Nyasaland show the opposite situation from the Azande: a majority of accusations are made against closely related kin, within the effective corporate group whose members hold property together and should support one another. Further south, among the Zulu, men of the equivalent patrilineal group do not accuse one another: common targets of accusation are the women who have married into this group. They may accuse one another, or be accused by mother-in-law, brother-in-law or sister-in-law. To the north of the Zulu, the Swazi and the Tsonga believe that the power of witchcraft is inherited like haemophilia: it is brought in by wives who transmit it to their children. Daughters take the power into the groups where they marry. Sons cannot pass it on.

A series of fascinating problems, on which considerable work is now being done, resides in the relation of the variations in beliefs, and the varying incidence of accusations, to other elements in the social organization of different tribes. It does not look as if any correlations will be simple and straightforward. For accusations vary in the extent to which they reflect direct animosities. Some arise out of open quarrels, which occur in chance encounters: jealousy over a girl, a quarrel over land, and so forth. Other accusations are made in standardized situations of competition, as between the fellow-wives of one man, between seekers after political office, or nowadays employees of the same white man. Yet other accusations reflect deeper conflicts in the social organization. I illustrate this last situation from the Zulu.

## WOMEN WITCHES

The Zulu are organized in patrilineal lineages, whose men marry ideally several wives. Each wife has an established position ranked in relation to her fellow-wives, and her rank largely determines the property and the position her sons will inherit. Hence when a woman accuses her co-wife of witchcraft she may act out of jealousy not only for their joint husband's favours, but also for the position of her sons. But wives are also accused by mother-in-law, brother-in-law, and sister-in-law. They are regarded as bringing quarrels into the ideally united patrilineal group. And in fact they do introduce disunity into this group. For each man is largely identified with his brothers—and beyond them his cousins—until he develops his own interests as an individual. These personal interests burgeon when he marries and has children, and begins to look to their welfare and to see them as the nucleus of a group which will establish his independence from his patrilineal kinsmen. Hence it is the wives who marry into the group that ultimately, by producing children, will lead to its break-up. Yet the highest duty of a wife is to bear children in order to maintain the line and strengthen the group. She suffers severely if she is barren. In the very course of fulfilling her creative duty and bearing children to maintain the patrilineal group, she sows the seeds of dissension and break-up in the group.

Some of us are working on the line that mystical beliefs and ritual practices are most significant where they 'cloak' fundamental discrepancies and conflicts between the principles on which a society is based, or between conflicting processes set at work in a society by an apparently definite single principle. Clearly we have such a situation here, focusing on the position of a Zulu wife. Note that I use 'conflict' to describe the incompatability and inconsistency between the duty of a wife to be fruitful and to strengthen her husband's group, and the actual resulting divisiveness of her fruitfulness. In this situation mystical belief ascribes an inherent evil of witchcraft to the woman which she obtains by acquiring animals and fabulous beings as sexual familiars. Out of this power she begins to take the health and lives of the group. Accusations are made against her by the men with whom her husband competes in the interests of her children and by her mother-in-law who represents the unity of the family. Her sister-in-law may accuse her for slightly different reasons: the sister-in-law has an interest in the continued unity of her brothers' group. Fortes shows that the Tallensi believe that there is a kind of ritual antipathy, handled by taboos, between a man and his sister. He relates this to the exclusion of the sister, by virtue of her sex, from the heritage to which her patrilineal descent otherwise would entitle her. Her position is the obverse of the wife who marries in. His analysis may be the clue to why sisters of the patrilineage accuse its wives of witchcraft.[5]

Among the Zulu the inherent evil of women is also represented in a whole series of other beliefs. Her menstrual blood, the source of her ambivalent fertility, is highly dangerous to all things virile, as is the blood of birth. Female ancestral-spirits are capriciously evil, and continue to send misfortunes even after sacrifices have been made to them: male ancestral-spirits send merited misfortune, and lift it after sacrifice has been offered to them. Dangerous forked lightning is female: sheet lightning is male. In short, men have deliberately to seek evil by palpably harming others, or by using sorcery: women have evil in their very nature.[6]

Women also have good in their very nature. Their fertility is highly regarded, and is often a source of mystical prosperity. It is the ambivalence of woman's ritual position that I am stressing. Directly it seems to reflect the ambivalence in her social position.

Those particular beliefs are important in the whole process of development of Zulu groups. For when a man's kin allege that his wife is bewitching them, he is able—if not compelled—to move off and establish his independence. Thereafter he can resume relations with his kin in a more attenuated form.[7] Or a man is entitled to move because a witch is attacking his wife and children.

This situation occurs among most neighbouring peoples who have patrilineal lineages like the Zulu, but according to reports the inherent evil of women is not so elaborately defined. Moreover, while *most* 'witches' are women, men also are accused of this offence.

There is evidence to suggest that a basic conflict inheres in women's position in all tribal societies, matrilineal and patrilineal. For while Zulu believe wives make mischief between brothers, so among the matrilineal Yao it is said that a man's difficulties arise from his problem of balancing his obligations to his wife and his obligations to his sisters. Sorcery or witchcraft enters a matrilineage because of backbiting among the women, even though frequent accusations are made by brother against brother, or sister's son against mother's brother, as they struggle to get control of the women of the matrilineage, in order to acquire a following.[8]

These beliefs may be largely formulated by the men of the tribe. But the tendency for witches to be women while men are sorcerers or wizards is so widely distributed throughout the world, that it must surely be related to conditions which are common to many societies. Perhaps the basic conflict lies in the fact that women bear the children who are to be the competitive heirs for social power, position and property that are formally held by men.

An important variant of this situation has been well analysed by Nadel for the Nupe. Among them, women are evil night-witches, while men are good day-witches. Women-witches kill, but must secure the permission and help of a male witch. Nadel shows that the position of many women in Nupe is quite out of accord with the formal ideal, that a woman should be a faithful wife staying at home as a subordinate to care for her husband and raise her children. In fact, many women by trade have become wealthy, and finance their husbands and sons (which also is approved); as they travel the country to trade they practise prostitution and use abortifacients to avoid having children. The conflict between ideal and the reality, Nadel suggests, produces the ascription by men of witchcraft power to women.[9]

The problem of why some societies select women as the main witches, while others apparently similar in organization select men, is still under investigation.[10] Similar witchcraft beliefs are not found always with the same types of social relations, though there is much congruence. In many patrilineal societies witchcraft beliefs are associated with the female line and women—but not in all. It seems to me that where this association does occur, femaleness also is associated with a much wider mystical evil. Among the Zulu this evil resides in menstrual blood, in lightning, in female ancestral spirits. The Tallensi, highly organized around the patrilineal line, ascribe almost all of their fortune and ill-fortune to patrilineal ancestors and to the Earth. But what there is of belief in witchcraft is focused on the purely matrilineal line, a line in which relationship produces the friendliest and least constricting of kinship relationships. In addition any person whose words or actions, even indirectly and without his awareness, lead to fighting which produces killing, bears a heavy mystical responsibility (*tyuk*). This may suddenly produce misfortune for him and his line, to be revealed by the diviner. A man who bears this *tyuk* guilt must be ritually cleansed from it. This guilt affects all persons related to the guilty man by uterine (matrilineal) ties. It is not inherited by child from mother, as witchcraft is: *tyuk* is rather a contagion which may suddenly become active in one of the uterine kin to produce further *tyuk* guilt.[11] Where men are believed to be witches, they go naked, commit incest, sodomy and bestiality, defecate in houses, have animal familiars and become were-animals, eat corpses: but maleness itself is not impregnated with evil.

## MYSTICAL AGENTS AND SOCIAL CONTROL: (2) ANCESTRAL SPIRITS

Witches are not the only answer to the problem, why have I suffered misfortune? Or in reverse, absence of witchcraft does not explain why I am prospering. The Tallensi ascribe the varying course of a man's good and ill fortune almost entirely to his ancestral spirits, and to his Personal Destiny or 'Fate' which is associated with his ancestral spirits.[12] Witchcraft is relatively unimportant. Other peoples, like the Nuer, also emphasize ancestral spirits and God. Other tribes, like the Zulu, select between witchcraft, sorcery, and ancestors, with God as an ultimate residual explanation of major misfortunes. Community disasters, as among the Plateau Tonga, may be accounted for by beliefs different from those that account for personal misfortune. In yet other tribes various 'wild' spirits, or gods, or fetishes, are believed to act in these ways. Breach of taboo, or the curse of a wronged senior person, may also be referred to. Why there should be these differences in the beliefs of various tribes, we cannot yet say; and we may never know the answer.

In the background of our understanding of witchcraft accusations, I can deal more briefly with a selected few of these other agents and causes. Ancestral spirits are believed to cause misfortunes for two kinds of wrongful action. The first is default in performance of obligations due to the spirits themselves. They are entitled to receive offerings and sacrifices on certain prescribed occasions during the round of the year's activities, and also in the development of an individual's life. If these offerings are omitted, they send illness or other misfortune. The second type of action which they penalize is default in performance of kinship obligations. Here we are particularly concerned with this kind of default.

It is difficult to state in general terms, what the role of ancestral-spirits is in safeguarding kinship norms. They are not always directly concerned with the immediate fulfilment of each duty owed to a particular kinsman. Their wrath seems to be provoked rather by actions which deny the validity of kinship itself, as establishing a network of mutual rights and duties between the ancestors' descendants. These rights and duties depend mainly on recognition of the superiority of elders of various kinds, since they represent among the living the power of the ancestors, whom they will in due course join. They alone can approach the ancestors on behalf of their junior dependants.[13] Hence an ancestral spirit is divined as the cause of misfortune when some descendant acts so as to deny his dependence on his senior kinsman. Among the living, this belief appears in the powerful effects of a curse by such a kinsman.

The cult of tendence on the ancestors serves to control relationships among living kinsmen in another way. In order to make offerings and sacrifices to the spirits all the kinsmen and women involved must assemble together. To eat of the sacrifice they must be in amity. Bad feelings and grievances in the heart spoil the sacrifice and endanger the living. Therefore a sacrifice is the appropriate occasion at which those who feel themselves to be wronged should state their grievances, in order that these may be discussed and if valid may be remedied. Fortes writes that 'to sacrifice together is the most binding form of ritual collaboration. According to the ethical and religious ideas of the Tallensi, it is totally incompatible with a state of hostility—that is, with an open breach of good relations. Personal feelings are of secondary importance in this connection. One can sacrifice with a person whom one despises or dislikes, as long as these feelings do not lead to an infringement of the ties of mutual obligation. . . . To sacrifice together means not only to acknowledge a common spiritual tutelage, but also to eat together of the sacrifice; in short to unite in a sacrament.'[14]

The effect of these rules is, that, until a section of a kinship group is sufficiently independent to make its own direct approaches to the ancestors, its members must be in sufficiently amicable relations with one another to join in common sacrifice. The establishment of the right to sacrifice independently marks a significant shift of social ties with their prescribed obligations. If is often a shift, and not a breaking, of ties: for the newly independent group may require the attendance of at least representatives of its former associates at major sacrifices. Indeed, as among the Tallensi this requirement is the main sanction for the superordinate network of relationships which binds the Tallensi into a polity.[15]

The ancestral-cult and its sacrifices mark both foci of unity and of distinction and more distant relationship among the groupings of kin in a tribal society. These foci change as men are born, mature, procreate children, and die: and these generational changes influence deeply the processes of development and struggle in groups. The ancestral-cult and its associated beliefs do not picture a straightforward relation between united congregations of kinsmen and their begetters. The inevitable changes in the structure of groups which result from the biological flow of a human population through a set social structure is productive of conflict, in which men and women come into dispute where they are both, by different rules, in the right. A man should always acknowledge his father's superiority: a man is entitled equally to his own measure of independence. Brothers should remain united: each brother has his independent interests. This conflict between social principles is obscured from the society's members by the raising of the axioms of kinship to a mystical plane where they are beyond question. There the principles are separately validated by ancestral power. But the ambivalence

PLATE XIX. POLITICAL ORGANIZATION

*a.* A Barotse councillor at the capital instructs the heir to a headmanship and his followers on the principle of good rule.

*b.* The Barotse councillor joins the heir and his followers in giving the royal salute to the king's palace.

(see pp. 216 f.)

PLATE XX. TALLENSI RITUAL

*a.* Prayer preceding Sacrifice to Clan-founder. An episode in the great sacrifice to Mosuor and the other founding ancestors, at Tongo, in 1936. Men of the sub-clan assembled at Mosuor's grave (stones in the foreground) and tree shrine (baobab tree). The photograph was taken as the prayer preceding sacrifice was being offered.

*b.* The widest politico-ritual community includes all the Tallensi. Part of the vast gathering people from all over Taleland who come to take part in or watch the concluding ceremon and dances of the Golib Festival. Note the dust cloud raised by the dancers.

*Photographs by M. Fortes*

(see pp. 22

remains. There is some element of capriciousness in all ancestral power: for ancestors may be divined as striking with misfortune even the apparently most upright. The cause of their wrath may be traced to fictitious neglect of themselves, or to incidents far in the past, even unto distant generations. Out of the past various ancestors may strike at one for neglect of dues to them or to the living. There is 'competition' even among ancestors.

## THE SELECTIVE ROLE OF DIVINATION AND ORACLE

When a misfortune occurs the sufferer or his close fellows may ascribe it immediately to infringement of a particular taboo, or omission of a ritual duty, or breach of a secular obligation. Divination is used to check this assumption. More often, any of several types of mystical agent may be causing the trouble. It is necessary to determine first what type, and second which agent within that category, is responsible. Divination, itself operating by mystical means, selects from among possible mystical agencies.

Divination operates in many ways. A detector of mystical agencies may speak out directly with insight strengthened by a possessing spirit or treatment with magical substances. Divination may proceed, as with the Azande 'chicken-oracle', through step by step selection. Or, at the other extreme, a diviner may have a whole collection of objects in the form of bones, shells, stone, and carved figurines which he casts. He reads the patterns in which they fall in relation to one another. Of the Tsonga diviner's collection, mainly of bones and shells, Junod wrote: 'It is a résumé of their whole social order, of all their institutions, and the bones, when they fall, provide them with an instantaneous picture of all that may befall them.'[16] For the bones represent males and females of different ages and status; the chief and princes; princesses and queens; foreign enemies; the tribe itself; warriors and loose women; wizards; doctors; villages; White people; ancestors; the mysterious power of Heaven; good fortune and ill fortune; maleness and its weapons and its qualities; female- ness and pregnancy and marriage cattle; medicines; luck and riches. The symbolism of the bones is very complex, and all I can note here is that the same important personages or qualities are represented by different 'bones', while one bone may represent several of these. For example, an ankle-bone of the hyaena represents counsellors, sycophants and parasites who batten on the powerful as the hyaena does on the lion; wizards because they eat the flesh of people which they steal, as the hyaena steals; the ancestral-spirits because they hide in their graves as the hyaena does in holes; and the chief himself, for he takes people's property and they cannot recover it, any more than one can recover what the hyaena has stolen. The multiple sets of symbolism represent the multiple and ambivalent effects of these real and reputed personages in social life. The chief's power has arbitrary aspects of tyranny, like the blows of wizards and spirits: its beneficent aspects are represented in other bones. Again, while the male duiker buck's bones represent warriors, who spill blood, the female's bone represents loose women, possibly because they both waste their own femaleness and cause the spilling of blood.[17]

More complicated divining apparatus of this kind thus brings out vividly the manner in which the multiple aspects, positive and negative, of all social persons and institutions are reflected among mystical agents. Hence a divinatory séance over a misfortune consists in working out what particular mystical cause has to be selected to be appropriately redressed. The selection is made in terms of alignments of relations in the group at that particular moment. In any village or group of kinsfolk the multiple cross-ties between persons produce inevitably a large number of current animosities, strains and quarrels, and frequent actual or felt derelictions from fulfilment of obligation. Since members of the group are variously associated with 'outsiders' in terms of kinship, common age-set membership, and political ties, these outsiders may also have an interest in the course of divination. A divinatory séance may therefore become in effect a complex jockeying process in which interested parties try to shift responsibility for the mischance of themselves and their protégé(e)s on to others. This process goes on even though all are interested in isolating the correct mystical agent, in order to put an end to the misfortune and restore chances of good fortune.[1]

Bohannan has a number of excellent accounts of this solemn and ritually controlled jockeying at Tiv séances.[19] These always are concerned with disturbances among relatively closely related persons, and the concatenations of possibilities are too complex for me to discuss here. Briefly, each party involved, and the set of his age-mates from the area, which represents him, consults a diviner in advance and brings to the séance the diviner's selection of possible causes of mystical disturbance, as related to misfortunes and quarrels in the group. Deaths and illnesses provoke séances, or brothers may be quarrelling over their rights to control the marriages of women or to inherit wives of dead members.

As the elders investigate these problems they may light on the omission of a ritual to a fetish, or witchcraft, as the cause of difficulty, or perhaps as the future outcome of some dispute among the close kin. In the course of the proceedings, they endeavour to set aright secular disorder: but the proceeding always end with a ritual. The characteristic of these proceedings, says Bohannan, is that they 'settle disputes between persons in relationships that can never be broken or ignored. The function of a moot [séance] is only incidentally the settlement of particular grievances: its main function is to make it possible for people who must live together to do so harmoniously. Marriage ties can be broken; marriage disputes can be heard in court. But ties of agnation [patriliny] are unchangeable, and are the basis of all citizenship rights of adult males. One must either get along with one's agnates or become an expatriate. . . . Tiv recognize that moots do settle disputes. But they also insist that the real purpose of the moot is not to settle the dispute itself but to allay the mystical factors which are behind it, which caused it, or which it caused.' Hence every moot ends with a ritual, either to allay or to be prophylactic against these mystical factors.

The elders who control the discussion are themselves interested in the internal politics of the group. They have also been involved in quarrels and alliances with the protagonists and with dead men and women who belonged to the group. They may have claims on the property and women discussed. Hence there is struggle for position, and not only 'judicial' assessment of facts in the light of law, though this is present. In an impasse, nothing may be done: and in the end divination decides the issue.

The decisive role of divination comes out in the fifth and final séance which Bohannan analyses. This séance followed on a man's death. The deceased's full sister had died three or four months earlier, and the divination said she had been killed by *tsav* (witchcraft or elders' powers used for community ends). Nobody asked the divining apparatus whose 'witchcraft-power' it was. When an autopsy was performed on her, she had no *tsav* (black substance) on her heart. It was clear that she did not die from her own *tsav*, but either from the *tsav* of an evil witch or from the *tsav* of the elders who needed a life for the community's fertility and prosperity.[20]     Loud and bitter accusations were made by her close male kinsmen, and a special pot 'of ashes and medicines [magical substances] which is the symbol of right and justice' was used to seek out the unnamed wrongdoer. He or she was 'cursed' upon the pot. When the woman's death was followed by her brother's illness and death, it was necessary to determine whether he was killed by the righteous medicine and his own evil, or as a sacrifice by his patrilineal kin, or by the witchcraft of one of them. Only autopsy on his corpse could settle the matter. His kinsmen opposed the autopsy. They protested that they knew he was innocent, and it was unnecessary. His age-set, composed of age-mates from outside the village, insisted on the autopsy. They protested that they knew he was innocent and demanded that his innocence be proved. Bohannan does not make this point clearly; but it seems that the kinsmen's objections to the autopsy are prescribed by custom and required of them. We may note that if he had been found to be 'innocent' of *tsav* on his heart the festering problem of which one of them was guilty would have remained. The age-set, who are outsiders, force the autopsy on the seemingly, and perhaps at heart really, reluctant kin. (Bohannan[21] says the age-set usually acts thus, or failing it representatives of the person's mother's lineage.) Outsiders here again seem to act to clarify moral relations within the kin-group. Perhaps something like this lies behind Evans-Pritchard's bare statement that in the past among the Azande a blood brother conducted an autopsy to test for witchcraft and was rewarded and cleansed if he found witchcraft.

The autopsy was performed by the leader of the dead man's age-set. It disclosed two 'sacks' of blood on the heart, one dull blue, the other bright red. The leader of the age-set pointed these out to the anthropologist as *tsav*, and added: 'But *tsav* need not be evil. But this *tsav* is evil. It is large and of two colours.' Slowly it was agreed that the man had been killed by the righteous medicines of justice which punished his witchcraft. The deceased's age-set, after argument with the agnates, symbolically took under its protection his younger brother and widows. The 'justice-seeking' medicine was then invoked again against anyone who had 'done evil deeds in this matter'.

This summary account cannot do justice to Bohannan's graphic description and illuminating analysis of these Tiv séances. He brings out the process of dispute arising from self-interest and from assertion of various rights in terms of complex relations, reaching back into the past, between the parties. He discusses the full duality of '*tsav*' whose potential power for good and evil is itself symbolic of the ambivalence inherent in social life.

M. Wilson in her *Good Company* (1951) similarly brings out for another tribe, the Nyakyusa, how closely associated may be the source of witchcraft and of righteous mystical defence. Among the Nyakyusa witches exist as pythons in the stomachs of certain individuals. Witches lust for meat and milk: and they kill individuals by gnawing at their insides. But they select as their victims those against whom they have a grudge, attacking those with whom they have quarrelled or of whose success or popularity they are jealous. People are protected against this evil by 'defenders' who punish the witches. The defender's power comes also from a python—but only one—in his stomach. The defenders punish not only witches, but also those who fail to provide prescribed feasts, and those who behave disrespectfully towards parents and parents-in-law as well as women who act thus to their husbands. They also punish incest and too frequent pregnancies. They attack the guilty witch by chilling him (or her) or striking him with fever. He may complain of 'witchcraft', but other people will consider he has sinned and been overtaken by just retribution.

Not all tribes associate the power of what we can call 'good magic' so closely with the power of witchcraft and sorcery in a form of belief where the single substance has potentiality both for good for the community and for selfish gain or lustful killing. But belief in the possibility that the good magician—the doctor—may at the request of a client or a chief use his power nefariously is widespread in Africa, Asia, Melanesia, and North America. The belief brings out what is a reality in the process of social life. The balance between legitimate ambition and lust for power, between good industriousness and over-conspicuous selfish success, between reasonable and too much luck, between admired skill and the exhibition of others' deficiencies, is a very fine one. In addition, as I described in Chapter II, the problem of distributing one's scarce means to satisfy all one's watchful and numerous fellows' rightful demands, and those of one's spirits, is almost insoluble. As people in these intricately interrelated groups try to satisfy their legitimate self-interests and meet the legitimate claims of others, an equally intricate web of quarrel and dispute is created. Upright behaviour to some becomes defaulting to others. As Lienhardt put it, one makes enemies in the course of making friends. Striving for legitimate power becomes rising at others' expense. The envy of witches, and righteous or capricious affliction by spirits, are equally possible explanations of misfortunes. Wilson relates the form of these beliefs to the fact that Nyakyusa dwell in villages composed mostly of unrelated age-mates, while cattle are 'owned' by members of patrilineages dispersed through several such villages. These kinsmen owe many duties to one another. There is an inherent 'conflict' between the claims of kinsmen and of age-mates within one village to one's cattle, one's hospitality, one's help.

The closeness of ancestral right and wrongful witchcraft to one another has been clearly demonstrated in Middleton's analysis of *Lugbara Religion* (1960) in Uganda. 'Lugbara realize that men are ambitious and want authority. They also realize that it is proper for them to do so, but that some men try to acquire authority which they should not possess and that others abuse it when they have acquired it.' The dilemma is: when should a man properly acquire and possess authority? As men mature they should seek it, and this breeds competition with elders. According to one's position in the society, one's judgment on the proper point when authority is due may vary. And when is a man with authority abusing it?

The Lugbara frame these universal problems in mystical terms. An elder in the system of patrilineal lineages—groups of kinsmen related through males—has the power legitimately to curse his subordinates by invoking ancestral spirits' wrath against them when they slight or offend him. Hence when such a subordinate (or his dependants) suffers a misfortune, his elders and even his competing near-equals will strive to be divined as the righteous invoker of ancestral wrath. This validates a claim to be in authority over the subordinate. If a lineage segment is to be independent, then its senior male must resist such a divination, and perhaps be himself proclaimed as the invoker of ancestral wrath against his and his competitors' common dependant. Conversely, if it seems that the power of a competitor has caused the misfortune, the struggle is to have this declared to be a use of witchcraft, and not a rightful 'curse'.

It is painful for me to compress here into a few words an elaborate analysis—as I have also had to do with the work of other of my colleagues. Middleton expounds this and other themes with rich, detailed analysis of the history of particular groups. He shows how accusations shift and are countered as the relations within groups of this kind change through time. As men mature and marry and produce children, segments within the lineage become large enough to seek independence. They also begin to require more land than is available to them while they live with their fellows in one village. Social values demand that they remain together: ecological exigencies and 'legitimate ambition' drive them apart. This deep conflict of social principles is worked out in terms of the compulsions exerted by mystical agents, which reflect actual quarrels and disputes in social life.

## The 'Extended-case' Method

Early in the last chapter, I said that as my own generation of anthropologists analysed the morphology of tribal social structures, we gave as supporting evidence 'apt and isolated illustrations'. In these terms Evans-Pritchard worked out how witchcraft, oracles, and magic operated as an interconnected system embodying philosophies of causation and morality. Much work still remains to be done on these lines. But my citations from Bohannan, M. Wilson, and Middleton show that recently some field anthropologists are giving more than a generalized analysis of the system of beliefs and their consistency with secular relations and activities. They are now analysing the development of social relations themselves, under the conflicting pressures of discrepant principles and values, as the generations change and new persons come to maturity. If we view these relations through a longish period of time, we see how various parties and supporters operate and manipulate mystical beliefs of varied kinds to serve their interests. The beliefs are seen in dynamic process within day-to-day social life, and the creation and burgeoning of new groups and relationships. For want of a better term I call this the 'extended-case method'. Let me state now, explicitly, that I do not believe that the values of this type of analysis negate the values of other types of analysis, including more static comparative analysis.

Several books mark the development of this new type of analysis. First, while social anthropologists continue to seek for generalizations, as most historians do not, studies of tribal political systems now more commonly embody a historical treatment. This is exemplified, for example, in Evans-Pritchard's book on

*The Sanusi of Cyrenaica* (1949), Barnes' on *The Politics of a Changing Society* (Ngoni) (1954), Schapera's on *Government and Politics in Tribal Societies* (1956), Southall's on *Alur Society* (*c.* 1956), Fallers' on *Bantu Bureaucracy* (Soga) (*c.* 1956), and M. G. Smith's on *Government in Zazzau* (1960). As far as our present problem is concerned, a critical book was Mitchell's on *The Yao Village* (1956).

Mitchell surveyed a large number of Yao villages, and found that they varied in composition. Some consisted of single matrilineages, others were composed of a number of matrilineages linked in various ways to the village headman. Most Yao men have to go to live at their wives' villages. But the headman is allowed to bring his wife—or wives—to his village. Each wife produces a matrilineage of her own children, and her daughters' children. This is distinctive from the lineage descended from the headman's mother, with its segments proliferating from each female descendant. When a headman dies, his younger brother or sister's son succeeds him. The new headman lacks the authority of a husband and father over the associated lineages, each under the 'wardenship' of one of its own males. In time the latter will move out to form simple villages of single matrilineages, reducing the internal complexity of each parent, compound village. Since each such move is in defiance of strongly held values, which emphasize the unity of villages and the amity of all kin, the move is validated on the grounds that the headman is failing in his duty to protect the members of the other matrilineage against witches, or is himself bewitching them. And headmen who obtain their positions in face of competition, are liable to be suspected of doing so by eliminating their rivals through witchcraft power. At their installation they are tested for witchcraft power.

The dispute is even deeper and more bitter where it arises from conflict within the matrilineage itself. There, as discussed in Chapter II, elder brother and younger brother, maternal uncle and sister's son, may struggle for control over the women of their matrilineage through whose fertility alone they are able to obtain secure social power. Serious misfortune, such as severe illness among these women and their children, precipitates accusations by younger kinsmen of neglect and of witchcraft against the person who is at the head of the group. Ambition of the younger kinsmen here comes against the moral axioms that junior respects senior, and that all descended from the same ancestress's womb should remain united. Mystical fears alone justify a breach. If separation is effected, the erstwhile quarrelling pair resume relations at a safer distance. Embittered relations between the women themselves also produce accusations.

Put thus baldly, this analysis suggests that Yao life is one constant round of misfortune, quarrel and accusation. Mitchell gives a proper time perspective by analysing the series of accusations and counter-accusations that were made in a number of groups over a series of years. His analysis of these village histories reaches its climax in one which covers quarrels, accusations and divinations over the deaths of children through a period of seven years (his pp. 165–74). Various women in the two segments of the village's matrilineage accuse one another, and the headman is himself suspected. Other mystical causes of death are canvassed. But the main opposition is between two collateral cousins ('brothers' in Yao idiom) who each represent one of the two segments in the village. Their names are Kanyenga and Cilimba, and their segments are descended from two sisters, one of whose brothers is headman of the village. Mitchell comments that the two cousins 'are the representatives of the two lineage segments in this situation'. There is seldom any doubt about the affiliation of these two personalities. Consistently in the accounts of the divinations each rejects the diviner's finding if it accuses a member of his lineage segment. Note that the divinatory séance itself becomes a field in which the opposition of the segments is expressed. Kayenga continued consulting diviners until finally he got the answer he wanted. His opponents rejected these findings and eventually even discounted the chicken ordeal. The diviners' findings and the results of the poison ordeals therefore were bandied about between the opposed groups, and though the whole procedure of divination and accusations of sorcery is directed towards the extirpation of discordant elements in the community, in fact it is only a facet of the underlying cause of tension—the opposition of segments in an ever-segmenting lineage.

'In addition to the structural opposition of Kanyenga and Cilimba there is a certain amount of tension among [the headman] Cikoja's uterine sisters. Bt. Amisa, Asimama, Ayesi, and Asubiya have all had children. Bt. Amisa is the senior and the relationship between her and any of the other sisters is difficult.

In addition to this there is the tension between the generations seen in the attempts of the sons of Amisa to bring a compensation claim against [the headman] Cikoja himself.' The very growth of the lineage and the maturing of young men precipitates struggles between the sons of different sisters, and across the cleavage of generations, despite every emphasis on major lineage unity. Each death causes a crisis. But when Mitchell left the field the struggle was still going on: no one had left the village permanently, though there was talk of migration.

Turner followed Mitchell's lead with a very complex analysis of the struggles around the succession to headmanship of an Ndembu village. He called his book *Schism and Continuity in an African Society: A Study of Ndembu Village Life* (1957), for while he emphasizes how endemic schism is in village life, he shows how the pattern of social relations endures. Schism arises partly out of the personal ambitions and self-interestedness of members of the village. In addition, each major protagonist is pressed to pursue a certain course of actions because he represents the interests of a sub-group or category of persons within the village. Willy-nilly—like an Anuak candidate for headmanship or noble for kingship—he must strive on behalf of his lineage for power. He is further compelled to do so, like the Yao Kanyenga and Cilimba above, by his own belief in the mystical causes of misfortunes to his fellows—men, women and children—which he ascribes to the ill-doing of his competitors.

Ndembu rules of succession allow several persons to put forward claims to the headmanship. Brother should succeed brother, yet sisters' sons have claims. A man's ability to make an essay, and his modes of action, are affected by the complex of principles which affect his position, and which enable him to mobilize support. But these principles are in their nature independent of one another. They do not necessarily fit together logically. There is insistence on matrilineage unity at various levels in the genealogical system, with matrilineal succession to position going to seniors and with an approved alternation between sections of the lineage. Women form the nuclei about which their blood-kinsmen assemble, yet these women leave their natal homes to live with their husbands. Hence wives live in villages where sisters have power. And since the rate of divorce is high a woman may move to more than one husband, bearing children to each, before at her menopause she returns to join her children and her brothers. Village and neighbourhood ties are important. Each generation competes within itself yet is regarded as united, and also identified with the generations of grandparents and grandchildren against the intervening generations. The sexes form groups for certain rituals in which they act and feel hostility to one another, and this unity affects secular life. The operation of these principles is influenced by *ad hoc* distributions of power, authority, and numbers of followers as against an ideal distribution. Individual personality is accepted as being important in deciding issues of authority.

Turner illustrates how these principles operate, sometimes together, sometimes setting opposing processes at work, through twenty years in the life of one village. The chance occurrence of fertility and barrenness, of illness and death, of good and ill fortune, precipitates crises, since the people ascribe these chances to ancestral spirits, sorcery, breach of taboo and omission of rituals. Each crisis therefore threatens the unity of relationships in the village. This unity is threatened also by breaches of duty and quarrels between village members. As in Mitchell's village, the pattern of discord is shaped by the struggle of two lineage segments, each aiming to make its representative the new headman.

Turner's study emphasizes two important principles for our present analysis. First, each divination after misfortune, or rational judgment after a quarrel, itself alters the balance of power in the village. The divination at the next crisis takes account of this alteration. Hence different mystical agents are divined to be at work; and the new divination may cancel out the previous one. This emerges clearly in the career of one of the principal candidates for the headmanship—a man named Sandombu. Sandombu was moved by strong personal ambition and also by the pride of his sub-lineage to struggle for the headmanship, though the odds were all against him. The women of his sub-lineage had had few children. He himself was sterile, and rumour had it that his semen was red, indicating that he was a sorcerer. With his generosity and capacity for affection, he fought with his quick temper and the curse of his sterility, to achieve the headmanship. Turner shows out of his general analysis of the social alignments that Sandombu was bound to lose, and on the way to be accused of sorcery. There is a tragic doom in his fate. The final blow which defeated Sandombu was when he was accused by divination of killing a mother's sister, by whose death he was grief-stricken—most griefstricken for not even he could be sure he was guiltless. He had to leave, and build on his own, trying to attract a new following of people discarded from various villages.

But the most powerful values of Ndembu society prevented his rivals rejoicing permanently in his defeat. Their consciences began to trouble them over him. Was he not blood of their blood, born from the same 'womb'? Had he not been part of their corporate life? Had he not contributed to their well-being, paying for the education of their children, finding jobs for their young men when he was in charge of making roads? His plea to return was allowed. A new misfortune led to a new divination, which found that Sandombu was not guilty of sorcery, that an outsider had caused the death of which he had been found guilty. A ritual was performed, for which Sandombu paid a goat. He planted a tree symbolic of matrilineage unity to his dead mother's sister, and he and his main antagonist prayed there and were 'reconciled'. Powdered white clay, symbolizing the basic values of Ndembu society—good health, fertility, respect for elders, observance of kinship dues, honesty, and the like—was sprinkled on the ground round the tree and the several kinds of kin present were anointed with it.

The odds against Sandombu had shifted so much, that his rivals could accept him back without fearing his renewed competition.

Second, Turner develops a formula for handling this kind of recurrent situation in the life of a group. He calls the series of events a 'social drama', and demonstrates that it has 'a processional form'. It starts with breach of norm-governed social relations. This is followed by a crisis in which the effects of the breach spread to the limits of the relationship between the parties involved, threatening to mobilize the largest opposed groups of which they are members. Various adjustive or redressive mechanisms are then deployed to seal off or heal the breach, and these lead either to re-establishment of relations or social recognition of irreparable breach between the contesting parties. These redressive and adjustive actions may range from 'personal and informal arbitration, to formal and legal machinery, and, to resolve certain kinds of crisis, to the performance of public ritual' (pp. 98 f.). Turner has tried to classify the situations in which these different procedures are brought into action. He suggests (p. 126) that jural machinery, involving a judicial process, is employed when the parties are appealing to common norms, or if norms are in conflict, when they can appeal to 'a common frame of values which organize a society's norms into a hierarchy'. On the other hand, when a group feels itself to be in conflict with social norms because of the working out of social processes which conflict with one another, this produces disputes where '. . . judicial decision can condemn one or more of the disputants, but . . . cannot relieve the quarrels so as to preserve the threatened relationships . . .'. These conflicts in social norms are crystallized when misfortunes strike the group. Recourse can be had to judicial methods when the living quarrel. 'But when a breach in social regularity is made by some natural misfortune such as the death of a member of the group, or a famine, or a plague, and if the natural order is thought to be sensitively responsive to the moral condition of society, then the calamity allows of a number of alternative interpretations. A wide range of conflicts between persons and factions is brought to light. . . . When rules are broken by living persons, judicial action can follow and this action can speedily seal off conflict within the orbit of a single relationship or within a small sector of the social system. But when a severe natural misfortune precipitates crisis, practically every latent source of conflict in the system is made manifest. These may be disclosed in accusations of witchcraft-sorcery, or in confessions of guilt by those who feel that they have broken some crucial norm governing the intercourse of the living with the living or with the dead.' Since no specific norm has been broken, judicial action cannot be employed. Ritual emerges as a result of the 'moral discomfort' of the group, when confronted with a breach of the natural order. Whether the witch or sorcerer be expelled, or ritual performed, 'irremediable conflict is felt to exist between the major principles by which the group is organized. There is nothing for it but to lay stress on values to which all men subscribe regardless of their particular loyalties and interests.' This is what ritual, including sacrifice, does.

Here Turner is advancing a hypothesis to differentiate and explain the situations in which judicial machinery can redress breach, as against those in which mystical beliefs, selected by divination and redressed by ritual action, are considered to be

effective. The latter we see here are called on when the disturbances of the group's life arise from the processes inherent in
the group's growth and development as its members mature,
and multiply at varied rates, sicken, and die.

Into his story Turner has woven an analysis of schism of groups
and relationships, and of continuity of society and principle and
value above the schism—a continuity which among the Ndembu
is that of a 'community of suffering'. For it is misfortune which
assembles the cult-groups whose rituals dramatize that continuity.
As the story unfolds we see Ndembu beliefs and customs working
in the process of social life, where they both control people and
are exploited by people. Customs and beliefs are seen to be
systematized through social relationships: they are not mere
adjuncts to these. Incidentally, in this analysis Turner is able to
show how changes in, and multiplication of, values and principles
of organization under British overlordship enter into Ndembu
life partially to amend the structure of village life, and partially
to leave it unchanged in basis, but expressed in new idioms.
The establishment of peace, work for wages and cash-cropping,
the killing out of game which has struck at the dominant male
value of hunting, all influence present-day Ndembu activities.

## WHY BELIEF IN MYSTICAL AGENTS?

I have quoted Turner as speaking of the 'moral discomfort'
a group feels when confronted with a 'natural' misfortune. This
statement raises in crucial form a further problem: why do tribal
societies evaluate natural misfortunes in such highly moral and
mystical terms?

Initially, we must recognize that a tribal society seems to be
more exposed to the hazards of life than we are. The infantile
mortality rate is normally high and the expectation of life even
for those who survive infancy is relatively short. Illnesses are
frequent. Correspondingly medical techniques are inadequate.
The margin of security in productive activities is low. Drought,
crop-blight, cattle disease, overturning of simple craft, all threaten
supplies. Methods of storing and transporting food are poor.
Since tribal peoples are faced with these hazards and have only a
relatively simple technology to deal with them, it is easily understandable that they should attempt to control chance and misfortune by invalid, but anxiety relieving, magical techniques and

appeals to spirits. This was the gist of Frazer's and of Malinowski's central theoretical statements.[22]

But statements of this kind do not cope with a major attribute of mystical beliefs and rituals: these contain a strong moral element and they are referred to the moral relations between the members of various groups. Durkheim stressed this element. Radcliffe-Brown stated it succinctly for *The Andaman Islanders* (1922, p. 399): 'We may perhaps adequately state the Andaman notion by saying that moral law and natural law are not distinguished from one another. The welfare of the society depends upon right actions; wrong actions inevitably lead to evil results. Giving way to anger is a wrong action, as being the cause of social disturbance. In the legends the catastrophes that overwhelmed the ancestors are in many instances represented as being caused by some one giving way to anger. There is a right way and a wrong way of making such a thing as a bow. We should explain this by saying that the right way will give a good serviceable weapon, whereas the wrong way will give an inferior or useless one. The Andaman Islander tends to look at the matter from a different angle; the right way is right because it is the one that had been followed from time immemorial, and any other way is wrong, is contrary to custom, to law. Law, for the Andaman Islander, means that there is an order of the universe, characterized by absolute uniformity; this order was established once for all in the time of the ancestors, and is not to be interfered with, the results of any such disturbance being evil, ranging from merely minor ills such as disappointment or discomfort to great calamities. The law of compensation is absolute. Any deviation from law or custom will inevitably bring its results, and inversely any evil that befalls must be the result of some lack of observance. The legends reveal to our analysis a conception of the universe as a moral order.'

The moral order in the universe of a tribal society is a small-scale moral order. For their beliefs state that breaches of rule among men and women can disturb the course of natural events: and any disturbance in the course of natural events is ascribed to breaches of proper relations among men and women. That is, each disturbance of social relations has a spreading 'moral' effect which results in misfortune befalling either the wrongdoer or the wronged. Our courts punish explicitly wrongful action. However vicious a man's feelings, he is not punished if he does not translate these feelings into action. We have seen how under beliefs in witchcraft a man's (alleged) vicious feelings are endued with power to go out and cause harm to others, perhaps independently of his volition. Or rather, since in social life action originates at the opposite end, when a misfortune occurs it is ascribed to this sort of vicious feeling.

This type of belief in witchcraft—the Azande type—is the most vivid exemplification of a general situation. Failure in amity, feelings of hostility and unspoken grievances, also spoil a sacrifice and bring mystical retribution in the form of misfortune.[23] Or misfortune is due to a breach of taboo, or to a warranted curse by an elder, or even to the protective mystical activity of the accredited elders of a society.

This situation seems to arise from the complex interdependence between persons which is characteristic of tribal societies. I have described how groups of kin have to co-operate to achieve multifarious purposes: together they hold and utilize land and goods; they produce, distribute and consume goods in co-operation; they combine to arrange marriages, and rear and educate their offspring; they act as a unit in administration and political struggle; they worship as a congregation; they seek recreation together. The effect of this situation is that every action of any member of the group which departs from norms influences adversely many purposive activities. A quarrel between two brothers has wider effects than in our industrial society: it may imperil productive work, affect the solidarity of political action, and disturb the unity of a religious congregation. Hence each breach of norm has a spreading moral disturbance: many relationships and activities are affected. Conversely, if 'outside' events do not run normally, this points to secret disturbances in the moral relations of the members of the group. These moral relations are framed in mystical terms and their disturbed state is appropriately redressed by ritual action.

The best hypothesis yet advanced to explain why in these societies moral relations should be endued with mystical power and ritual efficacy is that advanced by Fortes and Evans-Pritchard in a section on 'The Mystical Values Associated with Political Office', in their 'Introduction' to *African Political Systems* (1940, pp. 16 f.). I can do no better than quote and summarize them.

They point out that African rulers have mythical and ritual warranty for their authority. In a stateless society this warranty attaches to the inter-relations between the various segments of the society. As we have seen, these societies are not 'models of continuous harmony. Acts of violence, oppression, revolt, civil war, and so forth chequer the history of every African state.' The stateless societies are also full of strife. But once the society has achieved a degree of stability, these internal struggles do not necessarily wreck the social system. In practice they are themselves either protective devices against abuse, or they set in motion processes which deploy representatives or symbols of the widest common values of the society. Since people have to think and feel about the interests which actuate them, and yet may be unaware of these interests, they are symbolized in various ways: 'myths, dogmas, ritual beliefs, and activities make his social system intellectually tangible and coherent to an African and enable him to think and feel about it'. The symbols, being themselves 'sacred', endow the social system with mystical values which evoke acceptance of the social order on a plane that secular force and sanctions cannot attain. The social system is, 'as it were, removed to a mystical plane, where it figures as a system of sacred values beyond criticism or revision'. The bad king or usurper is overthrown without the kingship being questioned. All individuals and sections accept these symbols as common values.

These common values refer to fertility, health, prosperity, peace, and justice—everything which gives life and happiness to a people. They are safeguards of both the material needs of existence and the basic relations of social structure—land, cattle, rain, bodily health, the family, the clan, the state. But if the 'universal aspect of things like land and fertility are the subjects of common interest . . . these matters also have another side to them, as the private interests of individuals and segments of a society'. Each person (or group) is interested in the productivity of his own land and the welfare of himself and his own fellows. It is precisely over such matters that disputes between individuals and sections of the society arise. 'Thus the basic needs of existence and the basic social relations are, in their pragmatic and utilitarian aspects, as sources of immediate satisfactions and strivings, the subjects of private interests; as common interests, they are non-utilitarian and non-pragmatic, matters of moral value and ideological significance. The common interests spring from those very private interests to which they stand in opposition.' Readers of this book have only to recall the Tonga land-shrines to appreciate this point.

Every social action thus has an immediate utilitarian content. Food is planted and produced, goods are exchanged, women are married, to achieve the purposes of individuals. But each social action also has a moral aspect: it embodies rights, duties, and privileges, it expresses sentiments, it mobilizes social relations. And each individual social action, with its particular rights, duties and sentiments, and its setting in social relationships, is performed within a whole system of 'common, reciprocal, and mutually balancing rights, duties, and sentiments, the body of moral and legal norms'. The stability and continuity of the society depends on the regularity with which the body of interwoven norms is maintained. Unless most obligations are fulfilled, the social order would be too insecure for people to maintain themselves. This is the end which the political system as a whole subserves.

The mystical form of the political system thus reflects the common interests of all members of the society in the interconnected rights, duties, and sentiments which make it a single community. It reflects also the interests of all in general fertility and prosperity, though it is over particular means of achieving individual success that persons and groups come into conflict, over particular items of land, offices, women, cattle. These common interests are brought home to the competing sections in the ceremonies which affirm them periodically, or in crisis. And the discharge of the ritual obligations connected with these ceremonies is therefore 'the most stringent responsibilities of office'. The duties involved are distributed through key personnel of the society, often in a way which cuts across the secular distribution of power. The distribution of ritual power helps achieve a balance against competing secular interests.

This general hypothesis can be applied to domestic relations as well as political relations. It emphasizes that ritual arises from situations where there is conflict between the general moral order and the interests which lead individuals and groups to compete with one another. And it seems that ritual develops most strongly in those situations where moral judgments on action may affect many social relationships. I shall argue later that this situation influences the form of rituals. First we must examine further the nature of other conflicts involved.

We have seen that moral disturbance occurs at several levels. First, there is the straightforward breach of duty in pursuit of self-interest, as well as straightforward competition. Second, there is apparent breach because every individual has an immensely difficult, and almost impossible, task in distributing his or her scarce resources between the rightful demands of a variety of kin, so as to offend none. Third, each individual in a group of this kind is linked by customary allegiances in diverse ways to different outsiders from his fellows. Individuals in the group do not have precisely the same set of loyalties: this produces different calls on them, and makes difficult unity of action in the group. Fourth, as individuals mature and sections of each group grow in size, separate interests develop in which sectional loyalties conflict with the moral unity of the major group. Fifth, the structural principles which organize the society and the values which motivate its members are not logically consistent with one another: they are independent of one another, and furthermore sometimes discrepant, and situationally at least in conflict, with one another. These varied structural principles set in train conflicting trains of development.

Mystical beliefs and ritual action may be referred to the simplest situations where there is straightforward conflict of self-interest and duty. But in those situations, which are defined by a single principle or value, judicial action can be applied. It cannot be applied where principles and value are themselves in conflict. It is particularly to disputes arising out of these conflicts that natural misfortune is ascribed, in complex divinations. Ritual action is employed as the redressive, reconciling mechanism, for ritual reaffirms basic loyalties without careful examination of the underlying causes of disharmony. In fact disharmony of this kind, as shown by Tiv, Lugbara, Nyakyusa, Yao and Ndembu séances, is never settled. Fresh misfortunes provoke fresh, and again disputed, searches by divination for the source of mystical ills.

The major difficulty of this interpretation is that it does not of itself deal with the variation in the extent to which tribal—or tribal-type—societies explain natural misfortunes by mystical agents, or to which deep-rooted conflicts between social principles endow persons at critical points with evil mystical power. A large area of comparative research is left. I believe it can only be worked when we have more 'extended-case' studies.

Furthermore, we have to ask at what point in the development of differentiation in a society does this interpretation cease to apply? Would it cover the Ancient Greek ascription of events to gods and fate?

I glance briefly at this problem in terms of the position of women. It is well known that Hindus ascribed the break-up of joint patrilineal families to the wives of the younger generation—the women who caused mischief, and who pushed the interests of their husband and children. Similarly Freedman in his study of *Lineage Organisation in South-Eastern China* (1960) says that 'family peace in reality depended fundamentally on the suppression of the potential conflict between a man and his father and brothers, but his wife as a relatively new member of the group, could the most readily be accused of mischief-making, and doubtless she may often have merited some of the blame cast upon her because of her attempts to secure the interests of her husband and her own children against those of other members of the family. The total configuration of stress in a patrilineal complex and the burden borne in it by women are exemplified by the Chinese case.' Elsewhere he writes that a wife's transfer of loyalty to her conjugal from her natal family 'forced her into the struggle which essentially turned upon the rivalry between her husband and his brothers' (at pp. 21 f., 134-5).

The position of these Hindu and Chinese women in the joint family is very similar to that of Zulu women. Are they regarded as full of mystical evil? In neither India nor China are they, according to my search, witches as against sorcerers. Both men and women use noxious substances to harm others. Nor are female ancestral-spirits or goddesses unusually evil. But at least in the high castes of Hinduism femininity is highly ambivalent. A woman can be worshipped. But the feminine also pollutes. Menstrual blood, the blood of childbirth, and the blood of defloration are mystically dangerous to all that is auspicious. Furthermore, sexual relations themselves pollute: and in some high castes a woman even as wife is repelling, dirty, and dangerous. The man who yields his semen yields something of his life and virtue. More attention here needs to be paid to this problem.

Cursory investigation—which is all I am competent to make—of standard books on China also gives clues to a similar position. Granet says that in Chinese thought the feminine principle of *Yin* 'embodied the moon, cold, winter', while the masculine principle 'embodied the sun, heat, summer', and 'the Chinese believed that during the cold season the *Yang*, the male principle, was tricked and imprisoned by the adverse forces of *Yin*'. Beyond this, Granet states that a chieftain at certain periods was believed to be able by proper observances to influence prosperity. But if he 'is a chief who is not perfect, if he despises harmony, if he cannot combine in himself "the bitter, the acid, the salt and the sweet", if above all he compromises the male vigour (*yang*) which is in him, with a thoughtless approach to women (who are *yin*) he will become the victim of *ku*—which is the penalty of all excess, the harmful result of improper tabus, misfortune and sickness (more powerful the greater the soul) maleficence in its full force'.[24]

Strikingly the malign power of women is emphasized apparently more among Chinese nobility, where the joint family was more important than among peasants. Thus Granet wrote in his *La Religion des Chinois* (1951): '... In each man there is a portion of public power; something sacred. In antithesis, women appear essentially inferior and as if imbued with a malign power: while in the midst of the fields the peasant fiancées co-operate in the renewal, the noble fiancées, after three months of severe confinement, are taken, veiled and at twilight, to the husband's gynaeceum, where, for another three months, they are confined. The separation of men and women preserves for the sexual act its mysterious character: it is in no way tied to the exceptional emotions of a time of festivities and concord; it becomes something domestic and secret, surrounded by a ceremonial which underlines feminine inferiority and allows the husband not to sully that which is august in him. In urban life with permanent relationships, in the life of the nobility, man has become a head, a woman a servant, the sexual act only keeps a maleficent efficacity, it has lost all religious virtue.' If this depicts the formal surface of a noble Chinese family's life, it is out of accord with the reality as represented in the Chinese novel *Dream of the Red Chamber*, where men are terrified of mothers and may even be in subjection to their wives. (One is reminded of Nadel's analysis of the Nupe.[25]) I note that the one example of sorcery in the novel is by a concubine jealous of the inferior position of her son *vis-à-vis* a wife's son, and envious of the secure position of her husband's elder brother's son's widow, who is also niece to her husband's wife.

The manner in which these beliefs may operate in a community is shown in a passage from Hsu's study of Chinese culture and personality, *Under the Ancestors' Shadow* (1949). There are wide ritual differences between boys and girls: 'Boys, for example, are never barred from any occasion of ritual importance; girls on the other hand, are excluded from most prayer meetings. Boys have very few taboos to observe; girls suffer from a good many ritual disabilities. A girl's clothes, because of their association with her body, cannot be displayed or sunned anywhere in the courtyard as are other clothes. Her menstrual blood, ritually speaking, is the worst kind of impurity. It offends and alienates all spirits. Therefore, during menstruation she must avoid any ritual activity. After the birth of a child she must observe numerous taboos which virtually immobilize her' (p. 219).

Indications of the wide spread of this type of mystical beliefs are there. The attempt to relate the beliefs to the conflicting processes inherent in social organization may focus attention more sharply on problems of how ritual deals with unavoidable disharmony. Why, we may ask, in Dahomey is the goddess of women also the goddess of witches?[26] These two facts are given us as separated pieces of information: together they lead us deep into the structure of society with all its conflicts.

## CONFLICT IN RITUAL

This hypothesis has stimulated important work, including Fortes' own studies of ritual in the social relations of the Tallensi. Among other studies, there are Turner's quoted work and two books by M. Wilson on rituals among the Nyakyusa of Tanganyika.[27]

Some societies whose basic social relations are akin to those of tribes, appear to have few beliefs by which misfortunes are ascribed to personal animosities and personal mystical evildoing. Beliefs in the power of a God—even if a God comparatively uninterested in men's morality—are more significant. This situation is found in tribal areas, but is more common where Christianity and Islam prevail.

There is another general characteristic of the small scale of tribal religions and rituals, and the manner in which these order people's lives. As quoted, custom is highly specific to each relationship. In many rituals persons and groups have to perform their roles in relation to one another. King, chiefs, relatives of the king, a royal bride from a particular clan, specific groups of commoners, have prescribed roles in the installation of the Shilluk king, to a degree not found, for example, in a British coronation. At a sacrifice, all kin participate according to determined categories and each category is entitled to specific pieces of the offering. Tallensi and Tsonga 'joking-partners' or 'joking-relatives' may steal part of the sacrifice. At a boy's or maiden's initiation ceremony the categories of men and women, mother and father, maternal uncle, local groups, may appear in special roles. The prescribed ritual actions of participants may include direct representation of the present or future role in everyday life, as when a bride fondles a child and sweeps and gathers firewood and cooks. Or each participant may perform some highly symbolic action. Or a participant may reverse his or her everyday role and mien, as when a Iatmul maternal uncle in the *Naven* dresses as a filthy old widow, and make himself grotesque and ridiculous in the honouring of his sister's son's achievements.

We define these highly conventionalized performances as 'ritual' because the people believe that they help—by mystical means outside of sensory observation and control—to protect, purify or enrich the participants and their group. 'Ritual' is here distinguished from 'ceremonial', highly conventionalized performances in which this 'mystical' element is not present. Among some peoples in 'tribal' situations, again particularly some of the adherents of Islam and Christianity, 'ritual' performance of roles is comparatively infrequent, but their social life is strongly marked by ceremonial. This does not apply to all members of these 'universalistic' faiths. Where and in what circumstances will we find ritual as against ceremonial? What other facts may exclude the development of this type of mystical idea, in which the moral rightness or disturbance of personal relations becomes involved with the natural order?

The Shilluk coronation ritual involved more than a straightforward appearance of persons, categories, and groups in terms of their secular roles. The ritual dramatized the surface struggles which mark Shilluk politics. Beyond this, it symbolically portrayed the underlying conflicts of social principles. The mock-battles between the king and Nyikang's effigy symbolized the fundamental conflicts arising from one prince occupying a position representative of all Shilluk unity. He is 'unworthy' to occupy that position both because he is associated with a single segment and group of maternal kin, and because each individual's human frailties make him fall short of the high ideals of office. The roles of the chiefs of the northern and southern divisions also focus the autonomous loyalties of territorial segments.

This open exhibition of strife as well as co-operation—and underlying conflict as well as cohesion—is common in tribal rituals and ceremonials. We speak of the prescribed actions within them as 'symbolizing' underlying conflict and cohesion, because (as Fortes and Evans-Pritchard stated) the participants themselves are not fully aware of the whole setting of the symbolic action and its associations throughout the social order. As these scholars add, if participants were aware of these associations, the symbol might cease to be effective in stimulating the approved sentiments of loyalty and solidarity over and above conflicts and the strife these engender. The problems involved in the social and emotional effectiveness of symbols are immensely complicated in social anthropology as in psycho-analysis. We do not yet know many answers clearly. But it is certain that we must distinguish 'symbols' from 'signals and signs'.[28] Signals and signs operate almost entirely at the rational and conscious level to convey compressed meanings which are known to the participants. Symbols proliferate meanings and associations in the unconscious mind and feelings. Symbols handle the conflicting as well as the unifying principles which move members of a society to action. They represent in their structure the multifarious discrepant purposes of persons and offices and groups, yet stimulate the sentiments which animate solidarity despite strife and the conflicts it represents. All this emerges from Fortes and Evan-Pritchard's initial discussion.

It is possible, then, that we have here a clue to one factor which inhibits the development of ritual and the use of symbolic actions and objects charged with mystical power. The conflicts within unity may be too well known to the participants, too openly threatening, and—this is most important—may be fully accepted by them. In this situation, they could not believe that performing the conflicts will in some manner bless them.

I have worked out this possibility in writing this book. Clearly it fits in with Fortes and Evans-Pritchard's statement that if a man understood the 'objective meaning' of symbols, 'they would lose their power over him'. Here there is a sharp contrast within the Shilluk coronation and the installation dance round the drums of an Anuak village headman, described by Lienhardt. The village drums are beaten before dawn. 'An hour or so after sunrise, such men of the village as are not otherwise employed on necessary tasks arrive at the headman's homestead carrying spears and rifles, and run about the dancing-ground shouting ox-names, and uttering war-cries, gesturing with their weapons in mock defence of and mock attack on the headman's home. In the course of this activity, at one dance, I frequently heard the word *agem*, "rebellion", shouted by the warriors, and a stranger might be under the impression that a real *agem* was about to take place, since the drums are beaten and an occasional shot is fired.' Later the company call the headman out and he dances fully armed, with his followers' wives, to whom he makes sexual approaches. The men again mime an attack on the drums, seizing of which marks a successful rebellion. Lienhardt states that this dance compels the person honoured to distribute gifts. He emphasizes that the mimed attack is on the drums. Hence it is 'a clear indication' (note that he does not use the word 'symbolize') that the action represents a village rebellion, and is not a war-dance of a raid on or battle with strangers. The headman is enticed to join the dancers by their singing, and when he courts the married women before the villagers it is 'as it were on their behalf'. On the other hand, his own wife late in the dance leads the people and dances with the men: and this 'is the time for greatest excitement and display'.[29]

Readers know the background to this dance. The dance is ceremonial, not ritual, for it does not influence the prosperity of the village. It 'signalizes' the temporary capacity of the villagers to reach an ephemeral unity and ability to have internal peace: it does not 'symbolize' and influence mystically their solidarity despite conflict. The word 'signalize' is here used in its full meaning: 'make noteworthy or remarkable, lend distinction or lustre to . . .' The dance, Lienhardt says, is 'a dramatic representation of the relation between a headman and his villagers', in contrast with the orgiastic dances of villagers in the bush to which they creep 'stealthily . . . , "like thieves and witches and the like",' say the Anuak themselves.

There is something unexplained, as yet, the headman's dance with married women and of his own wife with the warriors. But seemingly the frequency of village rebellions—each few years or sooner—makes the agreement to live under a temporary headman entirely conscious. Hence the dance openly represents the headman's accession and temporary incumbency, under the constant threat of rebellion. It is not believed to influence the whole well-being of the village. It is ceremonial, not ritual.

This Anuak dance contrasts sharply with the great rejoicings and national dances which the Swazi enact at their first fruits.[30] These Swazi rituals focus on the king. But while periodically in the course of the rituals the unity of the nation is affirmed triumphantly, there is also a symbolic representation of the seeds of strife within the nation. The most sacred songs of the ritual, sung only during its course, lament the fate of the king who is hated and rejected by internal enemies, surrounded by treason.

At crucial phases of the ritual, princes, his potential rivals, aid in the ritual by withdrawing from the arena, as foreigners must withdraw. Even an unborn prince must withdraw, for pregnant wives of royal princes are excluded. Yet at other phases the princes aid the king. When he has been heavily medicated they entice him out from his seclusion. He appears dressed in razor-edged grasses, and heavily painted, to execute a wild crazy dance: he is a 'Monster', perhaps Nature itself. He casts an evergreen gourd, 'symbolizing the past' year, on to the shield of one of the warriors. This man, it is said, would in the past have been the first killed at war. At specific points in the ritual people hurl insults at the king.

Even this brief abstract shows the degree to which the pattern of social relations, with its inherent conflicts as well as solidarities, enters into the form of the ritual which is believed to bless the nation. The ritual embodies a small-scale view of the universe. For the universe, as far as the Swazi are concerned, is directly influenced by this performance of social roles. The Zulu had similar national ceremonies at first fruits, and also at sowing season.

In addition, at the time of sowing the women and girls of local districts performed ceremonies to honour a goddess. The women marched singing lewd songs to plant a garden for the goddess far out in the bush, and they poured libations of beer to her and solicited a good harvest. They attacked any man they met. At the same time girls donned their brothers' clothes, and, carrying warriors' weapons, they herded the cattle which were normally taboo to them. The course of 'natural' events is influenced favourably for people by women and girls reversing their normal modes of behaviour. To understand these rituals, we have to trace, as we have above, the normal roles of Zulu women and examine the deep conflicts which centre in their position.[31]

Similarly, when a Tsonga village is moved, rituals are performed to secure blessings at the new site. Headman and principal wife have ritual sexual relations to bind the new site to them. A month of taboo on sexual relations between villagers follows. Significantly, breach of this taboo may make the headman, not the offender, ill. The roofs of the old huts are carried to the new site by the men who sing obscene songs insulting the women. When the women smear the floors with mud they retaliate with obscene songs at the men's expense. When the village is ready, it is fenced magically against witchcraft and each couple has sexual relations in order of precedence. Then the headman is established in his position by his principal wife, who carries his spear and shield, closing the gate. She offers to the ancestral spirits and prays for the people: 'Be not tied by the village! Bring forth children; live and be happy and get everything. You gods, see! I have no bitterness in my heart. It is pure. I was angry because my husband abandoned me, he said I was not his wife; he loved his younger wives. Now, this is finished in my heart. We shall have friendly relations together.' They then feast together.

Again, to understand the symbolism by which this performance of roles, with its emphasis on conflict, blesses the village, we have to penetrate deeply into the structure of the village. Earlier analysis has shown us that the conflicts which will eventually split the village arise from the independence of each family. Sexual relations, the source of this independence, are banned while men, representing unity, and women, representing break-up, insult one another in obscene songs whose words Junod unfortunately has not given us. These songs are not allowed when only one hut is moved. The headman whose authority is threatened by his juniors' possible defections—likely when the village is moved—is threatened by their breach of taboo. His principal wife's prayer refers to the major source of dissension, the independence of each wife's family within the unified village.[32] This ritual thus symbolizes major sources of conflict as well as solidarity.

I have cited here rituals which I have elsewhere analysed because compression robs the descriptions of their full flavour.

It would be difficult for readers to see this process in terms of secular relations not analysed above. But the same process is to be found in report after report by many anthropologists from tribe after tribe. In rite after rite we see how moral difficulties as well as the demands of secular life are enacted in ritual to bless the community.

The outstanding characteristic of this type of ritualization is that it involves the details of particular social relationships— between various kinds of kinsfolk, between spouses, between men and women, between rulers and subjects. The performance of these ritual duties for the significantly related persons is one of the heaviest obligations of any role. It is severely enforced. Failure to act may bring down severe mystical penalties on the person for whom the ritual is performed, on the defaulter, and possibly on a whole group. Thus these ritual roles are on the one side an essential right, and on the other a pious duty. Their specificity demarcates the several relationships of closely knit groups. It is now possible to appreciate more fully the importance of the Northern Rhodesian Tonga clan-joking partners, who can substitute for any kinsman or kinswoman in any ritual.

Ritual demarcates roles and relationships from one another in an additional manner. The dominant characteristic of these societies is that people interact with the same sets of fellows to achieve several purposes. The village's, the kinship group's, even the nation's, social system embodies several sub-systems of purposive relations—familial, productive, distributive, consuming, educational, religious, organizing. In industrial society these purposive relations constitute separate sub-systems. But the multi-purposive relations of tribal society are for the outside observer divisible in terms of these several purposes. And they are in fact divided culturally from one another, each tending to be marked by highly specific conventional modes of behaviour and sometimes by ritual. There is a marked occurrence in these societies of ritual at each change of activity and each change of role.

This tendency is related also to the fact that the material apparatus of a tribal society is limited. I quoted earlier Evans-Pritchard's analysis of how in a meagre material culture all objects tend to acquire high social value because they have 'to serve the media of many relationships and they are, in consequence, often invested with ritual functions'.[33] This statement can now be further expounded. The same places and houses are used for many purposes: part of the living-hut may be the abode of the spirits of ancestors, whose bodies lie under the hut floor, or in the cattle corral. Or shrines are built on to the wall, or placed at the door, of living-quarters. In or nearby the same spots men meet to discuss group affairs, children are reared and are educated and play, women perform their domestic tasks. From these centres men go, often together, to plant and herd; they bring back their products to the same places, where these are distributed and consumed. There also are manufactured tools and household goods. Even a king's palace is not too distinctive from ordinary huts and activities.

This tribal situation emerges more clearly if we compare it with the situation in urban civilizations. Few men work at home: they go to factories, offices and other places of employment. Children go to school and institutions of higher education. There are separate buildings for congregations larger than the family, and for the discharge of political duties, the treatment of the sick by specialists, and so forth. The impersonal production and distribution of goods are also located in separate buildings from those in which these goods are consumed.

What the high specificity of custom and ritual does for tribal society is to 'segregate' the same place according to the purpose for which it is being used, or to mark off slightly specialized spots from one another. When a shrine is being used as a shrine, even if not always, it is approached in conventional manner. And as an individual changes his activity to achieve varied purposes—as he adopts one of the several roles which are involved in his total social personality—he may mark this change by undergoing ritual, observing taboos, or enjoining taboos on others. Ritual of this kind segregates the roles which one person plays, where the material circumstances do not move him to separate buildings in association with distinctive sets of fellows. The segregation may be of one man's multiple roles in relation to a single other person, or of his specific roles in relation to diverse others.

The rituals I have summarized demonstrate that ritual isolates roles largely by exaggerating the prescribed behaviour appropriate to the role involved.[34] This exaggeration may be carried as far as complete reversal: this again points to the problem, why are strife and underlying conflict stressed, when the purpose is blessing? I suggest that this is because there is what I have called 'conflict' of principle between actions in the several roles of an individual's social personality. This has been exhibited in considering, for example, production and consumption, and property-owning, in tribal society.

The major problem is: how does the licensed, nay the prescribed, expression of deep conflicts affect social life so as to bless the community by emphasizing unity? Social anthropologists have now, I think, demonstrated convincingly that ritual is related to the inherent conflicts within social structure. We can go further and say, with Fortes and Evans-Pritchard, that forms of ritual employing social relations themselves are characteristic of societies whose basic axioms and principles of organization are not questioned by the participants. Internal enemies may wage rebellion against a particular king: they do not attempt to subvert the political system. Rebellion is the theme of rituals of national unity. Zulu women and girls behave lewdly, even act as men: they do not question their roles as wives and mothers to form a party of suffragettes. Their ritual licence is believed to bless them and those who allow this licence. Statement of conflicts blesses the revered moral order and its related natural order.

If this view is correct, open ritual statements of conflicts are correspondingly not used in our ceremonies, perhaps because we do not all accept unquestioningly that our social order is not only good, but also hallowed. National ceremonies are marked by adulation only. Internal hate and rejection are not expressed. The enemies of the Nazi and Stalin regimes were in concentration camps.

I have been setting out a still not fully worked out or validated approach to the analysis of ritual. Many problems remain. But I think we begin to see more deeply into the underlying mechanisms by which the prescribed statement of conflict procures blessing. Turner has analysed ritual symbols to show that they have attached to them different levels of meaning. At one level they represent the social and moral order: values, loyalties, bonds of unity, groups and relationships, morality, law. At another level they refer to natural and physiological phenomena and processes, such as birth, breast-milk, blood, semen, urine and faeces, coitus, parts of the body, crops, rain. He calls these levels the *ideological* and the *sensory* poles of meaning. The sensory meanings of a symbol—whether object or action— evoke gross emotions. These are stimulated also by the inherent conflicts of a society. According to Turner, what the ritual symbol does, is to effect 'an interchange of qualities between its [ideological and sensory] poles of meaning. Norms and values, on the one hand, become saturated with emotion, while the gross and basic emotions become ennobled through contact with social values. The irksomeness of moral constraint is transformed into the "love of goodness".' The thesis obviously 'fits' with the Freudian theory of sublimation—but it states a social process. I cannot here set out Turner's full argument.[35] I have given enough to show the lines on which he is working.

## SOCIAL OR PSYCHICAL INTERPRETATION

I have stated that Turner's hypothesis 'fits' with the Freudian theory of sublimation—but it states a *social* process. It is essential to realize that when in the preceding analysis I have spoken of 'conflict', it has been of conflict between social principles, and not of conflict in individual psyches. In the analysis of state rituals we are concerned with the enactment of hostility against the king, an enactment that portrays the divisiveness in the spread of population practising a simple husbandry, which, with poor communications and the absence of integrating economic systems, leads to strong loyalties in segments of the Swazi nation—loyalties manifest in the rebellions I have described. I do not imply when I call them 'rituals of rebellion' that the subjects present are about to rebel, and feel rebellious—unless the performance makes them feel thus. Indeed, the opposite is true. The rituals are performed on hallowed occasions: the ancestral spirits (of the Swazi king; among the Shilluk the great culture-hero, Nyikang himself) are believed to be there. The king is medicated to purify and strengthen him as representative of the nation. Everyone of us has felt the well-being and the sense of community with fellows that comes with dancing, and possibly drinking. At the great Swazi festival the whole nation, in theory, was assembled, united in great dances, enjoying food and drink after dearth, feeling the full pressure of social relations. In this situation, the ceremony in effect states that 'however divided we may be, we are in fact united'. Princes may covet the throne: but they are part of the nation, they support the kingship, and even the incumbent king. In short, the prescribed statement of social conflicts affirms that there is a solidarity—and that when you ritually act (note, 'act', not 'act out') your institutionalized hostility, it is to strengthen the moral values implicit in the system. On these ritual occasions people are united and unanimous. They all want the nation to be strong and victorious, rain to fall, crops to be plentiful, locusts to stay away, epidemics not to assail, cattle and women to be fertile.

Turner postulates that the ceremonies awaken deep aggressions in the participants' psyches, and that the energy released is directed to social goals and cultural moral values. But neither he, nor I, make any statement about these psychological processes: to analyse these, a different kind of data and different techniques are required.

Similarly, I do not assert that when Zulu women don men's clothing and behave obscenely, they are rebels against their lot. Indeed, I clearly state the opposite: they are performing prescribed, socially approved actions, for communal good. The conflicts enacted are conflicts in social principles. Some women may unconsciously resent their lot, desire to be men, and get particular emotional satisfactions from appearing in the ritual, while other women, content to be women, treat the rites as a masquerade, enjoyable if hallowed. We have not evidence to decide, but it seems reasonable to assume that psychological study would show variations here.

I stress the social dimension of this analysis, because it has been constantly misinterpreted as a psychological analysis. One common misreading has been to change the phrase, that participants 'act' their roles, to 'act out' their roles—which certainly suggests some process of emotional purging. I have elsewhere dealt with this misunderstanding:[36] but it has recently been made again in an article published as this book goes to press. In his *African Rituals of Conflict* (December, 1963), Norbeck treats the type of analysis I have been outlining as basically psychological. He makes many good points. Here I can note only his failure, in my opinion, to appreciate that symbolic actions can refer to many conflicting processes and objects in social life. He argues that the same type of symbolic rite must always operate in the same way. If in Zulu women's rites the women, by donning men's clothing and carrying their weapons, enact a social statement of what I call 'rebellion' against their subordinate position, must this not imply that when men don women's clothes they too are in rebellion? He cites an analysis I made elsewhere of circumcision ceremonies in which men wear women's clothes,

PLATE XXI. Divination

*a.* Having cast the bones, a Pedi diviner discusses the future
patterning of social relations.

*Photograph by B. I. Sansom*

*b.* A Tallensi diviner.

*Photograph by M. Fortes*

(see pp. 229 f.)

PLATE XXII. A WITCHCRAFT ORDEAL IN CENTRAL AFRICA

A poor man, bound hand and foot, lying on the ground, was the offender: the chief crime of which he was accused being his relationship to certain parties in a neighbouring senzala who, by means of fetishism, had brought about the death of the Sova's son. The unhappy prisoner was condemned to be sold or put to death, unless he were ransomed by his friends.

(from H. Capello and R. Ivens, *Benguella to the Territory of the Yacca*, 1882) and women men's clothes, to express the identity of their interests in their sons who are to be circumcised.[37] I do not agree that every symbolic rite must have the same meaning always: each symbolic statement has to be interpreted in its multiplicity of meanings within a particular context. Turner has demonstrated the multiple meanings of symbols, and before him Richards drew attention to this fact.[38] Men donning women's clothing may make themselves ridiculous, as in the Iatmul *Naven* ceremony,[39] or they may temporarily subordinate themselves to women, or they may show that while they harshly drag boys away to be circumcised, they feel towards the boys the 'maternal tenderness' of their wives. These statements say nothing about the psychological processes at work: in the rituals some men may express constantly present, because not properly sublimated, desires to be women and to bear children—as theories of psycho-analysis teach us many men feel. Emotionally they may be in revolt against their maleness: socially the ritual may symbolize something quite different. It is essential in approaching the analysis of rituals to realize that there are several dimensions of interpretation, ranging from the biochemical and physiological, to the psychological, to the sociological. Each type of interpretation answers some problems, but not all: and one must be clear in which dimension one is operating. For actions may have quite different significance in the different dimensions.

Finally, the analysis above deals only with the form of rituals. It does not answer the problem, why at all levels of social development, are beliefs in mystical powers so often anthropomorphic, involving a hierarchy of spirits. The spirit-world is modelled on the world of men. This difficult problem lies outside my problem here, which is the connection of rituals with social order and social sanctions.

## THE NEGATIVE CASES

If this analysis was correct, I decided I would not find ritualization of social relations in any highly differentiated society, particularly where the existing structure of society is not accepted as hallowed. This 'prediction' was fulfilled when I checked the political rituals of more developed states. It is perhaps significant that peasants appear not to figure in the national rituals of the Ruanda, of Zazzau, of Nupe, and even of Dahomey, in the kind of complex pattern described for the Shilluk and Swazi.

The king may be religious head of the nation, and sacrifice or pray on its behalf. But Nadel, for example, says the ancient Nupe royal ritual taboos, sacred emblems and forms of magic linked with kingship disappeared under the conquering Mahommedan Fulani Emirs. Crowds attend ceremonial processions: they do not perform actions in relation to the ruler which help procure blessing; and they do not to this end help act the conflicts inherent in the polity.

At the other extreme there is the situation of the Anuak headman, and presumably the Anuak 'king'. Here the conflicts involved in political relations are too clearly seen and too fully accepted to appear in political rituals operating to cloak fundamental disharmony.

In between these two extremes, there is considerable variation in the extent to which social relations are ritualized. I think the indications are that the greater the degree of secular segregation (by place, material object, or elaborated social organization), the less the extent of ritualization. The Lozi ruling tribe in Barotseland associate the life of the king with the land, and extinguish fires at his death. They light new fires for the new reign. But while they flock to escort the king on his ceremonial moves between flood-season and dry-season capitals, offerings for success are made by priests. Subjects do not have ritual roles *vis-à-vis* the king, though their individual prosperity may be influenced by dead kings. In her 1934 study of the Baganda, Mair wrote that 'another peculiarity of Baganda religion is that there was no ceremonial in which it was obligatory for any one, outside the servants of the temple, to participate, no occasion for a national gathering such as are recorded almost everywhere among the Bantu, and certainly no gathering of kinsmen at the temple of the clan *lubale* [exceptional dead persons who were treated as divinities]. The cult of the *lubale* by the king himself was certainly regarded as performed on behalf of the nation, but the active participants in it were only the chiefs whom he designated as his messengers. The one tribal gathering took place in connection with the king's accession, and did not include a religious element.' Mair ascribed 'this rather loose association between the religious and the political system' perhaps to the fact that the kingdom was established by foreign invasion (at her pp. 241-2). But so were the Swazi, Zulu and Shilluk kingdoms. In short, after I worked out the morphological series of states in Chapter IV, I was sure

I would find that the Baganda, and 'more developed' states, would have a temple-cult, and not role-revealing rituals of the Swazi type. When I checked this in Mair and other books, I was proved correct. It was successful prediction.[40]

Family relations in the tribal situation are heavily ritualized, and conventions and mystical taboos create social distance between spouses and between parents and kin.[41] Nevertheless, conflict does not appear so markedly in ritual: it cuts too near the bone in so intimate a group as the family.

Finally, if the type of analysis set out above is to stand we have also to examine further those areas of social life, akin to the tribal situation, but where universalistic religions like Christianity exclude both reference of misfortunes to personal mystical evil doing and the ritualization of social relations. We know these practices survive in very poor and isolated, and internally integrated, areas. But where these mystical ideas are not found, it is important to check whether mechanisms alternative to ritual are present. For presumably disputes arising from conflicts in the community structure itself can still not be examined in the clear light of 'judicial' reasoning. Do such communities have mechanisms of redress which operate in ways similar to rituals in tribal societies? That is, are there mechanisms to cloak fundamental disharmonies, while the wider faith relates blessings and misfortunes to God?

I can here refer to only one study which has looked at these problems—Frankenberg's already cited analysis of a Welsh village. He explicitly compares with African rituals the mechanisms by which the community maintains its sense of unity. This community largely expresses its unity in the organizing of communal recreations. All true villagers take part at least indirectly. Success and prestige are sought in competition with other villages. The organization of the activity is co-operative; but co-operation is beset with struggles between men and women as groups and by feuds between families and individuals. Frankenberg shows how the committees debate by allusion and hint, which keep disputes from coming into the open. Under the surface innuendo and gossip and scandal both clarify and obscure issues. The secretary does not keep minutes or fails to produce them in crises so that major problems and strife are not dealt with continuously. Tribal rituals cannot settle fundamental disharmonies: the strife they engender recurs again and again so that new divinations and rituals are required. Similarly, the devices used in the Welsh village do not prevent quarrels erupting anew. Procedures akin to ceremonial and ritual give only temporary solutions. When the dispute comes finally to a head, some stranger to the total nexus of village ties is manipulated to make the proposal which drives one party out of the current activity. This stranger—resembling both scapegoat and diviner from afar—is then blamed for the break. The villagers feel that they would be in harmony if strangers did not make trouble. They feel further that they are therefore compelled to drop that recreation, purging their animosities with it. They start a new activity. Old animosities continue into it. Even though they know that many of them are in fact on bad terms, despite appearing friendly on the surface, by these devices they maintain the belief and the 'fiction' that they are a united community. Each crisis of this sort leads to a reassertion of that doctrine, which indeed is true.[42]

## SUMMARY: LAW AND RITUAL

This concludes our examination of strife and its adjustment. Disputes may be simple, and be handled by rational 'judicial' or 'proto-judicial' process. In stateless societies they may entail mobilizing various social pressures to achieve one's dues. The ability to mobilize pressures of this kind depends partly at least on the sense of justice, of law, in the community. As we analyse how disputes are settled, we have to specialize a varied vocabulary to clarify our problems.

Strife also arises on the surface of social life out of fundamental conflicts within social organization itself. Both parties to the dispute may be in the right in their own view as they act by independent, approved principles. Here beliefs in mystical agents relate these disputes to the occurrence of misfortunes. Divination of varied degrees of complexity isolates the responsible mystical agent, partly in terms of the state of personal relations in the group concerned. Individuals and sections seek to manipulate the divination and the beliefs entailed to their own ends. But ultimately the decision is given by the oracle, the divining apparatus, or the diviner, through mystical power. Once the mystical agent is selected, this indicates appropriate modes and rituals of adjustment.

The existence of these sorts of beliefs in tribal society cannot be ascribed to the mentality of the people concerned. The beliefs are slowly altered both by the increasing differentiation of society and the emergence of universalistic religions like Christianity, but only begin to disappear when the full industrial revolution breaks up closely knit groups. Many Hindu, and even Islamic, rituals are organized out of social relations.

Tribal rituals entail dramatization of the moral relations of the group concerned, for mystical power pervades the moral order. Performance of roles in social relations is believed to release beneficent power. But ritual is effective because it exhibits all the tensions and strife inherent in social life itself. Major loyalties are affirmed through the dramatic representation both of many bonds of unity and of the conflicts that lie in these varied bonds.

Conversely, in tribal society all changes in social relations—birth, a youth's growing up, a transfer of land, moving a village, changing one's activity, the alterations that accompany seasonal changes—tend to be regarded as threatening disturbances of the natural world, to correspond with the amended relations between people. Hence these sorts of changes are handled with much more ritual than in modern industrial society. This ritual, as well as ceremonial, not only mark special occasions, but also segregates roles in a situation where they are not materially segregated.

We can understand the beliefs and rituals of tribal society by relating them to the same conditions that explain the course of economic activity and political struggle, as well as the structure of law and order in the widest sense. These conditions are the relatively undifferentiated nature of social relations. Persons are intricately involved with the same sets of fellows in varied systems of purposive activity. Cross-cutting allegiances and processes of internal development within sets of relations establish ambivalence and conflict within each group. Ritual cloaks the fundamental disharmonies of social structure by affirming major loyalties to be beyond question.

Tribal religion and rituals are small-scale in their view. In each tribe they have a high degree of particularism in that the order of the universe is referred to the details of that tribe's own structure. Other tribes *may* be put on the fringe of mankind in these systems of belief. They certainly cannot just join the congregation at an important ritual. Yet these particularistic religions deal with problems general to human and social existence, which have faced men everywhere. Why should there be good and evil, prosperity and misfortune? How is human society set in the natural world? What is man? Whence does he come and whither does he go? How should men and women, parents and children, rulers and subjects, deal with one another? The answers are given in legend and myth, and also dogma, even though— with very important exceptions—dogmas are often simple. Professional priests, armed with writing, are required to elaborate theology. The complications of the universe for tribal society are mostly elaborated in the complexity of the ritual of social relations.

[1] It is a book which will fascinate every reader. I have abstracted a few of its riches in Chapter IV, 'The Logic in Witchcraft', in my *Custom and Conflict in Africa* (1955).

[2] This is again a proposal for the conventional specialization of terms such as I plead for with 'law'. It too fits English categories.

[3] A situation very well analysed for the Nyakyusa by M. Wilson in *Good Company* (1951) and by Bohannan for the Tiv (*Justice and Judgment among the Tiv*, 1957).

[4] See for an example outside of Africa, Pospisil, *Kapauka Papuans and their Law* (1958), pp. 154–5.

[5] *The Dynamics of Clanship* (1945), pp. 147 f.

[6] I elaborate on this position of Zulu women in 'The Licence in Ritual', Chapter V of my *Custom and Conflict in Africa* (1955). Middleton and Winter state in their editorial 'Introduction' to *Witchcraft and Sorcery in East Africa* (1963, at pp. 14 f.), that 'accusations of witchcraft against specific women tend to occur only in those patrilineal societies characterized by the presence of the house property complex'—i.e. where a man distributes his property among his wives, and each wife's sons have rights in the property allocated to their mother, as against their half-brothers by their father's other wives. This is the Zulu situation. It contrasts with the situations where a man's property is shared among all sons, or passes first to his brothers.

[7] Hunter (Mrs. M. Wilson) makes part of this point for the nearby Mpondo: *Reaction to Conquest* (1936), pp. 44, 313. V.q. her (with others) *Social Structure* (1952), pp. 183–94. The general operation of this process with reference to other tribes is discussed in the chapter on 'The Logic in Witchcraft' in my *Custom and Conflict in Africa* (1955).

[8] Mitchell, *The Yao Village* (1956): summarized above, p. 59 and pp. 236 f.

[9] Nadel, *Nupe Religion* (1954), Chapter VI.

[10] Middleton and Winter, in editing *Witchcraft and Sorcery in East Africa* (1963), have attempted some correlations: since the book was published after I completed my manuscript, I can only include footnote references, as above at fn. 6.

[11] Fortes, *The Web of Kinship among the Tallensi* (1949), pp. 32 f.

[12] For an excellent, and brief, analysis see Fortes, *Oedipus and Job in West African Religion* (1959).

[13] For a recent comparison of how beliefs are related to variations in organization, see Goody, *Death, Property and the Ancestors* (1962), pp. 407 f.

[14] *Dynamics of Clanship among the Tallensi* (1945), p. 98. See also from among many Evans-Pritchard, *Nuer Religion* (1956), p. 150.

[15] See above, pp. 100 f. and 127.

[16] *The Life of a South African Tribe* (1927), Vol. II, pp. 571 and preceding.

[17] The clearest discussion I know of how the 'ambivalence' inherent in social life is symbolized in a divinatory apparatus is Turner's analysis of the 'bones' in Ndembu *Divinations: its Symbolism and Techniques* (1961).

[18] In a book published as this one goes to press, van Velsen (*The Politics of Kinship*, 1964) shows the complexity of alignments, and pressures operating in a group, organized

on a few simple principles, when seeking to divine why a young girl died. Seemingly the simpler and the fewer the principles of organization, the more scope is allowed for jockeying for position.

[19] *Justice and Judgment among the Tiv* (1957), p. 169 f. Bohannan calls them 'moots', not 'séances', as Evans-Pritchard calls the corresponding gatherings among Azande. I consider 'moot' is better applied to a meeting with judicial-like procedures, and not to divination.

[20] I use the vernacular *tsav* here to bring out its multiple implications in belief, which reflect the duality of people's talents in actual social life (see above, pp. 233 f.).

[21] *Justice and Judgment among the Tiv* (1957), p. 189.

[22] See Malinowski, 'Magic, Science and Religion' (1925).

[23] M. Wilson, *Good Company* (1951), p. 100.

[24] Granet, *Chinese Civilization* (1950), pp. 169, 201, 254.

[25] See above, p. 225.

[26] Herskovits, *Dahomey* (1938), vol. ii, pp. 287, 300.

[27] On *Rituals of Kinship among the Nyakyusa* (1957) and *Communal Rituals among the Nyakyusa* (1959).

[28] I follow, summarily, an illuminating essay by Turner on 'Symbols in Ndembu Ritual' (1964), in which he cites authorities on this distinction. See also Nadel, *The Foundations of Social Anthropology* (1951).

[29] Lienhardt, 'Anuak Village Headmen' (1957), pp. 352–3.

[30] These rituals are brilliantly described by Kuper as 'The Drama of Kingship' in *An African Aristocracy* (1947). I analysed them as one of a series of what I called 'rituals of rebellion' in a Frazer Lecture (republished in my *Order and Rebellion in Tribal Africa*, 1963). I considered them also in a more general and 'popular' form in 'The Licence in Ritual' in *Custom and Conflict in Africa* (1955).

[31] These rituals are described and analysed in citations in a previous footnote.

[32] Analysed from Junod, *Life of a South African Tribe* (1927), vol. i, pp. 318 f., in my *Custom and Conflict in Africa* (1955).

[33] See above, pp. 46–7.

[34] The preceding analysis is argued at greater length in my essay on 'Les Rites de Passage' in Gluckman (editor), *Essays on the Ritual of Social Relations* (1962). The other essays in that book by Forde, Fortes and Turner, bear on all the problems raised in this chapter.

[35] See Turner, 'Symbols in Ndembu Ritual' (1964); also 'Three Symbols of Passage in Ndembu Circumcision Ritual' (1962).

[36] In the 'Introduction' to my *Order and Rebellion in Tribal Africa* (1963).

[37] In 'The Role of the Sexes in Wiko Circumcision Ceremonies' in Fortes, editor, *Social Structure* (1949).

[38] See her *Chisungu: A Girl's Initiation Ceremony* (1956).

[39] See above, p. 178.

[40] I had not worked this out when I wrote my 'Introduction' to *Order and Rebellion in Tribal Africa* (1963).

[41] Well worked out in Fortes, *The Web of Kinship among the Tallensi* (1949). On the general thesis see my 'Estrangement in the Family', in *Custom and Conflict in Africa* (1955).

[42] Shortly due from Manchester University Press is a study of *Sorcery in its Social Setting* among the Chewa of Northern Rhodesia. The Chewa are similar in organization to the Yao, and Marwick follows on and develops Mitchell's analysis, with additional social-psychological hypotheses. (Book not listed in bibliography at end.)

# CHAPTER VII

# CUSTOM IN STABILITY AND CHANGE

## TIME IN TRIBAL HISTORIES

Anthropologists in the nineteenth century were concerned to make sense of the odds and ends of customs drawn from accounts of peoples scattered over the world. They mostly looked at customs torn out of their context in social relations. They used these customs to establish the general evolution of human society from its primitive origins. Most of these evolutionary reconstructions appear crude: a few were more sophisticated but still were involved in speculative and conjectural history. Maine and Durkheim and some others produced more penetrating analyses of the interdependent development of forms of law and morals. I have in fact set modern analyses of tribal societies within the contrast which they drew between, in Maine's words, societies dominated by status and societies dominated by contract.

It is significant that Maine's important work was based on societies about whose development we have some, if inadequate, precise historical knowledge. Durkheim too in his analysis of how increasing division of labour influenced law, morals, and religion relied mainly on historical records of Hebrew, Greek, Roman, and more recent times. Their conjectures about tribal peoples were used to thrust their studies deeper into the past. If we eliminate the errors which they committed in the course of this exercise, their analyses still stand as bold attempts to understand major tendencies in the development of historic societies. Many of their errors about tribal peoples can be ascribed to the poor data with which they had to work.

Many modern field anthropologists have had to work without good historical records on the tribes they studied, and some had none at all. In a number of tribes they found that there was not even any history of the tribes, in our sense of 'history'. This is, of course, most marked in the stateless societies which could not mark events by the putative reigns of kings. For example, Radcliffe-Brown wrote that 'in the cosmology of the Australian natives the cosmos, the ordered universe, including both the order of nature and the social order, came into existence at a time in the past' which he calls the World-Dawn, for this name corresponds to certain ideas he had found amongst the aborigines of some tribes. 'This order (of nature and society) resulted from the doings and adventures of certain sacred beings.' He calls these beings Dawn Beings. The explanations of topographical features, of natural species and their characteristics, and of social laws, customs, and usages are given in the form of myths about the happenings of the World-Dawn.

'The cosmos is ruled by law. But whereas we think of the laws of nature as statements of what invariably does happen (except, of course, in miracles), and of moral or social laws as what ought to be observed but are sometimes broken, the Australian does not make this distinction. For him men and women ought to observe the rules of behaviour that were fixed for all time by the events of the World-Dawn. . . .'[1] The beliefs, myths and rituals involved in the concept of these Dawn Beings are very complex. I refer to them here in order to emphasize that Australian Aborigines believed and acted as if they lived in a society whose form and order were laid down virtually at creation.

This attitude is representative of many peoples. The Pueblo Red Indians of the American Southwest, like the Aborigines, perform rituals which are rationalized by reference to myths about the creation of the universe and society, both of which they aspire to maintain in their pristine form. Whitman concluded, for the Indians of San Ildefonso: 'History as they knew it, was represented by mythological legends preserved by the priests.'[2]

We must be clear here on three points. First, these statements refer to history in the sense of a progressive development of social institutions. In both myths and legends as seen in citations in preceding chapters from Malinowski on Trobrianders (pp. 26 f.) and Radcliffe-Brown on the Andamanese (p. 243), there is affirmation of the age-old warranty of the natural and social orders as they are, and of the importance of ritual to keep those orders working. Griaule and Dieterlen sum up their analysis of the immensely complicated cosmology of the Dogon of West Africa: 'The Dogon, in this system of myths and symbols, are able to express a correspondence between their social organization and the world order as they conceive it. For them social life reflects the working of the universe and, conversely, the world order depends on the proper ordering of society.'[3] In short, there is knowledge in these tribes of a series of events in recent times which have affected social life: but those events are regarded as irrelevant intrusions into the course of maintaining the mythologically validated order. In this way the Indians of the Pueblos have tried to exclude the incursions of Spanish as well as other Indians, and even their own difficulties when declining population interferes with the maintenance of their rituals.

Second, in reporting the views of peoples studied Radcliffe-Brown and other anthropologists were not asserting that they themselves accepted that there had been no social change, even in recent times. They described how these changes have been absorbed into the stationary view which dominates the system of beliefs.

Third, there are societies which state that definite historical events instituted their existent order. The Shilluk believe this: but they add that their culture-hero, Nyikang, was divinely connected—as the Romans related Aeneas to the gods. Nyikang's rituals reflect dispositions during this founding period. The Ruanda have a clear knowledge of how their kingdom was constituted: but their ruler too was associated with God. The Swazi and the Zulu also are clear about how their royal families established kingdoms by conquest: but their present natural and social orders are mystically involved in their kingships. The Luapula Lunda traditions tell how the first of their kings left Mwatiyamvo's kingdom in the Congo to conquer a realm for himself. What is significant in the present context is that the king and those chiefs regard their present relations, and their rituals, as controlled by the respective actions of their predecessors *vis-à-vis* one another. As cited (above p. 120) the historical establishment of certain important political relations between the incumbents of perpetual positions is recounted by them both in the first person and the present tense.

This tendency to incapsulate past in present occurs of course even in commemorative ceremonials in modern society. In Britain, when the House of Commons is summoned to listen to the Monarch's speech from the throne in the House of Lords, the royal messenger knocks three times before they answer. They still resist Charles I's attempt to dominate their predecessors—whom they continue to represent.

The stateless peoples also record their migrations, and their battles and conquests. But this is what Evan-Pritchard wrote of the Nuer: 'Valid history ends a century ago, and tradition, generously measured, takes us back only ten to twelve generations in lineage structure, and if we are right in supposing that lineage structure never grows, it follows that the distance between the beginning of the world and the present day remains unalterable. Time is thus not a continuum, but is a constant structural relationship between two points, the first and last persons in a line of agnatic descent. How shallow is Nuer time may be judged from the fact that the tree under which mankind came into being was still standing in Western Nuerland a few years ago!'[4]

A lineage system as a system of organized social relations embodies a fixed stretch of time, from the origin of men to their present-day descendants. Fortes says of the similar Tallensi system: 'Unbroken continuity of descent, persistence of self-identical corporate units, stability of settlement—these are the essential characteristics of the [Tallensi] lineage system. It requires the assumption, which the ancestor cult places beyond question, that the social structure is the same as it was in the past. . . .

'The Tallensi, therefore, have no history in the sense of authentic records of past events. The memories and reminiscences of old men are part of their biographies and never contribute to the building up of a body of socially preserved history. Their myths and legends are one means of rationalizing and defining the structural relationships of group to group or the pattern of their institutions.' Some of the legends may refer to actual persons, 'but there is no objective evidence. [Tallensi] myths and legends counterfeit history; they do not document it. They are a part of [Tallensi] social philosophy, projected into the past because the people think of their social order as continuous and persistent, handed down from generation to generation.'[5]

The fixed depth in time of social history is particularly marked in tribal systems where political relations between groups depend on their position *vis-à-vis* one another on a genealogy. Any factual alteration in political relations in the present, is met by altering the positions of critical ancestors in the genealogy. Laura Bohannan in her article on 'A Genealogical Charter' (1952) describes how the Tiv do this quite consciously, even though the correctness of their genealogies is an article of faith with them. In working out how 'drumming the scandal' operates we have met at least an incipient situation in which the relative strength of groups demanded some adjustment. Evans-Pritchard and Fortes in their studies dealt with similar situations. In these societies political and social obligations depend upon nearness and distance on the genealogy and also upon territorial propinquity. Hence adjustment of the flexible genealogy is essential to meet the inflexible demands of territorial distribution. Many social devices enable this adjustment to be effected, some of which I considered in citing analyses by Cunnison, Mitchell and Watson.[6] These devices are customary rules, such as naming children after their grandparents or having one term of reference for brothers, grandparents and grandchildren. The fairly widespread African institution by which a woman can give cattle to marry a 'wife' by whom she becomes 'father' to children begotten by men, may be important not so much because this kind of marriage is frequent, but because it may in later generations enable people, who are related to a group through a woman, to claim that they were in fact related through her in a father's and not a mother's capacity. In Tikopia married people are known by the names of their houses, and these names endure through generations. It is taboo to speak the personal names of a father or grandfather which presumably in this patrilineal system become submerged in the house-name. These customs obviously allow considerable manipulation of genealogies.

In tribal societies of this type the genealogy can therefore be amended to fit existing patterns of relations. Some of the methods by which this is achieved have to be worked out in analysis of what is going on in the present, which is all that the anthropologists have records on. Peters has been able to check these amendments among the Bedouin of Cyrenaica with some historical records on characters in the lower levels of the genealogy, to show how the genealogy is kept at a constant depth of eleven generations. That the genealogy must have been kept short is evident from the fact that the Bedouin tribes' major invasion of the region occurred in 1050 or 1051 A.D. Yet all the tribes are believed to be descended from one ancestress who lies some eleven generations back.[7]

In her article on Tiv genealogies, Mrs. Bohannan says that 'the way in which Tiv learn genealogies and the lack of written record allow changes to occur through time without a general realization of the occurrence of that change; social change can exist with a doctrine of social permanence'. Peters has been able to show that even where genealogies are written, the form in which they are written may allow amendments to be made to accommodate present-day relations, particularly where many persons bear similar names.[8] And Freedman concludes in his study of *Lineage Organization in Southeastern China* (1958) which he wrote from the reports of others, that 'the evidence that genealogical principles of arrangement [of ancestral tablets] were modified by the social status of the dead and their living descendants is not abundant; the question probably did not occur to many observers; but when the evidence is given it is very convincing' (p. 79). Their initial experience with societies which had no progressive view of history, and on which historical records defining social changes were scarce, has deeply influenced social anthropologists.

The timeless ideology as represented in ritual is not unique to these types of societies. The crucial rites of even a religion like Christianity are also referred to long-past events, like the Birth and Crucifixion of Christ, but these events transcend time. The Jewish Passover commemorates not only a past event which manifested the grace of Jehovah to his Chosen People, but it is a timeless covenant of that grace.[9] Where '. . . . the very stuff of religious reality . . . ' in its mass of detail '. . . is co-ordinated, woven together into a significant pattern by a scheme of beliefs closely integrated with the particular native social structure' (Firth),[10] this timeless quality has to be related to the nature of social relations themselves. Hence in studying these societies, anthropologists had to analyse why they were 'timeless'.

Rights and duties between Nuer are ostensibly set by their genealogical relations to one another. The more closely related they are, the more stringent their duties and the greater their rights. As their point of common ancestry recedes into the past, the more tenuous are their ties. Evans-Pritchard therefore formulated the concept of 'structural time' to cover the political distance between groups on the genealogy and on the ground. This rule did not apply so much to individuals, though it was effective in relations between men of the dominant or aristocratic lineages of small local sections inhabited by Nuer of diverse origin and by absorbed Dinka. The spread of men on the ground he called 'structural space'. Structural time was directly proportional to structural space.

Nuer historical thought about the relations between groups was conditioned by the structural time built into their genealogy as a reflection of relations between groups. Both structural time and structural space are independent of, though influenced by, ecological time—set by seasons, sun, etc.—and ecological space—set by topography and man's use of the land. This meant that to understand how Nuer thought about their relationships with one another, Evans-Pritchard had to envisage a political process going on through the full 11-12 generation period embodied in the lineage genealogy which was their ideology. The whole of this time-period was present in the relations between groups and their members, even when these were viewed over a very short period of time. For this time-period had to be a framework within which were analysed the allegiances and hostilities imposed by common and diverse descent on different men. These allegiances and hostilities determined in what associations men would pursue their various interests—making a living, acquiring prestige, marrying and rearing children, securing and defending their rights. To analyse how the political system controlled the activities of men, in the present moment, Evans-Pritchard had to make an analysis over 11-12 generations.

Anthropologists were confronted with the same situation in other tribes. Genealogies of 11-12 generations in depth are found in many tribes scattered through the world: Ashanti and Tallensi lineages in West Africa, the Bedouin in North Africa, the Zulu when first recorded in the 1820s, all show this depth. Firth's limited genealogies on Tikopia appeared to be of this depth, and on his visit twenty-five years later he found some signs of lengthening. There are other societies with greater and less depth. But where genealogies organize political relations, we seem to have at the bottom 4-5 generations which may correctly reflect the relations between living men, and above that a varying number of ancestors in perpetual relationships with one another, because they reflect relations between groups which are not as ephemeral as those between individual men. I have cited how among the Luapula Lunda, Cunnison established that the system of kinship terminology kept the top levels of the generations in two generations, covering the relationships of mother's brother to sister's son, and of 'brothers', since grandparents and grandchildren were placed in one category. However among the patrilineal Mambwe, Watson found that three fixed levels covered the positions of grandfather and father and grandson, since new political groups were formed by breaking off new units from inherited positions with permanent titles. As a position at the head of a new unit was established, the mother of the man occupying that postition was treated not as the wife of the present incumbent of the superior post, but as a wife to the enduring position. Wives moved up the genealogy to be 'married' to the original founder of the position. Among the matrilineal Lunda, if a man separated from a brother occupying a perpetual position, their mother as the focus of differentiation would in time become the sister to the founder of the position. The two positions, old and newly founded, would be perpetual brothers. The same process of moving a woman upward to be sister to the position occurred if the person moving off was sister's son to the incumbent, but the two positions would be linked perpetually as sister's son to mother's brother.

We are not yet clear why so many lineage systems should have 6–7 generations on top of the basic 5–6 generations of probably real relationships. Duties and rights alter critically at certain levels in the genealogy: and these changes presumably are recurrent and determine critical points of segmentation.[11]

I have touched on this very complex problem to emphasize that when tribal peoples think about many of their social relationships they do so with a stationary, or repetitive, perspective on time. We see that they think thus not because they are unable to distinguish between past, present and future: in fact, some tribal languages inflect their verbs to express fine grades of time where we have to use adverbs. These concepts of social time are inherent in the structure of particular types of social relations themselves. For each type of group, or social relationship, has imposed on it a certain time-scale by the purpose for which it exists and the nature of its personnel.[12] The manner in which these people think about time in relation to social activities and organization may appear to be irrational. It reflects a living reality of social life.

## ANTHROPOLOGICAL ANALYSIS AND TIME

This situation applies to ourselves as well as to tribal peoples. This is apparent if we think of relationships in the family.[13] In our own society we have the means to measure the life of a marriage by wedding anniversaries, and annual birthday celebrations mark the advance of each child to adolescence and adulthood. But it is common for the birthdays of children to be more noteworthy than the birthdays of parents. Each year of a child's growth is related to an elaborate set of institutions involved in our specialized educational process: entrance to nursery school, infant school, primary school, secondary school. Within each of these stages most children are promoted annually to a higher class. Hence, I suggest, each year of the child's life is significant, and distinguished. The position of parents is different. In some ways they lose count of years, for their view of the family is set in a different cycle of activities, whose periodic critical periods are not set by annual social movements. In the professional classes the father's career is likely to advance in intermittent spurts. As a father, he is involved with his wife in a movement from marriage through the phases before the first child is born into a phase dominated by the infancy of the first and subsequent children, into a phase when elder children become adolescent and then leave home and marry, until all the children leave home. This phasing stamps itself deep on the way in which the persons involved think about the time-scale of their family relations. They think and calculate in terms of years for the children's educational progress and for holidays. But professional parents' conversation and plans are also dominated by such ideas of time as: when the eldest child can be responsible for the youngest; when the youngest can look after himself; etc. The view of time in a working-class family may be somewhat different.

The manner in which ideas of time influence politicians is similar. These ideas not only include a calendrical reckoning to cope with sessions of the legislature, but they are also surely dominated by the four-year or five-year cycle of election on the longer run. Beyond that, they probably involve calculations about the respective ages of various party leaders, and how the ages of potential successors to these may influence the individual's own opportunities. A 'parliamentary' structure has its own time-scale.

When Evans-Pritchard began to write in terms of 'structural time' he was doing far more than invent a handy phrase to translate the bizarre modes of thought of an out-of-the-way Sudanic people. He was providing a key to expose the depths of social relationships to our view. For he showed us that in order to examine the inter-relationships of Nuer with one another for even the shortest period of time, we had to throw our analysis into a much longer time-scale. This is the time-scale which it takes a particular set of relationships to work themselves out fully.

If we are to analyse family relationships, we must look at their development through the full cycle of birth of children, their

PLATE XXIII. CEREMONIAL ROLES AT AN MBUNDA BOY'S INITIATION CEREMONY

*a.* Barotse women form a chorus for a masked dance who represents the kindly aspects of the presiding ancestral spirits.

*b.* Barotse women flee from a dancer who represents their cruel aspect. But both care for the initiates.

(see pp. 265 f.)

PLATE XXIV. SOCIAL SANCTIONS

*a.* The court was complete (a local judge settles a dispute between the explorers and their carriers).

(see p. 174)

(from H. Capello and R. Ivens, *Benguella to . . . Yacca*, 1863)

*b.* An Eskimo 'at home'.

(see p. 308

(from F. Nansen, *The First Crossing of Greenland*, 1890)

growing up and departure to found new families, and the entrance of their parents on grandparenthood. The last phase is essential in the study of a tribal family: it influences much earlier relationships in the family cycle. I think this influence also exists in our modern family, affecting the relations of parents to each other and to their children, even if their own parents are not alive. (In tribal society, there will of course be substitutes for the parents' parents if these are dead.) The total cycle determines the shape of each arc along its course. In short, to understand a short period of family life, we must look at it as if it were part of a three-generational repetitive cycle. Nuer and Tallensi political relations have to be analysed as if they were part of an 11-generational cycle. The period for the Mambwe lineage is 8 generations, and for the Lunda 7 generations. My colleagues have shown that these varying scales of structural time are controlled by the customs of each tribe.

Similarly, if we want to understand a day in the life of a legislature we must look at it in terms of the full cycle of a series of elections (I believe at least three in Britain). For day-to-day politics are influenced by the fact that the legislature runs through a series of elections. In an African state to analyse former day-to-day politics we must work out the cycle of rebellions. These did not occur anything like every day: but the possibility of rebellion influenced the motives and actions of everyone involved in politics.

Political scientists, economists, and historians in practice work with scales of structural time of this type. But few of them—as far as I know—have tried to work out the significance of time in varied social relations in this way. Anthropologists even more than sociologists have done so because their field material has thrust the problem at them.

Anthropological analyses may therefore appear to have a timeless quality. It looks as if the institutions they are examining go on and on for ever in an interminable cycle. Superficial readers—including some fellow-anthropologists[14]—therefore assume that these anthropologists are unaware of the possibility, and even the actual facts, of historical change. This, of course, is nonsense. A good anthropological analysis at the same time as it presents the structural development through time of a particular set of relations, also considers the various standardized alternatives that offer. A family may be childless or children may die, divorce or premature death of one of the spouses may interrupt or shift the course of development. And if external events are influencing the cycle these are also taken into account, even if they are to some extent haphazard. But no systematic analysis at all can be made unless the central analysis in structural time is made.

It is this kind of analysis that, for example, Mitchell made of Yao villages.[15] In reality he found in Yaoland villages composed of varying numbers of matrilineages, as well as villages of single lineages. As he examined their histories and investigated co-operation and strife in each village, he showed that he could explain everyday relations in the village if he put these villages at different points on a cycle running through some three generations. Compound villages hive off simple villages, which grow into compound villages which hive off simple villages. The headmen of these villages remain linked by perpetual kinship within the major political structure, which has a different time-scale. Here relations of villages are fixed 'forever' in Yao thought. This analysis is in structural time, not actual 'chronological' time. Mitchell does, in the course of his analysis, deal with villages in chronological time, in actual history: for he considers the effects of British occupation, men going afar to work for wages, the introduction of cash-crops, on the history of villages.

Clearly Mitchell can only analyse village life in this cycle. For only by looking at social processes in these terms can he make sense of the manner in which ecological and economic interests, and individual ambition and public feeling, operate within the setting of the biological cycle of men and women, the use of land, and the framework of custom and belief. These processes we have explained in detail. We have seen how co-operation is enjoined on persons, and how in time conflict of processes emerges from this enjoined co-operation.

In making such an analysis the anthropologist does not necessarily imply that the social relationships concerned have operated in precisely that way from the beginning of time, or that they will operate in precisely that way in the future. He may make a reasonable prediction for the future, but much will depend on future events which are haphazard.

One sound warning for research is contained in this cyclical analysis. We must be careful in making observations during a period of general social change, to try to distinguish real changes in action from what may well be new means of expressing established phases of the cycle. Schapera, for example, has shown that when young Tswana go out to the towns of South Africa to work, they return apparently rejecting tribal mores, and elders' and chiefs' authority. When they marry, and reach middle-age with growing children, their interests turn often into achieving elderhood and position around the chief for themselves. The cycle of family development itself exercises considerable constraint. Similarly, factional disputes phrased in terms of modern situations often continue from the past into the present divisions in villages.[16]

Preceding analyses have demonstrated that as many social relationships develop, strife and disputes emerge from the very customs and rules, as well as interests, which structure the relationships. This strife is exacerbated by the fact at which I can only glance, that a society is composed of many independent sets of relationships. Each of these has its own time-scale. Where they influence one another, these scales may not be in mesh; and this too is productive of conflict. We do not yet know—and may never know—the full complexity of events which set the periodicity of the cycle of rebellions even in the relatively simple situation of South African tribes. It may have been influenced by the maturing of young men who found their way to power blocked by elders. This was the fruit of an independent structure of relationships, possessing possibly a different time-scale from the accumulation of grievances against the king.

## EQUILIBRIUM AND CHANGE[17]

Anthropologists analyse a society as if it were in a state of equilibrium. They clearly do not mean by this that the structure of society is a set of rigid relations between fixed points, any more than Rutherford implied that the internal structure of the atom was rigid when he built a model of it out of billiard balls and wire. In fact the inherent meaning of 'equilibrium' excludes rigidity. 'Equilibrium' is the tendency of a system to return after disturbance to its previous state. To make clear that this is what anthropologists mean by equilibrium, I have myself spoken of 'repetitive equilibria', but the adjective 'repetitive' is redundant. The correct view of equilibrium involves both the acceptance of internal disturbance and of the possibility of disturbance by external events. If a system is in equilibrium, adjustive processes will occur to absorb any disturbance so that the system will after the working of these processes be in the same condition as before.

In the case of a social system this does not mean that the system will be constituted of precisely the same parts. After a rebellion a new king is in power, different chiefs are his favourites, the population may temporarily drop in number because of deaths in civil fighting, different persons and groups have new degrees of control over resources. The new king may be different in character from the man he ousted: he may be kindlier, less liable to commit acts of tyranny. The pattern of political relations remains constant: but there is some give, some leeway, in its structure.

The equilibrium of natural systems is similar. After a period of time the internal constituents of an atom are different, but they are identical (in most cases) in type with their predecessors, and they occupy the same positions relative to one another. But there is far less leeway in this type of system than in a social system. In the equilibria of organic systems cells and other parts change constantly. But the system retains its structure, which has more leeway than physical structures, and less leeway than social structures. In all systems of all types sufficient variation may occur to alter the structure of the system itself.

As we see equilibrium in social systems, therefore, we deal with constant disturbance and change. Preceding analyses have in fact demonstrated that disturbance and change of parts is inherent in these systems. Disturbance arises because men are not perfectly moulded by their upbringing: some act against rules. Disturbance arises also as men compete with one another for scarce goods, scarce women, scarce prestige, and scarce positions of power. Regulative and redressive customs restrain and settle these disturbances. Even more difficult to deal with is the disturbance set up by the conflicting pressures of various customs and the allegiances they enforce. The energy in social life comes largely from the way in which men (and women) pursue various ends to satisfy organic and psychical needs, as these are shaped by upbringing in a particular society. But the customary, institutional structure of the society also determines with whom they shall co-operate and with whom they shall compete as they pursue these ends. It is a most complex situation, since allegiances are never wholehearted and one-sided. Custom establishes varied, often contradictory, allegiances, for each man. Even rebellion may be an approved custom,[18] like accusations of witch-craft. In result, processes are set in motion which through a period of time operate against one another to cancel one another out. Hence after a period of change and disturbance in particular actual relations, the pattern of society is re-established. In a particular area there may develop a quarrel within a village over land that is becoming short, or over the succession to headmanship, or disturbance may be created by the increase in numbers of all or some of the sections of the village. Intrigues may result, involving accusations of witchcraft against some person who is held responsible for one of the misfortunes which beset all people. On the basis of this accusation the village may split. A split is socially justified, despite the value of unity, if the split enables persons to escape from witchcraft or to expel witchcraft. A new village is set up, of the same type as the original village, though perhaps at an earlier stage in the cycle. There are now two similar villages, both smaller, and less diversified in different degrees, than the parent village. But if we examine all the villages in the society, we find that they range in complexity of internal organization from small groups of people to complex associations of several of these groups. The simple village is developing towards the complex, the complex village will at least shed simple villages even if it does not completely disinte-grate into them. Analysis of an equilibrium always involves analysis in time; and in social analysis it is analysis in structural time.

While we are concerned with tribal societies it is easier to make this type of analysis because they were restricted in their external relations and their economies were stationary. But the analysis depends nevertheless on exclusion of events external to the system; and to achieve this, we may have mentally to exclude such events, in the way that Galileo thought of a vacuum before this could be produced, or of frictionless movement which does not occur in the world. We know for a particular tribe that if the population increased continually to multiply villages, ultimately there would not be enough land to maintain the system. More radical change would be bound to occur, unless a section of the population moved off in a mass migration. An analysis of a repetitive social system is made over a certain range of time, for a particular limited area of space, and for certain purposes.

To effect this type of analysis, we have to circumscribe an area of social life in time, in space, and in terms of the purpose of the social relations involved. All scientists have to circumscribe fields of study.[19] In the study of social life this is very difficult to do, because we cannot isolate events in a test-tube to observe how they influence one another. But it has to be done by every social scientist and every historian: otherwise there would be not just no end to research, but there could not even be research. In looking at the equilibria of African states I have not dealt with either the psychological complications in the personalities of competitors for power, or with historical reconstructions that states in Africa may have been created by the dispersion in stages of rulers from the old North-Eastern African state of Meroe, after it was devastated by invaders.[20] For my purpose this was not necessary. I began with the established state: and analysed how it worked through a period of history, taking account of change.

The concept of equilibrium in repetitive systems thus covers complex processes of disturbance and readjustment. Nor is the cycle through which events pass simple. In his study of *The Political Systems of Highland Burma* (1954) Leach, cited[21] above, found that the equilibrium oscillated between a stage when one lineage exercised aristocratic prestige (rather than authority) over a number of other lineages, through a phase when that prestige broke down and lineages were equal in relation to one another, back to a stage in which an aristocratic lineage re-emerged. He thought he was dealing with social change, and used this example to argue, falsely, that other anthropologists had too static a view of equilibrium. He had himself confused an oscillating equilibrium with a process of radical change, in which the actual structure of the system, both in the character of many of its parts and in their inter-relationships, is altered.

To some extent in analysing what is in reality a constant process of disturbance and readjustment, it is necessary to establish certain fixed points. This may give the unwary reader the impression of a rigid structure. In social anthropological analysis these fixed points, aside from the limiting factors of environment, material technology, and the plastic demands of human biological and psychical constitution, are groups and social relationships with their attendant customs and beliefs. Parts of every

anthropological study consist of the setting out of these socio-
cultural facts, and of attempts to show the interdependence of
these customs and beliefs with one another. There is such an
interdependence, and it is being established by wide-scale comparison between the customs and beliefs of many societies. In
this book I have only incidentally used and referred to these
comparative studies, partly because most of them have been
concerned with domestic relations and relations of individual
kinship. Here I have dealt with the manner in which the customs
of a society, in their interdependence with one another, set the
paths along which men move in pursuing their interests, so that
they quarrel: their quarrels then set in motion other customary
processes of settlement and adjustment.

I must repeat yet again that we do not conceive of this interdependence of custom as being an interdependence of wondrous
harmony. It is a canon of belief among the members of the
society themselves that some such harmony is there. It is this
search for harmony, despite the reality of conflict within cohesion,
that anthropological investigation suggests is asserted in ritual,
validated by myth. But Malinowski, who drove home to us the
extent to which a culture—a body of customs—was integrated,
also stressed that myth and ritual cover much inherent disharmony. He demonstrated that 'Myth fulfils in primitive
culture an indispensable function: it expresses, enhances and
codifies belief; it safeguards and enforces morality; it vouches
for the efficiency of ritual and contains practical rules for the
guidance of man. Myth is thus a vital ingredient of human
civilization; it is not an idle tale, but a hard-worked active force;
it is not an intellectual explanation or an artistic imagery, but a
pragmatic charter of primitive faith and moral wisdom. . . . The
myth [as against folk-tale and legend] comes into play when rite,
ceremony, or a social or moral rule demands justification,
warrant of antiquity, reality, and sanctity. . . . [But] the strength
of the various mythological and legal principles is manifested in
that the myths of justification still contain the antagonistic and
logically irreconcilable facts and points of view, and only try to
cover them by facile reconciliatory incident, obviously manufactured *ad hoc*. The study of such stories is extremely interesting,
both because it gives us a deep insight into the native psychology
of tradition, and because it tempts us to reconstruct the past history

of the tribe, though we must yield to the temptation with due caution and scepticism. . . .' Malinowski then shows the dubious worth of throwing these contradictory elements in the myths into a series of historical events, and he concludes that 'as far as the sociological theory of these legends goes the historical reconstruction is irrelevant. Whatever the historical reality of their unrecorded past may be, myths serve to cover certain inconsistencies created by historical events, rather than to record these events exactly. The myths associated with the spread of powerful sub-clans show on certain points a fidelity to life in that they record facts inconsistent with one another. The incidents by which this inconsistency is obliterated, if not hidden, are most likely fictitious: we have seen certain myths vary according to the locality in which they are told. In other cases the incidents bolster up non-existent claims and rights.

'The historical consideration of myth is interesting, therefore, in that it shows that myth, taken as a whole, cannot be sober dispassionate history, since it is always made *ad hoc* to fulfil a certain sociological function, to glorify a certain group, or to justify an anomalous status. These considerations show us also that to the native immediate history, semi-historic legend, and unmixed myth flow into one another, form a continuous sequence, and fulfil the same sociological function.

'And this brings us once more to our original contention that the really important thing about the myth is its character of a retrospective, ever-present, live actuality. It is to a native neither a fictitious story, nor an account of a dead past; it is a statement of a bigger reality still partially alive. It is alive in that its precedent, its law, its moral, still rule the social life of the natives. It is clear that myth functions especially wherever there is a sociological strain, such as in matters of great difference of rank and power, matters of precedence and subordination, and unquestionably where profound historical changes have taken place. So much can be asserted as a fact, though it must always remain doubtful how far we can carry out historical reconstruction from the myth.'[22]

This statement of the problems considered above, and of our answers to them, cannot yet be bettered. Incidentally we may see how much doubt this analysis of Malinowski's casts on attempts to deduce from Ancient Greek myths that patriarchal peoples conquered matriarchal peoples who had worshipped a

Mother Goddess. Ritual and belief to cover the conflicts focused on the mother is even more important among patrilineal than among matrilineal peoples.

## THE STUDY OF RADICAL SOCIAL CHANGE

The manner in which social anthropologists have analysed radical social change lies outside the main scope of the present book. But I must refer to it briefly lest I leave the impression that the subject's capacity is confined to the analysis of repetitive equilibria. Many social and cultural anthropologists have written about radical change in particular societies, even if we exclude from our reckoning those who have produced large-scale evolutionary and diffusionist theories, both in past and recent times. Every study of a particular tribe that I have cited in the course of this book, after analysing the tribal equilibrium, considers the tribe's position since it came under European domination. Others deal with earlier radical development.

The concept of equilibrium continues to dominate these studies. What the anthropologist does is to draw cross-sections through the tribal organization at various periods. He then attempts to analyse the process by which new institutions and personnel, with their own validating dogmas, reach a temporary balance of co-operation, in which mechanisms of settlement and adjustment redress at least partially strife and disturbance. As we saw in earlier chapters, radical change proceeds as much by multiplication and diversification, in which the old survives alongside the new, as by substitution of new for old. In this respect, social anthropological analysis of change does not differ from historical analysis of change in social institutions. Anthropologists and historians have to assess the accommodation of institutions, through the actions of their personnel, to one another. This necessarily involves an analysis in terms of balance, of equilibrium. But the periods of structural time involved in these temporary equilibria are very short, in the sense that no process of accommodation is sufficiently effective to enable various cycles involved in old and new institutional arrangements to run their full cycle to produce a repeated pattern. Imperfect accommodation leads constantly to the alteration of relationships between persons, to new distributions of power, and to the emergence of new types of inter-related personnel. A new temporary equilibrium is set up, and adjustment may operate until some crisis results in the emergence of new institutional dispositions.

In the course of analysing these series of temporary equilibria, many anthropologists focus their attention on how the new situation influences traditional, tribal arrangements, and is influenced by them. If they deal with social change at the end of an analysis mainly devoted to the structure and equilibrium of the traditional tribal system, it is because most tribal systems have in fact absorbed *many* changes into their traditional equilibrium. This is a fact, not an anthropological bias, as Turner's work on the Ndembu shows, as well as Firth's follow-up a generation later, of his earlier research in Tikopia. Many anthropologists are interested in the fascinating complexities of tribal systems: if they weight their analyses towards these, it does not mean that they deny the occurrence of change.

This slanting also partially results from an aspect of the new situation in which tribes are placed. Dominant developments in this situation are determined by the major political and economic structure of the world, not by tribal structures. Tribal structures are, so to speak, now encysted in the major structure. They show great tenacity, and in practice capacity to absorb familial and even political changes into their indigenous equilibria.

Finally, anthropologists of all kinds have delineated the processes by which social changes in institutions occur. Here undoubtedly the most ambitious essay has been that of the late Godfrey and Monica Wilson on *The Analysis of Social Change* (1945). The Wilsons examine the changes going on in Central Africa in terms of differences of scale between nine elements of culture. Differences of scale produce radical and temporary adjustments. The whole analysis is in terms of temporary equilibria, with inadequate adjustment between cultural elements moving the system through change towards a more effective equilibrium.

The sources of radical change escape these analyses. Perhaps this is inevitable because social anthropology aims to be scientific. Scientific method cannot deal with unique complexes of many events. The accounts of the actual course of events which produce change therefore necessarily remain historical narratives, with attempts to assess the weight of the factors leading to change.

Each portion of narrative leads to an analysis of a period of temporary equilibrium before a new external factor or some internal crisis engenders new changes.

This type of analysis is well exhibited in anthropological studies of African tribesmen who have moved to become labourers in the copper-mining towns of Northern Rhodesia. A. L. Epstein analyses *Politics in an Urban African Community* (1958) by tracing temporary equilibria moving towards crises, which then produce new patterns of relations. These are in some sort of equilibrium for people are able to live ordered lives. During the duration of each temporary equilibrium changes are occurring in the relative values and strengths of various parties, and new parties form. Their positions relative to one another only become clear in the crisis, which at the same time precipitates a new social pattern. It is in the last respect that crises during a period of rapid social change differ from the sort of crises we have examined in traditional civil wars or divination séances.

One of Epstein's main themes is how, during the growth of a coppermining town, typical urban associations and industrial grouping ousted European attempts to work with authorities based on tribal affiliations. When the copper mine at Luanshya was established in the early 1930's, Europeans provided managerial staff and skilled working force: the heavy labour was performed by thousands of Africans from tribes spread over British, Belgian, and Portuguese territories. The mine, like many industrial enterprises in Europe's industrial revolution, had to provide both order and some social services for this heterogeneous population. Government resources were not adequate for these tasks, and in any case European and African mineworkers dwelt on the private property of the mine. The Africans were housed in compounds under a Compound Manager. He was responsible for the housing, part of the feeding, and some welfare work for the Africans, for dealing with their working conditions and complaints, and for maintaining order among them and settling their quarrels. Faced with thousands of Africans of different tribes, the mine officials, reasonably enough, thought that it would be wise to deal with them through representatives of the tribes as groups. Therefore the Compound Manager instituted a system of Tribal Elders, who were elected, and given special robes and special houses. He planned that the mine management could communicate with its African labourers through the Elders, while the Elders in turn would inform the management of the wishes and complaints of their tribesmen. In addition, the Elders would look after the welfare of newcomers, involved in the ceaseless drift of men within a system of migrant labour. Finally, the Elders came to judge the small disputes that arose between men and their wives. The people themselves welcomed this institution; and a similar system was established in Luanshya Municipal Location, which had grown up distinct from the mine's compound.

This system of administration worked fairly well until, in 1936, there were major disturbances throughout the copper-mining towns. These disturbances arose out of African demands for better pay and working conditions. A strike began at two other mines, and the Compound Manager at Luanshya asked his Tribal Elders what would happen there. They assured him that there would be no disturbances. The Manager asked the Elders to go among the miners and calm them, but one of the Elders, a senior man, was driven away from a meeting, and accused of being in league with the Europeans. A mob stormed the Compound Office, and the Elders had to seek sanctuary within it. Clearly they had neither influence nor power within the strike situation. Yet after the disturbances, the Elders resumed their previous role. By 1937 there were some forty accredited Elders at the mine, and Epstein says that 'the system of Tribal Elders operated satisfactorily in the main, and was appreciated by the mass of the people' (p. 36).

Epstein stresses the tribal background of the Elders—their frequent affiliation with the families of chiefs, their knowledge of tribal customs and values, their skill in adjudicating in disputes, and so forth. The authority hierarchies of the tribes were projected into the urban, industrial areas. Yet, in a way paradoxically, the Elders came simultaneously to be associated with the European mine management. During the strike they were driven away as in league with the Europeans. Two important elements in their position have therefore to be stressed. Firstly, as tribal representatives whose authority was based on the political system of the tribe they had no connection with the situations in which African miners worked in the mine itself. Here the workers were organized in departments and gangs within which tribal affiliation was irrelevant; and it was in this situation that common interests had brought the miners to joint action in the strike.

This was industrial action, in which tribal allegiances, and hence the Elders, lacked all influence. But, secondly, in the administrative system the Elders had become representatives of the mine itself, in dealing with its workers, and hence when those workers come into dispute with the mine, they regarded the Elders as enemies. When the strike had ended, the Elders could resume their former role.

This position changed slowly until a second series of strikes broke out on the Copperbelt in 1940. There were disturbances, with shooting of miners, at Nkana mine, but none at Luanshya. At Mufulira, a strike committee of seventeen men was set up to negotiate with the management. At all mines, the authority of the Elders was rejected. The strike committee at Mufulira was the beginning of a new regime which was to oust tribal affiliation as the basis for handling industrial matters among African miners. For after the war, the British Government (now a Labour Government) sent out trained trade unionists to help Africans form trade unions. The development of trade unionism was present among the Africans themselves, but it was now encouraged by Government policy. Eventually, the African Mineworkers' Union emerged as a powerful, organized, industrial union throughout the mining towns of Northern Rhodesia, negotiating with management. As its last step on the way to power, the Union insisted that the Tribal Elders system be abolished, for the trade union leaders saw the Elders as a threat to their own authority, and as a means which the mine might use to oppose them. An overwhelming vote of the miners approved of this abolition. The trade union finally ousted the formal organized power of tribal representatives from the industrial field, though tribal affiliation continued to influence trade-union politics.

In the Municipal Compound developments were not so clear-cut. Epstein suggests that the monolithic structure of the mine with its centralized power over the working, residential, etc., lives of the workers, provoked the response of a monolithic African trade union, also catering for many aspects of the miners' lives. The Municipal Compound, on the other hand, is inhabited by Africans who are employed in many trades and by many employers. But there similar developments have occurred, in that Government's attempt to work with institutions based on tribal affiliations had been opposed by the emergence of associations from life in the town.

Epstein goes on to point out that the dominance of the trade union did not eliminate tribal allegiances within the industrial field. To some extent, these allegiances have ceased to be so significant in industrial matters where the Africans are opposed in their interests to the European mine officials. But tribal affiliation is still important in matters between Africans. Thus elections within the union for official posts in the union have to some extent been fought on tribal lines: for example, other tribes complained that the leadership was dominated by the Bemba tribe; and tribalism entered into other activities.

Nevertheless even here it is not straight tribal hostility and loyalty that are operating. During the early years of the mine, the posts open for educated and semi-skilled Africans were largely taken by Nyasalanders and Barotse. Bemba, who are the most powerful tribe near the mine, filled many minor authoritative posts. While many Africans see the struggle for leadership on the mine in tribal terms, this covers a struggle between groups of different skills.

After the firm consolidation of the trade union's power, a dispute began with the mines and the European trade union not only for better pay for Africans, but also for the opening to Africans of better-paid posts demanding higher skill. A new crisis emerged. Was the union to press for a few highly paid openings for a few well-educated Africans, or for much better all round opportunities for the mass of relatively unskilled labourers? Out of this struggle, a new and militant leadership, more representative of the labourers, won many union elections. The struggle reached its climax when the mine management opened new skills to Africans and put them on a monthly salary, instead of payment by ticket or work done. It also insisted that they join a new and separate union, formed by salaried Africans and led by a Barotse. The old union came out on strike against this move; and eventually the Government, holding that this was a political strike, arrested sixty-two trade union leaders and deported them to their tribal areas.

The significance of this strike is that it brought into the open the emergence within the African urban population of affiliations based on what we can call 'class principles'. The African union, after its victory, has been split by a division of interests between component categories with independent interests. This division on 'class' lines has what Epstein calls a 'pervasive' effect spreading into many institutions. Mitchell has examined the effect of this situation on the activities of a popular dance team in the Copperbelt, in his analysis of *The Kalela Dance* (1956). It is danced by teams of Africans who come from single tribes. During their dances they mock other tribes, by alleging that these have, among many unpleasant habits, loose, and even perverted, sexual lives. Thus on the surface the dance proclaims proudly the virtues of the team's own tribe, and derides other tribes. Yet the members of the derided tribes attend the performance and laugh as loudly as any at the salacious wit against themselves. Mitchell is struck by the fact that, despite this surface of tribal competitiveness, the dancers have named their hierarchy of officials after the hierarchies of British military or civil dignity. Moreover, the dancers do not wear tribal dress: instead they are dressed in smart and clean European clothes, and they have to maintain their tidiness and smartness throughout the dancing. This is insisted on, although the dancers themselves are mostly unskilled, and poorly educated, labourers. He interprets the dance as reflecting the aspirations of all Africans for a European way of life, or civilization, and he shows from other data how the values implicit here form a prestige scale for all Africans. But, he argues, these unskilled labourers are not striving through the dance to participate in the European part of Central African society: this is cut off from them by the colour bar. They are striving in the dance to associate themselves with the new African elite. While in political activity the Africans may combine against the Europeans, internally they are differentiated on a class scale, which people are striving to ascend.

Yet the dancing team is a tribal team, deriding other tribes. Its actions have therefore also to be related to a persisting significance of tribal allegiances in the towns. Mitchell works out that tribalism in the town operates as a primary mode of classifying the heterogeneous masses of people, whom a man meets, into manageable categories. With his fellow tribesmen he can converse, and he shares their customs and way of life. In practice, Mitchell discovered that there is far less tribal intermarriage in the towns than is usually assumed, so that a man marries the sisters and daughters of his fellow tribesmen. More than this, by the use of social distance scales, Mitchell finds that all the many tribes in the towns are grouped into several limited categories by other Africans, and that specific institutionalized modes of behaviour have developed between various tribal categories. Thus he discovered that joking relationships between tribes in this region have developed in modern times, and are not, as previously thought, traditional. Mitchell thus stresses that tribes in towns form categories by which people group one another, and this categorization determines a lot of action in casual as well as intimate relationships. Both he and Epstein stress that in domestic situations, where as stated most marriages occur within tribes, tribal custom and practice are effective, though much modified by the demands of the urban situation.

In some towns in Central and South Africa, but not in the Copperbelt, membership of a tribe has become the basis for forming various kinds of associations.

These studies show that we can find plenty of systematic regularities in the new African towns. These regularities are obvious in that people live and go about their business within the town in relative security and absence of fear. Hence clearly there is some kind of working, integrated social system in these towns. But the social system must not be thought of as rigid, tight, closed, or self-consistent. The social field of the towns consists of many semi-independent areas of life, where people associate for specific purposes: to run a home and raise children, to be entertained with friends, to work and improve status, to achieve political objectives, etc. Different principles of organization may be effective in the various areas of relations. A trade union can oust Tribal Elders, and with them tribal authority from the town, without affecting tribalism as a category or even loyalty to a tribal chief in other situations. I would stress, too, that this situation is not confined to Africans. Tribalism acts, though not as strongly, in British towns: for in these Scots and Welsh and Irish, French, Jews, Lebanese, Africans, have their own associations, and their domestic life is ruled by their own national customs, insofar as British law and conditions allow. But all may unite in political parties and in trade unions or employers federations. Tribalism in the Central African towns is, in sharper form, the tribalism of all towns.

The urban studies emphasize that tribal association in these towns does not dominate political life. Tribalism is not an organized set of political relations. Here modern urban tribalism differs radically from tribalism in the rural areas. In the rural areas, under British rule, each tribe is an organized political unit, with a complex internal structure. At its head, in Central Africa at least, there is usually a traditional chief, with a traditional council of elders, and a system of villages and other political units. For here it has been Government policy to rule through the tribal organization. Government has thus lent its powerful support to the continued working of the African political systems, as systems. Continuing, and in the sociological sense conservative, loyalty to chief has also been important here. Moreover, since the new industrial and urban political associations develop in the towns, they only affect tribal allegiances indirectly. But the tribal system in the rural areas serves new needs of tremendous importance to the modern African.

In order to earn the money which they require, Africans in Northern Rhodesia mostly go out to work, for longer or shorter periods, in mines and other labour centres. (I have not space to deal with events in tribes which have gone in for cash-cropping or fishing.) But they consider they have little security in their life in the towns. It is difficult for them to rear their children as they would like there; till recently they could not own houses, and few could do so when the studies were made; there is no provision for unemployment; sickness and accident compensation may not exist and are always low; there is little provision for the old. The insecurity of town employment for each personally is great, and they remember the years of great depression when mines closed down, and thousands of African workers (indeed like American workers) had to return to the land. In this situation, they look for security to their tribal homes: ever-present needs in the modern total field where they make their living, as well as sentiment, tie them to the rural areas.[23]

These tribesmen are therefore earning their living in two widely separated areas, and ultimately they feel that their main security lies in the tribal land—and objectively this seems to be true. Watson says of the Mambwe that they raid the towns for money from their rural base. The success of tribes in achieving the required deployment of their men on two labour fronts varies according to a complex of variables I cannot here examine. But all tribes do turn in the end to their rights to land, for ultimate support.

Land here is not an individual item of land which a man owns for himself and by himself. For he secures his rights to land in two ways. Firstly, as a citizen of the tribe he is entitled to some arable and building land, and to the use of public pasturage, fishing waters, and wild products. Secondly, in all tribes except those who shift their gardens widely and have an abundance of land, he gets rights to land from membership of a village and a group of kinsfolk. That is, a man's right to land in the tribal home depends on his accepting membership of a tribe, with all its obligations. This right of every subject, while he is a subject, to land, is jealously safeguarded. I examined the development of landholding in all the Central and Southern African tribes, and found that in no case, as land got scarcer and more valuable, had chiefs expropriated to themselves an unreasonable quantity of land. Instead, they had in various tribes, as pressure on land increased, steadily legislated to safeguard the fundamental right of every tribesman to some land. The first step by the chief was to take power to commandeer land allocated to a subject which he was not using, for distribution to the landless. Then—in a developmental series—the chief took power to take over for the landless, land which had lain fallow for a certain period: the cycle of soil degradation has here begun. The final step was to restrict each family to a limited area of garden land. People get around these laws by various devices, but the trend of development in the view of both the leaders and the mass of the tribesmen is clear. Every·man who is a member of the tribe has a right to live and support his family on the tribal land.

Honest fellow-feeling and sympathy and justice surely have contributed to this legislation. In addition, those who remain behind have an interest in the work of these who go away to the towns, for these bring home the money which the people require. In a way, those who stay at home hold the land as security for support in money from those who go out to work. And those who go out to work pass money to those who remain, in payment for this security. So that they get security by their continued allegiance to the tribe, for they hold land from the chief in return for loyalty and support. Hence they adhere to their chiefs; and as they adhere to their chiefs, they accept with the chiefs for the rural areas, the organized system of tribal political relations. Very few tribesmen wish to overturn the tribal political system as such, though new interest groups and new elites in the tribes may struggle for power in tribal councils. With acceptance of the tribal political system goes acceptance of many customs and observances built into that system.

In tribes where land is worked in co-operating groups of kindred, or where kin organize their departures to town so that some remain at home to work the land and care for dependants, security in holding of land also involves acceptance of kinship obligations, and with these of many parts of the tribal culture.

We see, in short, that tribalism persists in the rural areas because of Government support, and because the tie to tribal land is of the utmost importance to a man. With this tie goes acceptance of the tribal political system with its culture, and of its smaller constituent units with their culture. In short, tribalism in the rural areas consists of participation in a highly organized system of social relations, based strongly on the chief's rights as trustee for his people over the tribal land. Tribalism in the towns is not such an organized system of political and other social relations. It is an important basis for grouping people in categories, and it is most important in social life. Associations form between fellow tribesmen, and tribal loyalties and hostilities may influence the working of urban-type groups. But here specific urban and industrial groups have developed, and ousted attempts by Europeans to transplant African tribal authority systems to deal with urban-industrial problems. Class linkages are also beginning to pervade the life and culture of the new towns. In all these respects, Central African towns differ only in degree from any town, anywhere in the world probably. In crisis, common interests arising from industrial and urban association seem steadily to overcome tribal ties and divisions.

Nevertheless some of these developments are peculiar to Northern Rhodesia. They are duplicated in part in South Africa, which has much the same kind of system of employing African labour. Variations are produced by differences in Government policy, which bans African trade unions but cannot prevent African strikes. In addition, South African Africans have had open to them entry to Christianity and education for a much longer period than have Northern Rhodesian Africans. Many decades ago some tribal families opted for Christianity and schooling: others rejected these. The descendants of these two categories of families have quite different patterns of life in their leisure-time in a town studied by Mayer.[24] In the work situation, they are affected by the structure of urban and industrial systems.

The situation differs in yet other ways where towns have sprung up where there are few whites, and it differs even more in the large cities indigenous to West Africa and Asia. But tribal, or district, or in India caste,[25] ties seem to operate in somewhat similar ways in all situations, though variations are important.[26]

The Northern Rhodesian and Nyasaland situation which I have summarized will alter rapidly in important respects when these territories become independent under British rule. British officers, despite initial battles with a few chiefs, did not consider chiefs as rivals to their power. They exercised authority in quite different spheres. Officials were backed by Government power and dealt mainly with tribesmen's relations with the White system. Chiefs' prestige and authority lay in tradition and among Africans. The new African leaders will regard the chiefs much more as competitors, and as obstacles to the new democracy they hope to create. They are likely to attempt to reduce, and even eliminate, the power of the chiefs. The equilibrium described above was established for some decades: recent major political changes may overset it.

We may expect tribal ties to survive this crisis, though how they will fit into the new independent states of Africa and Asia it is impossible to tell. So long as there is some basis for a community life, tribal ties show tremendous tenacity. This is shown by the situation which Colson found among *The Makah Indians* (1953) of Washington State in the U.S.A. The American Indian Service set out in the 1870's to Americanize the Makah. All things Indian were forbidden. Children were sent to boarding-school to be broken from the culture of their parents. This policy of almost forcible indoctrination was continued until 1932 when the Indian Service began to encourage Red Indian cultural individuality. But many forces from general American life—radio, magazines, newspapers, cinemas, and friendly contacts with other Americans as well as work in outside enterprises—had influenced the Makah. By 1942 only 400-odd dwelt as Makah on the Reservation under Treaty with the U.S.A. Government: smallpox and other vicissitudes had early reduced their numbers from about 2,000. These 400 were not pure-blooded Makah owing to intermarriage with Whites and other Indians.

In result, few Makah in 1942, when Colson studied them, spoke Makah. Most of the younger and even middle-aged members of the tribe spoke English. The overt practice of Makah customs, and particularly those connected with the competitive *potlatch*, had died out, though many religious beliefs and ideas about the cause of sickness continued to flourish. These persisted even though many Makah worshipped as Christians alongside Whites. Both on the Reservation and in the cities and farms of the West Coast, Makah mixed on good terms with other Americans. On the Reservation Colson often found it difficult to tell if a man was Makah or White by his surface relations with others.

The Makah have clung together as a tribe partly because of their common rights in the Reservation, which entitle them to certain privileges denied other Indians as well as Whites. They have made a good living on that Reservation, first at sealing, then at halibut fishing, then working for the lumber-company exploiting their forests. As wards of the United States Government they are also entitled as Indians to a number of privileges in freedom from taxation as well as grants of social services. But primarily it is the Reservation which focuses their interests. Since it is small in size, and will bring in a limited sum if it is sold, they strive to keep their numbers small: individuals resist the addition to the tribal roll of all who are not related to them themselves. Interests in the Reservation are to some extent competitive between Makah.

This small group is hostile in many ways to the Whites with whom they associate on such good terms. They feel that the Whites despoiled them and their Indian brothers of both culture and land. They do not express this hostility by maintaining united relations among themselves. The community is torn by internal dissension and struggles for status, and they constantly use scandal to keep one another in proper place.

Colson found that Makah in their internal relations were dominated by ideas of status. Someone claimed high status by virtue of birth on both sides from chiefly lines: others would counter that he or she was descended from a slave, and was low class. Another would argue that status depended in the past on the achievements of a person, and add that his father had had great achievements. Others would run these pretensions down. Under the old *potlatch* system a man had to give feasts to establish status. So today a man ought to be generous if he is to be esteemed. Now anyone can earn money, if a man gives feasts his rivals will say he is trying to cover his low-class, since people whose high-class status is well known do not have to demonstrate this ostentatiously. But others will accuse these of meanness, inappropriate to high-class, until they become prodigal, when they are regarded as *nouveau riche*. Makah assured Colson that 'We Indians are just like Whites. We class up.' But everyone accused everyone else of being low-class and not 'entitled to speak for the Makah or hold up their heads in front of the really good people'. Makah could not make a success of business enterprises on the Reservation, since they had to give credit to close kin who did not pay them, while unrelated people would not patronize them lest they rise in status. Sniping gossip drove out of public life Makah who attempted to run various joint political activities.

On the surface it looks as if this whole picture of rivalry is disruptive of community life. Colson points out that in some respects the opposite is true: 'The incessant gossip and back-biting which goes on can be viewed as an important feature holding the Makah in a set of social relationships which is distinctive within wider American society. . . .' The Makah criticize others in terms of a set of values which operate within the group to govern the behaviour of members of the group. 'The constant criticism, gossip and back-biting' reassert these old Makah values, which in modern conditions cannot be expressed in any other way. Hence, says Colson, if the Makah 'repressed the gossip and back-biting, the values themselves would disappear, and with them much of the feeling that the Makah are a distinct people'.

Colson goes further than this. She points out that 'the back-biting itself has become a game . . . into which the Makah have thrown themselves with a zest and a determination, which have brought the art of verbal denigration to a high peak . . . [From] the zest with which they recount their experiences in the field of slander, it is apparent that they have developed this type of behaviour into a game with its own rules and interest. Like all artists or sportsmen, the Makah delight in playing with their own technical skill. And only others of their own community have the technical knowledge to compete in the game, or to appreciate the skill with which a point is scored.'

In this analysis, Colson establishes the important point that specific and restricted scandal within a group marks it off from other groups, both like and unlike. The gossip and scandal which are so biting in Makah life unite them into a group outside of general American society. And since this gossip and scandal involve the criticism and assessment of people against traditional values of the Makah, it maintains the tribe as Indians against Whites, and as Makah against other Indians. These Makah values and traditions largely persist in the gossip and in no other way. To be a Makah, you must be able to join in the gossip, and to be fully Makah you must be able to scandalize skilfully. This entails that you know the family histories of your fellows; for the knowledgeable can hit at you through your ancestry, and you must be able to retort in kind. You have also got to have some knowledge of old Makah customs.

Thus the Makah survive as a 'community', with many of the attributes of a tribal society, looking inward on itself. Colson shows that though the whole economic base of their social system has been altered and they disperse widely to earn their livings, they are held together by new economic forces: by the privileges of being wards of the United States Government and the privileges of being a Makah with rights in the Reservation. For Makah seem to remain Makah in order to gain these privileges. And these privileges make membership of the tribe a matter of competition between individuals and families. Hence it seems that among the Makah gossip does not show merely that general interest in the doings, and the virtues and vices, of others, which characterizes any group: the gossip passes into scandal, aimed at demonstrating that the other parties are not worthy to be Makah. The different groups and individuals in the tribe fight an unceasing battle to demonstrate their own true Makahship, as against the failures of others to attain Makahship. But this involves them in a continual process of remaining Makah, which (as Colson says) gives high importance to the scandalizing itself, as a means of maintaining the Makah as a distinctive group in the American nation, whose other members are excluded from this war of scandal.

## SOCIAL ANTHROPOLOGY AND CUSTOM

I have chosen to cite this study of the Makah partly for its own brilliance, but largely because it demonstrates how a social anthropologist focuses attention on the role of persistent custom in maintaining a social system in equilibrium. In the setting of quite different economic and political interests Makah customs, even if only as traditions since in many respects they are no longer practised, continue to influence Makah behaviour. Colson's insight went further. She demonstrated more clearly than any other anthropologist had done, that gossip and scandal are customs. They take standardized forms, and they are sanctioned by rules. For she shows also that the unskilful scandalmonger, who is too gross, overreaches himself or herself and falls in status.[27]

This study shows, too, that even if social anthropologists were to confine themselves to the study of tribal societies, there is likely still to be plenty for them to do, as these tribes adjust to the new world. Small groups have great tenacity: wholesale changes can sweep over them. In fact social anthropologists have begun to study also villages of peasants, and rural communities in the west, as well as schools, groups in factories, and the like.

If I ask what distinguishes a social anthropological study of, say, a factory from a study of the same group by other types of social scientist, I would point to an emphasis on customs. This is not to say that sociologists concerned with small-groups do not also take full note of custom, as Homans (who is part anthropologist) shows in *The Human Group* (1950). But the social-anthropological study seems to go further in stressing that customs themselves have an interdependence, which controls the behaviour of those who practise such customs. Customs are greater than any of these individual practititioners. Each individual finds most customs already in existence, and is constrained by their force. Customs develop an autonomy of their own, in view of their interdependent effects on one another. They are more than tools which men can manipulate.[28]

Another strain in anthropological analysis is that it shows the logic in apparently irrational customs. We have seen this in the analyses of witchcraft, of myth, of civil war, of seemingly silly taboos, such as that you do not eat your own pig. In this respect, I believe that social-anthropological insight is not confined to the analysis of small groups (as leading anthropologists have maintained). At all levels of society we find customs: and wherever there is custom, there is scope for anthropological analysis.[29]

For it is this interest in custom which continues to distinguish all branches of anthropology. Cultural anthropologists look for relations between customs themselves without as much reference to social relationships. They have tended, at least in the past, to see customs as forming patterns with dominant themes. What does not fit, is discrepant. I hesitate to quote from an essay of Mead's which she wrote twenty-five years ago,[30] and to represent in so simple a form a highly complex form of analysis. But I wish here merely to indicate that cultural anthropology concentrates also on customs, and it is helpful to cite a problem which I have analysed at length above. She defines the Bathonga (now called the Tsonga) as a 'co-operative political society'. In it 'the struggle for the kingship which occurred after the death of each king and in which competition was very keen and fierce' is 'one highly discrepant note in the Bathonga social structure'. This weakness she ascribes to the polygynous structure of the royal household. She deduces from the summary made by Goldman of Junod's material on family relations that after the death of a family headman succession is peacefully achieved because 'peaceful relationships between brothers are socially insured and guaranteed by the existence of the state, personified by the king'. This cannot be done for the kingship. Rules of inheritance for the kingship are also less clear. 'The resolution of this conflict in many monarchies makes it clear that the dynastic wars of the Bathonga are not the inevitable outcome of a monarchical system, but an instance of a flaw in the social system due to reliance upon conflicting mechanisms.' Mead might not now abide by that particular judgment; and I use it here only to illustrate a difference in approach to the inter-relationships between customs, to solve different types of problems.

The psychological anthropologist is again interested, as against the psychologist, in the specific effect of interdependent customs on personality; and beyond this, on how the customs under which children are reared influence the customs and beliefs of the adult world. These anthropologists have deeply influenced the development of many branches of personality psychology. Here I make this bare statement, to emphasize how the original focus of anthropological interest in the nineteenth century on custom, continues to demarcate each of the varied disciplines which that study of conglomerates finally engendered.

## SOCIAL ANTHROPOLOGY: SCIENCE OR ART?

My last problem in this book is to try to answer the question whether social anthropology is a science. In some of its forms— particularly its comparative analyses of kinship systems—it would never be confused with literature. But what of the kind of extended-case study made by Turner? This does in many respects resemble a novel or play. It describes how the relationships between the various characters in the village are affected by their social positions and their individual personalities, as well as by the course of events like illness and death and Government orders to move the village. We see how some individuals develop with changing social relationships and in reaction to what happens to them. Through the developments and changes we are given a view into the traditional life of Ndembu, and the way it has been, and is, altering under British rule. The study focuses on the tragic figure of Sandombu who wins our sympathy since we can see, as he cannot, that defeat is inevitable for him.

All this might have been done in the form of a novel. But the differences are important. Turner does not leave any of the 'social factors' which influence what happens implicit, taken for granted, unmeasured. Each form of relationship and the structure of each group involved has been carefully set out in earlier chapters. Wherever he could, he has given numerical form to these statements. The extent to which principles of organization are independent of, or dependent on, one another has been assessed. He does not shirk the statement of the obvious, since the problem of explaining what is obvious is often the most difficult in science. Both the obvious and the obscure are repeated and recapitulated because the same things must be considered in several different contexts: I excuse my own repetitiousness. For example, as Turner discusses the course of events in Sandombu's village he recapitulates the influence and strength of varying and often conflicting principles upon one another at particular points in time. The story is an analysis marked throughout by the manner in which each principle is stated explicitly. To be explicit, and to labour at accurate definition, means avoiding the evocative words on which playwright and novelist rely, and creating a technically specified vocabulary.

Explicitness against implicitness, insistence on the obvious as against avoidance of the obvious, numerical assessment as against avoidance of figures, recapitulation as against variety, accurate definition as against evocativeness: the former qualities are part of the rigorous code of scientists. As Homans says, '. . . it could not be better calculated to make their books and articles hard reading'.[31] There is the world of difference between Freud's exposition of the Oedipus Complex and Sophocles' presentation of it by implicit insight in *Oedipus Rex*, or Shakespeare's in *Hamlet*. Even the introductory reflections and presentations of historical forces in Tolstoy's *War and Peace* or Steinbeck's *The*

*Grapes of Wrath* are literary, not scientific. They may be full of valid insight into social processes. They write by evocation, by implication, and by metaphor—all of which should be shunned by the anthropologist.

Turner also asks himself constantly how typical his village is of all Ndembu villages. This question a novelist does not put, a least not explicitly. Turner tries to assess typicality in his initial general discussion of the structural principles of Ndembu society, where he tries to measure the strength of matriliny; the extent to which wives go to live with their husbands; the rate and incidence of divorce; the degree to which matrilineal kinsmen live together, etc. He is interested in extended-case analysis in order to probe the mechanisms of redressing and adjusting disputes, and the role of custom and belief. He produces constantly quantitative as well as qualitative evidence to support his analysis. Evidence is essential in science.

Finally, Turner's work, as he clearly denotes, depends on the accumulation of knowledge and analytic propositions by his predecessors. I have tried in the body of Chapter VI to show how our analysis, for example, of divinatory séances has developed. While writing this book I have, I hope, advanced a little the theory of the cycle of rebellions first put forward in social anthropology in 1940, and the theory of joking-relationships. Science is cumulative. The apprentice in this generation can outdo his master of the last. Art is not cumulative, however much study of past masters may improve the novice's skill. A relatively poorly equipped anthropologist in intellectual terms can on the basis of sound training produce good work; and it is now very difficult, if not impossible, for an untrained amateur to produce work which stands alongside the work of professionals. A fledgling novelist or playwright can burst upon the world. If art were cumulative, Dryden with all his ability could have written in *All for Love* a better play than Shakespeare's *Antony and Cleopatra* which he had as guide; and Shaw's *Caesar and Cleopatra* would have been yet better.

## Conclusion: The Eskimo Song-Contest

I have referred occasionally in previous chapters to analyses of the Eskimo singing-contest as a 'legal' mechanism of 'law' and indicated that these analyses do not satisfy me. I propose as a final exercise to apply some of the principles worked out above to advance a hypothesis of how this singing-contest may operate to sanction derelictions from norms. This will illustrate, I hope, both that social anthropology is cumulative and that propositions worked out in one social context can be applied to other contexts. They are propositions which are generally true. Both these characteristics stamp a science.

I shall try to analyse the contest as it operates in two widely separated, specific Eskimo communities. I here put together information which is somewhat scattered, but my summary accounts do not distort the original sources. In the case of the Greenland Eskimo I have had to rely on a secondary source, since the Danish original in which the records of disputes is contained is not available for me to secure translation.

A young Dutch anthropologist, Van den Steenhoven, recently studied *Leadership and Law among the Eskimo of the Keewatin District* (1962) of the Canadian Northwest Territories. He reports that 'derision' is a common and characteristic means by which they keep one another in check. They use derision in three situations: (a) constantly in daily intercourse; (b) in spontaneously sung lampoons during common gatherings in the large winter festival house; and (c) in formal 'song-duels' in the same situation. Derision is not confined to cases of private or social misconduct. Improvising songs is a popular everyday occurrence. But derisory songs are 'in season' in winter when many people gather in the large igloo 'and when the intensity of social intercourse culminates'. The two contestants sing songs against each other with the appreciative audience arbitrating by its applause, which gradually deserts the loser. The audience derives fun and amusement from watching the two opponents crush one another by 'Splitting off sharp words, little sharp words, like the wooden splinters which I hack off with my axe', said one Eskimo.

The opponents accuse each other of incest, bestiality, murder, avarice, adultery, failure at hunting, being henpecked, lack of manly strength—'in short anything with which the singer hopes to get the audience on his side and thus his opponent on his knees'. The songs are accompanied by antics and buffets. Several of the songs heard had no reference to private grudges. Van den Steenhoven goes so far as to say that it may be sometimes bad manners or policy to refer openly to private grievances, with which anyway the community may be well acquainted.

He lists, however, a case in which a singer indicated that he was left hungry one winter because his opponent, his maternal uncle, without necessity robbed his cache and fed his dogs on its contents. This is the only instance of public exhibition of a private grievance he cites; and it may be that this is a case where kinship norms excluded taking any open punitive action.

Van den Steenhoven quotes Rasmussen as saying of these Eskimo that 'these songs of derision are received in the best spirit and often repair friendships that have been broken'. He rather doubts if this is always the case, nor did his informants 'point in that direction'. But he himself saw few of these 'duels': he notes that as communal winter-hunting out on the ice has decreased, the sessions in the large igloo which are the setting for these duels are less frequent than they used to be.

The second study is of the Ammassalik Eskimo in Greenland, analysed by Mirsky in Mead's *Co-operation and Competition among Primitive Peoples* (1937) from the reports of Boas and Thalbitzer.[32] Here drum matches are held in summer and winter. Though they are said to be a method of settling disputes, they are mainly a pastime of the long winter nights. A match of this kind may be carried on for years; the parties take turns to visit one another and train assiduously in new songs, 'in which the crimes are vastly exaggerated, or, if they can find no new material that is suitable, they may father new crimes on to their opponents or reproach them for deeds which may have been merely intended but never committed. They can enumerate the faults of the opponent's family living and dead.'

The singer here also butts his opponent, breathes in his face, and performs other antics. In one match, over a stolen wife, the 'complainant' while singing put a stick in his opponent's mouth, pretended to sew his mouth up, gagged him with blubber, and so forth. This opponent 'showed his indifference by encouraging the onlookers to shout and laugh at him'. For the listener must accept all with composure. The 'same pattern that is found in . . . juridical drum matches is found in matches similarly carried on just for pleasure'. They are the Ammassalik's chief pastime.

Men do not here accuse others of incompetence as hunters, of laziness or of cowardice. The song-duels, we are told, arise largely over women, though charges are concealed under allegations of stealing food, poisoning a man, using a dead relative's name. But from this start the 'initial hostility gets lost in a pleasant social pastime'. It becomes 'a co-operative act in which the two principals and the onlookers all enjoy the "show" '.

I think we can now in the light of our several analyses see this institution in proper perspective. As in the joking-partnerships analysed above, a standard pattern of abuse and derision is established between men, who indulge in it competitively for fun and prestige. It fits into the general derision used on all occasions. The game is played according to rules, among which is the rule that to win a man must not show that he has taken offence. When real grievances and charges are involved, statements of these have also to be taken with equal composure. But is it possible that truth and rightness affect the audience's support, as Hoebel quoted? Then the songs might punish the defaulter by causing him to lose the match. Other methods of redress are either feeble or involve drastic killing, so that only thus can a man be publicly shamed, without a worse chain of mutual reprisals being started.

Since the songs allege misdemeanours against Eskimo morality, the contests are in a way ceremonies which, like rituals, assert the code, and a man must sharpen his wit in terms of that code. They also require that a participant to compete successfully must know the past interrelations of members of the community. The songs depend on sly allusions and puns; and a man can only make his taunting jibes effective in terms of scandalous knowledge of the opponent's past record and his family connections. Here the songs act as scandal does among the Makah: they keep the members of the community informed about and interested in one another. I suspect from the songs I have read that there is a commentary which probes into the past.

The occurrence of this institution among the Eskimo right round the shores of the Arctic is remarkable. It indicates the hard tenacity of customs. But it also suggests a general occurrence of similar types of social relations. Among both these sets of Eskimo families scatter to hunt through the summer but come together in the long winter season, presumably compelled by necessity to live together. They have no leaders. Men murder lightly. Wives are loaned by hospitable hosts to their guests and may strike up liaisons. Men sometimes share wives. Men also steal others' wives lightly, and wives desert and are deserted freely. At night, in winter, there is a game when the lights are put out; men and unmarried or unattached women (theoretically at least not the married women) couple, avoiding only breaches of incest taboos. Men also kill each other over women. There is a theory that men do not show jealousy over sharing women, but obviously some do. One Ammassalik song derided a sterile man who allowed others access to his wife to get a child, and then became jealous and beat her.

Finally, there is sometimes the problem of having enough food to survive through the harsh winter. Mead classifies the Eskimo as individualistic except under the threat of starvation, when they become co-operative. It is a big 'except'. Women are reported in extremity to eat their own children and grand-children, and this is accepted as a necessity: it was bad taste in a particular singing-contest to pain two such women and cause them to weep by referring to their cannibalism.

The winter gathering, as an association of very small summer bands, living closely together, dominated by the problem of food, troubled by multiple sexual associations between members, may explain the institution of joking-partnerships in deliberately instituted song-contests which resolve contrary elements in relationships.[33] They then become a means of asserting a moral code and community unity. Within this pattern of joking the institution may act as a mechanism for rebuking specific wrongs. The contest ends with a reconciling feast (presumably if there is food) and exchange of gifts: even if, as Van den Steenhoven says, it raises future sources of strife—like the Welsh recreations, like all ritual.

It is even possible, I believe, that an adequate mapping of the positions of the pairs of men who duel thus for years would show that they stand as representatives of component units within each community, and sometimes between communities. These particular duels, at least among some Eskimo, are inheritable when one party dies. There may be levels of set duels, ceremonial pairings, which give an enforcing moral arrangement to single communities, and over several communities, and which are akin to the joking partnerships of Tonga clans.

In order to bring out the modes by which a social anthropologist makes his analysis, I have on occasion as I worked over a number of problems in writing this book shown the process of formulating and checking hypotheses. Thus I have stated that when I began to develop the differences between the politics of South African states and 'politics of the capital' I decided that in the latter there would not be elaborate national rituals in which subjects by enacting conflicts within the state would be believed to give mystical support to king and nation, but there would only be temple cults under royal patronage. My 'prediction' proved correct when I consulted Mair on the Baganda, and other studies which I have not cited. I have done the same with the Eskimo song-contest, starting early in the book by expressing my doubts about Hoebel's handling of the institution, and step by step trying to interpret it by reference to joking-relationships, to ceremonial and ritual, to the social role of scandal and gossip. After discussing whether social anthropology is art or science, I tried to pull these threads together. Was this interpretation correct, i.e. did it have predictive value? Before I could check it on other studies of the Eskimo not at hand when I wrote my tentative analysis, I had the good fortune to visit the United States and lecture on this theme at the University of Minnesota. After I had delivered my lecture, Professor Robert F. Spencer presented me with a copy of his book on *The North Alaskan Eskimo: A Study in Ecology and Society* (1959). I found that many of the ideas set out above had been worked out in it; and I therefore summarize Spencer's analysis of the institution among that group of Eskimo—for the institution varies in different groups of Eskimo.

These Eskimo consist of two main groups, those living on the coast off the sea, and those living inland off herds of caribou. Persons in each of these groups tend to remain in their own habitat, but to move freely within it, changing their locale. These moves, and requirements for other goods, were helped by voluntary partnerships formed outside the links of close kin. Individuals freely entered into economic partnerships: 'this was tantamount to friendship; indeed, with one exception, it was the only recognized way of establishing relations with nonkin'. Secondly, men formed co-operative associations for hunting caribou or for whaling, and whaling-crews had their bonds cemented by membership in a men's house (*karigi*), important in ceremonial and ritual activities. Between trading partners joking was also important.

There were several kinds of partnerships, but all were basically economic, connected with trade. Between caribou hunters and coast dwellers partnerships were highly important: they were made 'meaningful in the exchange of commodities in which each group specialized and . . . such trade was effected almost exclusively by means of established trading partnerships'. These partnerships did not develop into formal joking partnerships, as did partnerships within a single ecological area. But the partnerships between inland nomad and coastal seaman set up a special relationship, which might be cemented by exchange of wives. Each partner was protected by his fellow in the other's area. Partners might meet only once a year, but then in trade your partner ' "always treated you right". There was no bargaining and haggling with partners; each member of the partnership team attempted to extend himself in favour of his partner.' (This is a theme we have met frequently in other tribal societies.) Ties of this kind might be inherited also by a son or other close relative, 'and so perpetuated after the death of one of the principals'. The institution thus tended to stabilize relations between family groups. When partners met, after gossiping, exchange of goods began, 'each taking, in an ideal situation, what the other had brought without question. Between partners, every effort was made to the other's benefit. A poke of oil, for example, might go to one's partner for 7 green caribou skins when five would be the usual number traded. A good partner, it is said, was always overgenerous.' When the relationship was formalized, each would spend the first year collecting as much wealth for the other as he could. Men of like wealth and social position tended to become partners, and a successful man might have several partners, all aiding him in maintaining 'his position of wealth and enhancing his social position'.

Within each of the ecological areas, the partnership 'was in effect an institutionalized friendship'. Again partners were generous to each other: 'the partner was given whatever he asked for, even if it meant deprivation on the part of the giver'. Partners might lend or exchange wives, and their children might thus be kin to one another.

Partnerships of this kind might evolve into a joking partnership, though joking partnerships also existed independently of trade. Men who were not related to each other and who grew up together 'played jokes and made sport together. Two members of the same crew, for example, might behave in this way and employ the pattern of joking in order to indicate their mutual esteem and friendship. This was the least formal kind of joking partnership and had few direct economic implications.' For among the Eskimo 'the general life situation is hemmed in with a great deal of humour. Joking, poking friendly fun, "kidding", making humorous remarks on any and all occasions make up an important aspect of daily life.' This kind of joking partnership was 'essentially on an equal basis', and Spencer translates the Eskimo term for it as 'pal'. It could not exist between kindred, for 'indeed, "one does not make fun of one's relatives". Men who hunted together, shared various kinds of experiences, worked together, could develop this kind of relationship merely out of the situation of being thrown together and in terms of the joking which was a pattern inherent in the culture.' Wealthy and important men did not enter these relationships, which were intra-community, involving mutual aid.

There was also a 'more formalized, intercommunity pattern of joking'. Spencer compares this with the insult song situation found among Eskimo farther to the east, for 'sarcasm, irony, and a certain spiteful humour made their way into the exchanges of songs which characterized this relationship'. Men in different places formed the partnership, and they sent songs, each from his community to the other's community. The relationship grew generally out of a trading partnership, which led to an invitation to the ceremonial occasion of a Messenger Feast (see below), and then resulted in exchanges of songs. In this Messenger Feast, 'where a wealth display feature is uppermost, the happier trading relations between partners tended to be set aside and the feast itself became characterized by a definite rivalry between principals. Here, friendship was put aside and attention given to the notion of besting one's partner in the display. And in keeping with this, songs of a nature reflecting patterned rivalry were sent from one principal to another.'

These songs involved plays on words, puns, and mild insults. The song might be composed to go with a new dance, and was sent with a gift to the 'partner-opponent'. Song and dance might be taken up by the community, which took great interest and derived entertainment from the exchange. The competition might go on for some time, apparently without the principals meeting. These contests 'arose between communities and out of the context of the trading relationship', which seemingly was thus stabilized and given formal expression. This came to its peak during the Messenger Feast, not a ritual or religious occasion, says Spencer, but 'a ceremonial in the sense that the activities were patterned in an elaborate and complex way'. The Feast aimed at enhancing the individual status of each community's important men, all in the community contributing to the gift exchanges these men made with important men from other communities (shades of Melanesia in the far north!). The Feast was held in January, in a slack time of economic pursuits, and a village could not afford a feast every year. For the hosts had to outdo the guests in their presentations, and guests could ask the hosts to meet extravagant demands. Though there were competitive races and games, the songs were not insulting, only mildly ridiculing, though a joking partnership might exist between partners in the Messenger Feast exchanges. Thus it seems to me that the insulting pattern is shown only in songs sent by others to distant partners; they are not sung when these partners meet face to face, and insults might provoke quarrels.

Meanwhile within a community 'insult singing, while fairly well developed, was not used as a social device for settling formal disputes as was the case among the Eskimo farther to the east. That it was a means of exerting certain social pressures is, of course, not to be questioned, since such songs and singing took place within communities and between them.' These insulting songs might be started spontaneously by one man against another, not a joking partner, in the men's house. 'Clearly, this was an accepted way in which to indicate hostility and to take out feelings resulting from any grievances. The man to whom the song was directed had to return the song with another. A person's mistakes, his misdeeds, his faults of character were all freely aired. . . . When one or the other ran out of ideas, or indeed, became so angry that he could no longer continue, the contest ended, and the loser, he who had been unable to reply with a suitable song, was the butt of jokes for some time thereafter. "Maybe you won't sing any more; maybe you just better go away" was said to him. In so far as he could a man was expected to contain himself and not to show resentment or temper in such exchanges. When he became angry, he naturally became the butt of further jokes. The two men who sang impromptu songs were called *iivireyik*, "two against each other".' But established joking-partners did not sing against each other.

In these groups of Eskimo, we see that joking partnerships operate at several levels, and each has its own rules appropriate to the context and relationships involved. At the highest level there is the most formal, least insulting, of relationships, those which establish apparently important and possibly enduring, inheritable relationships between important men in different communities. At the lowest level, pals who work together, but are not kin, indulge in free banter. In between are the less important trading partnerships, which can become joking partnerships, and the insult-songs of the *karigi* house. These houses were occupied by men from whaling-crews, and in them there was constant rivalry in games, feats of endurance and athleticism. Contests were also held between members of different houses. In these and in intra-house contests, 'a feeling of general good will was held to exist. To show anger, although some did, was to be a "spoil-sport". . . . Good manners, and indeed, the whole culture pattern in this respect demanded that one ignore the poor loser. If he persisted, the weapon of the insult song can be turned against him.' Men were bound to the house so long as they belonged to one of its whaling-crews, and to live adequately a man had to belong to some crew, formed by a leader with the resources to provide a boat and gather a crew about him. Though these 'whaling-crew houses' were peculiar to the Alaskan Eskimo, they show the same characteristics as the community-houses of the other Eskimo discussed: men (sometimes attended by women) brought together by hard necessity, men divided in many ways but linked in co-operation and community. And here in the pattern of joking relationships, existing at all levels of the society, grievances are expressed (unfortunately Spencer does not record any of these insulting songs) and morals reaffirmed in a setting where it is particularly reprehensible to manifest anger.

Mead stated that fierce quarrels and killings over women among the Eskimo arose because they did not have the means to handle the problem in the better controlled manner available to 'more organized societies' also faced with 'an objective limitation of women'. She therefore sees these quarrels and killings as standing in sharp contrast with the 'unorganized co-operativeness' which is the major emphasis of Eskimo culture and social system. 'This more usual emphasis is so strong that it tends to reduce drum-matches, which are phrased as contests and originate in quarrels—usually over women—to friendly partnerships in which the contestants continue the match in affectionate co-operation.'[34] In this case, I consider that the approach from social relationships and their interdependence with customs, towards institutions and procedures seems to offer chances of a complementary understanding. The sociological approach may solve problems which are anomalies for the cultural anthropologist: and I have skirted over many problems, that cannot be handled by social-anthropological techniques, but which yield to cultural-anthropological analysis.

[1] *Structure and Function in Primitive Society* (1951), p. 166.

[2] 'The San Ildefonso of New Mexico' (1940), p. 396.

[3] These themes are elaborated in an essay (at p. 83), one of nine, on the cosmological ideas and social values of African peoples, as well as in Forde's editorial introduction to *African Worlds* (1954).

[4] *The Nuer* (1940), p. 108.

[5] *The Dynamics of Clanship among the Tallensi* (1945), p. 26.

[6] See above, p. 120, and below, pp. 274–5.

[7] Peters, 'The Proliferation of Segments in the Lineage of the Bedouin of Cyrenaica' (1960).

[8] Peters, 'Aspects of Status and Rank in a Lebanese Village' (1964).

[9] Malinowski brilliantly emphasized the relation of a tribe's sense of time and religion to an original miraculous event in 'Myth as a Dramatic Development of Dogma' and in 'The Foundations of Faith and Morals' (1936), both republished in a posthumous collection of lectures and essays: *Sex, Culture and Myth* (1963).

[10] *The Work of the Gods in Tikopia* (1940), vol. II, p. 376.

[11] Peters on *The Bedouin of Cyrenaica* (1960), develops this point on the basis of work in which Evans-Pritchard, Firth, and Fortes were pioneers.

[12] For Fortes' analyses of time, see his *Dynamics of Clanship among the Tallensi* (1945) and 'Time and Social Structure: An Ashanti Case Study' in Fortes, editor, *Social Structure* (1949), especially at p. 84.

[13] The following type of analysis is presented in Goody (editor), *The Developmental Cycle in Domestic Groups* (1958).

[14] See e.g. Leach's criticisms of Evans-Pritchard, Fortes. and what he calls 'most anthropologists' in Chapter I of *The Political Systems of Highland Burma* (1954). In fact the books he criticizes for their lack of historical perspective are full of historical analysis.

[15] Cited above, pp. 236 f.

[16] I give references to such analyses in my 'The Crisis in the Folk Societies' (1962).

[17] Homans has an excellent discussion of what a social equilibrium is in his *The Human Group* (1951), pp. 301 ff. See also Nadel, *The Foundations of Social Anthropology* (1951), p. 343 and elsewhere; and also Bateson, 'Bali: The Value System of a Steady State' in Fortes, editor, *Social Structure* (1949), at pp. 52–3.

[18] The right to rebel was acknowledged into European feudal times, and explicitly granted—indeed, ordered—by King John in the first version of Magna Carta: see my *The Ideas in Barotse Jurisprudence* (1965), Chapter II, and 'Civil War and Theories of Power in Barotseland: African and Medieval Analogies' (1963).

[19] The problems involved in this procedure, and the modes of carrying it out, are discussed in M. Gluckman (editor), *Closed Systems and Open Minds* (1964).

[20] See Oliver and Fage, *A Short History of Africa* (1962). Recent finds near Lusaka in N. Rhodesia, announced as this book goes to press, lend weight to their suggestions (at pp. 48 f.) of very wide spread for 'Sudanic' influences.

[21] Above, p. 143.

[22] Malinowski, *Myth in Primitive Psychology* (1926), pp. 23, 36, 59, 77–8.

[23] On this problem see Gluckman, *Essays on Lozi Land and Royal Property* (1943), and Watson, *Tribal Cohesion in a Money Economy* (1958).

[24] *Townsmen and Tribesmen* (1962).

[25] Srinivas, *Caste in Modern India* (1962).

[26] See e.g. Southall (editor), *Social Change in Africa* (1961).

[27] I have used Colson's analysis of the Makah for a more general discussion of gossip and scandal as cultural institutions in 'Gossip and Scandal' (1963).

[28] I disagree strongly with Homans' conclusion 'that the ultimate explanatory principles in anthropology and sociology, and for that matter history, were ... psychological': 'Autobiographical Introduction' to *Sentiments and Activities* (1962), p. 29.

[29] This point is elaborated in Gluckman and Devons, 'Conclusion' to *Closed Systems and Open Minds* (edited by Gluckman) (1964).

[30] 'Interpretative Statement' at conclusion of Mead (editor), *Co-operation and Competition in Primitive Societies* (1937), at pp. 474–77. The statement is not amended in the 1961 edition, but since it is a paperback produced by photographic methods, presumably emendations in the main text were not possible.

[31] See the short but illuminating paragraph on this theme in *The Human Group* (1951), p. 17.

[32] Since this book went to press I have found a statement criticizing her use of the original sources as well as her interpretation: see Hughes, 'Anomie, the Ammassalik and the Standardization of Error' (1958). Mirsky (1961 edition of *Co-operation and Competition in Primitive Societies*, p. 530) acknowledges some of Hughes' points and points out the situation in which she made her pioneer effort to analyse Eskimo cultural materials while a graduate student. None of Hughes' points are relevant to my own problem, and I used Mirsky's essay as the best available to me in Manchester.

[33] On this see also L. Marshall, 'Sharing, Talking and Giving: The Relief of Social Tensions among Kung Bushmen', (1961), at pp. 232–3.

[34] Mead, *Co-operation and Competition in Primitive Societies* (1937), pp. 464–5. I emphasize, as in an earlier footnote, that this statement was written in 1937, and the conditions of republication of the 1961 edition excluded any possibility of amending the main text. Hence we cannot tell if Mead might not be able to make a more fundamental reconciliation of these facts. For instance, Gorer persuaded Barton, on the basis of a *Co-operation and Competition* hypothesis, 'to make a more thorough investigation of his Ifugaos, whom Barton in his popular book had painted as warm, generous lovers, but whose institutions suggested quite different kinds of motivation. Barton went back to the Philippines, and the result was *Philippine Pagans, the Autobiographies of Three Ifugaos*, which demonstrated that the same motives that operated in the rest of life also came into play in love affairs' ('Appraisal 1961', by Mead in 1961 edition, p. 517). Other examples are also given there.

# BIBLIOGRAPHY

ALLAN, W. *The African Husbandman*, Edinburgh: Oliver and Boyd (1965).

ASHTON, H. *The Basuto*, London: Oxford University Press for the International African Institute (1952).

BAILEY, F. G. *Caste and the Economic Frontier*, Manchester: Manchester University Press (1957).

BARNES, J. A. *Politics in a Changing Society: A Political History of the Fort Jameson Ngoni*, London: Oxford University Press for the Rhodes-Livingstone Institute (1954).

BARTH, F. *Political Leadership among Swat Pathans*, London: Athlone Press for the University of London; New York: Humanities Press (1959).

—— 'Segmentary Opposition and the Theory of Games: a Study of Pathan Organization', *Journal of the Royal Anthropological Institute*, vol. 89 (1959).

BARTON, R. F. *Ifugao Law*, University of California Publications in American Archaeology and Ethnology, vol. 15 (1919).

—— *The Kalingas* (posthumously published and edited by E. A. Hoebel), Chicago: University of Chicago Press (1949).

BATESON, G. *Naven*, Cambridge: Cambridge University Press (1936).

BEATTIE, J. *Bunyoro: An African Kingdom*, New York: Holt, Rinehart and Winston (1960).

BENEDICT, R. *Patterns of Culture*, London: Routledge (1934).

—— *The Chrysanthemum and the Sword*, Boston: Houghton Mifflin (1946).

BERNDT, R. M. *Excess and Restraint: Social Control among a New Guinea Mountain People*, London and Chicago: University of Chicago Press (1962).

BIEBUYCK, D. (editor) *African Agrarian Systems*, London: Oxford University Press for the International African Institute (1963).

BLOCH, M. *Feudal Society*, translated from the French (*La Société Féodale*) by L. A. Manyon, London: Routledge and Kegan Paul (1961).

BOHANNAN, Laura. 'A Genealogical Charter', *Africa*, vol. xxii, no. 4 (1952), pp. 301-15.

BOHANNAN, P. J. *Justice and Judgment among the Tiv*, London: Oxford University Press (1957).

BOHANNAN, L. and P. *The Tiv of Central Nigeria*, Ethnographic Survey of Africa, London: International African Institute (1953).

BOHANNAN, P. J. and DALTON, G. *Markets in Africa*, Northwestern University African Studies, No. 9. Evanston, Illinois: Northwestern University Press (1962).

BROOKFIELD, M. C. and BROWN, P. *Struggle for Land: Agriculture and Group Territories among the Chimbu of the New Guinea Highlands*, Melbourne: Oxford University Press (1963).

CODERE, H. *Fighting with Property*, Monographs of the American Ethnological Society, No. 18 (1950).

COHN, N. *The Pursuit of the Millennium*, London: Secker and Warburg (1957).

315

Colson, E. *The Makah Indians: An Indian Tribe in Modern American Society*, Manchester: Manchester University Press; Minneapolis: University of Minnesota Press (1953).

—— *Marriage and the Family among the Plateau Tonga of Northern Rhodesia*, Manchester: Manchester University Press for the Rhodes-Livingstone Institute; New York: Humanities Press (1958).

—— 'The Role of Bureaucratic Norms in African Political Structures' in *Systems of Political Control and Bureaucracy in Human Societies*, Proceedings of the Annual Spring Meeting of the American Ethnological Society (1958).

—— *The Plateau Tonga of Northern Rhodesia: Social and Religious Studies*, Manchester: Manchester University Press; New York: Humanities Press (1962).

Colson, E. and Gluckman, M. (editors) *Seven Tribes of British Central Africa* (1951), 2nd impression, Manchester: Manchester University Press; New York: Humanities Press (1959).

Coser, L. A. *The Functions of Social Conflict*, London: Routledge and Kegan Paul (1956).

Cunnison, I. G. *The Luapula Peoples of Northern Rhodesia: Custom and History in Tribal Politics*, Manchester: Manchester University Press for the Rhodes-Livingstone Institute; New York; Humanities Press (1959).

Dugdale, J. (editor) *Further Papers on the Social Sciences: Their Relations in Theory and Teaching*, London: Le Play House Press (1937).

Durkheim, E. *De la division du travail social*, Paris: Alcan (1893); translated by G. Simpson as *The Division of Labour in Society*, Glencoe, Illinois: Free Press (1933).

—— *Les Règles de la Méthode Sociologique*, Paris: Alcan (1895), translated by S. A. Solovay and J. H. Mueller as *The Rules of Sociological Method*, Glencoe, Illinois: The Free Press (1938).

—— *Les Formes Elémentaires de la Vie Religieuse*, Paris: Alcan (1912), translated by J. W. Swain as *The Elementary Forms of the Religious Life*, London: Allen and Unwin; New York: Macmillan (1912).

Elias, T. O. *The Nature of African Customary Law*, Manchester: Manchester University Press (1956).

Engels, F. *The Origin of the Family, Private Property and the State*, first published in German in 1884: many English versions.

Epstein, A. L. *Juridical Techniques and the Judicial Process*, Rhodes-Livingstone Paper 23, Manchester: Manchester University Press (1954).

—— *Politics in an Urban African Community*, Manchester: Manchester University Press for Rhodes-Livingstone Institute (1958).

Evans-Pritchard, E. E. *Witchcraft, Oracles and Magic among the Azande of the Anglo-Egyptian Sudan*, Oxford: Clarendon Press (1937).

—— *The Nuer*, Oxford: Clarendon Press (1940).

—— *The Political System of the Anuak of the Anglo-Egyptian Sudan*, London: Percy Lund, Humphries, for the London School of Economics and Political Science (1940).

—— 'Further Observations on the Political System of the Anuak', *Sudan Note and Records*, vol. xxviii (1947), pp. 62–97.

EVANS-PRITCHARD, E. E. *The Divine Kingship of the Shilluk of the Anglo-Egyptian Sudan*, Frazer Lecture, 1948, Cambridge: University Press (1948); published in his *Essays in Social Anthropology*, London: Faber and Faber (1963).

―― *Kinship and Marriage among the Nuer*, Oxford: Clarendon Press (1951).

―― *Social Anthropology*, London: Cohen and West; Glencoe, Illinois: Free Press (1951).

―― *Nuer Religion*, Oxford: Clarendon Press (1956).

―― *Essays in Social Anthropology* London: Faber and Faber (1963).

FALLERS, L. A. *Bantu Bureaucracy: A Study of Integration and Conflict in the Political Institutions of an East African People*, Cambridge: Heffer (*c.* 1956).

FIRTH, R. *We, The Tikopia*, London: Allen and Unwin (1936).

―― *Primitive Polynesian Economy*, London: Routledge (1939).

―― *The Work of the Gods in Tikopia*, London: Percy Lund, Humphries, for the London School of Economics and Political Science (1940).

―― *Social Change in Tikopia*, London: Allen and Unwin (1959).

―― (editor). *Man and Culture: An Evaluation of the Work of Bronislaw Malinowski*, London: Routledge and Kegan Paul (1957).

FORDE, C. D. *Habitat, Economy and Society*, London: New York: Dutton (1954) (reprinted in paperback, 1963).

―― (editor). *African Worlds*, London: Oxford University Press for the International African Institute (1954).

FORTES, M. *The Dynamics of Clanship among the Tallensi*, London: Oxford University Press for the International African Institute (1945).

―― *The Web of Kinship among the Tallensi*, London: Oxford University Press for the International African Institute (1949).

―― 'Malinowski and the Study of Kinship' in R. Firth (editor) *Man and Culture*, London: Routledge and Kegan Paul (1957).

―― *Oedipus and Job in West African Religion*, Cambridge: Cambridge University Press (1959); reprinted in C. Leslie (editor), *Anthropology of Folk Religion*, New York: Random House (Vintage Books) (1960).

―― (editor). *Social Structure: Studies Presented to A. R. Radcliffe-Brown*, Oxford: Clarendon Press (1949).

FORTES. M. and EVANS-PRITCHARD, E. E. (editors). *African Political Systems*, London: Oxford University Press for the International African Institute (1940); reprinted in paperback.

FRANK, J. *Law and the Modern Mind*, New York: Coward-McCann (1930); edition cited, London: Stevens (1949).

FRANKENBERG, R. J. *Village on the Border*, London: Cohen and West (1957).

FRAZER, J. G. *The Golden Bough*, abridged edition, London: Macmillan (1922).

FREEDMAN, M. *Lineage Organization in South-eastern China*, London: Athlone Press for the London School of Economics and Political Science (1958).

FREUD, S. *Totem and Taboo* (first translated from German into English in 1919), in many editions.

GIBSON, J. Y. *The Story of the Zulus*, London: Longmans, Green (1911).

GLUCKMAN, M. *Essays on Lozi Land and Royal Property*, Rhodes-Livingstone Paper No. 10, Livingstone (Northern Rhodesia), (1943).

―― 'The Lozi of Barotseland in North-Western Rhodesia' in Colson and Gluckman, editors (above) (1959).

GLUCKMAN, M. *The Judicial Process among the Barotse of Northern Rhodesia*, Manchester: Manchester University Press; Glencoe, Illinois: Free Press (1955).

—— *Custom and Conflict in Africa*, Oxford: Blackwell; Glencoe, Illinois: Free Press (1955) (reprinted as paperback, 1963).

—— 'Ethnographic Data in British Social Anthropology', *The Sociological Review*, N.S. vol. 9, no. 1 (1961); and Transactions of the Third International Congress of Sociology, Stresa, 1959.

—— 'The Crisis in the Folk Societies' in H. D. Lasswell and H. Cleveland (editors), *The Ethic of Power*, New York: Harper for the Conference on Science, Philosophy and Religion (1962).

—— *Order and Rebellion in Tribal Africa*, London: Cohen and West; Glencoe, Illinois: Free Press (1963).

—— 'Gossip and Scandal: Essays in Honor of Melville J. Herskovits', *Current Anthropology*, vol. 4, no. 3 (1963), pp. 307–16.

—— 'Civil War and Theories of Power in Barotseland: African and Medieval Analogies', *Yale Law Journal*, vol. 72, no. 8 (1963), pp. 1515–46.

—— *The Ideas in Barotse Jurisprudence*, New Haven and London: Yale University Press (1965).

—— (editor). *Essays on the Ritual of Social Relations*, Manchester: Manchester University Press; New York: Humanities Press (1962).

—— (editor). *Closed Systems and Open Minds: The Limits of Naivety in Social Anthropology*, Edinburgh: Oliver and Boyd (1964).

GOODHART, A. 'The Importance of a Definition of Law', *Journal of African Administration* iii, 3 (1951).

GOODY, J. *Death, Property and the Ancestors*, London: Tavistock; Stanford, California: Stanford University Press (1962).

—— (editor). *The Developmental Cycle in Domestic Groups*, Cambridge: University Press (1958).

GRANET, M. *Chinese Civilization* (trs. by K. E. Innes and M. R. Brailsford), London: Routledge and Kegan Paul (1950).

—— *La Religion des Chinois*, Paris: Presses Universitaires (1951).

GULLIVER, P. H. *Social Control in an African Society. A Study of the Arusha: Agricultural Masai of Northern Tanganyika*, London: Routledge and Kegan Paul (1963).

GUTKIND, P. C. W. *The Royal Capital of Buganda: A Study in Internal Conflict and External Ambiguity*, The Hague: Mouton (1963).

HERSKOVITS, M. J. *Dahomey, an Ancient West African Kingdom*, New York: Augustin (1938).

—— *Economic Anthropology*, New York: Knopf (1952).

HOBSBAWM, E. J. *Primitive Rebels*, Manchester: Manchester University Press (1959).

HOEBEL, E. A. *The Political Organization and Law-Ways of the Comanche Indians*, American Anthropological Association Memoir 54: Contribution from the Santa Fe Laboratory of Anthropology, 4 (1940).

—— *The Law of Primitive Man*, Cambridge, Massachusetts: Harvard University Press (1954).

—— 'Three Studies of African Law', *Stanford Law Review*, xii, 2 (1961).

—— *The Cheyennes: Indians of the Great Plains*, New York: Henry Holt (1960).

HOGBIN, H. J. *Law and Order in Polynesia*, London: Christophers (1934).

—— *Experiments in Civilization*, London: Routledge (1939).

—— *Transformation Scene*, London; Routledge and Kegan Paul (1951).

HOLMBERG, A. R. *Nomads of the Long Bow, The Siriono of Eastern Bolivia*, Publication No. 10, Washington: Institute of Social Anthropology, Smithsonian Institution (1950).

HOMANS, G. C. *The Human Group*, New York: Harcourt Brace (1950); London: Routledge and Kegan Paul (1951).

—— *Sentiments and Activities*, Glencoe, Illinois: Free Press (1962).

HOWELL, P. P. *A Manual of Nuer Law*, London: Oxford University Press for the International African Institute (1954).

HSU, F. L. K. *Under the Ancestors' Shadow*, London: Routledge and Kegan Paul (1949).

HUGHES, C. C. 'Anomie, the Ammassalik, and the Standardization of Error', *Southwestern Journal of Anthropology*, vol. xiv, no. 4 (1958), pp. 353-77.

HUNTER, G. *The New Societies of Tropical Africa*, London: Oxford University Press for the Institute of Race Relations, London (1962).

HUNTER, M. *Reaction to Conquest*, London: Oxford University Press for the International African Institute (1936, 1961).

JORDAN, A. C. 'Towards an African Literature: II. Traditional Poetry', *Africa South*, vol. 2, no. 1 (1957), vol. 2, no. 1, pp. 97-105.

JUNOD, H. A. *The Life of a South African Tribe*, London, Macmillan (1927); reprinted New York: University Books (1962).

KARDINER, A. *The Individual and his Society*, New York: Columbia University Press (1929).

—— *The Psychological Frontiers of Society*, New York: Columbia University Press (1945).

KLINEBERG, O. *Race Differences*, New York: Harper (1935).

—— *Race and Psychology* in 'The Race Question in Modern Science' series, Paris: Unesco (1951).

—— (editor). *Characteristics of the American Negro*, Carnegie Corporation of New York, Vol. 4. New York: Harper (1944).

KLUCKHOHN, C. *Mirror for Man*, New York: McGraw-Hill (1954): citations here from Premier Book Edition, New York: Fawcett World Library (4th printing, 1961).

KLUCKHOHN, C. and MURRAY, H. A. *Personality in Nature, Society and Culture*, London: Cape (1949).

KRIGE, J. D. 'Some Aspects of Lovedu Judicial Arrangements', *Bantu Studies*, vol. xiii, no. 2 (1939).

KRIGE, E. J. and J. D. *The Realm of a Rain-Queen*, London: Oxford University Press for the International African Institute (1943).

KROEBER, A. L. *Zuni Kin and Clan*, American Museum of Natural History, Anthropological Papers, vol. 18, part 2 (1917).

KUPER, H. *An African Aristocracy: Rank among the Swazi*, London: Oxford University Press for the International African Institute (1947).

LABOURET, H. *Les Tribus de Rameau Lobi*, Travaux et Mémoires de l'Institut d'Ethnologie, vol. xv, Paris (1931).

LEACH, E. R. *Political Systems of Highland Burma*, London: Bell (1954).

LE GROS CLARK, W. 'The Humanity of Man', *The Advancement of Science*, vol. xviii (September 1961).

LÉVY-BRUHL L. *La Mentalité Primitive*, Paris, Presses Universitaire (1922).
—— *Primitive Mentality*, translated by Lilian A. Clare, New York: Macmillan (1923).

LÉVI-STRAUSS, C. *A World on the Wane*, London: Hutchinson (1961), translated by J. Russell from *Tristes Tropique*, Paris: Libraire Plon (1959).

LEWIS, I. M. *A Pastoral Democracy: A Study of Pastoralism and Politics among the Northern Somali*, London: Oxford University Press (1961).

LIENHARDT, G. 'The Shilluk of the Upper Nile' in *African Worlds: Studies in the Cosmological Ideas and Social Values of African Peoples*, edited by C. D. Forde, London: Oxford University Press for the International African Institute (1954), pp. 138–63.
—— 'Nilotic Kings and their Mothers' Kin', *Africa*, vol. xxv, no. 1 (1955), pp. 29–41.
—— 'Anuak Village Headmen', *Africa*, 'I: Headmen and Village Culture', vol. xxvii, no. 4 (1957), pp. 340–55, and 'II: Village Structure and "Rebellion",' vol. xxviii, no. 1 (1958), pp. 23–36.

LINTON, R. (editor). *Acculturation in Seven American Indian Tribes*, New York: Appleton-Century (1940).

LIPS, J. E. *Naskapi Law: Law and Order in a Hunting Society*, Transactions of the American Philosophical Society, vol. 37, pt. 4 (1947).

LLEWELLYN, K. N. and HOEBEL, E. A. *The Cheyenne Way*, Norman: University of Oklahoma Press (1941).

LOWIE, R. H. *The Crow*, New York: Farrar and Rinehart (1935).
—— *The History of Ethnological Theory*, London: Harrap (1937).

MAINE, H. S. *Ancient Law*, London: Murray (1861).

MAIR, L. P. *An African People in the Twentieth Century* (Baganda), London: Routledge (1934).
—— *Primitive Government*, Harmondsworth: Pelican Books (1962).

MALINOWSKI, B. *The Family among the Australian Aborigines*, London: London University Press (1913) (reprinted as paperback, with an introduction by J. A. Barnes, 1963).
—— *Argonauts of the Western Pacific*, London: Routledge (1922).
—— 'Magic, Science and Religion' in J. Needham (editor), *Science Religion and Reality*, London: Macmillan (1925); republished in B. Malinowski, *Magic, Science and Religion and Other Essays*, Glencoe, Illinois: Free Press (1948).
—— *Myth in Primitive Psychology*, London: Kegan Paul, Trench and Trubner (1926); reprinted in B. Malinowski, *Magic, Science and Religion, and other Essays* (as above).
—— *Crime and Custom in Savage Society*, London: Kegan Paul, Trench and Trubner (1926).
—— *Coral Gardens and their Magic*, London: Allen and Unwin (1935).
—— *Sex, Culture and Myth*, London: Hart-Davis (1963).

MAQUET, J. J. *The Premise of Inequality in Ruanda*, London: Oxford University Press for the International African Institute (1961).

MARSHALL, L. 'Sharing, Talking, and Giving: Relief of Social Tensions among Kung Bushmen', *Africa*, vol. xxxi, no. 3 (1961), pp. 231–49.

MAYER, P. *Townsmen or Tribesmen*, Cape Town: Oxford University Press (1961).

MEAD, M. *Growing up in New Guinea*, New York: Morrow (1930).

—— *Coming of Age in Samoa*, New York: Morrow (1928).

—— *Sex and Temperament in Three Primitive Societies*, New York: Morrow (1938).

—— *Male and Female*, New York: Morrow (1949).

—— (editor). *Co-operation and Competition among Primitive Peoples*, New York, and London: McGraw-Hill (1937) (republished as a paperback, 1961).

MEGGITT, M. J. *Desert People: A Study of the Walbiri Aborigines of Central Australia*, London and Melbourne: Angus and Robertson (1962).

—— *The Lineage System of the Mae Enga of the New Guinea Highlands*, Edinburgh: Oliver and Boyd (1965).

MIDDLETON, J. *Lugbara Religion: Ritual and Authority among an East African People*, London: Oxford University Press for the International African Institute (1960).

MIDDLETON, J. and WINTER, E. H. (editors). *Witchcraft and Sorcery in East Africa*, London: Routledge and Kegan Paul (1963).

MITCHELL, J. C. *The Yao Village*, Manchester: Manchester University Press for the Rhodes-Livingstone Institute (1956).

—— *The Kalela Dance*, Manchester: Manchester University Press for the Rhodes-Livingstone Institute (1956).

—— *Tribalism and the Plural Society*, London: Oxford University Press (1960).

MORGAN, L. H. *Systems of Consanguinity and Affinity of the Human Family*, Smithsonian Contributions to Knowledge, xvii (1871).

—— *Ancient Society*, New York: Holt (1877).

NADEL, S. F. *A Black Byzantium: The Kingdom of the Nupe of Nigeria*, London: Oxford University for the International African Institutue (1942).

—— *The Nuba*, London: Oxford University Press (1947).

—— *The Foundations of Social Anthropology*, London: Cohen and West, (1951).

—— *Nupe Religion*, London: Routledge and Kegan Paul (1954).

NORBECK, E. 'African Rituals of Conflict', *American Anthropologist*, vol. 65, no. 6 (1963), pp 1254-79.

OBERG, K. 'The Kingdom of Ankole in Uganda', in Fortes and Evans-Pritchard (editors), *African Political Systems*, London: Oxford University Press for the International African Institute (1940).

OLIVER, D. L. *A Solomon Island Society: Kinship and Leadership among the Siuai of Bougainville*, Cambridge, Mass.: Harvard University Press (1955).

OLIVER, R. and FAGE, J. D. *A Short History of Africa*, Harmondsworth: Penguin African Library (1962).

PERISTIANY, J. G. 'Pokot Sanctions and Structure', *Africa*, vol. xxiv, no. 1 (1954), pp. 17-25.

PETERS, E. 'The Proliferation of Segments in the Lineage of the Bedouin in Cyrenaica', *Journal of the Royal Anthropological Institute*, vol. 90 (1960), pp. 29-53.

—— 'Aspects of Status and Rank in a Lebanese Village' in J. Pitt-Rivers (editor), *Mediterranean Countrymen*, Paris: Mouton (1963).

POLANYI, K., ARENSBERG, C. M. and PEARSON, H. W. (editors) *Trade and Markets in the Early Empires*, Glencoe, Illinois: Free Press (1957).

POSPISIL, L. *Kapauka Papuans and their Law*, Yale University Publications in Anthropology, No. 54 (1958).

PROVINSE, J. 'The Underlying Sanctions of Plains Indian Culture' in F. Eggan (editor), *Social Anthropology of North American Indian Tribes*, Chicago: Chicago University Press (1937).

RADCLIFFE-BROWN, A. R. *The Andaman Islanders*, Cambridge: Cambridge University Press (1922).

—— *Structure and Function in Primitive Society*, London: Cohen and West, (1952).

—— *A Natural Science of Society*, Glencoe, Illinois: Free Press (1957).

RATTRAY, R. S. *Ashanti Law and Constitution*, Oxford: Clarendon Press (1929).

REAY, M. *The Kuma*, Melbourne: Melbourne University Press for the Australian National University (1959).

RICHARDS, A. I. *Land, Labour and Diet in Northern Rhodesia*, London: Oxford University Press for the International African Institute (1939).

—— *Chisungu: A Girl's Initiation Ceremony among the Bemba of Northern Rhodesia*, London: Faber and Faber (1956).

RICHARDSON, J. *Law and Status among the Kiowa Indians*, American Ethnological Society, Monograph I (1940).

RITTER, E. A. *Shaka Zulu*, London: Longmans, Green (1955) (republished as a paperback).

ROBERTSON, D. H. *Money*, London: Nisbet; Cambridge: University Press (1922).

SAHLINS, M. D. *Social Stratification in Polynesia*, Seattle: University of Washington Press (1958).

SAHLINS, M. D. and SERVICE, E. R. (editors). *Evolution and Culture*, Ann Arbor: University of Michigan Press (1960).

SARGENT, S. S. and SMITH, M. W. *Culture and Personality*, New York: Viking Fund (1949).

SCHAPERA, I. *The Khoisan Peoples of South Africa*, London: Routledge (1930).

—— *A Handbook of Tswana Law and Custom*, London: Oxford University Press for the International African Institute (1938).

—— *Native Land Tenure in the Bechuanaland Protectorate*, Lovedale, South Africa: The Lovedale Press (1943).

—— *Tribal Legislation among the Tswana of the Bechuanaland Protectorate*, London: Lund, Humphries, for the London School of Economics and Political Science (1943).

—— *The Political Annals of a Tswana Tribe*, Communications from the School of African Studies, University of Cape Town, N.S. no. 18 (1947).

—— *Government and Politics in Tribal Societies*, London: Watts (1956).

SCHNEIDER, D. M. and GOUGH, K. (editors). *Matrilineal Kinship*, London: Cambridge University Press; Berkeley and Los Angeles: University of California Press (1961).

SEAGLE, W. *The Quest for Law*, New York: Knopf (1941); 2nd edition entitled *The History of Law*, New York: Tudor Publishing Co. (1946).

SHEDDICK, V. G. *Land Tenure in Basutoland*, London: Her Majesty's Stationery Office (1956).

SIMMEL, G. *Conflict and the Web of Group Affiliations* (translated by K. H. Wolff and R. Bendix), Glencoe, Illinois: Free Press (1955).

SMITH, M. G. *Government in Zazzau*, London: Oxford University Press for the International African Institute (1960).

SMITH, W. and ROBERTS, J. M. *Zuni Law: A Field of Values*, Peabody Museum of American Archaeology and Ethnology, Harvard University, vol. 43, no. 1 (1954).

SOUTHALL, A. W. *Alur Society: A Study in Processes and Types of Domination*, Cambridge: Heffer (no date: 1953–54).

—— (editor), *Social Change in Africa*, London: Oxford University Press for the International African Institute (1961).

SOUTHWOLD, M. *Bureaucracy and Chieftainship in Buganda*, East African Studies No. 14, London: Kegan Paul, Trench, Trubner (n.d.-*circa* 1960).

SPENCER, R. F. *The North Alaskan Eskimo*, Smithsonian Institution, Bureau of American Ethnology Bulletin 171, Washington: Government Printing Office (1959).

STEWARD, J. H. *Basin Plateau Aboriginal Socio-Political Groups*, Bureau of American Ethnology Bulletin No. 120, Washington: Government Printing Office (1938).

—— *Theory of Culture Change*, Urbana: University of Illinois Press (1955).

STONE, J. *The Province and Function of Law*, London: Stevens (1947).

SRINIVAS, M. N. *Caste in Modern India and Other Essays*, Bombay, London and New York: Asia Publishing House (1962).

TAX, S. (editor). *Horizons in Anthropology*, Chicago: Aldine Press (1964).

THOMAS, E. M. *The Harmless People* (Bushmen), London: Secker and Warburg (1959).

THOMSON, D. F. *Economic Exchange and the Ceremonial Exchange Cycle in Arnhem Land*, London and Melbourne: Macmillan (1949).

TURNER, V. W. *Schism and Continuity in an African Society: A Study of Ndembu Village Life*, Manchester: Manchester University Press for the Rhodes-Livingstone Institute (1957).

—— *Ndembu Divination: its Symbolism and Techniques*, Rhodes-Livingstone Paper No. 31, Manchester: Manchester University Press (1961).

—— 'Three Symbols of *Passage* in Ndembu Circumcision Ritual' in M. Gluckman (editor), *Essays on the Ritual of Social Relations*, Manchester: Manchester University Press (1962).

—— 'Symbols in Ndembu Ritual' in M. Gluckman (editor), *Closed Systems and Open Minds*, Edinburgh: Oliver and Boyd (1963).

TYLOR, E. *Primitive Culture: Researches into the Development of Mythology, Philosophy, Religion, Language, Art and Custom*, London: Murray (1871); many later editions, including paperback.

—— 'On a Method of Investigating the Development of Institutions, applied to Laws of Marriage and Descent', *Journal of the Anthropological Institute*, vol. xix (1889).

UBEROI, J. P. S. *Politics of the Kula Ring: An Analysis of the Findings of Bronislaw Malinowski*, Manchester: Manchester University Press; New York: Humanities Press (1962).

VAN DEN STEENHOVEN, G. *Leadership and Law among the Eskimos of the Keewatin District, Northwest Territories*, Rijswijk: Excelsior (1962).

VAN VELSEN, J. *The Politics of Kinship: A Study in Social Manipulation among the Lakeside Tonga of Nyasaland*, Manchester University Press for the Rhodes-Livingstone Institute (1964).

VINOGRADOFF, P. *Common-sense in Law*, Home University Library, London: Thornton Butterworth (1913).

WARNER, W. LLOYD. *A Black Civilization: A Study of an Australian Tribe*, New York: Harper (1937, 1958).

WATSON, W. *Tribal Cohesion in a Money Economy*, Manchester: Manchester University Press for the Rhodes-Livingstone Institute; New York: Humanities Press (1958).

WELSFORD, E. *The Fool: His Social and Literary History*, London: Faber and Faber (1935) (republished as a paperback).

WHITE, L. A. *The Science of Culture*, New York: Farrar, Straus (1949).

—— *The Evolution of Culture: The Development of Civilization to the Fall of Rome*, New York: McGraw-Hill (1959).

WHITMAN, W. 'The San Ildefonso of New Mexico' in R. Lindon (editor), *Acculturation in Seven American Indian Tribes*, New York: Appleton-Century (1940).

WHYTE, W. F. *Street Corner Society*, Chicago: University of Chicago Press (1943) (republished with an appendix, 1961).

WILSON, G. 'An Introduction to Nyakyusa Law', *Africa*, vol. x, no. 1 (1937).

—— *The Constitution of Ngonde*, Rhodes-Livingstone Paper No. 3 (1939).

WILSON, G. and M. *The Analysis of Social Change*, Cambridge: University Press (1945).

WILSON, M. *Good Company: A Study of Nyakyusa Age-Villages*, London: Oxford University Press for the International African Institute (1951).

—— *Rituals of Kinship among the Nyakyusa*, London: Oxford University Press for the International African Institute (1957).

—— *Communal Rituals of the Nyakyusa*, London: Oxford University Press for the International African Institute (1959).

WILSON, M., KAPLAN, S., MAKI, T. and WALTON, E. M. *Social Structure: Kerskammahoek Rural Survey*, vol. iii (on Xhosa).

WITTFOGEL, K. A. *Oriental Despotism: A Comparative Study of Total Power*, New Haven: Yale University Press (1957).

WORSLEY, P. *The Trumpet Shall Sound: A Study of 'Cargo' Cults in Melanesia*, London: Macgibbon and Kee (1957).

# INDEX

absorption of non-kin, 85 f.
abuse of power, in Melanesia, 119
adjudication: and mediation, 183; Bohannan on Tiv, 185; definition of, 183
Admiralty Islands: tokens of value in, 66
African kingdoms: women rulers in, 134
age: basis for social differentiation, 19
age-mates: regiments of, 140–1
Allan, W.: on African crops, 72
allegiances: among Tonga, 117; cross-ties, 110 f., 114; division of, 111 f., 165; in Buganda, 148 f., 153 f.; in Ruanda, 156 f.; in total system, 165; in tribal societies, 164
alternate generations: identification of, 18
Alur: history, 236
ancestor-worship, 9
ancestral spirits, 7; and kinship obligations, 227; and misfortunes, 227; obligations due to, 227
Andamanese, 269
Andaman Islands, 24
Anglo-Saxon feud, 113
Ankole, 147
anthropology: and economics, 80 n. 29; and sociology, 33; books on psychological —, 35 n. 41; branches of, 30 f.; growth of, 1 f.; history of, 34 n. 1; modern, 22; social, 23, 31; specialization of, 29, 30, 38 n. 35
Anuak, 216; authority among, 123 f., 135 f.; Evans-Pritchard on, 123 f.; headmanship among, 134; installation of village headmen, 253; land shrines among, 130; leaders among, 123 f.; Lienhardt on, 124 f.; rebellions among, 123 f.; ritual emblems among, 124, 128 f.; rotation of headmen, 124 f.
apartheid, 111
Arapesh, 76
arbitrator: and authoritativeness, 189
Ashanti, 274; complicated structure, 167 n. 37
Australia: ceremonial partners in, 15
Australian Aborigines, 268–9; ideas on procreation, 11–12
authoritativeness: scale of, 189
authority: among Anuak, 123 f.; among Bemba, 145; among Swazi, 145; among Zulu, 145; Colson on, 146; division of—in Barotseland, 144 f., 148; division of—in Buganda, 148; division of—among Zulu, 148; Hogbin on—in Melanesia, 119; in Nupeland, 160 f.; in Ruanda, 154 f.; in stateless societies, 123 f.; instituted, 119 f.; institutionalization of, 118; in tribal societies, 123 f., 158; secular—and priestly office, 127 f.; succession to, 118; types of, 116 f.
Azande: mystical disturbances, 217 f.

Bacon, F.: as scientist, 4
Bachiga, 76
Baganda: see Buganda
Bailey, F. G.: on India, 74; on Indian economics, 80 n. 42, 121 n. 3
Bamangwato: 'towns' among, 147
Bantu Kavirondo: as political unit, 84
Barnes, J. A.: history of Ngoni, 236; tribal legislation, 214 n. 2
Barotse (Lozi), 143 f., 174, 199–200, 219; and 'rightness', 20 f.; and Tswana terms for law, 215 n. 51, 215 n. 52; British support for king, 214 n. 5; disputed succession among, 146 f.; division of authority in, 144 f., 148; economic system, 70; land-tenure laws, 37; legislation among, 214 n. 4; on Copperbelt, 290; position of chiefs, 88; rebellions among, 145, 146; ritual roles, 262; sanctuaries, 216; stability of state, 144; tribute among, 146
Barotse capitals: size of, 146
Barotseland: barter and exchange in, 144; trading relations in, 14